CONSTITUTIONALISM AND DEMOCRACY

STUDIES IN RATIONALITY
AND SOCIAL CHANGE

STUDIES IN RATIONALITY AND SOCIAL CHANGE

Editors: Jon Elster and Gudmund Hernes

Editorial Board:
Fredrik Barth
Amartya Sen
Arthur Stinchcombe
Amos Tversky
Bernard Williams

Edited by Jon Elster and Rune Slagstad

CONSTITUTIONALISM AND DEMOCRACY

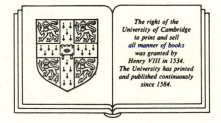

The right of the
University of Cambridge
to print and sell
all manner of books
was granted by
Henry VIII in 1534.
The University has printed
and published continuously
since 1584.

Cambridge University Press

Cambridge

New York – Port Chester – Melbourne – Sydney

Published in collaboration with Maison des Sciences de l'Homme, Paris

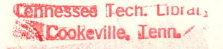

Published by the Press Syndicate of the University of Cambridge
The Pitt Building, Trumpington Street, Cambridge CB2 1RP
32 East 57th Street, New York, NY 10022, USA
10 Stamford Road, Oakleigh, Melbourne 3166, Australia
and in Scandinavia by Norwegian University Press, P.O. Box 2959 Tøyen, 0608 Oslo 6,
Norway

First published 1988
Reprinted 1989

Printed in Great Britain at the University Press, Cambridge

British Library cataloguing in publication data

Constitutionalism and democracy. –
(Studies in rationality and social change).
1. Democracy
I. Elster, Jon II. Slagstad, Rune III. Series
321.8   JC423

Library of Congress cataloguing in publication data

Constitutionalism and democracy.
(Studies in rationality and social change)
Includes index.
1. Constitutional history. 2. Democracy. 3. Comparative government.
I. Elster, Jon, 1940–   . II. Slagstad, Rune, 1945–   . III. Series.
JF51.C627   1988   321.8   87-24300

ISBN 0 521 34530 8 (excluding Scandinavia)

ISBN 82 00 18483 8 (Scandinavia only)

CE

Contents

Notes on contributors

Bruce Ackerman is Sterling Professor of Law and Political Science at Yale University

Jon Elster is Professor of Political Science and Philosophy at the University of Chicago

Stephen Holmes is Professor of Political Science at the University of Chicago

Jennifer Nedelsky is Professor of Law and Political Science at the University of Toronto

Adam Przeworski is Professor of Political Science at the University of Chicago

Francis Sejersted is Professor of History at the University of Oslo

Rune Slagstad is Editor-in-chief of the Norwegian University Press

Cass Sunstein is Professor of Constitutional Law at the University of Chicago Law School

Introduction

JON ELSTER

Ten chapters, most of them published here for the first time, make up the bulk of this book. In addition, the editors commissioned an epilogue from Cass Sunstein, to bring out more clearly implicit agreements and disagreements among the contributors, and to engage in a discussion with them. The present introduction has a more limited purpose. It attempts to map some of the main problems raised by the contributors and to bring out their relation to one another. I shall emphasize three issues. First, I shall argue that the tension between constitutionalism and democracy is only, as it were, the two-dimensional projection of a three-dimensional issue. The third dimension which provides depth to that tension is the goal of efficient decision-making, unencumbered, if necessary, both by popular participation and by constitutional constraints. Next, I attempt to survey some of the proposed answers to what is perhaps the central question in the volume: why would a society want to limit its own sovereign power? Why would a democratic society tolerate what might appear to be a dictatorship of the past over the present? Finally, I shall explore some of the multiple links, discussed in the chapters below, between democracy, constitutionalism and private property. Is constitutionalism only a tool deployed in the self-interest of the property-holding class? Or are constitutional guarantees for property in the interest of everybody?

I A three-cornered dilemma

Democracy I shall understand as simple majority rule, based on the principle "One person one vote." For the present purpose it is useful to construe the notion quite broadly, so as to include regimes in which,

1

for instance, slaves, foreigners, women, the propertyless or minors are excluded from the electorate. Even when the electorate is narrow, the tension between untrammeled majority rule and the need for constitutional constraints can arise. I discuss this in some detail below with reference to fourteenth-century Florentine politics. One may say, of course, that restriction of the electorate is a constraint on democracy, but it is not a constitutional constraint, as I shall use that term, since the excluded individuals almost invariably are not allowed to vote in the decision to exclude them.[1]

Similarly it is useful to include direct as well as representative democracy within the scope of our inquiry. The direct form of democracy practiced in classical Athens had self-imposed constraints which correspond to the spirit of constitutionalism. New legislation was subject to control by the *nomothetai*, a group of individuals chosen by the Assembly with the authority to approve or reject laws passed by the assembly.[2] Another institution with a similar purpose was the *graphe paranomon*, whereby an individual might be punished for having proposed an illegal law in the Assembly, even if it had already been passed.[3] Indeed, one might argue that direct democracy has a special need for such constraints, to prevent demagoguery and restrain the passions of the moment.

Constitutionalism refers to limits on majority decisions; more specifically, to limits that are in some sense self-imposed. The limits can take a variety of forms. They can be procedural or substantive; they can block or merely slow down the process of legislative change. Many countries have a written constitution which, among other things, prescribes complicated procedures for changing the constitution itself, including delays, qualified majorities and the like. Lower-level clauses can be either procedural or substantive. They include detailed regulations of the electoral process and of assembly voting, as well as guarantees for various individual rights, civil as well as political.

The central rights-protecting element in modern constitutions is the "principle of legality": to be punishable, an act must be explicitly

---

[1] An exception is the referendum on lowering the voting age in Denmark in 1953. Here the individuals whose enfranchisement was contemplated were allowed to vote.

[2] D. M. MacDowell, *The Law in Classical Athens* (London, Thames and Hudson, 1978), pp. 48ff.

[3] *Ibid.*, pp. 50ff.

forbidden by a law which was in force at the time it was committed. The effect of the principle of legality is to exclude arbitrary punishment and, very importantly retroactive legislation. It should not be confused with the requirement, sometimes referred to as "the rule of law,"[4] that laws should be (relatively) stable and predictable. The principle of legality blocks the present from legislating for the past, whereas the rule of law allows it to legislate for the future. Both are important to ensure the security and peace of mind without which no well-functioning society is possible, but the former is the more fundamental condition.

Not all regulations are properly thought of as limits to majority rule. Many of them are better thought of as forms without which majority rule could not exist. There must be rules which determine when elections are to be held; electoral districts must be drawn; mechanisms for transforming votes into winners must be chosen. These forms of majority rule can also, however, be chosen with a view to being limits on majority rule. For instance, majority rule is constrained by a system of rigidly periodic elections, which prevent the government emanating from the majority from picking the moment at which its chances of being reelected are most propitious. Another example is provided by the periodically arising need, due to demographic changes, to redraw the boundaries between electoral districts. Notoriously this gives rise to strategic manipulation, often with the result that the districts are drawn up so as to favour the majority party. To avoid this, the constitution might lay down that the redrawing of electoral districts shall happen automatically whenever a certain inequality is attained, and that the new boundaries shall be drawn at random from a set of boundaries satisfying the condition of equipopulousness as well as certain topological conditions of connectedness and the like. This would be a constraint on majority rule.[5]

As described in this volume, constitutions serve two (overlapping) functions: they protect individual rights, and they form an obstacle to certain political changes which would have been carried out had the majority had its way. The latter function is served in several ways: by declaring certain changes unconstitutional; by making the process of change so complicated and demanding that few proposals will be able

---

4 See for instance the discussion by Sejersted below, pp. 131–52.
5 For a discussion of electoral boundaries, see also Holmes below.

to clear the hurdles;[6] or by irreversibly delegating certain tasks to independent institutions like the Federal Reserve Board.[7] Of these various tasks, only the two last-mentioned can be carried out mechanically and without recourse to interception. The others usually require judgment and interpretation, and so for obvious reasons are placed outside the political system proper. If the majority could interpret the statutes limiting its authority, the temptation to bend the interpretation its way could be overwhelming. Whenever mechanical processes (including randomization) are unavailable, judicial review becomes essential. It is no accident that constitutionalism is closely associated with the Supreme Court, although it should be emphasized that limits on majority rule go beyond judicial review.

Very broadly speaking, and with the qualification just stated, we may associate democracy with the elected assembly and constitutionalism with the Supreme Court (or its equivalent, like the French *conseil constitutionnel*). The third branch of the political system is the executive. The assembly embodies popular participation; the Supreme Court embodies constitutional constraints; and the executive embodies the need for action. At times, the executive may feel that its action is encumbered or hindered by each of the other branches. This shows itself most clearly, perhaps, in warfare. Tocqueville argued that in war an aristocratic or monarchic leadership would deploy a given amount of resources better than a democratic government could do, although he was careful to add that in the long run a democracy will create more resources than an aristocracy.[8] Similarly, when war breaks out or is impending the government may decide that constitutionally guaranteed civil liberties must be suspended.[9] Carl Schmitt argued that the power of the state to declare a state of emergency shows that it is at bottom a *Machtstaat* rather than a *Rechtsstaat*.[10] In his opinion, the essence of the state is revealed at moments of crisis, not through its day-to-day operations. Although this view is farfetched, the government's desire to be as unconstrained as possible is a constant fact of politics.

Any government wants to be free, to have wide discretionary

---

[6] In this volume this is stressed especially by Ackerman.
[7] In this volume this is stressed especially in Sejersted's first contribution (chapter 5).
[8] See my discussion below, pp. 81–102.
[9] See the discussion below in Sejersted, pp. 275–302.
[10] See the discussion in Slagstad below, pp. 103–30.

powers of action. Against this there are several reasons why it needs to be restrained. Most obviously, there is the risk that it may use its powers for particularistic purposes; that it will violate the rights of some individuals simply to promote the interest of other individuals. The *lettres de cachet* of the pre-revolutionary French regime have come to epitomize this danger. In modern democratic societies, other risks loom larger. In its effort to promote economic growth, military success or whatever other goal it has been mandated to achieve, the government may decide that civil and political liberties ought not to stand in its way, because it is really acting for the general good.[11] What, indeed, is the right of a few against the good of all? The argument rests on a fallacy of composition. From the fact that in any of a large number of cases the general good is promoted by violating individual rights one cannot conclude that a regular habit of rights-violation whenever the general good seems to require it will have the same effect. (In addition the premise of the argument is frequently shaky, since governments tend to overestimate the certainty that their policies will yield the desired results.[12])

Economic planning exhibits the same problem in a somewhat different form. Discretionary use of the state's economic powers may detract from the stability and predictability which is a condition for long-term economic growth.[13] To this proposition[14] we should add another, which is that *predictable* discretionary behaviour may also yield undesirable results.[15] Consider a plain which is regularly inundated with many houses destroyed each time. After any given flood, the best policy from the point of view of the government may be to subsidize the house-owners to rebuild their dwellings. In a long-term perspective, however, it may be better if the government declares that

[11] An example is the Pentagon Papers case, as discussed in G. Calabresi and P. Bobbit, *Tragic Choices* (New York, Norton, 1978), pp. 39–40. See also the case of requisition of housing, discussed by Sejersted, pp. 275–302 below.

[12] On this point, see B. Ackerman, *Private Property and the Constitution* (New Haven, Yale University Press, 1977), pp. 51ff.

[13] Of these desiderata, predictability is the more fundamental. In the legislative realm, it may be difficult to conceive of a predictability not based on stability, but in, say, monetary policy a predictable, non-zero rate of inflation may serve as well as no inflation at all. On this point, see J. Buchanan, "Predictability: the criterion of monetary constitutions," in L. B. Yeager (ed.), *In Search of a Monetary Constitution* (Cambridge, Mass., Harvard University Press, 1962), pp. 155–81.

[14] Explored by Sejersted in chapter 5 below.

[15] See F. Kydland and E. Prescott, "Rules versus discretions: the inconsistency of optimal plans," *Journal of Political Economy*, 85 (1977), 473–92.

it will under no circumstance offer such subsidies, since then people will have an incentive to locate themselves elsewhere.

These remarks reflect the familiar theme of act-utilitarianism versus rule-utilitarianism. The natural tendency of governments to *act* on a case-by-case basis must be countered by *rules* which take account of the cumulative effect of many individual acts. Many defenders of constitutional constraints would, of course, put their case differently. Rather than admitting that rights are an output of the utilitarian calculus, they insist that rights are independently given constraints on that calculus. Some of them might perhaps be prepared to accept the utilitarian defense of property rights, but not accept that the protection of privacy or the freedom of religion are similarly dependent on the argument from utility. In the history of constitutional thought the utilitarian argument and the pure rights-based argument for constraints have been constantly intertwined and not infrequently confused.[16]

Whichever side one takes in this controversy, one side of constitutionalism can certainly be summed up as "rules versus discretion." This is the face that constitutionalism bears in its struggle with the day-to-day wielders of power, whether these be embodied in a monarchy or in a government emanating from a majority party. Another side can be summed up as "reason versus passion" or as *"politique politisante* versus *politique politisée."* Constitutionalism then stands for the rare moments in a nation's history when deep, principled discussion transcends the logrolling and horse-trading of everyday majority politics, the object of these debates being the principles which are to constrain future majority decisions.[17] Needless to say, it must not be possible to undo these principles by simple majority decision if they are to serve their function of constraining the majority. Nor would they be seen as binding were it possible to adopt them by simple majority decision. The general problem which haunts constitutionalism – why should any generation be bound by the decisions of its predecessors? – would be exacerbated if 51% of one generation could bind the next generation to principles which could be undone only by a two-thirds majority or even by unanimity.[18]

---

[16] In the present volume this is brought out in the chapters by Sejersted and Nedelsky.

[17] In the present volume this opposition is especially emphasized by Ackerman and in Sejersted's first contribution.

[18] See my discussion below, pp. 81–102.

Constitutionalism, then, fights a two-front war: against the executive and against the legislative branches of government. In addition, there is a constant tension between these two branches. Any government wants to receive its mandate in a general form that allows for efficient use of discretionary judgment, whereas any assembly wants to specify as much as possible how the mandate is to be carried out. To guard against the abuse of governmental power the assembly may, however, decide to use the tools of democracy rather than those of constitutionalism.[19] The procedural principles of openness and of participation in administrative decisions by those most deeply affected by them are democratic values, not derived from constitutional thought.[20]

A similar point can be made with respect to John Ely's reinterpretation of constitutional theory.[21] Ely insists that the purpose of judicial review is to protect democratic procedures from bias and distortion, and that the laying-down of substantive principles of justice is the task of the legislature, not of the courts. The task of the Supreme Court is to protect the political rights of the citizens, not their civil rights, since by exercising their (suitably protected) political rights they can define and protect their civil rights themselves. If this view is accepted, should we say that these procedural values serve as a constraint on democracy – or that they are simply part of what we mean by democracy?

The general conclusion suggested by the last two paragraphs is that both the wars fought by constitutionalism, as traditionally conceived, may be becoming less important. Constitutional constraints on governmental action are to some extent being replaced by democratic checks and controls. Similarly, the substantive constitutional constraints on majority rule are, or should arguably be, replaced by (or reinterpreted as) procedural controls. It is not my task here to argue for or against this view. I want only to suggest that this shift toward procedural justice may be the logical continuation of some lines of

[19] For discussions, see K. C. Davis, *Discretionary Justice* (Urbana, University of Illinois Press, 1971) and J. L. Mashaw, *Due Process in the Administrative State* (New Haven, Yale University Press, 1985). Many useful insights are also found in the contributions to R. G. Noll (ed.), *Regulatory Policy and the Social Sciences* (Berkeley, University of California Press, 1985).

[20] See the discussions below by Nedelsky, pp. 240–74 and Sejersted, pp. 275–302.

[21] J. H. Ely, *Democracy and Distrust* (Cambridge, Mass., Harvard University Press, 1981). For comments, see Ackerman below, pp. 153–94 and Holmes.

argument developed in the chapters below. If laws are promulgated by
a properly elected assembly and administered by proper participatory
procedures, the need for constitutional constraints may appear less
urgent.

II Self-binding

Why would a political assembly want to abdicate from the full
sovereignty which in principle it possesses, and sets limits on its own
future actions? In an intergenerational perspective, the question is
what right one generation has to limit the freedom of action of its
successors, and why the latter should feel bound by constraints laid
down by their ancestors.[22] A natural (although possibly misleading)
point of departure is to consider individual analogies.[23] Why, for
instance, would two individuals want to form a legal marriage instead
of simply cohabiting? What possible advantages could they derive
from limiting their future freedom of action and by making it more
difficult to separate should they form the wish to do so?[24] One obvious
answer is that they want to protect themselves against their own
tendency to act rashly, in the heat of passion. By raising the costs of
separation and imposing legal delays, marriage makes it less likely
that the spouses will give way to strong but temporary impulses to
separate. By increasing the expected duration of the relationship,
legal marriage also enhances the incentive to have children, to invest
in housing and make other long-term decisions. These decisions, in
turn create bonds between the spouses and reinforce the marriage.

These answers have partial analogues in the constitutional domain.
It is a truism that constitutional constraints make it more difficult for
the assembly or the society to change its mind on important questions.
Groups no less than individuals (although not in quite the same sense
as individuals) are subject to fits of passion, self-deception and
hysteria which may create a temporary majority for decisions which
will later be regretted. But then, one may ask, why could the members

---

[22] For the distinction between these two ways of asking the question see Holmes
below, pp. 195–240.

[23] For discussion of the disanalogies, see also Holmes, pp. 195–240. See also D. H.
Rubin, "Of bindings and by-products: Elster on rationality," *Philosophy and Public
Affairs*, 15 (1986), 82–95, at pp. 90–1.

[24] The marriage analogy is used below by Ackerman, pp. 153–94 and by Holmes,
pp. 195–240.

of the assembly not simply undo the decisions if and when they come to regret them? The presumption must be, after all, that the assembly knows what it is doing, not that it needs to be protected against itself.

Part of the answer to this question is suggested by the marriage analogy. The expected stability and duration of political institutions is an important value in itself, since they allow for long-term planning. Conversely, if all institutions are up for grabs all the time, individuals in power will be tempted to milk their positions for private purposes, and those outside power will hesitate to form projects which take time to bear fruit. Moreover, if nothing could ever be taken for granted, there would be large deadweight losses arising from bargaining and factionalism.[25]

Another part of the answer is that not all unwise decisions can be undone. Imagine that a majority untrammeled by constitutional constraints decides that an external or internal threat justifies a suspension of civil liberties, or that retroactive legislation should be enacted against "enemies of the people." In the first place, such measures have victims whom one cannot always compensate at later times. Examples abound: the internment of the American Japanese during the Second World War, the excesses during the Chinese Cultural Revolution, the *Berufsverbot* against Communists in several countries. When society again comes to its senses, the victims may be dead or their lives destroyed. In the second place, the temporary suspension of rights easily leads to the permanent abolition of majority rule itself and to its replacement by dictatorship. It suffices to cite the years 1794 and 1933. This is possibly the central argument for constitutional constraints on democracy: without such constraints democracy itself becomes weaker, not stronger.[26]

To flesh out some of these general considerations I shall consider fourteenth-century Florentine politics, as an example of a democratic society in search of, or at least in need of, constitutional constraints.[27] The development of the Florentine electoral system in this period could be summarized, perhaps, as the transformation of "instant politics," in which no institutions could ever be taken for granted, into

[25] See the discussion by Holmes, pp. 19–58 below, of the similar problems that would arise if the constitution were to be periodically remade from scratch.

[26] See the concluding remarks in Holmes's second contribution, pp. 195–240 below.

[27] The following draws upon J. M. Najemy, *Corporatism and Consensus in Florentine Electoral Politics 1280–1400* (Chapel Hill, University of North Carolina Press, 1982).

(or at least towards) a regime capable of commanding durable assent. To understand the tensions which the political process was supposed to resolve, we can first note that Florentine society in this period was divided both vertically and horizontally. The vertical divisions were, first, between the aristocratic oligarchy and the guildsmen, and, secondly, between various groups of guildsmen. The horizontal divisions were factions within the oligarchy, similar to if less violent than those between the Guelfs and the Ghibellines in the preceding century. Many of the electoral struggles in the period concerned the modalities of guild representation in city politics. Although corporatism, a political system based directly on the guilds, was regularly proposed and occasionally realized, the general tendency was toward a regime based on loyalty to the city and its political regime rather than to one's profession.

The object of the electoral politics was the election of members to the city government (the Signoria) and to various committees. Every two months these bodies were appointed anew, by a process which in general included four stages. First, candidates had to be nominated; then the nominated candidates had to be scrutinized for approval; then among the approved candidates a certain number had to be selected; and finally among the selected candidates those were rejected who did not satisfy various conditions of eligibility, the main ones being that neither the candidates themselves nor their close relatives should recently have held office. Each of these stages was, naturally, the focus of controversy, since the formal rules for nomination, scrutiny, selection and rejection shape and bias substantive outcomes.[28] Before we consider the process more closely, we should observe the very short time of office, constant throughout the period. The Florentines, presumably, did not trust anyone to hold power for long. In this they may well have acted wisely, but on the other hand it is clear that the high turn-over rate invites problems of stability, continuity and legitimacy. Their ingenious solution to these problems will occupy us in a moment.

Before we consider the solutions to the two specific problems of guild representation and high turn-over rates, the ground rules for proposing solutions and getting them accepted must be explained. The legislative assembly chose the mode of election of the government. In

---

[28] On this point see also Przeworski below, pp. 59–80.

part of the period the assembly deliberated anew for each election, thus creating an extremely unstable system in which not only the set of office-holders but also the methods for electing them could change every two months. This extreme of untrammeled democracy was, however, the exception rather than the rule, since the assembly, or those to whom it delegated its authority, could in principle choose many successive governments with one fell stroke. I shall return to this important, indeed unique, feature of the Florentine system.

To create a system which transcended guild interests, numerous solutions were proposed, and some of them put to test. Although there was general agreement that guild representation on the Signoria must be ensured, there was controversy over how it should be realized. The guilds, naturally, wanted to be able to nominate their representatives. The oligarchy wanted the representatives of the guild to be nominated from the outside, for instance, by the existing Signoria. Intermediate proposals were to have representatives from any given guild nominated by members of the other guilds, or to have guild nominators convened by district rather than by guild. These conflicts can be viewed cynically, as an attempt by the oligarchy to break the power of the guilds or by the major guilds to break the power of the minor ones (or vice versa), but they can also be viewed as an effort to overcome guild particularism in favor of loyalty to the city as a whole. From the last point of view, one should note the "constitutional" element of checks and balances in the intermediate proposals.

The more important task was to overcome the destabilizing forces resulting from the short period of office. The solution that came to be worked out was to have the officials for many successive governments nominated, approved and selected simultaneously, with a selection process based on lottery. Disregarding numerous variations and qualifications, the system in force in the third quarter of the century worked roughly as follows. Every three years various bodies, the most important of them the advisory colleges from the sixteen administrative districts, nominated candidates for office. The nomination process resulted in a large number of candidates, usually several thousand. These were presented to a scrutiny committee of 144 members, most of whom were appointed directly by the existing government. The committee voted in secret on each candidate, a two-thirds majority being required for approval. The names of the approved candidates were then placed in bags, from which were drawn at random, every two months, those of the candidates who would serve on the Signoria for the next period. Since the bags were not exhausted during the three-year period or discarded after the end of the period, there were always several overlapping bags in existence. The rule was to start with the oldest bags and to proceed to the more recent as the oldest became exhausted or the names drawn from them were ineligible for some reason. As a consequence there was a many–many correlation between governments and scrutinies, as distinct from the one–one correlation of modern elections.

The consequences of this complex arrangement were manifold. The fact that a large part of the citizens were nominated for office contributed to the legitimacy of the system, especially since it was never made public who survived the scrutiny. The knowledge that "my turn may come" on some future extraction of names from the bags probably prevented many citizens from rocking the boat. In addition, since the random element in the system prevented anyone from knowing who would hold office when, no faction could influence or bribe future office-holders. This was an important guarantee for the guilds against the powerful oligarchy, as were the restrictions on eligibility which prevented individuals from the same family from holding office frequently. Moreover, the lack of clear correlation between scrutinies and governments ensured that electoral discontent lacked any obvious target of attack. Randomness in itself ensures that a corrupt government cannot be directly traced to a corrupt electoral mechanism, and the system of overlapping bags must have made it even more difficult to perceive any malevolent hand at work behind a bad outcome.

Against this, of course, both the temporal lag between nomination and office-holding and the element of randomness have clear inconveniences, well summarized by Leonardo Bruni in the early fifteenth century:

> Experience has shown that this practice was useful in eliminating the struggles that so frequently erupted among the citizens competing for elections [under the previous system]. But as much as extraction by lot is beneficial to the republic in this respect, just as

much and even more is it harmful in another, namely, that because of the chance of the draw many unworthy persons are placed in the magistracy of the priorate. For the same care is not taken in staffing offices to be drawn in the future as in electing present ones, and we certainly give more attentive consideration to present matters and tend to be more negligent in judging those things ordained for an uncertain future. This practice of extraction by lot also extinguishes any motivation for prudent conduct, since, if men were forced to compete in direct elections and openly put their reputations on the line, they would be much more circumspect [in their life and behavior].[29]

In other words, the system reduced the pre-scrutiny incentive of the nominated candidates to behave well, since the motive of the scrutinizers to pay attention to behavior was reduced by time and uncertainty; and it also reduced their post-scrutiny incentive, since in a random draw nothing they did could affect their probability of being chosen. For these reasons, perhaps, the system was later modified into a two-track system, in which nearly half of the government was drawn from another set of bags filled with names carefully selected by and from the oligarchy. With this final modification the system survived for another century. The de facto elite dominance ensured stability and continuity, as well as legitimacy among the oligarchy, while the broad popular participation made for legitimacy among the citizens at large.

The Florentines did not think of themselves as engaged in constitution-making, but the problems they encountered in their experiments with democratic forms are similar to those which preoccupied later and more self-conscious "founders" or "framers." On the one hand democracy must rest on popular participation, but on the other hand it must be protected from the particularism and myopia which can easily result from unchecked popular rule. By trial and error the Florentines arrived at a practice that ensured efficiency as well as legitimacy, stability as well as participation. Needless to say, the strong oligarchic element of Florence disqualifies the regime from being democratic in anything like the modern sense, but this is a pointless observation from the present point of view. The tension

29 Cited after Najemy, p. 313.

between democracy and the need for stabilizing constraints is a perennial one, and arises in embryonic democracies as well as in full-fledged ones. The Florentines and the Greeks solved it by trial and error: their regimes survived, for a while, because they hit upon stabilizing devices that limited the self-destructive forces inherent in unconstrained democracy.[30] Modern approaches have, as I have said, been more self-conscious, but the problems they have addressed are largely the same.

III Property, democracy and constitutionalism

A frequently held left-wing view of the place of private property in the debate over constitutionalism and democracy is that the rich would never accept democracy unless they had a constitutional guarantee against confiscation by the propertyless majority.[31] An equally frequent right-wing view is that the right to free and undisturbed enjoyment of one's property follows from the more basic right to the free use of one's powers and faculties.[32]

A corollary of the left-wing view is the following. Assuming that the rich have veto power over the political regime and that they do indeed require political guarantees to accept majority rule, it is in the interest of the propertyless majority to give them such guarantees.[33] The majority must bind or limit itself to gain the indispensable minority support. The situation is somewhat analogous to that of a firm inviting outside shareholders: it must incur "costs of bonding," such as conservative principles of accountancy, in order to attract capital.[34] Yet that analogy also suggests a limitation of the left-wing view. One may ask, namely, why outside investors could not simply rely on the self-interest of the firm instead of requiring formal guarantees. Given that the firm is likely to need capital again in the future, it will tend to satisfy its current shareholders out of enlightened self-interest. Similarly, the propertied classes might reckon that the propertyless

[30] See Holmes's observation below, pp. 195–240: the problem is not how to create democracy, but how to make it endure.

[31] For statements of this view, see Przeworski below, pp. 59–80, and Nedelsky, pp. 241–74.

[32] For statements of this view, see Holmes below, pp. 195–240, and Sejersted, pp. 275–302.

[33] See Przeworski below, pp. 59–80 and Holmes, pp. 195–240.

[34] See M. C. Jensen and W. H. Meckling, "Theory of the firm: managerial behavior, agency costs and ownership structure," *Journal of Financial Economics*, 3 (1976), 305–60, esp. pp. 325–6.

majority will find it in its self-interest not to tamper with vested property rights, since the prosperity of everybody, including the majority itself, depends on the secure enjoyment of property by the bourgeoisie.[35]

This argument in turn invites two comments. First, the propertied classes might fear confiscation not just of the fruits of their property, but of their property itself. They might, in other words, fear the introduction of social ownership or workers' ownership of the means of production rather than excessively high taxes on profits. If the majority believes that a capitalist regime is not the best road to prosperity, or that prosperity is not the only political value, formal guarantees are required to prevent expropriation. Next, even if the propertied classes do not in fact expect a revolutionary change in the ownership of the means of production, they may not trust the propertyless classes to behave in their enlightened, long-term self-interest. Even though a high rate of taxation on profits undermines the tax base in the long run, it does bring in money in the present which can be used to satisfy popular demands. One might expect to find, therefore, the propertied classes demanding a constitutionally guaranteed ceiling on the rate of taxation. This, however, is rarely if ever observed. What we find instead is that they demand and get procedures which will, in their opinion, make confiscatory taxation an unlikely outcome.[36]

The "bonding" referred to above is subtly different from the constitutional "binding" discussed in many of the chapters below. As stated, the need for bonding referred explicitly to the *introduction* of democracy. The more general need for constitutional self-binding is, however, a permanent feature of democracy as a going concern.[37] As argued in (II) above, it arises out of the vulnerability of democracy to myopia and particularism, not out of the temporary vulnerability to the power of the pre-democratic elite. The question then arises why a democracy which has found its "assiette permanente et tranquille" (Tocqueville) should feel bound by the compromises it had to accept in the transitional period. The answer lies in the inherently controversial character of the distinction. In any given case it will be very

[35] For a discussion of this argument and of its limits, see my *Making Sense of Marx* (Cambridge University Press, 1985), ch. 7.1.

[36] This is the central argument in Przeworski's contribution below.

[37] For this distinction, see my contribution below, pp. 81–102.

difficult to sort out from each other the constraints which were set up
to make the creation of democracy possible and those which were set
up to make it endure. Many will defend the former by subsuming them
under the latter. To avoid destructive conflict, one usually has to treat
all constraints as essentially alike and thus to accept some measure of
ancestor dictatorship, even when it *cannot* be justified as self paternalism.

The right-wing argument for the constitutional protection of property is not very prominent or plausible today.[38] Unlike, say, privacy,
autonomy or participation, property does not, to the contemporary
mind, appear as an inherently valuable right. The growth of the
modern state and the need for complex regulations of private
economic affairs have restored the "bundle-of-rights" conception of
property to the place from which it had been temporarily dethroned
by classical liberalism. None of the components of the bundle appear
as especially sacred, and each of them is in fact regularly violated or
overridden. Any suggestion that a particular component ought to
enjoy particular security will have to be justified on squarely consequentialist grounds. Natural-rights arguments may occasionally
reinforce the rule-utilitarian arguments for security of property, but
are no longer effective on their own.[39]

There may even be an emerging trend in the opposite direction,
towards constitutional guarantees for the dilution or diffusion of
private property. It has been widely argued that an egalitarian
distribution of property is a condition for the effective exercise of
democratic political rights.[40] In a well-functioning democracy in which
all citizens are well informed and no one exercises disproportionate
power, there should be minimal as well as maximal levels on property-
holding. One way of realizing this goal could be by making workers'
ownership of enterprises mandatory, i.e., by outlawing wage labor
and private property of the means of production,[41] but other solutions
could also be imagined.[42] Secondly, one may argue that the demo-

[38] As is also observed by Nedelsky below, pp. 241–74.
[39] On this point see Sejersted below, pp. 275–302.
[40] See for instance R. Krouse and M. McPherson, "On Rawlsian justice in political
economy: capitalism, 'property-owning democracy', and the welfare state," forthcoming in A. Guttman (ed.), *Democracy and the Welfare State.*
[41] See my discussion below of this alternative, pp. 303–26.
[42] R. Krouse and M. McPherson, "A 'mixed' property regime: equality and liberty in
a market economy," *Ethics*, 87 (1986), 119–28.

cratic value of participation is no less relevant for economic life than for political decisions.[43] It is not simply that the relation between property rights and civil rights is reversed:[44] the very distinction may be disintegrating. These emerging tendencies towards an extension of democracy would, if confirmed, fit well with the trends sketched towards the end of (I) above towards procedural and democratic controls. But these are speculative remarks, to be entertained as hypotheses, not as assertions.

[43] R. Dahl, *A Preface to Economic Democracy* (New Haven, Conn., Yale University Press, 1985); M. Walzer, *Spheres of Justice* (New York, Basic Books, 1983), pp. 291ff.

[44] As argued by Nedelsky below, pp. 241–74.

1. Gag rules or the politics of omission

STEPHEN HOLMES

A conversation is invariably shaped by what its participants decide not to say. To avoid destructive conflicts, we suppress controversial themes. In Cambridge, Massachusetts, old friends shun the subject of Israel in order to keep old friendships intact. Burying a divisive issue, of course, can be viewed censoriously – as evasiveness rather than diplomacy. But conflict-shyness is not merely craven: it can serve positive goals. By tying our tongues about a sensitive question, we can secure forms of cooperation and fellowship otherwise beyond reach.

Strategic self-censorship occurs in a variety of settings, from international summits to midnight trysts – including perhaps the limiting case of amnesia. In collective life, unmentionables abound. Within every group, speaking about tabooed subjects will provoke general consternation and embarrassment. After all, no one should wash his dirty linen in public. At faculty meetings, even garrulous professors will not prattle interminably about their alcohol problems or marital relations. Such universally appreciated uncommunicativeness can be easily explained. For one thing, no group's information-processing capacity is infinite. People cannot talk about everything at once; life is short; to avoid cognitive overload, different groups focus on different topics at different times.

Other reasons for sealing one's lips are less general and more pertinent to democratic theory. Sometimes an issue appears "unspeakable" because open airing would mortally offend prominent individuals or subgroups and permanently injure the cooperative spirit of the organization. Alternatively, a group can utilize its scarce resources more effectively if it dodges an irksome issue. By refraining from opening a can of worms, discussion leaders can prevent its lively contents from absorbing 100% of everyone's attention – at least for the time being. Despite the warnings of popular psychology, in other words, repression can be perfectly healthy.

Some preliminary examples

In law, statutes of limitation preclude prosecutions for temporally remote crimes. Similarly, various nonjusticiability doctrines enable the Court to silence itself about difficult legal issues. The "political questions" doctrine, as well as "case and controversy," "ripeness" and "standing" are all "devices for deciding not to decide,"[1] strategies by which members of the Court limit the range of problems on which they are required to pronounce. Every institution is equipped to resolve certain difficulties better than others. By staying its hand, the Court can improve its overall performance. By refusing either to uphold or overturn a governmental action, it can avoid decisions that might damage its credibility and overtax its limited problem-solving capacities.

Scholarly communities similarly regulate the area of permissible and pertinent speech. Universities, for example, are generally thought to have a limited mission. True, controversy rages about how audible or muted, say, the university's political voice should be. Conservatives assert that divestment from companies doing business in South Africa is not a suitable subject for formal consideration by a university faculty. But liberals, while castigating what they perceive as moral evasiveness, concur that the docket of faculty meetings must be confined in *some* ways, for example, that they should not leave time for an exhaustive diagnosis of faculty spouses.

Finally, to select a quite different example, John Rawls has argued for the political utility of what he calls "the method of avoidance."[2] In any group, a cleverly formulated gag rule can profitably shift attention away from areas of discord and toward areas of concord. Certain metaphysical assumptions about the human person are now, and will probably remain, controversial. To establish a public conception of justice acceptable to all members of a diverse society, we must abstract from questions which elicit radical disagreement. In a liberal

---

[1] Alexander Bickel, *The Least Dangerous Branch: The Supreme Court at the Bar of Politics* (New Haven, Yale University Press, 1962), p. 133; and, in general, pp. 111–98.

[2] John Rawls, "Justice as fairness: political not metaphysical," *Philosophy and Public Affairs*, vol. 14, no. 3 (summer, 1985), 223–51.

social order, the basic normative framework must be able to command the loyalty of individuals and groups with widely differing self-understandings and conceptions of personal fulfillment. As a result, theorists of justice can achieve their principal aim only by steering clear of irresolvable metaphysical disputes.

Similar side-stepping techniques are familiar in political life. Like "self-binding" in general, tongue-tying may be one of constitutionalism's main gifts to democracy. Some constitutional limits, at least, can be usefully redescribed as expressing a community's decision to silence itself, or its representatives, on selected issues. Legislators are enjoined from officially discussing questions which, if placed under the control of electoral majorities, would (it is thought) induce governmental paralysis, squander everyone's time or exacerbate factional animosities.

Self-denying ordinances

Conspiracy theorists have taught us to conceive agenda-narrowing as a technique by which sinister elites exert power over their hapless victims: "power may be, and often is, exercised by confining the scope of decision-making to relatively 'safe' issues" or, less circumlocutiously: "He who determines what politics is about runs the country."[3] Indeed, power-wielders do not always act surreptitiously when silencing others or constricting the range of issues which can be freely discussed. By limiting campaign contributions or discontinuing legal aid to the poor, public officials effectively stifle the voice of certain citizens without actually commanding them to remain silent. But direct censorship, at least since the invention of printing, has easily rivaled the withdrawal of resources as an instrument of political control. Today, for example, state legislatures no longer forbid doctors to distribute contraceptive information; but they may well, to choose another random example, restrain tobacco companies from advertising cigarettes.

Freedom of speech, in point of fact, does not outlaw every sort of gag order. Judges seal records, tell lawyers not to inform the jury

---

[3] Peter Bachrach and Morton S. Baratz, "Two faces of power," *American Political Science Review*, 56 (1962), 948; E. E. Schattschneider, *The Semisovereign People: A Realist's View of Democracy in America* (Hinsdale, Illinois, The Dryden Press, 1975), p. 66.

about a defendant's earlier mistrial for the same offense. More rarely, a judge may prohibit lawyers from discussing a case with reporters while the trial is going on. Various laws regulate disclosure by government employees. The Justice Department can, in exceptional circumstances, impose prior restraint to prevent newspapers from publishing a story that might endanger national security. Similarly, and more generally, libel law is a system of rules about what people cannot say.

In sum, one individual or group can gag another, using threats or paying hush money. But individuals and groups can also gag themselves. Self-denying ordinances are perfectly possible. Witnesses plea the Fifth Amendment, declining to testify for fear that what they say may incriminate them. Analogously, nominees to the federal bench duck senatorial cross-examination, averring that they must never rule in advance and without benefit of a concrete case. Panel members recuse themselves because of conflicts of interest. Legislators abstain from voting when countervailing pressures cannot be reconciled and when taking a position one way or the other might cost them essential electoral support.

Such garden-variety examples of strategic self-censorship could be multiplied indefinitely. Legislative bodies interdict debate on delicate issues in a somewhat more systematic manner. In the early American Senate and House, a parliamentary technique (then called "the previous question") was employed "for avoiding either undesired discussions or undesired decisions, or both."[4] Like individuals, in other words, organizations and collectivities can leave selected topics undiscussed for what they consider their own advantage. In order to present a united front, members of a political party may refrain from publicizing internal conflicts. To attract public attention, by contrast, members of rival parties may choose to highlight their differences, remaining mute about the principles and goals they share in common. Sometimes important objectives can only be achieved so long as they are left unspoken. Marriages may founder on attempts to delineate, in a written contract, precisely who is to do what and when. Affirmative action may be yet another example: if the government talks too freely

---

[4] Joseph Cooper, *The Previous Question: its Standing as a Precedent for Cloture in the United States Senate* (87th Congress, 2d Session, Document No. 104) (Washington, D.C., U.S. Government Printing Office, 1962), p. 2.

about what it is trying to do (for instance, create the conditions for self-respect among minorities), it may needlessly throw obstacles in its own path. In such a case, public officials are wise to gag themselves. At the very least, soft-spokenness is desirable because it may help prevent not unwanted conflict but rather unwanted humiliation. To make their policies successful, in sum, groups too find it prudent to cultivate the arts of omission.

Positive uses of negative liberty

No issue is more frequently classified as "worthy of avoiding" than religion. Sectarianism, is understandably considered to be divisive, a serious threat to communal cooperation. Religious disputes, it is said, cannot always be resolved politically, or even rationally. On this premise, many communities have decided to draw a "line" between the public and the private – to consign religious attachments to the nonpolitical sphere, beyond the jurisdiction of majorities and officials. Paradoxically, such compartmentalization is thought to reinforce social cohesion. Other controversies will be easier to resolve if religious schisms do not crystallize into political factions.

If accepted, such a claim throws interesting light on the doctrine of nonentanglement. Viewed from this perspective, the "wall" between church and state does not merely shelter the private sphere from unwanted incursions; it also unburdens the public sphere of irresolvable problems. In general, students of "negative liberty"[5] have neglected the disencumbering or agenda-uncluttering function of private rights. Limits on the government's jurisdiction are typically justified by reference to the fragility and intrinsic value of protected domains. But why not invert the picture and examine what benefits accrue to public life if certain issues are excluded from the public agenda? While screening one realm, private rights may simultaneously lighten the

[5] For present purposes, I shall define *positive liberty* as collective self-government (not as "the realization of the real self" or "the exercise of authentic capacities," to which self-government is often narcissistically assimilated); *negative liberty*, by contrast, can be preliminarily defined as the absence of coercive interference by the government or other wielders of power. It is profoundly confusing to identify positive liberty with both democracy and individual self-realization, I believe, because (1) the absence of coercion is typically prized as a necessary precondition for the development of human faculties, and (2) obligatory and full-time political participation may condemn many humanly important capacities to wither on the vine.

charge on another. Negative liberty "privatizes" certain questions, erasing them from the list of problems to be resolved politically. This unloading tactic makes all remaining controversies more amenable to compromise. When viewed from a slightly different angle, what formerly seemed a protective device now appears as a disencumbering strategy. By gagging themselves about religion, to return to that example, public officials seem to gain as much freedom as do private sectaries. The autonomy of politics increases simultaneously with the autonomy of religion.

According to Isaiah Berlin, "there is no necessary connection between individual liberty and democratic rule." This connection, he continues, "is a good deal more tenuous than it seemed to many advocates of both."[6] If my suggestion has any merit, Berlin is at least partially mistaken: private rights contribute vitally to democratic government by expunging irresolvable disputes from the public sphere. By the narrowing of the political agenda to problems manageable by discussion, certain individual rights may be said to subserve self-government. Their function, once again, is not merely to shield the private but also to disencumber the public.

Issue-suppression sounds tyrannical: to gag is to choke. But self-denial may be indispensable in self-regulating polities. For one thing, conflict-resolution often presupposes conflict-avoidance. Democracy becomes possible, according to many democratic theorists, only when certain emotionally charged solidarities and commitments are displaced from the political realm. By keeping religious questions off the legislative agenda, as I have been suggesting, the principle of nonentanglement may help fashion a certain kind of public – a public susceptible to democratic methods of conflict-resolution. Self-gagging is thus a form of self-control, not of self-strangulation. To repeat: by agreeing to privatize religion, a divided citizenry can enable itself to resolve its *other* differences rationally, by means of public debate and compromise.

Democracy is conventionally associated with *glasnost*, freedom of speech and the overthrow of censorial government. Thus, it seems perverse to focus on the contribution of gag rules to self-rule. Nevertheless, the shape of democratic politics is undoubtedly determined by the strategic removal of certain items from the democratic

---

[6] Isaiah Berlin, *Four Essays on Liberty* (Oxford University Press, 1969), pp. 130–1.

agenda. Some theorists have even argued that issue-suppression is a necessary condition for the emergence and stability of democracies. According to Joseph Schumpeter, for instance, one of the essential prerequisites for a successful democracy is that "the range of political decision should not be extended too far."[7] Robert Dahl argues that moral conflict need not subvert democracy: disagreement about goals is compatible with collective self-rule so long as there remains ample group autonomy within a society, i.e., plenty of lee-way for groups to follow their own goals unharassed.[8] Because he views religion as a prime source of rationally irresolvable conflict, Samuel Huntington asserts that cultures lacking a sharp separation between religion and politics, between spiritual and secular domains, are not "hospitable to democracy."[9] When ultimate ends color all concrete political acts, compromise or piecemeal reform becomes next to impossible. Democratization is doomed from the start, according to this line of argument, without some sort of socially acknowledged boundary between religion and politics.

Types of gag rule

Gag rules can be either autonomous or heteronomous, i.e., self-imposed or imposed by others. Self-imposed gag rules, in turn, can be ratified by unanimity or only by a majority. They can also be either formal or informal. For example, some legislative vows of silence are explicitly incorporated into the constitutional framework, while others are based on a tacit agreement among political elites. The autonomous/heteronomous, unanimous/majoritarian and formal/informal distinctions will prove very useful in our analysis, below, of two classic attempts at issue-avoidance: the efforts, in the United States, to suppress political controversy first about slavery and then about religion. Several other variations among kinds of gag rule should also be mentioned at the outset.

Some gag rules are designed only to postpone a discussion or avoid a

---

[7] Joseph Schumpeter, *Capitalism, Socialism, and Democracy* (New York, Harper and Row, 1962), p. 291 (see also p. 297).

[8] Robert Dahl, *Preface to Democratic Theory* (University of Chicago Press, 1956), p. 80.

[9] Samuel P. Huntington, "Will more countries become democratic?," *Political Science Quarterly*, vol. 99, no. 2 (summer, 1984), 208.

precipitate decision; others are meant to bury a topic definitively.[10] Some gag rules debar everyone from raising a ticklish question; others are more narrowly targeted, silencing only a selected class of speakers. For instance, when a technical question arises, laymen ordinarily defer to specialists. Modern democracies contain many semi-autonomous institutions, each with its own agenda. Thus, we must also distinguish between the universal suppression of a theme and the mere transferral of that theme to a different institutional context. Unspeakable in one room or *devant les enfants*, embarrassing revelations may be thoroughly canvassed in a more secluded part of the same house. Rather than tinkering with an explosive issue, a high official may pass the buck, handing it over to expendable functionaries not too closely associated with the party in power.

Less deviously, some topics are excluded from the national legislative agenda only to be consigned to state legislatures or to the courts. Contrariwise, by decamping from the political thicket, the Court silences itself; but it simultaneously invites executive and legislative officials to speak out. In such cases, gag rules institute a division of labour which can help clarify responsibilities for all parties. Much more radical is the decision to remove an issue from the jurisdiction of all branches and levels of government.

Finally, some items are excluded from the political agenda without any conscious decision having been made. Agendas are not infinite; and it would be preposterous to assume that all issues are naturally on the agenda and only fail to appear because they are consciously taken off. Parochial habits of mind, cultural blinders or a lack of imagination all help explain why politicians fail to seize upon (what seems to us) an important theme. In the United States, unlike European nations with Communist Parties, the legitimacy of private property is never debated in formal legislative settings. But the issue was never deliberately suppressed because, for a variety of reasons, it was never raised.

Political agendas are constantly expanding and contracting. Why an issue captures or escapes public attention is an important subject for historical and sociological research. To analyze processes of agenda-narrowing and agenda-broadening would require, among other things, careful attention to the conditions for successful and abortive

---

[10] The opposite of postponing a discussion is cloture: the decision to prohibit discussion *after* a certain point.

social movements. Understandably, my concerns are more narrow. At least some issues which would otherwise be at the center of political attention are consciously deleted from the range of subjects to be discussed.[11] To make the concept of a *gag rule* useful for comparative analysis, we must restrict it to such overt, fully purposive and tactically justified acts of omission.

The transition to democracy

Consider the decision of several recently restabilized democracies to offer immunity from criminal prosecution to military leaders who wielded power in the old regime.[12] Although guilty of atrocities, some of these officers have been willing to relinquish power peacefully to a civilian government. But they did so only in exchange for a legislative and judicial vow of silence about their past wrongdoings. Amnesties, in fact, are classic examples of democracy-stabilizing gag rules. They embody what Nietzsche called *aktive Vergeßlichkeit*,[13] but on a national or at least governmental scale. By closing the books on the past, keeping retribution for former crimes off the political agenda, the organizers of a new democracy can secure the compliance of strategically located elites – cooperation which may be indispensable for a successful transition from dictatorship to self-government. Without an overriding desire for national unity, however, we can assume that opposing groups will be unlikely to silence themselves about the issues that most radically divide them.

Freedom is sometimes defined as a coincidence of desires and capacities. Governments presumably strive to ensure that their abilities and resources are adequate to the problems they face and the objectives they intend to pursue. Deleting unanswerable questions from the political agenda is thus a natural strategy for any state, especially a recently founded one. New regimes have shallow roots

[11] Freudian repression must suppress not only the event to be forgotten but also the act of repressing itself (J.-P. Sartre, *L'Etre et le néant* [Paris, Gallimard, 1943], pp. 88–93). An effective gag rule, by contrast, requires all parties to know that – and remember why – they are avoiding a touchy question.

[12] Juan J. Linz, "The transition from authoritarian regimes to democratic political systems and the problems of consolidation of political democracy," unpublished manuscript, presented at the IPSA Tokyo Roundtable, March 29–April 1, 1982.

[13] Friedrich Nietzsche, "Zur Genealogie der Moral," *Werke*, edited by Karl Schlecta (Darmstadt, Wissenschaftliche Buchgesellschaft, 1966), vol. II, p. 799.

and may be destroyed by the first storm that strikes, as Machiavelli observed. A newborn government is especially unlikely to survive if forced to make controversial decisions about historically intractable problems.

According to Dankwart Rustow, an intense but obviously unwinnable struggle is an essential precondition for the transition to democracy.[14] All parties will soon become weary of interminable hostilities. If they possess the talent and will, key elites can then negotiate a settlement – a system of power-sharing and mutual accommodation in the interest of all major factions. This bargain among subgroups and sections may assume the form of a constitution. Eliminating divisive questions from the jurisdiction of state officials is likely to be an essential element in any such regime-founding compromise.

If the government is to survive, Rustow argues, the original constitutional settlement must be a boot-strap operation. The constitution cannot be imposed autocratically from above. To have the exemplary power essential to any successful act of founding, the initial peace treaty must at least appear to be designed cooperatively by the rival factions.[15] In other words, consensus on fundamentals should not be overrated as a precondition for democratization. Without major divisions, there would be no incentive to devise democratic institutions in the first place. These institutions, we may add, will only succeed in handling latent conflicts if they incorporate mechanisms for side-stepping divisive issues.

Paradoxically, as Clifford Geertz has argued, citizenship and community are sometimes incompatible.[16] At the very least, communal loyalties present serious obstacles to the integration of recently created national states. Geertz is concerned with the consolidation of any sort of national state, not solely with the creation of democracies.

---

[14] Dankwart Rustow, "Transitions to democracy: toward a dynamic model," *Comparative Politics*, 2 (April, 1970), 337–63.

[15] "The first grand compromise that establishes democracy, if it proves at all viable, is in itself proof of the efficacy of the principle of conciliation and accommodation. The first success, therefore, may encourage contending forces and their leaders to submit other major questions to resolution by democratic procedures" (*ibid.*, 358).

[16] Clifford Geertz, "The integrative revolution: primordial sentiments and civil politics in the new states," *The Interpretation of Cultures* (New York, Basic Books, 1973). Geertz writes of "the looming headlong clash of primordial and civil loyalties" (*ibid.*, p. 309).

But his insights are nevertheless revealing for our inquiry. "Primordial attachments," as he describes them, can be religious, racial, linguistic, tribal, regional or customary; but they are always tinged with sectoral xenophobia and are thus in tension with membership in the state as a whole. Some of the world's most intractable problems arise when primordial ties are politicized by attempts at national integration.[17]

Minority security is a common good – good for the majority as well as the minority. By designing a constitution to allay the fears of defenceless ethnic subgroups, the framers of a regime-founding compromise can secure the national cooperation necessary for economic prosperity and military independence. Any nation split into "primordially defined groups" must discover a "form competent to contain the country's diversity." This "form," once again, is a political constitution in the broad sense. It establishes law-making and law-enforcing bodies, but also organizations, such as political parties, "within which primordial conflicts are being informally and realistically adjusted."[18]

Party organization, the domestication of factional loyalties and the diplomatic skill of elites are essential for social stability in a religiously and ethnically diverse country. But such factors must be supplemented by a strategic narrowing of the national political agenda. Primordial loyalties must be shielded from the police and not only directed into "proper" political channels but also (at least to some extent) channeled away from politics altogether.[19] De-politicization, in conjunction with other forces, can increase the chances for rational compromise in a divided society.

One traditional solution to the problem of primordial divisions is secession or partition. Another is ethnocracy: a single religious, linguistic, racial or regional group can expel, assimilate or subjugate all others. This is "community" in the strong and antiliberal sense. But if diversity can be neutralized constitutionally, it can also be

---

[17] *Ibid.* pp. 263, 272.

[18] *Ibid.*, pp. 282–3. What leaders must strive to establish is "an effective civil framework within which very intense primordial issues can be adjusted and contained rather than allowed to run free in parapolitical confusion" (*ibid.*, p. 285).

[19] This must be what Geertz means by the importance of "divesting [primordial loyalties] of their legitimizing force with respect to governmental authority" (*ibid.*, p. 277).

accommodated within the four corners of a single state. Clever framers can design institutions which cushion conflict. By so doing, they are laying the foundations for "a civil politics of primordial compromise."[20]

A compromise-minded politics of this sort has long been the focus of Arend Lijphart's studies of consociationalism. In primordially divided societies, self-government requires "cooperation by the leaders of different groups which transcends the segmental or subcultural cleavages at the mass level."[21] Paradoxically, elites must both represent and not represent their constituents. They must hold their followers' loyalty but not reproduce their uncompromising attitudes in national negotiations.[22] Such cross-sectarian cooperation among elites requires "a strengthening of the political inertness of the nonelite public and their deferential attitudes to the segmental leaders."[23]

The spirit of compromise among elites is a necessary but not sufficient condition for self-rule in a divided society. Equally important is "segmental autonomy" – Lijphart's expression for the removal of divisive issues from the national agenda. Ideally, there will be a "high degree of freedom for the segments in the conduct of their internal social and cultural affairs."[24] In other words, the national government must muzzle itself on certain issues. On matters of regional or sectarian but not national interest, "decisions and their execution can be left to the separate segments."[25] When national decisions cannot be avoided, each group must be granted influence proportionate with its numbers and, crucially, armed with a veto. The reason for taking such elaborate precautions is simple: "in a political system with clearly separate and potentially hostile population segments, virtually all decisions are perceived as entailing high stakes, and strict majority rule places a strain on the unity and peace of the system."[26] When the stakes are high, the jurisdiction of national majorities must be narrow. To ensure its own authority on other

[20] *Ibid.*, p. 310.
[21] Arend Lijphart, *Democracy in Plural Societies: A Comparative Exploration* (New Haven, Yale University Press, 1977).
[22] *Ibid.*, p. 53.   [23] *Ibid.*, p. 169.   [24] *Ibid.*, p. 151.   [25] *Ibid.*, p. 41.
[26] *Ibid.*, p. 28. "When such decisions affect the vital interests of a minority segment, such a defeat will be regarded as unacceptable and will endanger intersegmental elite cooperation" (*ibid.*, p. 36).

issues, the national majority must gag itself on issues destined to provoke sectarian animosity.

For divided societies, Lijphart advocates coalition governments, a mutual veto, proportionality in the allocation of civil service jobs as well as government subsidies and, as I mentioned, segmental autonomy. He favors three or four parties over two, a parliamentary to a presidential system, proportional representation to majority rule and federalism over a unitary government. He also prefers a "coalescent" to an adversarial style of decision-making. Political choices should be made in secret negotiations among rival elites (on the basis of log-rolling, package deals and so forth) and should be arrived at by virtual unanimity. Consociationalism, in other words, means democracy without an opposition. According to Lijphart, the societies in question are too deeply divided to withstand open political contestation.

The gag rule of 1836

Before the Civil War, the United States itself was a profoundly divided society. Its leaders, too, shied away from open conflict over the most divisive of all issues. In 1836, for example, the U.S. House of Representatives adopted the first in a series of gag rules:

> *Resolved*, That all petitions, memorials, resolutions, propositions, or papers, relating in any way, or to any extent whatsoever, to the subject of slavery, or the abolition of slavery, shall, without being either printed or referred, be laid on the table, and that no further action whatever shall be had thereon.[27]

This act of legislative self-censorship and the parallel measure adopted in the Senate were tactical compromises, "coalescent" attempts to split the difference between North and South. Only a self-denying ordinance would permit mutual adjustments and rational discussion of other issues among the sections. Only a gag rule could scale back the responsibilities of the federal government, making them roughly

[27] *Register of Debates*, vol. XII, 24th Congress, 1. session (May 18, 1836), p. 3757. The last of the congressional gag rules was rescinded in 1845, largely through the efforts of Adams: see Samuel Flagg Bemis's chapter entitled "Slavery and the gag rule," *John Quincy Adams and the Union* (New York, Knopf, 1956).

proportionate to its modest problem-solving capacities. Curiously enough, Congress's decision to stay its own hand was attacked not only, as one would expect, by abolitionists; it was also assailed by proslavery advocates of states' rights (such as John Calhoun) who themselves yearned for absolute congressional silence on the slave question. The precariousness of all self-gagging arrangements is usefully underlined by southern hostility to this bill.

The debate of 1836 about gagging Congress occurred under the shadow of a larger controversy about gagging the abolitionist press. Northern antislavery societies had decided to use the mails to flood the South with emancipationist tracts. Predictably, southerners refused to allow these works to circulate freely. In their view, such pamphlets threatened their very survival, i.e., constituted open invitations to slave insurrection. The federal government, unwilling to enforce its own laws on such a sensitive issue, turned a blind eye while southern states proceeded to censor the mails.[28]

Staunching the flow of abolitionist literature across southern borders was not sufficient for the proslavery forces. They were equally anxious to quell unending congressional debates about slavery. President Jackson himself argued, in the words of his biographer, that "all discussion in Congress of the slave issue" was "ultimately undemocratic."[29] Incessant slavery agitation was crippling the national legislature's capacity to deal with other issues. Talk of slavery was simply disruptionist. Mutual recriminations between proslavery and antislavery forces had even led some congressmen to arrive at the House and Senate chambers armed with knives – a sure sign that parliamentary courtesy was fraying at the edges.

Of particular concern to the South were petitions requesting Congress to abolish slavery, or at least the slave trade, within the District of Columbia. The antislavery position was that all citizens had a right to petition the government for redress of grievances.[30] According to slavery's advocates, by contrast, Congress should refuse even to

[28] William W. Freehling, *Prelude to Civil War: The Nullification Controversy in South Carolina 1816–1836* (New York, Harper and Row, 1966), pp. 346–8. I am indebted to Freehling's entire discussion of the gag rule debate.

[29] Robert V. Remini, *Andrew Jackson and the Course of American Democracy, 1833–1845*, vol. III (New York, Harper & Row, 1984), p. 406.

[30] A significant majority from *both* sections, however, voted to gag the slaves themselves, i.e., to deny them a right to petition Congress (*Register of Debates*, vol. XIII, 24th Congress, 2. session [February 11, 1837] p. 1733).

receive these petitions on the grounds that the federal government had no authority to abolish slavery anywhere. Exactly like the abolitionists, Senators and Representatives should be fully gagged on the slave question: "The subject is beyond the jurisdiction of Congress – they have no right to touch it in any shape or form, or to make it the subject of deliberation or discussion."[31] While appealing to formal rights and lines of jurisdiction, Calhoun was essentially concerned with political consequences. The abolitionists were fanatics and incendiaries. Their "insulting petitions" vilified the South, taught hatred and threatened to destroy the Union. Attempts publicly to disgrace and humiliate slaveholding states could not be profitably discussed in Congress. Such discussions, however perfunctory, could only further polarize the nation.

As a compromise measure, Henry Pinckney introduced a series of resolutions in the House stipulating that Congress could not, as a matter of constitutional principle, regulate slavery in the South, and should not, as a matter of expedience, regulate slavery in the District. The attached gag-rule clause, cited above, declared that petitions concerning slavery would be formally "received" by Congress; but they would then be automatically tabled and never discussed.

As I said, Calhoun in the Senate and fellow nullificationists in the House "considered Pinckney's gag rule a disastrous southern defeat."[32] It struck Congress dumb, but not deaf. In retrospect, proslavery objections to the rule seem almost hysterically legalistic. The resolutions, they argued, implicitly granted Congress the right to discuss slavery and to abolish it in the District, even though Congress currently refused to exploit these rights.[33] Abolition petitions, at any rate, should not be received and tabled but simply not received. Congress's mouth should be gagged; but its ears must also be plugged. The initial reception of petitions, Calhoun explained, was "our Thermopylae." We must, he added, "meet the enemy on the frontier."[34] Half-hearted gag rules were too loose to still the emanci-

[31] *The Papers of John C. Calhoun*, vol. XIII (1835–1837), edited by Clyde Wilson (Columbia, University of South Carolina Press, 1980), p. 393.

[32] Freehling, *Prelude to Civil War*, p. 355.

[33] For similar reasons, Calhoun rejected President Jackson's offer to debar incendiary publications from being circulated in the South: to accept federal help on this matter would be dangerously to extend federal authority into the internal affairs of the states.

[34] *The Papers of John C. Calhoun*, vol. XIII, p. 105.

pationist tongue. Indeed, Calhoun and his compatriots wanted the impossible, for Congress to be so tightly handcuffed and corseted on this issue that it could never even aspire to slip its bonds: "nothing short of the certainty of permanent security can induce us to yield an inch."[35]

The gag rule of 1836, precisely because it was a political compromise, is emblematic of the mainstream approach to the slavery question in American politics from the Founding to the Civil War. First the emergence and subsequently the maintenance of national self-rule presupposed the strategic avoidance of this divisive theme. At the very outset, a clause opposing the slave trade was dropped from the Declaration of Independence. The Constitution itself discreetly abstained from using the words "slave" or "slavery." The Framers acknowledged the institution of slavery, of course.[36] But they resorted to euphemism and indirectness when describing it – as if the disagreeableness of the thing could be mitigated by fastidiousness about the name. The sectional compromise at the heart of the Constitution, one might say, demanded that the issue remain latent and largely unspoken.[37] Discussing the bargains by which divided nations are united, Geertz comments that "the mere prejudices that must be tolerated in order to effect such reconciliations are often repugnant."[38] The creation of a national republic in the United States seems to be a case in point. As time went by, many northerners became more

---

[35] *Ibid.*, p. 106.

[36] For example, by agreeing to tolerate the slave trade until 1808 (Art. I, sec. 9, para. 1), and by accepting the three-fifths rule (Art. I, sec. 2, para. 3), which helped balance northern and southern power in the House.

[37] The classical "pro-democratic" argument for suppressing a divisive issue was made by Senator Benton in 1848: "This Federal Government was made for something else than to have this pestiferous question constantly thrust upon us to the interruption of the most important business ... What I protest against is, to have the real business of the country, the pressing, urgent, crying business of the country stopped, prostrated, defeated, by thrusting this question upon us. We read in Holy Writ, that a certain people were cursed by the plague of frogs, and that the plague was everywhere. You could not look upon the table but there were frogs, you could not sit down at the banquet but there were frogs, you could not go to the bridal couch and lift the sheets but there were frogs! ... Here it is, this black question, forever on the table, on the nuptial couch, everywhere! ... I remember the time when no one would have thought of asking a public man what his opinions were on the extension of slavery any more than what was the length of his foot" (*Congressional Globe*, 30th Congress, I session, appendix, p. 686; cited in Andrew McLaughlin, *A Constitutional History of the United States* [New York, Appleton-Century-Crofts, 1935], p. 509).

[38] Geertz, "The integrative revolution," p. 310.

and more morally opposed to slavery. Most remained even more averse to dismembering the Union, however. Nationalism, as is often the case, made them unwilling to stir up sectional hostilities.

The Constitution as a bargain

Under any system of majority rule, members of an outvoted minority must agree to an outcome they oppose. That is, they must consent to a decision to which they do not consent. Majoritarianism is thus inherently paradoxical. It escapes inconsistency only because *consent* can be aimed at different targets. Even if they do not consent directly to the decision being made, members of an outvoted minority can consent to the procedures by which that decision was reached and even bind themselves indirectly to abide by whatever outcome the accepted procedure produces. But the difficulty here cannot be so easily dismissed. Why *do* minorities accept majority rule? Without a minority's acquiescence in decisions which its members, by definition, dislike, democracy would be impossible. But how is a minority's acquiescence politically guaranteed?

One answer is offered by the theory of "multiple membership." If every individual belongs to several groups at once, then most citizens will be aligned with both majority and minority coalitions on different questions. Outvoted on one issue, citizens will have good self-regarding reasons to accept an unwanted decision: in other circumstances they, too, will benefit from majority rule. Contrariwise, members of an obviously temporary majority will be inspired to display self-restraint. Cross-pressured by their rival group allegiances and expecting to be outvoted on other issues, the winners-of-the-moment will be unlikely to run roughshod over the deepest values of the losers.

When majority and minority coalitions become stable across the most important issues, no system of mutual restraint and accommodation based on multiple membership can gain a purchase. Such was roughly the situation in the United States before the Civil War. Only a Constitution placing strict limitations on majority power could foster minority security and thereby induce a southern minority to accept the decisions of a northern majority. Federalism, paradoxically, was the structural provision most essential for securing national cooperation in the face of "primordial" divisions. Relative decentralization gave all states a stake in the system and guaranteed that their deepest values would not be trampled upon by national majorities.

In every deeply divided society, majoritarianism must be qualified by segmental autonomy. Not surprisingly, southern unionists conceived American democracy in proto-consociational terms.[39] For democracy to function in a morally disunified country, national majorities must tactfully yield to intense sectional minorities. Simple outvoting on highly charged issues would bring the entire system crashing down. In the American case, the moral status and political future of slave ownership was too hot to handle and touched nerves too deep to be subjected to majoritarian politics on the national level.

Northerners offered southerners the following *quid pro quo*: if the slave states would submit other issues to majority control, the free states would agree to exclude the slave question from the national majority's jurisdiction. Legislative self-censorship was justified as essential to national cooperation. This strategy of avoidance seems to have been a working principle of American government in the first half of the nineteenth century. Pinckney's gag rule of 1836 simply codified a generally accepted practice and applied it to a particular case. The Union could be preserved only by removing the slave issue from the Congress's agenda. The Missouri Compromise corroborates this interpretation; it, too, was a package deal in the classic consociational manner.

Calhoun came very close to formulating the argument in precisely this way. Slave-holders had a constitutionally guaranteed private right to hold their property. But the prohibition against federal regulation of slavery did not merely protect a private sphere and the attendant values of personal autonomy; it also unburdened the public sphere and thus subserved the values of democracy. Orderly democratic consideration of *other* problems would become impossible if such a passion-charged and divisive issue were placed at the center of legislative deliberation.

This pro-democratic defense of agenda-narrowing follows directly from Calhoun's general theory of constitutionalism. Constitutions, he

---

[39] Lijphart, in fact, expressly modeled his own theory on Calhoun's doctrine of "concurrent majorities"; for his references to Calhoun, see *Democracy in Plural Societies*, pp. 37, 125, 149.

argued, are bargains. Indeed, the development and acceptance of a constitutional framework can occur only as the contingent result of irresolvable conflict:

> The constitutions [of both Rome and Britain] originated in a pressure occasioned by conflicts of interests between hostile classes or orders and were intended to meet the pressing exigencies of the occasion, neither party, it would seem, having any conception of the principles involved or the consequences to follow beyond the immediate objects in contemplation.[40]

And, he adds, it seems "impossible" for constitutional governments of this sort to arise in any other manner.[41]

The initial willingness of rival factions to compromise on a constitutional framework is usually motivated by battle fatigue and a yearning for the fruits of peaceful cooperation. But all parties must be assured that "ultimate values" – the things they care about most – will not be dragged through the mud of contestation. When factions negotiate, they put their differences aside and build on common ground. Both northerners and southerners desired peace and detested the thought of being ruled by foreigners. Burying differences, in Calhoun's view, meant removing them from the national political agenda in order to concentrate on problems likely to mobilize greater social consensus.

Despite all gagging efforts, the slave issue would not subside. Eventually, it cracked the frame, that is, became too explosive to be handled within the institutional structures established by the Framers and reaffirmed by the Missouri Compromise. Abolitionists, of course, had always been repelled by the bargainish character of America's quasi-consociational system. William Lloyd Garrison, for example, denounced the Constitution as "a covenant with death, and an

---

[40] John C. Calhoun, *A Disquisition on Government* (Indianapolis, Bobbs-Merrill, 1953), pp. 78–9.

[41] Like Rustow, Calhoun believes that it is inconceivable for a constitution to be created within a faction-free society: "[i]t is difficult to conceive that any people among whom [constitutions] did not exist would or could voluntarily institute them in order to establish such governments, while it is not at all wonderful that they should grow out of conflicts between different orders or classes when aided by a favorable combination of circumstances" (*ibid.*, p. 79).

agreement with hell."[42] Slavery was sinful and odious; and it was the essence of immorality for legislators to silence themselves about such an abomination. If forcing slavery on to the legislative agenda caused the breakdown of national democracy, so be it. An issue of this magnitude was worth a civil war.

What cannot remain unspoken

To a surprising degree, the great Lincoln–Douglas debates of 1858 hinged precisely upon the question of what should and should not be said. According to Douglas, any discussion of the moral status of slavery was a grave insult to southerners, tending to put the Union at risk. By unceremoniously branding slavery as "evil" and declaring that slaves had an inalienable right to the fruits of their own labor, Lincoln was acting no differently than extreme abolitionists such as Garrison. He, too, was threatening the Union and inviting sectional war. Basically, according to Douglas, Lincoln was an agitator who refused to let sleeping dogs lie, a *Gesinnungspolitiker*, driven by abstract idealism and unappreciative of the tactical compromises implicit in the Constitution. By announcing that slavery must be placed on the course of ultimate extinction, he was terrorizing a vulnerable southern minority, engaging in a "conspiracy to wage war against one-half of the Union."[43] The slave question was so charged with "passion," moreover, that rational discussion about it was precluded.[44] Theorists of negotiation and mediation typically urged that "[w]hen anger and misperception are high, some thoughts are best left unsaid."[45] Douglas would have concurred. Lincoln simply did not understand that preserving the American republic required self-censorship about the most emotional and galling of all issues.

While painting Lincoln as an extremist, Douglas portrayed himself as a moderate and a *politique*. He was willing to compromise about

[42] Cited in C. Vann Woodward, "The northern crusade against slavery," *American Counterpoint: Slavery and Racism in the North/South Dialogue* (Oxford University Press, 1983), p. 142.

[43] *The Lincoln–Douglas Debates*, edited by Robert Johannsen (New York, Oxford University Press, 1965), p. 121.

[44] *Ibid.*, p. 265.

[45] Roger Fisher and William Ury, *Getting to Yes: Negotiating Agreement without Giving In* (Harmondsworth, Penguin, 1983), p. 37.

almost anything except union and peace. The peace party of sixteenth-century France had believed that national unity was compatible with religious diversity, i.e., that a divided house could stand. Three centuries later, the unionist Douglas asserted that national unity was compatible with a diversity of laws and customs concerning slavery. The nation was not based upon moral consensus about black slavery: northerners thought it evil, while southerners thought it good. The Constitution was nevertheless able to unify the country by abstracting from this underlying normative dissonance. Instead of demanding that all citizens adopt a common attitude toward slavery, the Framers forged a modus vivendi among a morally divided people. The Constitution was a "form designed to contain the country's diversity." By their incessant ranting about the evils of slavery, Lincoln and the abolitionists were wrecking this skillfully wrought bargain from which great benefits had ensued.

Lincoln, needless to say, denied Douglas's fundamental premise. The basic division in the land was not between those loyal and those indifferent to the Union. Much more important was the disagreement between those who believed slavery was wrong and those who considered it comely and beneficial. In a valiant attempt to be even-handed, to ply an intermediate course between secessionists and abolitionists, Douglas struggled to say *nothing at all* about the moral status of slavery. As Lincoln ironically noted: "He has the high distinction, so far as I know, of never having said slavery is either right or wrong."[46] But tongue-tying neutrality on this issue was unacceptable. Especially in the final debates, Lincoln repeatedly maneuvered his opponent into an either/or situation: Douglas must throw off his conciliatory pose, ungag himself and take sides. To remove the slave issue from the political agenda may appear fair to all sections, but it actually "muzzled" the nation's conscience.[47] Self-gagging was simply immoral. To suppress this issue, in any case, was implicitly to take sides. According to Lincoln, Douglas was "in favor of eradicating, of pressing out of view, the questions of preference in this country for free and slave institutions; and consequently every sentiment he utters discards the idea that there is anything wrong in slavery."[48] No

---

[46] *The Lincoln–Douglas Debates*, p. 256.
[47] *Ibid.*, p. 233.   [48] *Ibid.*, p. 225.

would-be fence-sitter could avoid making a moral pronouncement one way or the other.

While cautious himself, Lincoln nevertheless ridiculed the idea that conflict-avoidance should be a politician's paramount concern. Douglas was opposed to discussing the slave issue in moral terms, he mockingly suggested, only because such discussions "will make a fuss."[49] Conflict was not amusing, of course; and Lincoln was willing to grant important concessions to the South to preserve peace and the Union. But there could be no lasting compromise with evil. Ultimately, political horse-trading must yield to moral conscience.[50] Not even a majority of voters, local or national, can make a wrong into a right. Here Lincoln appears at his most anti-propitiatory and anti-*politique*. The Framers were not solely concerned to establish a modus vivendi between morally discordant sections. They agreed to tolerate slavery, but only on the assumption that it would eventually disappear. The Constitution was not merely a bargain; it was also an acknowledgement of fundamental norms. Despite Calhoun, American democracy was never meant to be a consociational system. The "pluralism" of slaveholding and nonslaveholding states could not be accommodated indefinitely: a house divided cannot stand. The nation was founded on a unifying moral creed: all men are created equal. The institution of slavery was an affront to that creed and ultimately had to be extinguished if the nation was to endure.

Douglas was an eloquent spokesman for the democracy-reinforcing function of segmental autonomy. His basic thesis was that national harmony would reign if every state would leave the others alone. The sovereignty of local majorities promoted national concord by preventing one state from using federal powers to pester another. "Each state must do as it pleases" was his maxim.[51] This was a principle, he proudly announced, that travelled well, i.e., could be embraced in Illinois as well as South Carolina. Unfortunately for Douglas and for the unity of his party, deference to local majorities was *not* universally admired. By advocating what he thought was an intermediate posi-

---

[49] *Ibid.*, p. 256.
[50] For my understanding of Lincoln's position on this matter, I am indebted to J. David Greenstone, "Political culture and American political development: liberty, union, and the liberal bi-polarity," in *Studies in American Political Development*, 1 (1987), pp. 1–49.
[51] *The Lincoln–Douglas Debates*, p. 216.

tion, Douglas (like Pinckney) lost southern support. But why was segmental autonomy ultimately unacceptable in the South?

Even the most extreme nullificationists supported the fugitive slave clause in the Constitution.[52] This provision placed the weight of federal authority on the side of the individual slaveholder against the pretensions of local majorities who might be inclined to pass laws protecting runaway slaves. Despite talk of states' rights, in other words, southerners were never willing fully to embrace segmental autonomy. If safe havens were available, planters might be deprived of their property without due process of law.

Rights-based thinking is essentially antimajoritarian, impatient with local as well as national majorities. The *Dred Scott* decision, although an act of the federal government, was hailed by proslavery forces because it debarred local majorities from interfering with property rights in slaves. As a shrewd polemicist, Lincoln exploited the contradiction between Douglas's absolute deference to the Supreme Court and his absolute deference to local majorities. The compromise position to which Douglas retreated was remarkably illogical: the territories had no right to prevent the entrance of slave property, but they could exclude slavery in practice by enacting unfriendly legislation. Naturally enough, this "solution" (whereby territorial majorities could make slave property worthless) proved unpopular in the South.

To deny the federal government a power is to assign that power somewhere else. Everything depends on the arena to which forbidden decisions are subsequently transferred. To take a question off the national agenda may be to place it on the local agenda and to subject it to the control of local majorities. On the other hand, a decision may be withdrawn from all branches and levels of government and consigned to private individuals. Some conspicuous examples are whom to marry, how many children to have, what career to pursue, where to live, what religion if any to embrace and (to introduce a discordant note) where to establish a plantation with one's slaves. That, according to Lincoln, was the individualistic logic of *Dred Scott*. Given planter concern for property rights, it is small wonder that Douglas's enthusiasm for local majorities alienated southern Democrats.

Lincoln stressed another weakness of segmental autonomy. Local

[52] Article IV, sec. 2, para. 3.

communities might be just as divided by the slave question as the national community. Kansas, in fact, was cursed with just such a division. Territorial sovereignty there, which Douglas believed would place a quietus on slavery agitation, had led instead to bloody conflict.[53] Even from a pure *politique* standpoint, Douglas's *cuius regio, eius religio* solution was inadequate. Local control did not cause any abatement of the slavery turmoil. On the contrary, the struggles in Kansas reopened old wounds and increased rather than decreased national tensions.

The modus vivendi between North and South was destroyed by a thirst for expansion. As Lincoln said: "we have generally had comparative peace upon the slavery question, and ... there was no cause for alarm until it was excited by the effort to spread it into new territory."[54] The open question of whether the new states to be carved out of the western territories would be slave or free perturbed both factions and enfeebled congressional vows of silence. Slavery in the South was the real evil; but what ultimately mobilized northern indignation, that is, provoked mainstream northern politicians into talking openly about the immorality of slavery, was the mere anticipation of slavery in the federal territories. Reticent about repealing an old gag rule, northerners were nevertheless unwilling to accept a new one.[55]

The old Whig and Democratic parties had purchased internal cohesion by intra-party decisions to suppress the slave issue. Thus, both parties had adherents in the North as well as in the South. After slavery had been placed squarely on the national agenda by the acquisition of vast new territories, however, the old nation-straddling parties were doomed to disintegration. Once slavery had become the outstanding political issue, a massive realignment was inevitable:

[53] *The Lincoln–Douglas Debates*, pp. 199, 236. As one commentator puts it: "To publicize Kansas as an arcadia for homesteaders and planters alike, and then to legislate that the people in the territory would decide the burning issue of slavery on the basis of squatter sovereignty, was to thrust two gamecocks into a barrel" (James MacGregor Burns, *The Vineyard of Liberty* [New York, Knopf, 1982], p. 550).

[54] *The Lincoln–Douglas Debates*, p. 136.

[55] Arthur Bestor, "The American Civil War as a constitutional crisis," *American Law and the Constitutional Order: Historical Perspectives*, edited by Lawrence Friedman and Harry Scheiber (Cambridge, Mass., Harvard University Press, 1978), pp. 219–34.

sectional parties arose, notably the Republican.[56] And fissiparous tendencies began to threaten the Union as well.

Strategic self-censorship did not prevent conflict between the proslavery and the antislavery forces in the long run. Although it could be successfully squeezed off the legislative agenda for several decades, the slave issue was never off the agenda of public discussion. Congress could gag itself temporarily; but it could not effectively gag the public or the press. The temporary and selective nature of gag rules, however, does not necessarily destroy their usefulness. By 1860, many historians have argued, the North was finally strong enough to impose abolition on the South. Abolitionists could never have achieved military and industrial superiority without a provisional agreement to silence Congress on the slave question. By *postponing* the discussion of a difficult issue, in other words, a group or a nation may increase its capacity to solve the underlying problem when it can no longer be repressed.

The political divisiveness doctrine

This brief overview of efforts to keep the slave issue off the national agenda suggests the usefulness, for historical analysis, of a theory of gag rules. As a second example, offered in the same tentative spirit, consider now the question of self-government in *religiously* divided societies. I will be focusing here on recent constitutional disputes. While attempts to side-step the slave issue were morally questionable and ultimately unsuccessful, collective self-censorship about religious disagreements seems to be a happier arrangement all around.

Even when obviously useful for preventing sectarian conflict, legislative gag orders may be annulled if they appear repugnant to the Free Exercise Clause.[57] But the Establishment Clause has led the Court to issue gag orders of its own. Most notably, school prayers – even silent prayers conducted on a "voluntary" basis – have been declared unconstitutional.[58] Religious conservatives claim that the

---

[56] According to Douglas, "the great revolution" was that the new parties "seem to be divided by a geographical line" (*The Lincoln–Douglas Debates*, p. 116).

[57] Classically, *Cantwell* v. *Connecticut*, 310 U.S. 296 (1940), where a law construed as barring Jehovah's Witnesses from playing anti-Catholic records in a Catholic neighborhood was declared unconstitutional.

[58] *Engel* v. *Vitale*, 370 U.S. 421 (1962); *Wallace* v. *Jaffree*, 105 S. Ct. 2479 (1985): the paradoxical, though not completely unreasonable, decision to gag silence.

Court has prohibited children from praying. But the Court's intention has been only to impede children of a majority sect from harassing, embarrassing and pressuring children with different beliefs. More importantly, the school prayer rulings seem reconcilable with free exercise values because the gag orders in question are not aimed principally at children at all but rather at public employees. The government must gag itself (i.e., its functionaries) on religious questions to avoid conveying a message that the state endorses or approves any sectarian practice. To send such a message would insultingly suggest that non-adherents of the endorsed religion are second-class citizens. By refusing to be a party to sectarian controversies, public officials can not only do their jobs more effectively but can also promote an atmosphere of cross-sect cooperation essential for the proper functioning of the political processes outlined in the Constitution.

Consider, as one historical illustration, the New York state school law of 1842. A fiery, brick-heaving conflict was raging around this time between antiforeign Protestants and recent Irish-Catholic immigrants. Catholics sought public financial support for their own schools, while anti-Irish nativist forces aimed to reserve all state aid for Protestant schools. Moderate politicians agreed that "it was imperative that this disruptive issue be removed from the political arena."[59] The problem would not subside, however, unless Catholics could be appeased without Protestants being outraged. Various segmental solutions were proposed, allowing local majorities to determine the religious content of publicly financed education. But the New York legislature ultimately rejected segmentation among districts and embraced the separation between church and state: no public funding would go to schools where sectarian practices were inculcated.[60] The gag rule imposed by the bill was quite narrowly targeted. Publicly paid teachers could not indoctrinate students on school premises. But religious indoctrinators remained free to practice their arts outside school walls.

[59] J. W. Pratt, *Religion, Politics, and Diversity: The Church–State Theme in New York History* (Ithaca, Cornell University Press, 1967), p. 185.

[60] The bill of 1842 actually contained a mixed strategy: the attempt to separate politics from religion was complemented by a concession to the religious loyalties of local majorities. Bible-reading survived the general ban on sectarian practices in the schools; but the King James version was used in Protestant areas and the Douay edition in Catholic districts (*ibid.*, p. 189).

In this century, at least, when the Supreme Court has removed religious questions from the national agenda, it has not transferred them to local majorities: that would have been a consociational solution. Conservative and religiously inclined scholars, to be sure, claim that such a decision would have been more faithful to the Constitution.[61] But it is difficult to believe that the Framers wished to pacify and harmonize the national political scene by fostering political divisions along religious lines within the states. In any case, a strategy of segmentation remains incompatible with the Court's present attitude towards separation between church and state. When the Court removes religious questions from the control of national majorities, it privatizes them, i.e., turns them over not to localities but to individuals.

If religion can be made into a wholly private matter, then religious attachments will no longer provide the basis for "politically salient subgroup solidarity." Political divisions will not directly reduplicate religious cleavages. The de-politicizing of religious conflict is accompanied by the desacralizing of political conflict. When both occur, the benefits of an adversarial style of decision-making begin to outweigh its dangers. The apparent ease with which a government-versus-opposition pattern has been sustained in the United States may be due not merely to the "Lockian consensus" stressed by Louis Hartz, but also to the robustness of a public/private boundary which inhibits religious antagonisms from ossifying into political oppositions.

Like other protective devices, as I said earlier, the "wall" of separation between church and state can also serve as a disencumbering strategy. On the one hand, it shelters the integrity of individual conscience. On the other hand, its contribution to social cohesion was noted from the start. Unifying a divided nation may not require a "naked public square." But a political sphere marked by general indifference to sectarian practices may well be a significant precondition for nation-building in a country such as the United States. Neutral territory – a schoolroom where all sects were debarred from stigmatizing others as un-American – seems to have played an essential role in unifying this religiously pluralistic society.

---

[61] The No Establishment clause is commonly said to have denied the right to establish a church to the national government only in order to protect established churches in the states. For a counterargument, see Leonard Levy, "The original

Justice Frankfurter, calling the public school "the symbol of our democracy," advanced this argument for the democracy-reinforcing function of a secular education:

Designed to serve as perhaps the most powerful agency for promoting cohesion among a heterogeneous democratic people, the public school must be kept scrupulously free from entanglement in the strife of sects. The preservation of the community from divisive conflicts, of Government from irreconcilable pressures by religious groups, of religion from censorship and coercion however subtly exercised, requires strict confinement of the State to instruction other than religious, leaving to the individual's church and home, indoctrination in the faith of his choice.[62]

In a multidenominational society, rival and exclusive religious communities pose a potential threat to inclusive political citizenship. Frankfurter did not contrast affectless legal neutrality with affective moral community. Rather, he argued that *political* community cannot flourish unless the government adopts a modest institutional neutrality toward all sects. In essence, by gagging indoctrinators on public premises, we can promote a sense of shared identity among Catholics, Protestants and Jews. Relieved from sectarian harassment, local religious minorities will not develop "a feeling of separatism."[63] Frankfurter emphatically denies that the secularization of public life diminishes the social importance of religion. The vitality of religion in nonpolitical domains may usefully prevent citizens from deifying their country. But a nonsectarian school system can help children develop the "habits of community"[64] essential for the proper functioning of democractic institutions.

During the last fifteen years, the need to avoid political divisiveness has become a central – although controversial – theme of Estab-

---

meaning of the Establishment clause," *Constitutional Opinions* (New York, Oxford University Press, 1986), pp. 135–61.

[62] *McCollum* v. *Board of Education* (1947) 333 U.S. 203, 231, 216–17. Reviewing the history of the state–church issue as it affected public education, Frankfurter also noted that "In Massachusetts, largely through the efforts of Horace Mann, all sectarian teachings were barred from the common school to save it from being rent by denominational conflict" (*ibid.*, at 215).

[63] 333 U.S. 203, 227.   [64] *Ibid.*, 203, 227.

lishment Clause jurisprudence.[65] Because it may "strain a political system to the breaking point," Judge Harlan wrote, "political fragmentation on sectarian lines must be guarded against."[66] According to Paul Freund, too, "[w]hile political debate and division is normally a wholesome process for reaching viable accommodations, political divisions along religious lines is one of the principal evils that the First Amendment sought to forestall." Clinching his case, Freund added that "President Kennedy, as a candidate, was able to turn off some of the questions addressed to him on church–state relations by pointing to binding Supreme Court decisions."[67] Lucky the politician who can gag reporters by gagging himself!

A well-functioning majoritarian democracy, as political scientists, too, have argued, may require cross-cutting cleavages. Consociationalism, secession and civil war seem to become the only available options when political divisions map neatly on to religious schisms. All three solutions, however, are plainly unacceptable in the United States. Thus, a coincidence of political and religious cleavages must be avoided at all costs. Artfully crafted gag rules can be justified whenever they help prevent the consolidation of religiously defined political constituencies.

In *Lemon* v. *Kurtzman*,[68] the locus classicus of the divisiveness doctrine, Chief Justice Burger explicitly echoed Freund's argument. The entanglement between church and state produced by public aid to parochial schools is dangerous precisely because of its community-splintering potential. The religious provisions of the First Amendment, too, are meant to foster democratic politics:

Ordinarily political debate and division, however vigorous or even

---

[65] Already in *Everson* v. *Board of Education*, Justice Black associated church–state entanglement with "civil strife" (330 U.S. 1, 8 [1947]. Consider also *Committee for Public Education & Religious Liberty* v. *Nyquist*, 413 U.S. 756, 794–8, Powell's plurality opinion; *Meek* v. *Pittenger*, 421 U.S. 349, 372 (1975), Stewart's plurality opinion; *Wolman* v. *Walter* 433 U.S. 229, 258 (1977), Marshall, concurring in part and dissenting in part; *March* v. *Chambers*, 463 U.S. 783, 799–806 (1983); *Aquilar* v. *Felton*, 105 S. Ct. 3232, 3239 (1985). For a recent summary by the champion of the divisiveness test, see *Meek* v. *Pittenger*, 421 U.S. 349, 374–85, Brennan, concurring in part and dissenting in part.

[66] *Walz* v. *Tax Commission*, 397 U.S. 664, 694–5 (1969).

[67] Paul Freund, "Public aid to parochial schools," *Harvard Law Review*, 82, 7 (May, 1969), 1692.

[68] 403 U.S. 602 (1971).

partisan, are normal and healthy manifestations of our democratic system of government, but political division along religious lines was one of the principal evils against which the First Amendment was intended to protect ... The potential divisiveness of such conflict is a threat to the normal political process.[69]

More concretely, "[t]o have States and communities divide on the issues presented by state aid to parochial schools would tend to confuse and obscure other issues of great urgency."[70] If Protestants, Catholics and Jews began to battle over yearly school appropriations, the community's capacity for collective self-rule would be severely damaged. To preserve a climate of national cooperation and thus secure the majority's authority on other more pressing issues, citizens must agree to let their public officials gag themselves on religious questions.[71]

Conservatives, worried that the general prohibition against church–state entanglement is somehow demeaning to religion, have recently raised numerous doubts about the utility of the divisiveness test.[72] Divisiveness cannot be measured; sectarianism in America has become almost unbearably bland; sects are no different from other interest groups; the danger of explosive conflict among denominations is vanishingly remote. At the very least, the potential for divisiveness alone, without other factors, does not suffice to make a statute unconstitutional.[73] Some antiseparationists even suggest that the idea of political divisiveness along religious lines is a twentieth-century

---

[69] *Ibid.*

[70] *Ibid.* See also *Aquilar* v. *Felton* 105 S. Ct. 3232, 3240 (1985), Powell concurring.

[71] Recall, once again, that an overriding desire for national unity is probably an essential precondition for the willingness of rival groups to set aside their differences. Only a shared concern for military security, for example, seems to have induced secular and fundamentalist Israelis to postpone any clear-cut decision about the status of religion in their country (Nadav Safran, *Israel: The Embattled Ally* [Cambridge, Mass., Harvard University Press, 1981], pp. 200–19).

[72] Justice Rehnquist, for example, refers slightingly to the "rather elusive" inquiry into divisive political potential (*Mueller* v. *Allen* 463 U.S. 388, 403, n. 11 [1983]); consider also: "The Court's reliance on the potential for political divisiveness as evidence of undue entanglement is also unpersuasive" (*Aquilar* v. *Felton*, 105 S. Ct. 3232, 3247 [1985], Justice O'Connor, dissenting); and "In my view, political divisions along religious lines should not be an independent test of constitutionality" (*Lynch* v. *Donnelly*, 104 S. Ct. 1355, 1367 [1984]).

[73] Brennan concurs but stresses that political divisiveness remains a useful signal of impermissible entanglement (*Lynch* v. *Donnelly*, 104 S. Ct. 1355, 1374 [1985]).

coinage unknown to the eighteenth-century Founders.[74] The idea that collective self-censorship might help avert religious conflict, however, had already occurred to peace-makers soon after the Reformation split the Christian world into rival sects.[75] To eighteenth-century *philosophes*, and thus to the framers of the First Amendment, it was a truism.

Another hostile critic asks: "Does a potential for even minor division justify silencing the churches in public debate over fundamental values?"[76] But such a question reveals an elementary misunderstanding: the divisiveness doctrine requires the government to gag not citizens but itself.[77] Religious groups and individuals can freely express their views; the government, however, is debarred from providing aid which, because it benefits one religion at the expense of other sects and of nonbelievers, would significantly deepen sectarian animosities.

More theoretically interesting is the objection that the norm of conflict avoidance exposes a society to manipulation by anyone willing to threaten conflict. In the Pawtucket crèche case,[78] for example, the Court noted that the challenged nativity display had caused no sectarian dissension in its forty-year history. It is ludicrous for litigants to adduce their own complaint as evidence that an offending govern-

[74] Leonard F. Manning, *The Law of Church–State Relations* (St Paul, Minn., West Publishing Co., 1981), p. 235.

[75] Free discussion exacerbates the tendency of religious opinions to become dangerously sectarian. Thus, according to Jean Bodin, "the princes of the Germans at a great assembly at Augsburg, after destructive and lengthy wars, proclaimed that there would be no more discussion about religion among Catholics and priests of the Augsburg confession. When one man rashly violated this edict, he was put to death, and the uprisings in that city were quelled up to the present" (*Colloquium of the Seven about Secrets of the Sublime* [Princeton University Press, 1975], p. 167). By force of tradition, most sixteenth- and seventeenth-century political theorists believed that no nation could endure part Catholic and part Protestant. But moderates and *politiques* eventually realized that, if salvation were conceived as a wholly private matter, a divided house could stand. The no-more-discussion rule, mentioned here, was a first and somewhat crude attempt to maintain civil order by excluding religious controversy from the public square.

[76] A. James Reichley, *Religion in American Public Life* (Washington, D.C., Brookings, 1985), p. 167.

[77] According to the leading advocate of the divisiveness doctrine: "The State's goal of preventing sectarian bickering and strife may not be accomplished by regulating religious speech and political association" (*McDaniels* v. *Paty*, 435 U.S. 618, 641 [1978], Brennan, concurring).

[78] *Lynch* v. *Donnelly*, 465 U.S. 668 (1984), ruling that a publicly subsidized nativity scene did not convey government approval of Christians or disapproval of non-Christians.

mental action is politically divisive. Along the same lines, the goal of eliminating religious divisiveness does not justify judicial attempts to promote "safe thinking"[79] among citizens or even among public officials. Obviously enough, anodyne and useless political discussions would result if the divisiveness test were carried to extremes.

These and similar demurrers raise some doubts about the legal future of the divisiveness doctrine. But the very debate between its advocates and its opponents confirms once again that gag rules have played (and no doubt will continue to play) a central role in the functioning of democratic political institutions.

A note on abortion

No catalogue of recent acrimonious disputes could omit abortion. Some twentieth-century Americans feel as passionately as about this issue as nineteenth-century Americans felt about abolition. Walter Berns once wrote quite sympathetically of Calhoun's desire to repress emancipationist pamphlets and petitions.[80] More recently, he has argued that the success of the American legislative process depends upon "its ability to exclude issues – the abortion issue comes to mind – on which there can be only one winner and one loser."[81] Those who disagree about this question do not hesitate to smear each other publicly with hate-provoking names such as "murderer." One side, at least, seems religiously motivated. There may be no room for compromise here, and little capacity for either side to listen to the other. If such a burning issue became central to the legislative process, would not Congress's capacity to solve other problems be drastically curtailed? Why waste national resources on an issue that will never command widespread consensus, when there are equally pressing problems (such as teenage pregnancy) about which everyone agrees that something should be done?

These considerations are not without weight. But persuasive arguments have also been mounted on the other side – against the wisdom

[79] *McDaniels* v. *Paty*, 435 U.S. 618, 641.

[80] Walter Berns, *The First Amendment and the Future of American Democracy* (New York, Basic Books, 1976), pp. 119–28.

[81] Walter Berns, "Taking rights frivolously," in *Liberalism Reconsidered*, edited by Douglas MacLean and Claudia Mills (Totowa, N.J., Rowman and Allanheld, 1983), p. 62.

of removing the legitimacy of abortion from the legislative agenda. For one thing, dire predictions that the issue will necessarily overload and destabilize a democratic political system seem exaggerated.[82] Furthermore, restricting the political process to a limited range of issues is never a perfectly neutral procedure. Even when agenda-narrowing is not a tool in the hands of sinister elites, it still favors some parties and disfavors others. The congressional gag rules of the 1830s and 1840s were moderate but not impartial; on balance, they were much friendlier to slaveholders than to abolitionists. Similarly, withdrawing the legality of abortion[83] from the jurisdiction of Congress and state legislatures means affirming the status quo, i.e., resting content with a pro-choice stance. Legislatures may be compelled to adopt a "hands off" attitude; but winners and losers remain. In the case of abortion, when the Court constricted the agenda of state legislatures, it was wielding power and doing so for particular ends. Not surprisingly, some pro-life activists view wresting abortion from the Court and putting it back on the legislative agenda as their principal political objective.

Both slaveholders and abolitionists adduced unassailable rights (property rights, on the one hand, and the right to the fruits of one's labor, on the other). These rights were considered indefeasible, regardless of how political majorities happened to vote. Douglas's position fell between the two rights-based views: let the people of each state decide by majority rule. An uncannily similar pattern reappears in the abortion debate. Each side asserts an indefeasible right (the fetus's right to life and the woman's right to choose). This time, the intermediary position is occupied by Justice White: "Abortion is a hotly contested moral and political issue. Such issues, in our society, are to be resolved by the will of the people."[84] The Court, in other words, should loosen its grip on the abortion question and consign it to majority rule in the states.

In *Roe* v. *Wade*, the Court decided to take the issue of abortion out of legislative hands. On the basis of a fundamental right to privacy, it assigned the right to decide to the individuals directly involved. But

---

[82] This is more or less the conclusion of *The Abortion Dispute and the American System*, edited by Gilbert Y. Steiner (Washington, D.C., Brookings, 1983).

[83] But not the question of whether federal funds should be used to pay for abortions.

[84] *Thornburgh* v. *American College of Obstetricians*, 106 S. Ct. 2169, 2197 (1986), Justice White dissenting.

Roe also reallocated power from state legislatures to the Court. As a result, all sides in the dispute now argue for the moral, legal and political appropriateness of some sort of gag rule. Differences arise only over which branch of government should be gagged. What I have described as the intermediate position is antijudicial and deferential toward local majorities. From the divisiveness of the issue, Justice White interestingly concludes that abortion must be handled legislatively rather than judicially. The Court should gag itself because, by constitutionalizing such an explosive issue, it not only has thrown the legitimacy of judicial review into question but also has polarized the national community more radically than if it had allowed the problem to be solved on a decentralized basis by ordinary processes of pluralistic bargaining. Far from dampening conflict, *Roe* exacerbated a diffuse and latent antagonism, drawing it on to the national scene. After the decision, tempers flared and battle fronts hardened. Keeping abortion off the legislative agenda, far from consigning it peaceably to the domain of private conscience, has given it higher visibility on the agenda of public agitation and discussion. Removing abortion from the Court's docket might conceivably be a more effective political sedative than deleting it from the legislative agenda of the states.

In contrast to White, pro-life and pro-choice advocates cannot, on principle, consistently defer to the opinions of local majorities (or national ones, for that matter). Despite the tactics and rhetoric of antiabortion forces, they do not believe that a fetus's right to life hinges upon the election-day behavior of voters. Pro-life advocates, it is true, wish they could have gagged the *Roe* Court. But (apparently unlike White), they would welcome a judicial decision which declared abortion unconstitutional and, in a gagging maneuver, denied state legislatures any further power to authorize or fund it.

Like the slavery controversy, though on a less tragic scale, the abortion dispute raises questions about the wisdom of political self-censorship. It, too, underlines the lesson that gag rules, although often presented as impartial measures serving the cause of communal peace, can easily be turned into weapons in a partisan struggle.

Proscribing creationist legislation

In *Epperson* v *Arkansas*,[85] the Court overturned a state law prohibiting the teaching of Darwin's evolutionary theory in public schools and universities. The majority justified its decision on the grounds that "fundamentalist sectarian conviction was and is the law's reason for existence."[86] Antievolution statutes, in other words, were declared to breach the wall of separation. Only because they interpret Genesis in a literalist manner have fundamentalists attempted to gag schoolteachers who would otherwise teach Darwinist theories as a matter of routine.[87]

In his separate opinion, Justice Black suggested that a community could justifiably side-step this problem by deleting all mention of the development of the human species from classes in biology. Banning evolutionary theory on religious grounds violates the Establishment Clause. But state governments have a right to withdraw emotional subjects from the school curriculum; and nothing prohibits a blanket vow of silence designed to reduce disruptive conflict in the classroom. In Black's view, in sum, there is nothing objectionable about a community's self-muzzling decision that "it would be best to remove this controversial subject from its schools."[88]

For a student of self-imposed gag rules, *Epperson* is interesting for another reason as well. What would be the indirect effect upon democratic government if majorities were allowed to rewrite scientific textbooks? The rationalist outlook central to the development of seventeenth-century science had a decisive influence on the shaping of seventeenth-century parliamentary institutions. Could challenging the autonomy of science inadvertently threaten one of the essential preconditions of democratic government?

According to Robert Bork, what majorities are not allowed to do must be left up to individual freedom.[89] To protect democracy against

[85] 393 U.S. 97 (1968).   [86] *Ibid.*, 97, 108.

[87] *Ibid.*, 97, 103. Concern with the constitutional protection of the conditions of government by discussion is even more apparent in the U.S. District Court finding in *McLean* v. *Arkansas* 529 F. Supp. 1255 (E.D. Ark. 1982), holding unconstitutional a statute requiring balanced treatment of evolutionary theory and creation science; all the relevant documents are available in *Creationism, Science, and the Law*, edited by Marcel La Folette (Cambridge, Mass., M.I.T. Press, 1983).

[88] 393 U.S. 97, 112–13.

[89] Robert H. Bork, "Neutral principles and some First Amendment problems," *Indiana Law Journal*, vol. 47, no. 1 (fall, 1971), 3.

inherent self-destructive tendencies, the Court must defend the right of individuals to engage in political speech. Because most speech is not political, however, most speakers remain constitutionally susceptible to majoritarian censorship and control. Bork's ultimate concern here is to justify gag orders which his more squeamish colleagues are loath to impose: the Constitution is not a suicide pact, and the government has a right to silence anyone advocating its forcible overthrow. Generalizing about the need to gag the talkative, Bork adds: "Government cannot function if anyone can say anything anywhere at any time."[90] *En passant*, he also denies that the Court has a right to protect scientific inquiry against majority rule.[91] He even suggests that, constitutionally speaking, scientific conclusions are a matter of taste; and on questions of taste, the Court should remain aloof and allow majorities to have their way. If he retreated from this implausible claim, moreover, Bork would have only one available alternative: the discovery and propagation of scientific truths must be left to "individual freedom."

How adequate to the creationism controversy is this dichotomy between majority rule and individual freedom? For one thing, scientific theories are not preferences. Science is not an interest group (even though scientists may sometimes act like one); and the outcome of a scientific inquiry is not a free choice. Science has a logic and dynamic of its own; and its results cannot simply be "adjusted" to personal or political demands. By the Enlightenment standards on which our constitutional settlement was based, a community's attempt to compel scientific outcomes congenial to its nonrational attachments should probably be described as a form of self-injury. Creationists doggedly reinterpret fossil evidence to make it accord with their reading of Genesis. The conclusion they want to reach is fixed beforehand and is, in principle, a conclusion which no counterevidence could ever lead them to revise.[92] Why not view the Court's prohibition against creationist tampering with textbooks in this light? Keeping scientific

---

[90] *Ibid.*, 21.   [91] *Ibid.*, 20, 28.

[92] As is well known, some philosophers dispute the rationality of the process of scientific inquiry. But even Paul Feyerabend would be able to tell the difference between a criminal justice system in which the verdicts were set in advance and one where prejudgments were at least conceivably revisable in the light of evidence.

conclusions off the majority's agenda may protect "reason" itself, rather than merely individual freedoms. How could the scientific method, in a minimal sense of the examination of embarrassing facts and the hearing of rival viewpoints, be overriden without undermining an essential element of democratic government itself?

Keeping scientific results off the political agenda (and thus beyond indirect religious control) may allow a nation to shelter the preconditions of rational debate. A gag rule of some sort is obviously required to defend the integrity of science – and its standards of evidence, argument, inference and disproof – from nonrational attachments. To prohibit creationist legislation may also be to defend democracy from itself. A majority should be empowered to act for the nation, one might say, only if its religious motivations are neutralized constitutionally. By invalidating creationist legislation, arguably, the Court (implicitly, if not explicitly) intended to confer authority on what the Framers called the deliberate sense of the community, that is, on the opinions the majority holds when it discusses matters in a consecutive, disciplined, fact-minded and thoughtful way.

When a decision is withdrawn from national majorities, it may be consigned either to local majorities or to individuals: what majorities are not allowed to do must be left to individual freedom. But the creationist case raises a third alternative. Decisions may be withdrawn from all branches and levels of government and from individuals as well. The proper "place" for discussing evolution and determining the contents of biology textbooks is the social system of *science*, a system which operates under imperatives other than maximizing the independence and preference-satisfaction of its individual practitioners and which is largely indifferent to majority opinion. The Constitution nowhere mentions the autonomy and authority of science. But if the Court must protect the preconditions of democratic government, can it be completely oblivious to the attitude toward truth inculcated in public schools? In any case, neither Establishment Clause concerns nor the need to protect political speech and individual autonomy seem sufficient to explain what seems to be a rationally defensible countermajoritarian ban on antievolution statutes.

Some problems and a cautionary tale

While substantial, especially in divided societies, the benefits of agenda-narrowing are usually accompanied by significant drawbacks. Democracy is not only made possible but also made imperfect by a systematic thinning out of the issues under majority control. In a majoritarian democracy within a unified nation, bowdlerizing the legislative agenda will inevitably trivialize public life and drain it of human significance. To remove all issues of high moral importance and assign them to individual conscience or even to the courts may make democratic politics unbearably bland and useless as an arena for national self-education. Gag rules, moreover, are seldom neutral; they implicitly support one policy and undermine alternatives. Suppressing a theme may surreptitiously insure the victory of one party over its rivals. Finally, the strategy of avoidance can exacerbate pent-up social tensions, eventually engendering terrorism or a revolutionary explosion by denying legitimate expression to deeply felt beliefs.

At first glance, it seems reasonable to skirt an issue which promises to unleash paralyzing hostilities. Such evasiveness has serious disadvantages, however. For one thing, conflict-averseness makes a group hostage to anyone willing to threaten conflict. Prickliness and unwillingness to compromise may be feigned. If a group openly declares conflict-avoidance to be its highest priority, it invites the power-hungry strategically to misrepresent their preferences. Indeed, intractable conflict is not merely an independent variable to which gun-shy groups respond by imposing vows of silence on themselves. If a group habitually gags itself on divisive issues, it will give individuals and subgroups a powerful incentive for bluffing. If threats trigger collective silence, threats will be forthcoming. Willingness to yield will never pay; shortness of temper will always be rewarded. By redescribing their annoyance as utter horror, individuals and subgroups can prevent issues from being raised which could otherwise, and more justly, be resolved by compromise. Indeed, a policy of self-gagging may eventually produce a culture where the threat of violence or secession is a common political tactic.

Finally, the dangers of founding a relationship on a suppressed theme is strikingly illustrated in a tale recounted by Gregory of Tours.

Two noblemen could only remain friends and reveling companions so long as they kept silent about the embarrassing fact that, years earlier, Sichar had butchered Chramnesind's family. One evening, the healing silence was broken:

> Sichar drank far more wine than he could carry and began to boast at Chramnesind's expense. He is reported to have said: "Dear brother, you ought to be grateful to me for having killed off your relations. There is plenty of gold and silver in your house now that I have recompensed you for what I did to them. If it weren't for the fact that the fine I've paid has restored your finances, you would still today be poor and destitute." When he heard Sichar's remarks, Chramnesind was sick at heart. "If I don't avenge my relatives," he said to himself, "they will say that I am as weak as a woman, for I no longer have the right to be called a man!" Thereupon he blew the lights out and hacked Sichar's skull in two.[93]

Like the peaceful coexistence of slave and free states, the precarious companionship of Sichar and Chramnesind was destined not to last. An individual's thirst for wine, like a nation's thirst for expansion, may irreversibly destroy a long-established etiquette of omission. To win otherwise unattainable cooperation, people voluntarily muzzle themselves about divisive topics. Self-gagging may be a short-lived experiment, however. From moment to moment, there can be a return of the repressed.

Conclusion

Communities, like individuals, can silence themselves about selected issues for what they see as their own good. Although seldom studied in a systematic manner, strategic self-censorship seems to be an almost universally employed technique of self-management and self-rule. While somewhat slippery and difficult to control, the idea of gag rules, as I have been discussing it, does focus attention usefully on the advantages and disadvantages shared by widely varying techniques of

---

[93] Gregory of Tours, *The History of the Franks*,. book IX, ch. 19, (Harmondsworth, Penguin, 1977), pp. 501–2.

issue-suppression. As a result, the concept may well become a serviceable tool for comparative analysis.[94] To show how such a conception might be developed theoretically and applied to a few important cases has been the principal purpose of this chapter.

Many questions, of course, remain unanswered. Under what cultural and psychological conditions, for example, can gag rules be adhered to successfully? Normative theorists, on the other hand, will want to know when gag rules can be morally justified. Can we provide a principled rationale for removing one issue rather than another from the community's or an individual's agenda? While the slave issue could not (and should not) have been permanently suppressed, religious disagreements probably can (and should) be. I believe this, but can I explain it? On the abortion question, opinions differ about the advisability of gag rules – just as they do on every other aspect of the issue. In general, so it seems, the foregoing discussion emphasizes only the moral ambiguity of strategic self-censorship. To prevent overload, all individuals and groups must suppress *some* controversial problems. An essayist, for instance, may have no choice but to relegate an unanswerable question to a perfunctory conclusion where he can shiftily "postpone" it to a later work. But issue-avoidance, however attractive, will always be one-sided and potentially dangerous. We can neither dispense with gag rules nor allay the guilty consciences they inevitably produce.

[94] For an interesting example, see Beryl L. Bellman, *The Language of Secrecy* (Rutgers University Press, 1984).

2. Democracy as a contingent outcome of conflicts

I

Anyone who has lived through moments when a dictatorship was about to fall and democracy become a real possibility remembers almost constant tension, hopes that repeatedly alternated with fears, outbursts of enthusiasm and the pain of defeat. Every step seems difficult and yet nothing seems out of reach. But as one looks for the turning-points, a particular moment appears as a threshold, as a break. At one moment dictatorship has disappeared and has been replaced by democracy.

Since this is a "moment" in a world of stylized facts, let me first provide some context, a sort of logical chronology of the processes of transition from dictatorship to democracy. Without entering into a general discussion of authoritarian regimes, which has recently received extensive attention in the work of Juan Linz and Guillermo O'Donnell,[1] I wish to emphasize one characteristic of authoritarian

This is a revised version of a paper presented at the Conference on Constitutionalism and Democracy organized by the University of Oslo at Ustaoset, Norway, January 16–19, 1983. I should like to thank the participants, and in particular Aanund Hylland and John Elster for their comments. The chapter constitutes my personal reflections upon discussions and essays accumulated within the framework of the project on the "Prospects for democracy: transitions from authoritarian rule," sponsored by the Woodrow Wilson Center, Washington, D.C. and directed by Guillermo O'Donnell and Philippe C. Schmitter. Joanne Fox Przeworski and Philippe C. Schmitter persuaded me to revise several original formulations.

[1] Juan Linz, "An Authoritarian Regime: Spain," in Erik Allardt and Stein Rokkan, eds., *Mass Politics: Studies in Political Sociology* (New York, Free Press). Guillermo O'Donnell, *Modernization and Bureaucratic Authoritarianism: Studies in South American Politics* (Berkeley, University of California Press, 1973); David Colleir, ed., *The New Authoritarianism in Latin America* (Princeton University Press, 1979); Karen L. Remmer and Gilbert W. Merkx, "Bureaucratic Authoritarianism Revisited," *Latin American Research Review*, 17 (1982), 3–41, with a response by O'Donnell.

systems (which I will also call "dictatorships," abandoning some important distinctions). The essential feature of such regimes is that someone has an effective capacity to prevent political outcomes that would be highly adverse to their interests. That "someone" can be an individual, the leader, or an organization, such as the armed forces, the police, the party, or the bureaucracy, or even a less easily identifiable "ring" of groups and individuals. I will speak below of the "authoritarian power apparatus" and introduce distinctions only when they are enlightening for the problem at hand.[2] The authoritarian power apparatus has the capacity to prevent some political outcomes from occurring by exercising not only *ex ante* but also *ex post* control over the society. The power apparatus can intervene *ex post* to alter some state of the world which is the result of the functioning of the authoritarian institutions, as well as those that are not. In other words, the power apparatus in an authoritarian system exercises not only procedural but also substantive control over decisions. A Minister of Education is appointed; he charges a group of experts with preparing a mathematics text for elementary schools; the textbook is prepared; it is approved by the Minister, published and distributed. It then falls into the hands of the commandant of the local military zone, who orders that it be removed from schools. Note that the text at stake is not an underground pamphlet; it is the product of the authoritarian institutions themselves. Yet this does not make it immune from intervention.

In this light, then, a particular regime would be authoritarian if there existed some power apparatus capable of overturning the outcomes of the institutionalized political process. This definition may be too broad for several purposes, since the institutions are important in themselves. In particular, many regimes perhaps best described as "tutelary democracies" fall under our definition. These are regimes in which the military extricates itself from the direct performance of government and withdraws into barracks, but withdraws intact and contingently.[3] Thus while elections take place in such systems and the

[2] On the difficulties in identifying the authoritarian power apparatus see my "The Men of Iron and Men of Power in Poland," *PS* (February 1982). A more systematic analysis is offered by Fernando H. Cardoso, *O modelo politico Brasileiro* (Sao Paulo, Difel, 1972).

[3] For a discussion of the conditions under which the military extricated itself from government in Latin America see the article by Alain Rouquier in Guillermo

elected representatives govern, the armed forces remain in the shadows, ready to fall upon anyone who transgresses too far in undermining their values or their interests.[4]

For reasons discussed extensively in O'Donnell's and Schmitter's volume,[5] authoritarian regimes experience from time to time moments known generically as "liberalization" (also *odvilsh* or "the thaw," *apertura* or "the opening," *decompressão* or "decompression"). Liberalization is a situation or, when it involves a series of steps, a process of instituting civil liberties, most importantly the right of autonomous association, and of allowing or even creating some political organizations through which conflicts can be processed in an open fashion, but without transforming the power apparatus and undermining its capacity to control outcomes *ex post*. Thus liberalization is a process whereby the power apparatus allows some political organization and interplay of interests but maintains intact its own capacity to intervene. Liberalization is a controlled opening of the political space, continually contingent upon the compatibility of the outcomes of politics with the interests or values of the authoritarian power apparatus. The final outcome of the process of liberalization is thus a system described above as a "tutelary democracy": a regime which has competitive, formally democratic institutions, but in which the power apparatus, typically reduced by this time to the armed forces, retains the capacity to intervene to correct undesirable states of affairs.

As defined above, liberalization is not the same as democratization. To define the latter term, we need to focus first on the essential feature of democracy as a form of political organization. This feature is referential uncertainty: in a democracy outcomes of the political process are to some extent indeterminate with regard to positions which participants occupy in all social relations, including the relations of production and the political institutions. Clearly, all outcomes are

---

O'Donnell, Philippe C. Schmitter, and Laurence Whitehead, eds, *Transitions from Authoritarian Rule* (4 vols., Baltimore, Johns Hopkins Press).

[4] In such systems the competing political forces choose their strategies taking into account the threat and the fear of a military intervention. For an exemplary analysis see Guillermo O'Donnell, "The State and Alliances in Argentina, 1956–1976," *The Journal of Development Studies*, 15 (1978), 3–33.

[5] *Transitions*.

not equally likely and one can formulate reasonable predictions about them; I will say much more on this topic below. The point is that under a democracy no one can be certain that their interests will ultimately triumph. Capitalists do not always win conflicts which are processed in a democratic manner, and even one's current position within the political system does not guarantee future victories: incumbency may be an advantage, but incumbents do lose. In a democracy all forces must struggle repeatedly for the realization of their interests since no one is protected by virtue of their position. No one can wait to modify outcomes *ex post*; everyone must subject their interests to competition and uncertainty. This feature of democracy does not exclude the possibility that some generals would organize a conspiracy and overthrow democratic institutions: that is, unfortunately, possible all too often. In a democracy, however, generals do not have an organized capacity to overthrow the political institutions and the actors who subject their interests to democratic competition do not need to anticipate their reactions.

Let me emphasize that the difference between dictatorship and democracy is not one of absolute but of conditional uncertainty. Under a sufficiently capricious authoritarian ruler or a sufficiently divided power apparatus, the authoritarian regime may keep bewildering everyone with its twists and turns: *vide* the post-1948 agricultural policy in Poland. A democratic regime may, in contrast, yield highly predictable outcomes, even when parties alternate in government. Hence, the differences in certainty are only conditional in the following sense: in an authoritarian system it is almost certain that political outcomes will not include those adverse to the interests of the power apparatus, while in a democratic system there is no group whose interests would predict political outcomes with a near certainty.

Hence the crucial moment in any passage from authoritarian to democratic rule is not necessarily the withdrawal of the army into the barracks or the opening of the elected parliament but the crossing of the threshold beyond which no one can intervene to reverse outcomes of the formal democratic process. This is the moment beyond which, as Adolfo Suarez eloquently put it in the inaugural speech to the Constituent Assembly, "el futuro no esta escrito, porque solo el pueblo puede escribirlo": "the future is not written, because only the people can write it."[6] Democratization is a process of subjecting all interests to competition, of institutionalizing uncertainty. It is thus this very devolution of power over outcomes which constitutes the decisive step toward democracy. There is a moment before which the authoritarian power apparatus controls outcomes and after which no one does. Power is devolved from a group of people to a set of rules.

Clearly, this act of devolution need not be a discrete moment in time: in Spain, for example, it has been a long process in which attempts at *golpes* and rumors of them continued through the eve of the first democratic alternation of power. Moreover, at various points it may be unclear whether anyone still has the effective capacity to reverse the process. Even when the authoritarian power apparatus loses its cohesion and when the state bureaucracy, the armed forces and the police become independent of each other, even when the centralized command of the armed forces becomes constitutionalist, some units within the military may still be able to subvert the process. But in any successful process of democratization there must come a point of no return.

To finish setting the stage and to organize the analysis, let me observe that I have collapsed thus far two conditions that need not coincide theoretically (that is, need not have the same determinants) or chronologically. For it may happen – *vide* the French, the Soviet or the Iranian revolutions – that a new authoritarian regime rises to replace the overthrown one. The transition is to democracy if both conditions are fulfilled: (1) the old authoritarian power apparatus is dismantled and (2) the new political forces opt for democratic institutions as a framework within which they would compete for the realization of their interests. One must not forget that forces which join together to destroy a particular authoritarian regime often represent specific interests and offer distinct plans for the society. In pursuit of these interests they must not only dismantle the old regime but must create simultaneously conditions that would favor them in the newly established political system. Hence each group must struggle on two fronts: to abolish the old authoritarian regime and to create conditions that would be most conducive to the realization of its interests in the future conflicts against its current allies. The problem

---

6 This speech is reproduced in Pablo Lucas Verou, *Critica juridico-politica de la reforma Suarez* (Madrid, Editorial Tecnos, 1976).

of democratization, therefore, is to establish a compromise among the forces which are allied to bring down the authoritarian regime, not only to bring this regime down. Otherwise, the "anti-authoritarian alliance" quickly enters a second phase during which the weaker members are purged and a new authoritarian system is established.

I shall discuss first the problem of establishing a democratic system and then I shall focus on the difficulties of devolution of power. Hence the first section is intended to examine the conditions of the possibility of a democratic compromise in general, while the second section examines conditions under which the power apparatus of the authoritarian regime may be willing to devolve its power to a democratic system. Note that the entire analysis is couched, albeit informally, in the language of possibility rather than determination. The central question is under what conditions democracy becomes possible.

II

Solutions to the problem of democratization consist of institutions. Since this assertion may seem innocuous, let me emphasize that it is meant to exclude the possibility of democracy being a result of a compromise concerning exclusively substantive issues. Democracy is possible when the relevant political forces can find institutions that would provide a reasonable guarantee that their interests would not be affected in a highly adverse manner in the course of democratic competition. Democracy cannot be a result of a substantive compromise, but it can be a result of an institutional compromise.

One reason why democracy cannot result from a substantive compromise follows tautologically from the definition of democracy: in a democracy substantive compromises cannot be binding. Suppose that the leaders of various proto-parties within the Anti-Authoritarian Front sit down and agree that the rate of taxation of incomes will not exceed 53% in the new democratic regime. But the leadership of these parties may eventually change its mind under more auspicious conditions, or be replaced if it does not, or a new party could appear to capture electoral support with a program of redistribution of income.

Secondly, since substantive agreements cannot bind, some parties will always have an incentive to renege on their commitments. For suppose that a negotiation takes place and each party behaves strategically in its self-interest. The result will be a package that will constitute a compromise in the following sense: at least one of the parties will agree to an outcome which will be best for it given the eventual retribution of other parties but not as good as it would have been had the other parties bound themselves to a course of action. But once the agreement is concluded, the party or parties which were forced to anticipate others' reactions will prefer to act as if others had committed themselves to the negotiated agreement, that is, they will prefer to change the terms of the compromise.[7]

Finally, if there are no mechanisms to bind the parties to a compromise and if they have good grounds to expect that no compromise would be observed, they will not enter into one. Under conditions under which compromise solutions are highly uncertain each party will be better off seeking a full realization of its interests, that is, seeking to assert itself over others by whatever means. If the parties maximize expected utility they will opt for noncooperation as long as the probability of the compromise outcome is not greater than the likelihood that they would be able to destroy their adversaries. On these – admittedly schematic – grounds, a group would opt for a compromise only if the gain in the probability of the noncooperative outcome outweighed the loss of utility entailed in the compromise.

Consider a few examples, beginning with an extreme one: the issue of the guarantee of immunity for the members of the authoritarian power apparatus for the acts of repression they committed. Suppose that the power apparatus agrees to relinquish power, even to disband, on condition of the guarantee of immunity. It does; the first election takes place; a Revenge Party is formed, wins, and puts them all in jail. Or suppose that of the parties within the Multiparty Anti-Authoritarian Alliance one is confessional and one is anti-confessional and that they agree that religious schools would not be subsidized by public funds. Now authoritarianism is abolished as the result of allied efforts; the Religious Rebirth Party wins an overwhelming electoral victory, and passes legislation to subsidize religious schools. Finally, take the issue of class compromise, which I discuss in detail else-

---

[7] This is not a formal argument and it is based on a number of implicit assumptions. But if the solution to the negotiation is a Stackelberg equilibrium then it will be true that at least one and at most all but one participants will be better off returning to their best reply strategy when they conclude the negotiation.

where.[8] Workers offer wage restraint in exchange for the promise of future wage gains, but capitalists do not invest, output does not increase and no wage gains transpire. In none of these cases would a substantive agreement suffice to establish a compromise. As long as the potential parties fear that a compromise on their part would not be reciprocated, everyone will seek to impose their will and the outcomes will not be democracy but either the continuation of the old dictatorship or the establishment of a new one.

These examples, and the entire construction, are artificial insofar as no compromise could ever be purely substantive: some institutions exist even if they are not the object of negotiations. The model of "substantive" compromise is based on the assumption that no decisions have been yet made about the institutional framework or that the institutions are such that the probability of a substantive compromise holding is quite low. The *pacto de Moncloa* is a good example of a substantive agreement, but *nota bene*, one that did not hold.

My main thesis, therefore, is that democracy can be established only if there exist institutions that would make it unlikely that the competitive political process would result in outcomes highly adverse to anyone's interests given the distribution of economic, ideological, organizational and other relevant resources. This thesis is based on three assumptions: (1) that institutions have an impact upon outcomes of conflicts, (2) that the protagonists believe that they do and (3) that institutions that would provide the relevant political forces with reasonable security can be found under some circumstances.

The question why institutions affect outcomes or, in other words, what the justification is of explanations that cite institutions among causes, is much too basic to be discussed here.[9] As a preliminary answer, institutions affect both the repertoires of strategies from which groups can choose their courses of action and the mappings between outcomes and the selected strategies, but this form of explanation is not easy to apply under concrete circumstances. The

---

[8] Adam Przeworski, "Material Bases of Consent: Politics and Economics in a Hegemonic System," *Political Power and Social Theory*, 1 (1980), 23–68. Adam Przeworski and Michael Wallerstein, "The Structure of Class Conflict in Democratic Capitalist Societies," *American Political Science Review*, 76 (1982), 215–38.

[9] An interesting recent paper on this topic is by Robert Grafstein, "The Social Scientific Interpretation of Game Theory," *Erkenntnis* (in press). See also his "The Failure of Weber's Conception of Legitimacy: Its Causes and Implications," *Journal of Politics*, 43 (1981), 456–72.

abstract theory of public choice has accumulated a number of analyses of consequences of different voting systems, such as the majority, plurality, Condorcet tournaments, Borda's counts and exhaustive or approval voting.[10] We also know something about topics closer to political practice: in particular, we have a pretty thorough understanding of the effects of different electoral arrangements.[11] Recently, we have been rapidly accumulating evidence of the effect of different labor-capital systems, in particular of the laws regulating collective bargaining, upon the durability of income policies, strike intensity and labor strategies.[12] These are just a few examples.[13]

Given a distribution of economic, organizational and ideological resources, institutions determine the prior probabilities that particular interests will be realized to a definite degree and in a specific manner. This probability distribution – which is no less than political power –[14] is determined jointly by the resources which the parties bring into politics and the specific institutional arrangements. The point deserves attention since descriptions of democracy at times emphasize its formal character and the bias which results when resources are unequally distributed.[15] Clearly, a universalistic law which prohibits everyone from sleeping under bridges in fact prohibits only some people. But the converse is also true: given the resources, institutions do affect outcomes. The probability that a basketball team composed

10 The best review, from which this list is derived, is by Dennis C. Mueller, *Public Choice* (Cambridge University Press, 1979).

11 The classic book is, of course, Douglas Rae's *The Political Consequences of Electoral Laws* (New Haven, Yale University Press). This book is, however, exclusively empirical. In turn, attempts at a theoretical explanation of the number of parties have been singularly unsuccessful.

12 OECD, *Collective Bargaining and Government Policies in Ten OECD Countries* (Paris, 1979); Peter Lange, "The Conjunctural Conditions for Consensual Wage Regulations: An Initial Examination of Some Hypotheses." unpublished paper, 1981. Colin Crouch, "Conditions for Trade Union Wage Restraint," in Leon N. Lindberg and Charles S. Maier, eds., *The Politics of Inflation and Economic Stagnation* (Washington, The Brookings Institution, 1985).

13 One area in which quite a lot is known about the effect of institutions on outcomes is educational systems.

14 The notion of political power as the capacity of groups to realize their specific interests is due to Nicos Poulantzas, *Political Power and Social Classes* (London, New Left Books, 1973).

15 The most influential recent book along these lines was Ralph Miliband's *The State in Capitalist Society* (New York, Basic Books, 1970). Yet Miliband is inconsistent: he first argues that universalistic institutions simply reproduce economic and political inequalities but then he analyzes, most convincingly one should add, the bias due to the institutions. But if institutions can introduce a bias in favor of the Right, then they can introduce bias.

of players who are seven feet tall will beat a six-foot team by a number of points depends upon the height of the basket.

Suppose, for example, a system of proportional representation with sufficiently large districts. In such a system the distribution of seats is determined solely by the distribution of votes. Any given distribution of seats is therefore as likely as a given distribution of votes and the latter, in turn, is molded by the economic, organizational, ideological and other resources which parties bring into elections. In contrast, consider a system in which only the two parties which obtain the largest vote shares have the right to seats and distribute these proportionately: a single-member, single-district, first-past-the-post formula will approximate this result. In this system a number of distributions of votes will result in the same distribution of seats. Some outcomes are much more likely than other outcomes, independently of the resources of the participants.

It is this capacity of institutions that makes institutional compromises possible. If institutions determine the prior distributions of outcomes, always given the resources, then a particular institutional arrangement may render some outcomes quite unlikely. An appropriate institutional framework may provide a virtual guarantee that a newly formed party would not sweep elections, that no party would obtain the majority needed to alter basic laws, that corporatist arrangements would be enforced.

Even if at times they may have had inaccurate understandings of effects, politicians have long understood the importance of institutions.[16] The Upper House was the guarantee the Right wanted as the protection against the transfer of ministerial responsibility from the crown to parliament; indirect elections, plural voting, second ballot and eventually proportional representation were the protection the upper classes sought against extensions of suffrage. Negotiations were often complex. For example, in Sweden between 1902 and 1907 – the period of rapid industrialization, organization of classes and popular unrest – the package to be negotiated included the following issues: (1) whether to extend franchise and to whom, (2) whether the reform

---

[16] Perhaps the classical example is the understanding of electoral abstentions by the conservatives in several European countries at the turn of the century. They thought that it was the people with the most refined minds who abstain from voting, repelled by the vulgar clamor of campaigns. Hence they advocated compulsory voting. See Herbert Tingsten, *Political Behavior* (Totowa, Bedminster Press, 1932).

should include the Upper or only the Lower House, (3) whether seats should be allocated to single-member districts or multi-member constituencies with proportional representation, (4) if single-member districts were to be retained, whether it should be first past the post or there should be a run-off election and (5) whether the executive should continue to be responsible to the crown rather than the Rikstag. Each of these institutional details would have had an impact on the chances of particular groups, and each was seen as having an impact. Social Democrats would have preferred to extend franchise as widely as possible and to stay with a single-member, first-past-the-post system.[17] They were willing to agree to proportional representation but not to single-member districts with run-off since this arrangement would have favored the Liberals, who as a center party would have picked up the second round votes. Conservatives, once they recognized that an extension of franchise was inevitable, sought guarantees. Their guarantee was proportional representation which, they thought, would have prevented Liberals and/or Social Democrats from winning a majority. As their spokesman, Bishop Gottfrid Billing, put it, he would rather have "stronger guarantees and a further extension of the suffrage than weaker guarantees and a lesser extension."[18]

The most recent Brazilian elections (of 1982) were a spectacular case in which the authoritarian government used every possible legal instrument to secure *a priori* advantage for the pro-government party and to secure for itself the eventual majority in the presidential electoral college. First, the government allowed the formation of additional parties, hoping that the opposition, unwillingly united in the officially created movement, would factionalize. At the same time various obstacles were set up to prevent some parties from registering that might have preserved their appeal from the pre-1964 period: minimal number of members, geographical spread and a prohibition to use old party labels. Eventually, a law was issued forcing electors to vote a straight party ticket for elections at all levels of government: the

---

[17] Douglas Verney, *Parliamentary Reform in Sweden, 1866–1921* (London, Oxford University Press, 1957), p. 168.
[18] Dankwart A. Rustow, *The Politics of Compromise. A Study of Parties and Cabinet Government in Sweden* (Princeton University Press, 1955), p. 59. Rustow's 1970 article is still the classic work on the transition to democracy: "Transition to Democracy: Towards a Dynamic Model," *ComParative Politics*, 2 (1970), 337–63.

hope was that local ties to pro-government mayors and last-minute public spending would buy governatorial and congressional votes. At the last minute, when all this still seemed insufficient, casting ballots was made difficult for illiterates who could have been expected to vote against the government. This careful orchestration was a result of the bitter lesson of 1972, when the government did not prepare and, most importantly, allowed the opposition access to television.[19] This time, with television barred to practically all but the President and the rules continually manipulated, the outcome was more favorable to the government.

Agreements about institutions are thus possible, even if the political forces involved have conflicting interests and visions, because institutions shape the opportunities of realizing specific interests and the groups involved understand that institutions have this effect. Faced with the alternative of an open, possibly violent, conflict – the outcome of which may be highly beneficial but also quite risky – and of a democratic solution, which requires compromise but provides security, political forces involved in regime transformation may opt for the democratic compromise. This compromise is substantive in the sense that groups enter into it as the most promising framework for the realization of their interests. It is, however, only indirectly substantive: only to the extent to which substantive outcomes are shaped by institutions. What are at stake in any process of democratization are guarantees, and guarantees can only be institutional.[20]

III

Is an institutional solution always possible? This is basically the same as asking whether institutions always compensate for the distribution of economic, organizational, ideological and other politically relevant resources in such a way that all the major political forces would feel

---

[19] See Bolivar Lamounier, "O discurso e o proceso." Paper presented at the Conference "Prospects for Democracy: Transitions from Authoritarian Rule," Woodrow Wilson International Center, Washington, D.C., September 25–6, 1979.

[20] It is worth remembering that what can be guaranteed are only probabilities, but that unlikely events do transpire. My favorite example is the reaction of the Chilean newspaper El Mercurio to the electoral victory of Salvador Allende: "Nobody expected that a marxist president would be elected by means of a secret, universal, bourgeois franchise" (September 5, 1970).

protected under democracy.[21] The question can be posed in the following context. Suppose that the authoritarian power apparatus retains the capacity to reverse the process of democratization until and unless institutions can be found that would protect its interests and the interests of those forces in civil society that are allied to it. Can an institutional solution always be found under such conditions?

Note that the problem of democratization, attempted or successful, need not arise in this form: where the authoritarian power apparatus is destroyed as a result of military defeat, whether in a foreign or a civil war, or when it disintegrates under the pressure of internal divisions, most often still as a consequence of being defeated in a foreign war. We are limiting the analysis, however, to the problem of a negotiated devolution of power, a *ruptura* but a *ruptura pactada*. The use of these Spanish terms is obviously not accidental, since it was in Spain that the possibility of such a negotiated break was most recently demonstrated. I have in mind, also, however, cases that are still open, notably Brazil, and one which is interrupted by dictatorial reassertion, namely, Poland.

The interests and values which must be guaranteed by the democratic institutions if the authoritarian power apparatus is to accept democracy fall into two categories. Some interests are attached to those forces in civil society which provide the support for the authoritarian regime – the power block. Other interests are attached more narrowly to the power apparatus, that is, the amalgam of the armed forces, police, bureaucracy and whoever else participates in the exercise of dictatorial power.

The only effective guarantee that the interests of the forces associated with the dictatorship would be protected under democratic conditions is that these forces develop a significant political presence under democracy. This is possible, in turn, only if those forces which are placed on the right wing of the political spectrum by their economic interests are attached to democratic values. Where a democratic Right is in existence – where parties can find support

---

21 Needless to say this is not a new question. The issue of the relative importance of social structure and institutions preoccupied political sociologists during the 1950s (Duverger, Lipset). Somewhat later this issue became the center of controversies among political scientists, who divided between "institutionists" – those who thought that the study of institutions is sufficient because institutions determine behavior – and "behaviorists," who ignored institutions altogether.

appealing simultaneously to the values of property and democracy – the power block underlying the authoritarian regime can be quite certain that under properly designed institutions its interests will be quite well protected even in democratic competition. Where, in turn, the Right is antidemocratic – where it values protection of property more than its own political autonomy – there is no one to whom the authoritarian power block can delegate the representation of its interests under democratic conditions. In Marx's formulation the question was whether the mass of the bourgeoisie prefers to assume the responsibility for defending its own interests under competitive conditions or to renounce its own political autonomy in exchange for the protection of its economic interests. This is still a valid question and one to which answers have been different in different societies.[22]

What does it mean to say that a democratic Right "is in existence"? Historically, the following seems to be the case: only where the Left lost the first competitive election has the process of democratization not been reversed. Since the universe of cases has not been defined and since the terms "the Left" and "winning" are ambiguous, this generalization should not be pressed. But clear cases to the contrary are difficult to find. Thus it would seem that the Right must be sufficiently strong, and the Left sufficiently weak, to reassure those who still have the capacity of arresting or reversing the institutionalization of democracy.

The problem is that one would normally expect that the opponents of the authoritarian regime would sweep the first election. They are the ones who mobilize mass support when the opening is created. At the first stage of the process of democratization various forces within civil society organize outside the tutelage of the regime. At this stage, however, there are still no institutions that could serve these new autonomous organizations as a forum of expression and negotiation. Because of this *décalage* between autonomous organization of the civil society and the closed character of state institutions, the campaign for

[22] On this complicated topic see Fernando H. Cardoso, "O papel dos empresarios no processo de transicao: O caso brasilero," *Dados* 28 (1983), 9–27; Guillermo O'Donnell, "Notas para el estudio de la burgesia local, con especial referencia a sus vinculaciones con el capital transnacional y el aparato estatal," *Estudios Sociales*, no. 12. CEDES: Buenos Aires, 1978. Peter Evans, *Dependent Development: The Alliance of Multinational, State and Local Capital in Brazil* (Princeton University Press, 1979), and "Reinventing the Bourgeoisie: State Entrepreneurship and Class Formation in the Context of Dependent Capitalist Development," *American Journal of Sociology*, forthcoming.

democracy must assume a mass character. Mass movement is needed as a means of pressure, and the street becomes the chief arena of expression in the early stages, when no other channels exist.[23] Opponents of the regime mobilize mass support.

Workers are typically the first and the largest force to organize autonomously. This was true in Western Europe at the turn of the century as well as in Spain (Comisiones Obreras), Brazil (ABC unions) and Poland (Solidarnosc). This fact is not accidental. First, places of work are along with markets (the bazaar) the only places where people can meet naturally without police supervision. Secondly, political rights are necessary for workers if they are to be able to struggle for their economic interests. Thus workers organize autonomous unions and the unions embrace political demands that put them in the forefront of the struggle for democracy.

Note as well that while opponents of the authoritarian regime mobilize during the early stages of the campaign for democracy, the supporters of the regime are typically not ready to participate in politics. Authoritarian regimes do not mobilize: even in Eastern Europe, where the membership in official organizations is massive, real political activity is highly infrequent.

And yet, if our empirical generalization is valid, some time between the decision to hold elections and the elections themselves the forces associated with the authoritarian regime must constitute themselves as a political party or parties, must build an organization and must find means of popular appeal to the masses of previously unpoliticized supporters. The Left in turn must somehow demobilize. Practically in Spain demobilization meant that struggle was removed from the streets and factories and almost completely restricted to electoral competition. Moreover, left-wing organizations were willing to moderate their demands, including a fair dose of wage restraint.[24] As

---

[23] I am not arguing that the process of liberalization must begin and everywhere began with popular mobilization, as Rustow, "Transition to Democracy," suggests. Indeed, I am persuaded by Cardoso that in Brazil the initial impetus came from above and I can think of other cases when this was true, both Poland in 1956 and Czechoslovakia in 1968. See Cardoso in *Transitions*, as well as my own paper, "Some Problems in the Study of the Transition to Democracy," also forthcoming in *Transitions*. This paper examines critically those explanations of liberalization which attribute the causal force to the loss of legitimacy.

[24] For the description of demobilization in Spain and the divergent interpretations of this demobilization see Jose Maria Maravall, *La politica de la transicion, 1975–1980* (Madrid, Taurus, 1981), particularly pp. 28–31. Unfortunately, Maravall's own inter-

Santiago Carrillo put it, "We must have the courage to explain to workers that it is better to give a surplus to the bourgeoisie than to face an even worse fate.'[25] The result in Spain was the weakening of support for the Communist Party, both in relation to earlier estimates of its strength and in relation to its strength in the factories and streets. A similar phenomenon seems to have occurred with the Communist Party of the Exterior in Greece and with the Partido Trabalhista in Brazil.

Obviously I would not venture to argue that leaders of these parties deliberately sought to diminish their electoral strength. More likely the initial mobilization does not become transformed into electoral support of the otherwise apathetic, often predominantly rural, masses. The fact seems to be that somehow in a number of countries the parties which organized the mass mobilization against the authoritarian regime managed to arrive at the polls divided among themselves and not to win.

The existence of a democratic Right and even its electoral victory may be far from sufficient, however, to provide a guarantee for the authoritarian power apparatus. Here the problem is twofold. One problem is the responsibility of the repressive apparatuses for the acts they committed, often during the implantation of the authoritarian regime. Where repression had been massive and brutal and the memory is still vivid in the life of the same generation, the issue of personal immunity may be without solution. Even the electoral victory of political parties representing interests of the authoritarian power block does not provide sufficient protection for individual members of the apparatus of repression. This problem is now at the center of difficulties in Argentina and it is likely to constitute the central obstacle in Chile. It is noteworthy that in Spain the repressive apparatuses simply remained in place as democratic institutions were introduced.[26]

The second obstacle is perhaps specific to noncapitalist countries, where the question of economic survival looms importantly in the

pretation is far from conclusive and a detailed analysis of the relation between popular mobilization and party strategies remains to be conducted.

[25] Santiago Carillo, *Demain L'Espagne* (Paris, Seuil, 1974). I am quoting from memory.

[26] See some interesting reflections on this topic by Jorge Semrpun, *La Autobiografía de Frederico Sanchez* (Madrid, 1978).

considerations of the bureaucrats within the power apparatus. Under capitalism those members of the bureaucracy who have no skills that would enable them to live decently from private employment can accumulate while in power property that would make them wealthy for ever. Under noncapitalist conditions access to property, even if exercised privately by members of the *nomenklatura*, is open to them only by virtue of their position within the power apparatus. Hence the stakes are much higher: one is forced to play for economic and not only political survival.

Thus where bridges were burnt by repression and where additionally some members of the power apparatus are concerned about their private economic interests, the authoritarian power apparatus may resist the transition to democracy even when the forces within the civil society upon which the regime rests are willing to try their chances under democratic conditions.

The competitive strength of these forces seems again to be crucial. If the economic Right can organize itself as a party and successfully compete under democratic conditions, then the democratic coalition, composed of forces across the political spectrum, will place the power apparatus in complete isolation, in which its rule will be reduced to naked force or broken. Indeed, these are the moments of putschist fever, in which plots against democratization become more frequent but also less likely to succeed.

A stalemate occurs when the democratic Right is unable to mobilize popular support, when it is not legitimate in the sense of being able to evoke popular support by appealing simultaneously to values of property and democracy. Under such conditions the problem of democratization has no solution: the authoritarian power apparatus opposes the process, and the democratic Right has no power without the support of the power apparatus. Without this support the democratic Right is not a viable interlocutor; with this support it cannot opt for democracy.

Thus an institutional compromise is not possible under all circumstances: it is conceivable only if there exist some political forces to which the power block can delegate the defense of its interests and only if sufficient guarantees can be created with regard to particularistic concerns of the power apparatus. Such forces may be simply absent. They may be absent because of the macro-structural conditions identified by Barrington Moore[27] and they may be absent because the authoritarian regime was so narrowly based that no forces within civil society can be mobilized in defense of interests and ideas of the authoritarian power apparatus under democratic conditions. Institutions have an autonomous impact upon outcomes of political conflicts and this is why institutional compromises are possible. But their impact is in the end circumscribed by the historical conditions and under some conditions no negotiated solution may be possible.

IV

As the reader may have noticed from several examples, this chapter has a hidden thesis as well. I am persuaded that the logic of the transition to democracy, the choices present at different stages and the conditions under which democracy becomes possible can be analyzed in similar terms whether one speaks of Western Europe at the turn of the century or contemporary Latin America or Eastern Europe. Clearly, specific historical conditions are important. Moreover, there are some relevant systemic differences between the capitalist and the Eastern European countries: one was used above as an element of analysis. Finally, several categories which one is willing to apply intuitively to the analysis of capitalist societies – the Right, civil society, power block – seem awkward when applied to Eastern Europe. But having been educated about the transition to democracy in the context of Latin America and Southern Europe, I found in 1980 a ready-made framework for analyzing the events in Poland. In the end, the model of "Polonia" derived from the Latin American experience both elucidates the defeat of the democratic movement in Poland and provides material for subsequent analyses of democratic transition elsewhere.

The impetus toward democratization originated in Poland from workers. Reacting against economic conditions and economic decisions of the authoritarian government, workers sought to defend their collective interests by organizing autonomous, self-governing unions. Their original vision of reforms was both narrowly economicist and abstentionist: the principal demand was for union autonomy, but unions were seen as an instrument for exerting pressure upon the

[27] Barrington Moore, Jr., *Social Origins of Dictatorship and Democracy* (Boston, Beacon Press, 1965).

existing political institutions from the outside. During the initial stage, the union did not seek either a reform of political institutions or a place within them. This stance could not be maintained for long, however, as it soon became apparent that autonomous unions are not possible without some liberalization of the political system. Without political reforms union members could not communicate with each other and could not present and justify their demands in any regularized manner. Hence, the union movement quickly became "politicized," that is, it set political goals as an instrument for realizing economic interests. At the same time, the movement of workers gave impetus to numerous other groups, each of which organized autonomously from the government and swore to promote its interests vigorously. The result was a broad, massive and highly heterogeneous movement which, like so many movements of this kind in Western Europe at the turn of the century, had a political and a trade-unionist wing.

The power apparatus, in turn, saw the initial concessions as temporary compromises necessitated by the conjunctural relations of force. Neither the union nor the government viewed the existence of autonomous organizations as incompatible with the monopolistically controlled political institutions. Hence both sides thought at the beginning that the newly formed organizations would be somehow accommodated without any basic political reforms.

A division within the power apparatus went first through the middle of the Polish United Workers' (Communist) Party. A significant wing within the party was willing to find some institutional solution that would have allowed an effective role for unions and other organizations. Eventually a profound split developed between the reformist groups within the party on the one hand and the permanent apparatus of the party, the police and some groups within the bureaucracy on the other hand. Some party leaders were willing to transform the party back into a political from a purely administrative organization, back into an ideological from a thoroughly opportunistic force. Others, not easy to identify in generic terms because their power was always clandestine, opposed any reforms. They defended control and privilege against all attempts.

In some aspects the structure of conflict was one of a prisoner's dilemma.[28] The cooperative solution under which the Communist Party would have had an effective guarantee of winning a majority of seats in competitive elections (and forming the government by virtue of having won the majority) would have been preferred over the feasible alternatives by the moderate, trade-union wing of Solidarity as well as by reformist groups within the party. The radical strategy of factory take-overs ("active strike") seemed much too risky, partly because of the Soviet threat, to moderates within Solidarity.[29] On the other hand, the eventual outcome, the forcible repression of the movement, was not the preference of reformers within the party who would rather have shared power with consent than monopolize it by force.

Little is known about the details of negotiations which continued with interruptions throughout the fall of 1981, but there are good reasons to believe that these negotiations ultimately broke over the issue of the electoral formula. To the best of my knowledge the leadership of Solidarity was willing to accept a formula according to which (1) the government would be effectively responsible for the Seym (parliament) rather than the party, (2) the Communist Party alone or in some coalition would be guaranteed a majority of seats within the parliament and thus could form the government and (3) some competition for seats would be permitted. The problem was that these conditions could not be simultaneously satisfied. There was no electoral system that would permit real competition for seats and would guarantee the majority for the Communist Party. The reason was that the party had no popular support whatever: although clandestine and not quite reliable, foreign surveys conducted in Poland gave the Communists between 3% and 5% of the vote in an open election. Under such conditions no electoral formula could do the magic and no institutional compromise was possible. The moderate wing of Solidarity could not go any further in its concessions; in particular it could not compromise the principle of competition, because at this moment it would have lost control over the radicals within the movement. On the other hand, the reformists within the party were unable to offer any additional concessions because their

[28] A game theoretic interpretation of the situation was offered by Stefan Nowak in the fall of 1982, if I remember correctly in *Polityka*, Warsaw (October 1981).

[29] Indeed, I would claim that "moderates" are in general people who are risk-averse, not people who have more moderate goals.

power rested ultimately on the support of the power apparatus and this apparatus was opposed to any political concessions. The reformists could negotiate only as far as they could carry with them the power apparatus, and that was not very far. Without the support of the police, the bureaucracy and the army the reformist group would have been swept away by the popular movement.

This is not intended as a full account of the collapse of the democratic process in Poland. Several of its aspects – the emergence of the army as an autonomous actor, the role played by the Catholic Church and the pressures from the Soviet Union – would require a more complex analysis. The purpose of this analysis was to illustrate the general thesis, specifically, the fact that institutional compromises may be impossible even if they are desired and actively sought by the relevant political forces. In Poland an institutional compromise was impossible because the forces associated with the regime (including those who supported the alliance with the Soviet Union) could not find any support under democratic conditions and the authoritarian power apparatus could not risk a devolution of power because of the threat it presented to its most narrow personal interests.

V

This, then, is the answer to the original question. Democratization, understood as a discrete step of devolution of power from the authoritarian power apparatus to institutions that permit an uncertain interplay of forces, is possible if there exist institutions that provide a reasonable expectation that interests of major political forces would not be affected highly adversely under democratic competition, given the resources these forces can muster. Substantive agreements are possible only if they are institutionally guaranteed because institutions mold the prior probabilities of outcomes. The leaders of conflicting political forces can agree to the actions of institutions while they cannot agree to substantive outcomes in the absence of institutional guarantees.

Whether such institutional solutions can be found depends upon the distribution of resources. The authoritarian power apparatus may be willing to devolve power if the forces associated with the authoritarian regime can mobilize enough popular support to play an important role under competitive institutions. If, however, the Right is not politically democratic and if in addition, the power apparatus is afraid of reactions to its acts of repression or is concerned with individual economic survival, then the process of democratization may be effectively reversed and a narrowly based, highly repressive regime may deepen the authoritarian rule. Having someone to delegate the representation of interests and not having burnt its bridges seem to be crucial from the point of view of the authoritarian power apparatus. When these conditions are absent a negotiated transition to democracy is not possible; under these circumstances democracy may be possible only if the dictatorship is defeated by force.

Perhaps the most striking feature of the Spanish transition to democracy is that the political system was transformed without affecting the economic relations in any discernible manner: not only the structure of ownership, but even the distribution of income. Indeed, even the victory of the Socialist Party made one editor comment that "Before the center was Right; now it is Left." Having demonstrated that it is fit to exist, the Left must now show that it is "fit to govern" – the phrase used to justify the entrance of the Labor Party into government in 1924.[30] If the analysis presented above is invalid, social and economic conservatism may be the necessary price for democracy: political institutions that organize the democratic compromise must be designed in such a way as to protect interests of the forces associated with the authoritarian regime and thus to minimize the extent of eventual transformations.

Thus negotiated transitions to democracy present a dilemma: political democracy is possible only at the cost of limiting social and economic transformations. As Marx already observed, under such conditions the masses of the oppressed will seek to use their political rights to obtain social and economic change while those who enjoy economic and social privilege will be repeatedly tempted to seek the protection of force. The conclusion Marx drew – that the combination of political democracy with private property is impossible as a durable form of societal organization – was too strong.[31] But democracy continues to be rare and unstable: rare because it requires a class compromise, unstable because it is based upon one.

[30] See my "Social Democracy as a Historical Phenomenon," *New Left Review*, 122 (1980).
[31] See Przeworski and Wallerstein, "The Structure of Class Conflict."

3. Consequences of constitutional choice: reflections on Tocqueville

JON ELSTER

Tocqueville's *Democracy in America* is, among other things, an argument about the social consequences of constitutions. He draws attention to various features of the democratic constitution he observed in the United States, such as universal suffrage, the system of elected officials, the jury system and freedom of association and of expression. He then goes on to discuss how these institutions have various consequences for certain social values, such as prosperity, happiness and religious faith. His goal is clearly to *evaluate* democracy, as compared to other arrangements such as despotism, monarchy or aristocracy. For this he needs a method for tracing the full social effect of democratic institutions. It will not do to look at local effects, partial effects, short-term effects or transitional effects. Rather we must see the problem as one of general equilibrium. We must compare democracy as a going concern with other regimes also considered as going concerns.

Tocqueville is not generally considered an important figure in the development of social science methodology. He wrote as an historian, with the historian's peculiar brand of arrogance, which is to make the theories and methods employed as unobtrusive as possible. They serve as scaffolding, useful in construction but not to be left visible in the finished work. Hence posterity has tended to focus on Tocqueville's substantive views, notably his theory of liberty and equality as the main values of modern societies, sometimes in harness with one another, sometimes in conflict. I shall attempt to show, however, that Tocqueville had a profound understanding – unequalled in his time, unsurpassed in ours – of the nature of social causation. I hope the demonstration will be of interest in itself, in addition to the

implications it might have for constitutional design[1] and for democratic theory.[2]

I Local versus global consequences

Tocqueville warns us against two invalid inferences. First, from the
fact that a proposition may be (locally) true with respect to *any* unit of
analysis, we cannot conclude that it may be (globally) true of *all* units.
To make this inference is to commit the fallacy of composition.[3]
Secondly, from the fact that a proposition is true when applied to all
units, we cannot conclude that it remains valid when applied to one
unit separately *and exclusively*. This inference would be an instance of
the fallacy of division.[4]

An instructive example of the fallacy of composition is due to
George Katona. For the individual businessman, the effect of a tax
increase is the same as that of a rise in wages – it represents an extra
cost that he will try to pass on to the consumer through higher prices.
The local causal link is from higher taxes to higher prices. But this is
valid only under *ceteris paribus* assumptions, since the effect of a
general tax increase will be a reduction of aggregate demand and thus
a fall in prices. The global causal link goes in the opposite direction.[5]

Tocqueville offers a similar analysis of the effect of marrying for
love, a practice which is widespread in democracies. Here, as elsewhere, he was concerned with defending democracy against its
rearguard critics:

> Our ancestors conceived a singular opinion with regard to marriage.
> As they had noticed that the few love matches which took place in
> their days almost always ended in tragedy, they came to the firm

---

[1] Some of these implications I discuss in chapter 10 below.

[2] I make no pretension here to scholarship. I am engaged in a somewhat anachronistic dialogue with Tocqueville, in which I largely disregard the historical context in which
he wrote and the various ambiguities that a close reading of the texts might discern. I do
hope, of course, that Tocqueville scholars will find something here that speaks to their
concern, but mine lie elsewhere.

[3] See Elster (1978), pp. 97ff. for an analysis of this fallacy.

[4] The fallacy of composition is the inference from "For any x, possibly x if F" to
"Possibly for all x, x is F." The inverse inference is not fallacious, but valid. An invalid
deduction, however, is the inference from "Possibly for all x, x is F" to "For any x,
possibly x is the sole F." This I call the fallacy of division. I ought to add that this bears
only a distant relation to the standard logical terminology (for which see Hamblin 1970).

[5] Katona (1951), pp. 45ff.

conclusion that in such matters it was very dangerous to rely on one's own heart. They thought that chance saw clearer than choice. (596)[6]

Tocqueville goes on to point out two reasons why this view is untenable. First, to marry for love in a society where this is the exception is to court disaster, since going against the current tends to create hostility and in turn bitterness. Secondly, only very opinionated persons will go against the current in the first place – not a character feature conducive to happy marriages. The latter mechanism is a sampling effect, the former a real after-effect.[7] They are both related to the necessarily exceptional act of going against the current – something which it is possible for any one individual to do, but not for all. And Tocqueville concludes that

> There is therefore no just ground for surprise if, in an age of aristocracy, a man who chooses to consult nothing but his taste and inclination in selecting a wife soon finds that irregular morals and wretchedness break into his home life. But when such behaviour is part of the natural and usual order of things, when the social system makes it easy, when paternal authority supports it and public opinion recognizes it, one should not doubt that the internal peace of families will be increased thereby and conjugal faith better protected. (597)

A more consequential instance of this fallacy (or a closely related one) is pointed out in the notes to the second volume of the *Ancien régime*, in the course of a discussion of the summons of the Estates-General in 1789. Why did the King, disastrously, agree to let the third estate have double representation and to have voting in common rather than by estates? True, this system already existed in the Languedoc, where it seemed to produce class harmony rather than class conflict. Yet, Tocqueville argues, the fatal mistake was that of not recognizing that "an institution which in one province only led to slight changes in the local constitution could not fail to disturb it violently and profoundly

---

[6] Hereafter page references in the text are to Tocqueville (1969).
[7] For this distinction see Feller (1968), pp. 199ff.

the day it was applied to the whole nation."[8] Note that this is not exactly the member–set or any–all fallacy identified above. Rather it is the part–whole fallacy of thinking that whatever is true of a smaller entity must also be true of a larger one. Tocqueville is not here pointing to the dangerous effects of extending the Languedoc system to all provinces, but to the risk of extending it to the national assembly, which is at a higher level than the provincial ones.

Consider next the fallacy of division. It is an old axiom that "Qui peut le plus peut le moins." Whoever can lift ten pounds can also lift five. But there are cases in which the axiom is false, because in effect it embodies a fallacy of division. Thus an employer may be able to lay off all his workers, but unable to dismiss some but not all of his workers.[9] Similarly, Tocqueville notes, in connection with the practice of compulsory military service, "a democratic government can do pretty well what it likes, provided that its orders apply to all and at the same moment; it is the inequality of a burden, not its weight, which usually provokes resistance" (651–2). This, in his opinion, is due not to solidarity but to envy, an endogenous vice of democracies. One may object, however, that the resistance could also be due to the lack of legitimacy of a decision that singles out a few to bear a burden that benefits all. There is, in all such cases, a bargaining problem that comes on the top of the collective action problem which the political system is supposed to resolve. People are more willing to forgo the possibility of being free riders than to see others benefiting without contributing – even when their additional contribution would be pointless.

II Partial effects versus net effects

When tracing the consequences of a given institutional change, it is all too easy to focus exclusively on one causal chain, forgetting that there may be several paths from the independent to the dependent variable. Moreover, even if there is only one primary causal chain, the effect

---

[8] Tocqueville (1953), pp. 110–11.
[9] Nozick (1969), p. 480 refers to a ruling by the Supreme Court to the effect that "it is not an unfair labor practice for an employer to close his entire business, even if the closing is due to antiunion animus, but that closing *part* of his business is an unfair labor practice."

may call forth countermeasures that partially or totally offset it.[10] In both cases our interest ought to be in the net effect, rather than in any partial or *ceteris paribus* conclusions.

An amusing example in Tocqueville is the following. "As there is no precautionary organization in the United States, there are more fires than in Europe, but generally they are put out more speedily, because the neighbors never fail to come quickly to the danger spot" (723). The general structure of this argument is the following. We want to examine the effect of the independent variable, democracy, on some dependent variable, such as the number of houses destroyed by fire. We first observe that the effect is mediated by two intermediating variables: the number of houses that catch fire and the proportion of fires that are not quickly extinguished. We also note that the two mediating variables interact multiplicatively in their effect on the dependent variable, rather than additively. Finally we observe that the first of the mediating variables is an increasing function of the independent variable, whereas the second is a decreasing one. This implies that the net effect could go either way, in the absence of more information about the relative strength of the two tendencies.

Another example has to do with the impact of democracy on the strength of social interaction. Tocqueville argues that "the bonds of human affection are wider, but more relaxed" (507) than in aristocratic societies. Each person is tied to a greater number of other persons, but each tie is weaker. The substantive issue is whether what has been called "the strength of weak ties"[11] exceeds or falls short of that of the closer relations in earlier societies. The methodological point, again, is that the question can be resolved only by looking at the net effect, rather than by focusing on some partial mechanism.

A closely related form of argument is the following. Tocqueville first has the occasion to observe that democracy tends to increase people's opportunity set in some respect, and then goes on to point out

[10] The distinction between these two cases is well brought out by considering Marx's theory of the tendency of the rate of profit to fall and the countertendencies that work in the opposite direction (Elster 1985, ch. 3). Some of the countertendencies are produced by the very same cause (i.e., labor-saving innovations) that generates the "main" tendency, while others arise as reactions to the main tendency when businessmen see the rate of profit falling.

[11] Granovetter (1973) argues that "weak ties play a role in effecting social cohesion" and that the "local cohesion of ethnic communities goes together with an extremely fragmented global society."

that it simultaneously tends to weaken their desire to exploit the new opportunities. In the chapter in *Democracy in America* on "Why great revolutions will become rare," he argues that although men are less than satisfied with their present condition and feel no natural abhorrence toward revolution, they nevertheless are held back from it by their inclination. "The same social condition which prompts their longings restrains them within necessary limits. It gives them both greater freedom to change, and less interest in doing so" (636). Similarly he argues that the American Constitution "gave the president much power, but took away from him the will to use it" (138). The power stems from his prerogatives and veto, the lack of will to use it from the constant preoccupation with reelection. The same reasoning is applied to religion, as can be seen by juxtaposing two passages. "While the law allows the American people to do everything, there are things which religion prevents them from imagining and forbids them to dare" (292). And, "I doubt whether man can support complete religious independence and entire political liberty at the same time. I am led to think that if he has no faith he must obey, and if he is free he must believe" (444). Here the thrust of the second passage is that religion is endogenous to democracies, while the first argues that it tends to restrict the potentially dangerous freedom that is also part and parcel of democratic society.

Usually Tocqueville uses this kind of argument to defend democracy against its critics, by suggesting that the net effect in question is positive, although the critic may correctly have perceived that one of the partial mechanisms by itself has bad consequences, other things being equal. Thus in democracies each thing is less well done, for reasons that will become clear, but this tendency is more than offset by the fact that more things are done (244). In particular, although democracies may perform badly in the short run, they out-perform aristocracies in the long term.

III Short-term versus long-term consequences

This distinction, indeed, is only a special case of the preceding one, but its importance in Tocqueville's analyses is such that it needs to be singled out for separate consideration. There is an interesting comparison that suggests itself here, between Tocqueville and Schumpeter. One obvious affinity is that they both attempt to work out a theory of capitalist democracy – Tocqueville for an early stage and Schumpeter for a later stage of that system. The relation between the two theories would deserve an extensive analysis, which would fall outside the scope of the present discussion. I want to draw attention, however, to the close structural resemblance between Schumpeter's defense of capitalism and Tocqueville's defense of democracy. Schumpeter admitted – in fact, insisted on – the multiple weakness of capitalism, such as its allocative inefficiency and its proneness to crises.[12] He also argued that one should not judge capitalism as a system in the light of these defects, as they appear over a short span of time. The patent system or the excessively optimistic entrepreneurial expectations both involve short-term waste, but are also indispensable conditions for the dynamic efficiency of capitalism. In a famous passage Schumpeter makes the point in a very general manner:

> Since we are dealing with a process whose every element takes considerable time in revealing its true features and ultimate effects, there is no point in appraising the performance of that process *ex visu* of a given point of time; we must judge its performance over time, as it unfolds over decades or centuries. A system – any system, economic or other – that at *every* given point of time fully utilizes its possibilities to the best advantage may yet in the long run be inferior to a system that does so at *no* given point of time, because the latter's failure to do so may be a condition for the level or speed of long-run performance.[13]

In a very similar vein Tocqueville writes that "administrative centralization succeeds . . . in assembling, at a given time and place, all the available resources of the nation, but it militates against the increase of those resources" (88). Or again, "I think that in the long run government by democracy should increase the real forces of a society, but it cannot immediately assemble, at one point and at a given time, forces as great as those at the disposal of an aristocratic government or an absolute monarchy" (224). This holds in particular for warfare: "An aristocratic people which, fighting against a democ-

12 For discussion see Elster (1983), ch. 5.   13 Schumpeter (1961), p. 83.

racy, does not succeed in bringing it to ruin in the first campaign always runs a great risk of being defeated by it" (658). And if somebody objects to democracy on the grounds that it tends to tax the citizens too heavily, Tocqueville again has recourse to an argument of the same general form:

> Is democratic government economical? First, we must know with what we are comparing it. The question could easily be answered if we wanted to compare a democratic republic with an absolute monarchy. One would find public expenses in the former considerably greater than in the latter. But that is so of all free states compared with those not free. It is certain that despotism brings men to ruin more by preventing them from producing than by taking away the fount of wealth while often respecting acquired riches. But liberty engenders thousandfold more goods than it destroys, and in nations where it is understood, the people's resources always increase faster than the taxes. (208–9)[14]

IV Transitional effects versus steady-state effects

The short-term versus long-term distinction must be kept separate from another distinction that needs to be made with respect to the temporal flow of consequences that stem from institutional change. This I refer to as the distinction between the transitional effects of *introducing* a certain institution, and the steady-state effect of *having* that institution. The latter can only be observed when all other institutions have adapted to the change, including all the chain effects and feedback effects that are set in motion.

To bring out the difference between these two distinctions, we may first consider Tocqueville's discussion of freedom of association. As usual, he is concerned to defend this principle against the accusation that it perniciously undermines social stability. He admits that freedom of association might at first glance seem to involve a danger to society, but goes on to argue that through associations Americans also learn how to render the dangers of freedom less formidable:

---

[14] Tocqueville does not, of course, argue that a high tax rate leads to a high taxable income. Rather, the argument is that democratic institutions are the common cause of both phenomena.

By picking on one moment in the history of a nation it is easy to prove that political associations disturb the state and paralyze industry. But if you take the life of a people as one complete whole it may prove easy to show that freedom of political associations favors the welfare and even the tranquillity of the citizens. (534)

This is the pure Schumpeterian argument of (III) above. But Tocqueville also makes a subtly different defense of associations when he argues "that political association is not nearly as dangerous to public peace as is supposed and that it could happen that it might give stability to a state after having shaken it for some time" (523). This, I believe, is a distinction between the temporary effect of introducing the freedom of association and the steady-state effect of having it. This reading might seem tenuous, but I believe it is plausible in view of the central importance of steady-state reasoning in the other passages that I now go on to discuss.

Tocqueville is sympathetic to the usual conservative view that the stability of social arrangements is more important than their specific form. Speaking of the relation between master and servant, he observes that neither in stable aristocracies nor in stable democracies need there be anything degrading in either condition. Hence, he says, "It is not my business . . . to discover whether the new state of affairs which I have described is worse than what went before or simply different. It is enough for me that it is fixed and regulated, for what is important to find among men is not any particular order, but just order" (578). Correlatively, it is "in the journey from one social condition to the other" that "the lines between authority and tyranny, liberty and license" (579–80) become blurred. Either steady state, in other words, is preferable to the traverse from the one to the other.

This argument, however, is not all there is to Tocqueville. Although notoriously ambivalent and ambiguous in his attitudes toward democracy, he does in many respects prefer – at least with his intellect, if not with his passions – the state of democracy over the old order. And so he is concerned to defend democracy by arguing that as a steady state it is superior to aristocracy and monarchy, although the process of democratization may initially lead from bad to worse. One step backward, two steps forward is the pattern of the democratic revolution. Hence, "One must be careful not to confuse the fact of equality with the revolution which succeeds in introducing it into the state of society and into the laws. In that lies the reason for almost all the phenomena which cause our surprise" (688). I shall briefly refer to some central passages in *Democracy in America* that apply this principle to central democratic institutions.

(1) In his chapter on freedom of the press, Tocqueville argues that its steady-state effect is "to plunge mankind into universal doubt and distrust," while the transitional effect is to "daily change the object of their implicit belief." The former is a state of scepticism, the latter a series of firmly held and rapidly changing prejudices. That he clearly prefers the steady state to the traverse transpires from his warning: "Woe to these generations which first suddenly allow freedom to the press!" (187) Doubt is better than dogmatic belief, and although a justified conviction is better than either, it is rarely attained.

(2) He also argues that "there is a tendency in democracy not to draw men together, but democratic revolutions make them run away from each other and perpetuate, in the midst of equality, hatreds originating in inequality. The Americans have this great advantage, that they attained democracy without the sufferings of a democratic revolution and that they were born equal instead of becoming so" (509).

(3) As was pointed out above, he also asserts that freedom of political association is more dangerous during the traverse than in the steady state.

(4) Moreover, "while equality favours sound morals, the social upheaval leading to it has a very damaging influence on them." In an argument that can be applied to the aftermath of the October Revolution, he also asserts that even those revolutions "which in the end imposed stricter moral standards began by relaxing them" (599).

(5) Similarly, "although high ambitions swell while conditions are in process of equalization, that characteristic is lost when equality is a fact" (629).

(6) Invoking the same argument, Tocqueville rejects the notion that "there must be a hidden and secret link between equality itself and revolutions" (634), since it is rather the process of equalization which involves violent and profound disturbances.

(7) Lastly, and rather obviously, "the final result of a revolution might serve the interests of industry and trade, but its first effect will

almost always be the ruin of industrialists and traders, because it must immediately change general habits of consumption and temporarily upset the balance between supply and demand" (637). He might well have added the destructive effects on production.

One could not wish, I think, for a more clearly drawn contrast. Whereas a society in the process of democratization and equalization fosters rapidly changing dogmatic beliefs, hostility between the citizens, ambition, loose morals, social unrest and economic ruin, a well-established democracy is in all these respects the opposite.[15] Although Tocqueville is no unconditional defender of democracy, he is acutely aware that one can evaluate it only as a going concern. Observe that the distinction between short-term suboptimality and long-term optimality is drawn within democracy as a going concern. Both are features of the steady state, so that the defects of the short term are not to be confused with those of the transitional period. Also, note the link between partial and transitional effects on the one hand, and between net effects and steady-effects on the other. The initial consequences of institutional change may be offset later on by consequences that take more time to work themselves out or are called forth in reaction to the immediate effects. Finally, note the difference between the presently discussed distinction and the distinction between local and global effects. To use Tocqueville's example, it could be the case that love matches continue to be unhappy even after they become the rule rather than the exception, until the process of adjustment has worked itself out fully.

I add a few comments on Tocqueville's use of the distinction in other works. In the notes for the second volume of the *Ancien régime* he objects to the myopic character of Burke's *Reflections on the Revolution in France*. While Burke "is admirable when judging the details of the new institutions, their immediate consequences and the innumerable errors that resulted from the philosophical presumption and the lack of experience of the reformists," he is "only attentive to the forces that will be lost to France because of the Revolution, and not to those that will be gained."[16] Elsewhere he injects a note of

---

[15] "The opposite" is, however, an ambiguous phrase. It may mean the absence of the phenomenon in question, or the presence of the substantively opposite phenomenon. The opposite of a system that makes people run away from one another may be one that does not have this effect or one that positively draws them together (Elster 1984a).

[16] Tocqueville (1953), pp. 340–1.

scepticism concerning the character of those (steady-state) gains. "In my time I have already heard it proclaimed four times that the new society, such as the Revolution had made it, had finally found its natural and permanent state, and later on the next event proved that one was mistaken."[17] This is actually a quite momentous observation. It suggests that there may not be any steady state at all toward which the chain of consequences converges, either because of the inherent character of the process or because of exogenous shocks that constantly change it in its course.[18] There are hints of similar ideas in *Democracy in America*. Tocqueville believed that the American system he had observed contained potential for still further changes – toward an aristocracy of money, a tyranny of the majority or a despotism founded on the equal subjection of all. Yet by and large he appeared to have believed that the state of society he observed around 1830 was "the natural and permanent" one, which might be contrasted with the immediate consequences of revolutionary upheaval.

V Democracy and time

A central substantive concern of *Democracy in America* is the ability of political systems to learn from the past and to engage in long-term planning. This issue involves time from the subjective point of view of the actors. The issues discussed under (III) and (IV) concern time from the point of view of the external observer. Perhaps the most striking achievement of Tocqueville's work is how he brings together attitudes toward time and performance over time. One might say, simplifying, that in his opinion Americans achieve so much in the long term because their political system is so badly adapted to long-term planning. A more correct statement would be that any reform designed to improve the capacity for long-term planning would have bad long-term consequences.

Generally speaking, men are unique in that they can relate consciously to time – to events in the past and to possibilities in the future.[19] They relate to the past mainly by learning and remembering. They relate to the future in a number of ways. The most basic is

[17] *Ibid.*, p. 343.
[18] I explore this distinction further in chapter 10.
[19] This paragraph draws heavily on Elster (1984b). For useful surveys see also Crook (1980) and Staddon (1983).

grounded in the ability to wait, or to defer gratification. By an extension of this ability they can also deploy indirect strategies, of the form "one step backward, two steps forward." To say that men can behave in this way is not of course to say that they always do so when required. Impulsive behavior, or weakness of the will, is a constant threat to the ability to relate to the future. To neutralize the threat, it is sometimes possible to use a higher-order strategy, such as committing oneself in advance to a particular course of action from which one will be unable to deviate even should one later on want to do so. The problems created by one's inability to relate to the future may to some extent be alleviated by the ability to relate to that future inability. The air of paradox surrounding this statement is dissolved as soon as it is pointed out that precommitment today may require less will-power than resisting temptation will demand tomorrow.

The preceding remarks apply to men individually, but one may also ask whether groups and organizations are good at relating to the past and the future. It is clear, for one thing, that groups with a very high turn-over rate will not be good at learning from past mistakes, or remembering past successes.[20] Some continuity and overlap of membership is necessary. Similarly, if the tenure of managers and politicians is short, they will not be around to enjoy the benefits from innovations that do not yield immediate results. Hence with most types of incentive systems the organizations which they manage will have a short time horizon.

I shall consider Tocqueville's views on these issues. Does democracy foster specific time attitudes in individuals? Does the democratic method for collective decision-making have particular consequences for the ability to learn from the past and take account of the future, over and above the effect on individuals?

First, in democratic societies citizens tend to act on the assumption that techniques and preferences are in a constant state of flux, so that it is pointless to build anything too solid and durable. Tocqueville was apparently very impressed when he "met an American sailor and asked him why his country's ships are made so that they will not last long. He answered offhand that the art of navigation was making such quick progress that even the best of boats would be almost useless if it

---

[20] Elster (1978), pp. 141ff. also develops this idea.

lasted more than a few years" (453).[21] Also, in a democracy people "are afraid of themselves, dreading that, their taste having changed, they will come to regret not being able to drop what once had formed the object of their lust" (582).[22] This in turn explains a fundamental fact about democracies: although people do more things than in aristocracies, they do each thing less well. "They carry through many undertakings quickly in preference to erecting long-lasting monuments" (631). This attitude to time contrasts greatly with that of the Ancients, who tended to look at the world as basically unchanging, so that it made sense to communicate with posterity by constructing durable monuments.[23] Either attitude may be rational, depending on the rate at which techniques and preferences do in fact change.

Secondly, the incessant change of preferences is itself endogenous to democracies. "Americans cleave to the things of this world as if assured that they will never die, and yet are in such a rush to snatch any that come within their reach, as if expecting to stop living before they have relished them" (536). We find, therefore, "people continually changing path for fear of missing the shortest cut leading to happiness" (537). This echo of Descartes's famous argument[24] is highly suggestive. Democracy does not foster the capacity for consistent long-term planning, because of an excessive concern with short-term fine-tuning.[25]

Nor, thirdly, is democracy a good system for taking collective, future-oriented decisions. "A democracy finds it difficult to coordinate the details of a great undertaking and to fix on some plan and carry it through with determination in spite of obstacles. It has little capacity for combining measures in secret and waiting patiently for the

---

[21] For a discussion of this idea see Rosenberg (1976).

[22] See also Cyert and de Groot (1975) and Goodin (1982), ch. 9 for this idea.

[23] For a discussion of the attitudes towards time in Classical Antiquity see Veyne (1976), pp. 642ff.

[24] "Ma seconde maxime était d'être le plus ferme et le plus résolu en mes actions que je pourrais, et de ne suivre pas moins constamment les opinions les plus douteuses, lorsque je m'y serais un fois déterminé, que si elles eussent été très douteuses. Imitant en ceci les voyageurs qui, se trouvant égarés en quelque forêt, ne doivent pas errer en tournoyant tantôt d'un côté, tantôt d'un autre, ni encore moins s'arrêter en une place, mais marcher toujours le plus droit qu'ils peuvent vers un même côté, et ne le changer point pour de faibles raisons, encore que ce n'ait peut-être été au commencement que le hasard seul qui les a déterminés à le choisir; car, par ce moyen, s'ils ne vont justement où ils désirent, ils arriveront au moins à la fin quelque part où vraisemblablement ils seront mieux que dans le milieu d'une forêt" (Descartes [1897–1910], vol. VI, p. 24).

[25] Elster (1984b), ch. I.4.

result" (229). Tocqueville, in other words, is making two different but strongly convergent arguments about the attitude toward time fostered by democracies. Individual as well as collective decisions suffer from an attitude toward the future that can variously be characterized as incontinent, inconstant or inconsistent.[26] The fact of inconstancy, in particular, makes it rational not to invest too much in enterprises in which one may soon lose interest.

Lastly, democratic governments have difficulties in relating to and learning from the past. Tocqueville explains this fact by the high turn-over rate which characterizes the American political system and social life generally. He saw clearly that the high rates of change and mobility in democratic societies have advantages as well as inconveniences. He argues, for instance, that since "the rich are constantly becoming poor or retiring from business when they have realized their profits," the "class of the rich does not exist at all." Hence the aristocracy of money "does not know its own mind and cannot act," and for that reason is less of a threat to democracy than an enduring group of privileged would be (557). But in the case of politics, the fact that "each generation is a new people" (473), unable to learn from the past, has uniformly bad consequences. "After one brief moment of power, officials are lost again amid the ever-changing crowd," and "nobody bothers about what was done before him." The upshot is that "It is very difficult for American administrators to learn anything from each other . . . So democracy, pressed to its ultimate limits, harms the progress of the art of government" (208).

There seems to be an inconsistency in this part of Tocqueville's argument. He twice uses the phrase "the ability to make retrievable mistakes" to characterize the United States and to explain why democracy could succeed there and not elsewhere. In the first context he refers to the ability to learn by trial and error, to "profit by past experience" (225). But this is hard to reconcile with the argument about administrative instability which prevents learning from experience. Even in the first context, however, the argument is ambiguous, and he may have intended to say only what he definitely states in the

---

[26] For incontinence, or "weakness of the will," see Davidson (1980), ch. 2; for inconstancy, or endogenously changing preferences, see von Weiszäcker (1971); for inconsistency, or the inability to stick to past plans because of non-exponential time preferences, see Ainslie (1975). Tocqueville's discussions are too casual to allow us to determine to which of these closely related phenomena he is referring.

second passage. Here he invokes the principle of the steady state, and argues that if a nation is so placed as to afford retrievable mistakes, it can survive the initial step backward of the transitional period. "Suppose a society so organized by nature or by constitution that it can tolerate the passing effect of bad laws and can without disaster await the result of the *general tendency* of its laws, and in such a case you will appreciate that democratic government, for all its faults, is yet the best suited of all to make society prosper" (232).

I have referred twice to the notion of "one step backward, two steps forward" or, as Leibniz had it, "reculer pour mieux sauter."[27] First, democracy as a going concern does not promote the ability to deploy such indirect strategies in a deliberate and conscious way, because of the peculiar attitude toward time it fosters. Secondly, in the transition to democracy the situation will tend to get worse before it gets better – not as a result of strategic choice, but because of the general turmoil created by the lack of stable institutions. Tocqueville clearly saw that the fragility of the intermediate state might prevent the final state from emerging, and suggested two conditions under which this difficulty might be overcome. In the case of America the country was less vulnerable because of its relative isolation and autarchy. The ability to make retrievable mistakes is linked to the fact that "no one needs the Americans, and they do not need anybody" (131). A second possibility is that of a simultaneous transition in several nations, so that no single nation can exploit the weaknesses of the others during the traverse. The "relative weakness of democratic republics in time of crisis is perhaps the greatest obstacle preventing the foundation of such a republic in Europe. For a democratic republic to survive without trouble in a European nation, it would be necessary for republics to be established in all the others at the same time" (224).

How, then, shall we explain the fact that democracies prove their superiority in the long run even though they are badly suited for dealing with the future? I have already hinted at the general direction of Tocqueville's answer: democracy increases the forces of the nation, although it also causes them to be badly utilized. In the chapter on "The real advantages derived by American society from democratic government" Tocqueville elaborates as follows:

[27] For further discussions of Leibniz see Elster (1984b), p. 10, n.19 and especially Elster (1975), pp. 211ff., pp. 229ff.

That constantly renewed agitation introduced by democratic government into political life passes, then, into civil society. Perhaps, taking everything into consideration, that is the greatest advantage of democratic government, and I praise it much more on account of what it causes to be done than for what it does. It is incontestible that the people often manage public affairs very badly, but their concern therewith is bound to extend their mental horizon and shake them out of the rut of ordinary routine ... Democracy does not provide a people with the most skillful of governments, but it does that which the most skillful government often cannot do: it spreads throughout the body social a restless activity, superabundant force and energy never found elsewhere, which, however little favoured by circumstances, can do wonders. Those are its true advantages. (243–4)

The advantages of democracy, in other words, are mainly by-products. The avowed aim of democracy is to be a good system of government, but Tocqueville argues that it does not realize this goal. Democratic governments lack the ability to proceed in a systematic, coherent way; they cannot plan for the future, or stick to past decisions. Yet the very activity of governing democratically has as its by-product a certain energy and restlessness that benefits industry and prosperity. A similar argument is advanced for the jury system: "I do not know whether a jury is useful to the litigants, but I am sure it is very good for those who have to decide the case. I regard it as one of the most effective means of popular education at society's disposal" (275). Again, the main justification for the institution is found in side-effects, which could hardly be the main motivation of the participants. (They could, of course, enter into the motivation of the creators of the system.)

VI Conclusion

Tocqueville's *Democracy in America* uses democracy as an independent variable to explain various features of American life: religion, public opinion, family life, economic activities, military matters and numerous other phenomena. The independent variable itself may be characterized as *institutionalized equality and liberty*. The equality is both social and political, i.e., it pertains both to the absence of privilege and hierarchy, and to the principle of universal suffrage. The liberty consists in the traditional political freedoms: freedom of religion, of association, of expression. Yet beyond these formal institutions democracy must also have a specific content. In particular, there must be not only the possibility of mobility, but a high degree of actual mobility between the social classes. The freedoms must be exercised, not just guaranteed. Hence the considerable amount of ambiguity in Tocqueville's references to democracy, and his own difficulties in distinguishing form from content.[28] His intention, nevertheless, is fairly clear. Given that the democratic institutions exist *and* that the doors which they open are actually used, what are the further consequences for social life?[29]

This way of phrasing the issue poses a methodological problem: how can we distinguish cause from effect in stable democratic societies? Tocqueville's answer to this question had political as well as methodological benefits. In France the opponents of democracy were above all concerned with the abuses that followed in the wake of democratization. By arguing that these are not inherent in democracy as such, he offered a new brief to its defenders. At the same time he was enabled to justify his causal statements about the consequences of democracy. They appear as statements about the effect of a change in exogenous institutional variables upon the endogenous social variables. The change is measured by the difference between the old and the new equilibrium values of these variables, not by the difference that may be observed shortly after the change. Needless to say, this proposal begs several questions. For one thing, the distinction between the democratic form and the social content is not respected. The French abuses might have been due to the lack of the social concomitants of democracy, not to their merely transitional character. For another, the lack of any democratic revolution in America creates a difficulty for the argument that the French are only suffering from the revolution rather than from democracy as such. It could be – in

[28] Lamberti (1983) is very useful in this regard.
[29] An answer to this question would have the following form: If (p and q), then r. From this, of course, one cannot infer: If p, then (q and r). Yet one sometimes gets the impression that Tocqueville wants to use only the existence of the democratic institutions as the independent variable to explain both their observance and the more general phenomena of social life.

fact, Tocqueville himself makes this argument – that the virtues of American democracy are related to its relatively uncontested emergence, in which case the steady-state consequences of a revolutionary introduction could be quite different. In any case, however, the merits of the Tocquevillian methodology – as set out in (I) through (IV) above – are unaffected by these objections.

Tocqueville – like his older contemporaries Chateaubriand and Stendhal – was a democrat by reason, an aristocrat by heart. In particular, he was very sensitive to the aristocratic virtues of individualism and perfectionism. Yet he had an answer to the aristocratic criticism of the mediocrity of all things democratic: democracy does more things (or causes more things to be done), although each thing is done less well. The democratic era is the age of quantity, after that of quality. This links up with a classical argument for democracy in the sense of majority rule rather than rule by the elite: "If quality is equal (or, as Hobbes more exactly put it, quality must be taken to be equal as a condition of peace) the only differentiating factor left is quantity."[30] Tocqueville adds an instrumental argument for democracy to this legitimacy-oriented argument. In the modern age, he seems to say, no one can stand up and proclaim for himself a superior political wisdom, however superior he might in fact be. Yet the admission of the many to the political system also galvanizes them into action, to the extent of offsetting the loss of excellence. Democracy is unavoidable: once mankind has eaten the fruits of equality, there is no way back. Yet, although inefficient as a system for decision-making, it can be justified by its non-political side-effects. Universal participation in politics is the price we have to pay if we want society to be energetic and prosperous; and in any case we do not have the choice.

[30] Barry (1980), p. 193.

References

Ainslie, G. 1975. Specious reward. *Psychological Bulletin*, **82**, 463–96

Barry, B. 1980. Is democracy special? In P. Laslett and J. Fishkin (eds.), *Philosophy, Politics and Society*, Fifth Series, pp. 155–96. Oxford University Press

Crook, J. 1980. *The Evolution of Human Consciousness*. Oxford University Press

Cyert, R. M. and de Groot, M. H. 1975. Adaptive utility. In R. H. Day and T. Groves (eds.), *Adaptive Economic Models*, pp. 223–46. New York: Academic Press

Davidson, D. 1980. *Essays on Actions and Events*. Oxford University Press

Descartes, R. 1897–1910. *Oeuvres complètes*, ed. C. Adam and P. Tannery. 11 vols. Paris: Vrin

Elster, J. 1975. *Leibniz et la formation de l'esprit capitaliste*. Paris: Aubier-Montaigne

1978. *Logic and Society*. Chichester: Wiley

1983. *Explaining Technical Change*. Cambridge University Press

1984a. Active and passive negation: an essay in Ibanskian sociology. In P. Watzlawick (ed.), *The Invented Reality*, pp. 175–205. New York: Norton

1984b. *Ulysses and the Sirens*, rev. edn. Cambridge University Press

1985. *Making Sense of Marx*. Cambridge University Press

Feller, W. 1968. *An Introduction to Probability Theory*, vol. 1, 3rd edn. New York: Wiley

Goodin, R. 1982. *Political Theory and Public Policy*. Chicago University Press 1982

Granovetter, M. 1983. The strength of weak ties. *American Journal of Sociology*, **78**, 1360–80

Hamblin, C. L. 1970. *Fallacies.* London: Methuen

Katona, G. 1951. *Psychological Analysis of Economic Behavior.* New York: McGraw-Hill

Lamberti, J.-C. 1983. *Tocqueville et les deux démocraties.* Paris: Presses Universitaires de France

Nozick, R. 1969. Coercion. In S. Morgenbasser et al. (eds.), *Philosophy, Science and Method: Essays in Honor of Ernest Nagel,* pp. 440–72. New York: St Martin's Press

Rosenberg, N. 1976. On technological expectations. *Economic Journal,* **86,** 525–35

Schumpeter, J. 1961. *Capitalism, Socialism and Democracy.* London: Allen and Unwin

Staddon, J. E. R. 1983. *Adaptive Behavior and Learning.* Cambridge University Press

Tocqueville, A. de. 1953. *L'Ancien Régime et la révolution,* vol. 2: *Fragments et notes inédites sur la révolution.* In Tocqueville, *Oeuvres complètes,* vol. II. Paris: Gallimard

1969. *Democracy in America.* New York: Anchor Books

Veyne, P. 1976. *Le Pain et le cirque.* Paris: Le Seuil

von Weiszäcker, C. C. 1971. Notes on endogenous change of tastes. *Journal of Economic Theory,* **3,** 345–72

4. Liberal constitutionalism and its critics: Carl Schmitt and Max Weber

RUNE SLAGSTAD

Carl Schmitt occupies a special position within the field of modern legal and political theory. On the one hand, Schmitt is one of the foremost specialists in liberal constitutionalism; but on the other hand, he is also one of its keenest critics. His *Verfassungslehre* of 1928 dissects the constitution of the Weimar Republic, interpreting it along the lines drawn up by the German constitutional tradition from Wilhelm von Humboldt and Lorenz von Stein to Georg Jellinek and Max Weber. In all of his writings, Schmitt unites themes drawn from both conservative and radical critiques of the ideology of constitutionalism. He asserts a discrepancy between idea and reality, and, turning reality against idea, finally rejects the concepts of the liberal *Rechtsstaat* and the parliamentary legislative state as outdated bourgeois ideology. His alternative is absolute state power.

This chapter is built around Schmitt's theory. I shall begin with a brief introduction to the liberal theory of the *Rechtsstaat* based on Schmitt's *Verfassungslehre* [I]. The tension existing between the liberal *Rechtsstaat* and the Hobbesian *Machtstaat* forms the basis of Schmitt's criticism and rejection of liberalism [II]. In his alternative theory of politics and law, Schmitt combines two motifs: political Machiavellianism and normative decisionism [III]. Examination of Schmitt's work sheds considerable light on the political theory of Max Weber. Weber – who may rightly be considered a forerunner of Schmitt – also occupies a position opposed to Schmitt's in seeking to incorporate Machiavellian power-politics within a constitutional-democratic framework [IV].

I am very grateful to Stephen Holmes and Susan Höivik for their help with my English in this chapter.

I The liberal Rechtsstaat

In his *Verfassungslehre*, Carl Schmitt attempts to delimit what he terms "the ideal concept of the constitution of the bourgeois *Rechtsstaat*." He is referring explicitly to the kind of state constitution which had been established in Western Europe and North America since the eighteenth century. Since that time "the only constitutions designated as constitutions have been those which correspond to the demands of civil freedom and which contain definite guarantees of this freedom."[1] Schmitt emphasizes two basic features of this type of constitution. First, the constitution contains a system of guarantees of freedom. Fundamental here is freedom in the sense of freedom *from* state interference, especially in the field of legislation. As constitutional embodiments of this sort of freedom, Schmitt lists the following: "recognition of basic rights, the division of powers, and a minimum of popular participation in the legislative process by means of a civil assembly."[2] The proclamation of basic human rights – *Grundrechte* – implies the establishment of a general concept of freedom. The principle of division of powers is meant to ensure that this principle of freedom has an organizational guarantee, against misuse of the power of the state. Without this principle and this guarantee, the result will be "despotism, absolutism, dictatorship – terms which are not simply rhetorical, but which receive legal meaning through a contrast: they denote the union of (the organisational principle of division of) the legislative, executive and judicial powers."[3] Secondly, the constitution is to be based on a written document more difficult to alter or amend than other legislation. This is to ensure a greater degree of stability and permanence.[4] Such a view of the constitution as a written contract is in line with the tendency reflected in the U.S. Declaration of Independence of 1776, as distinct from the English tradition.

The guiding purpose of the *Rechtsstaat* is to protect the freedom of the individual citizen against the *power of the state*. In this connection, Schmitt formulates two main principles for the liberal constitution: a distributive principle, and an organizational one. By "distributive principle" is meant the following: "The sphere of individual freedom

---

[1] C. Schmitt, *Verfassungslehre* (1928) (Berlin, 1970), pp. 37f.
[2] *Ibid.*, p. 38.   [3] *Ibid.*, p. 39.   [4] Cf. *Ibid.*, pp. 39f., 16ff.

is simply presupposed insofar as the state is concerned; indeed, the freedom of the individual is *in principle unlimited*, whereas the authority of the state to intervene in this sphere is *in principle limited.*"[5] According to this principle – which implies that whatever is not forbidden is permitted – the individual possesses certain basic rights of a pre- or meta-political nature. These include both rights concerning each individual as such (freedom of religion, inviolability of private domicile, private property) and rights concerning the individual in interaction with others (freedom of speech, freedom of the press, freedom of organization):

> These basic rights receive their content not through any laws or acts, but according to legal standards or within legal limits; rather, they designate the – in principle – unbound scope of individual freedom; the state serves to protect them, thereby finding the true justification for its existence. The individual's right of resistance is the final guarantee of these rights; it is an inalienable right but one which cannot be organized.[6]

From the point of view of the *Rechtsstaat*, all state interventions in the private sphere of the individual are to be regarded as exceptions, "and indeed as in principle limited and measurable, generally regulated exceptions."[7] State intervention will thus represent a deviation which must be justified. This view is quite in line with a classical theme of the liberal philosophy of freedom: the free individual is subject not to the rule of other persons, but only to that of reason. The light of reason may eventually bring an individual to see a limitation of his freedom perfectly justified to the extent that the freedom of one individual is not to be sacrificed to that of another. This is why free individuals enter into a contract establishing state regulation of their exercise of freedom: to make the freedom of one compatible with that of all the others.[8]

The second main principle – the organizational principle – serves the realization of the first one: the power of the state – which is in

---

[5] *Ibid.*, p. 126. [6] *Ibid.*, pp. 163f. [7] *Ibid.*, p. 166.
[8] Cf. Kant, *Die Metaphysik der Sitten. Werke in zwölf Bänden* (Frankfurt a.M., 1978), vol. VIII, p. 399.

principle limited – is to be divided into legislative, executive and judicial branches, combined in a normative system designating spheres of competence. In this way, provision is made for mutual control and binding of the state apparatus.

The liberal *Rechtsstaat* is a *legal* state, in the sense that the only form of intervention into the free sphere of the individual which is legitimate is intervention *based on law*:

> A state may be termed a *Rechtsstaat* only when all administrative authority – especially that of the police – is subject to the conditions and procedure of law, and when intervention into the sphere of individual freedom is permissible solely on the basis of a law. Its identifying characteristic is the lawlike nature of the administration. The guarantee of its citizens' freedom lies in its law.[9]

According to liberal constitutionalism, rulers act "on the basis of a law" ("auf Grund eines Gesetzes") or "in the name of the law" ("im Namen des Gesetzes") – this is "the rule of law": "The laws rule – not persons, authorities or administrators. More precisely: laws do not rule – they only serve as norms."[10] Governors "rule" only in the sense that they follow the existing positive norms in a competent way: "The fundamental 'principle of legality' of all state activity ultimately means that, in the end, there will be no more 'ruling' or 'commanding,' because only impersonally valid norms will be enforced."[11] The legitimacy of the liberal state rests on the general "legality of all its exercise of power." However, not just any kind of law can be regarded as law, from such a point of view. The "rule of law," liberally understood, implies more than simply that all actions of the state should be legal. According to liberal constitutionalism, laws must fulfil specific criteria. In this respect, then, constitutionalism may be characterized as a doctrine specifying which characteristics particular rules need to possess in order to be regarded as law. These characteristics distinguish a law from a command or an ordinance. The main characteristic of law, in the constitutional sense, is the *generality* of the

---

[9] Schmitt, *Verfassungslehre*, p. 130.
[10] C. Schmitt, "Legalität und Legitimität" (1932), in *Verfassungsrechtliche Aufsätze* (1958) (Berlin, 1973), p. 264.
[11] *Ibid.*

norm involved. This is, according to Schmitt, the Archimedean point: "One quality cannot be announced without nullifying the *Rechtsstaat*: this is the *general* character of its legal norms. Herein lies the final guarantee of the traditional *Rechtsstaat*'s distinction between a law and a command, between reason and will – and thus the ultimate foundation of the *Rechtsstaat* itself."[12] This constitutional concept of law is opposed to pure formalism, "which designates as law whatever comes into being through the proceedings necessary for legislation": "Whatever can be said of the rule of law or the rule of norms, all talk of 'normativity' is contradictory and confused if the general character of rules is abandoned and any single command, and legislative measure whatever, can be considered a valid 'norm' or a 'law.'"[13] The generality of the law makes it possible for individuals to predict state intervention. Moreover, the general character of laws is meant to make them as binding as possible on the legislators – be these democratically elected or not. If legislators were not bound by and to their own laws, there would be no preventing the abuse of legislative authority, the arbitrary exercise of power and the reduction of legislation to a mere instrument of power: "A legislator whose individual measures, special edicts, exemptions or decrees are just as legally valid as are his general norms – such a person is in no way bound by his own laws. Being bound by law is, for those who can make any 'laws' they wish, but a meaningless turn of phrase."[14] The state – "the strictly controlled servant of society" – is thus seen as identical with a system of norms, "so that it is nothing but norm or procedure."[15] In this regard, the liberal *Rechtsstaat* is a normative system of "Gesetzmässigkeit, Kompetenzmässigkeit, Kontrollierbarkeit und Justizförmigkeit": "It is pretended first, that the constitution is nothing but a system of legal norms and prescriptions; second, that this system is a closed one; and third, that it is 'sovereign' – i.e. that it can never be interfered with, or indeed even influenced, for any reasons or necessities of political existence."[16] The ideal of the liberal *Rechtsstaat*, writes Schmitt, culminates "in a general 'juridification' of the entire life of the state." From this perspective, the independence of the courts of law

---

[12] Schmitt, *Verfassungslehre*, p. 142.
[13] *Ibid.*, p. 142.   [14] *Ibid.*, p. 139.   [15] *Ibid.*, p. 125.   [16] *Ibid.*, p. 131.

becomes "a particularly important organizational characteristic" of such a state.[17]

Dominant in this perspective of the *Rechtsstaat* is the negative point of view – the protection of individual citizens against the possible abuse of power by the state: "It is not so much the state itself which is organized by the principles of the *Rechtsstaat*, but rather the means and methods by which it is controlled; guarantees against state abuse are created, and an endeavour is made to secure checks on the exercise of state power."[18] The central purpose of liberal constitutionalism is to institutionalize a system of defense mechanisms for the citizen vis-à-vis the state. Given the unequal relationship between citizen and state, such institutions should enable the citizen to withstand and check the potentially overwhelming power of the state. The institutions of the *Rechtsstaat* consist of "a series of bars and checks as regards that state, a system of guarantees of the freedom of the citizen and the limitedness of state power."[19] Thus the *Rechtsstaat*, as the controlling arrangement of law, presupposes the existence of the *Machtstaat*, the political power apparatus to be controlled:

> All the effort of the bourgeois *Rechtsstaat* goes into repressing the political, compressing all expressions of the life of the state into a series of prescriptions, and transforming all state activity into actions performed within precisely articulated, and in principle limited spheres of competence. As a consequence, the bourgeois-*Rechtsstaat*-element can at most comprise but a part of the total state constitution, while another part must register a positive decision concerning the form of political existence.[20]

II The total Machtstaat: constitutionalism as ideology

The various arrangements of the *Rechtsstaat* sketched above serve to make more concrete the pivotal concept in the constitutional tradition of Locke and Kant: *the power of the state must be limited and bound by legal norms.* However, such liberal constitutionalism makes sense only if one also presupposes a major political concept in the tradition

---

[17] *Ibid.*, pp. 131ff.   [18] *Ibid.*, p. 41.   [19] *Ibid.*, p. 200.   [20] *Ibid.*, p. 41.

from Machiavelli and Hobbes: *the establishment of the power monopoly of the state.*

According to Schmitt, Hobbes bases his political state on fear of the state of nature. The goal to be achieved is a civilian, state-guaranteed peace and security.[21] Against the background of the religious civil wars and their controversies over competing politico-religious truths, Hobbes launched his *Leviathan*:

> For Hobbes, the point was to overcome, by means of the state, the anarchy of feudal, local or church rights of resistance, as well as affiliated danger of civil war: to medieval pluralism, church demands for dominion, and other "indirect" powers, he opposed the rational unity of a clear, effectively protective and predictable functioning system of legality. Such a rational state power must above all assume all risks, and in this sense, take full responsibility for the protection and security of the state's subjects. Should this protection cease then the state itself will cease to exist and all duty to obedience subside. Then the individual regains his "natural" freedom.[22]

The state of nature is left behind not only by virtue of a *social* contract based on a general consensus: social peace is guaranteed by the establishment of a *state* contract, in which political power is ceded to a higher third instance, "the sole guarantor of peace":

> The sovereign-representative person is far more than simply the sum of the powers of all contracting individual wills. The accumulated *angst* of individuals fearing for their very lives calls into being the Leviathan, a new power: a god more conjured up than created. So far, this new god transcends the sum total of individual subjects – but only in a legal, not a metaphysical sense.[23]

Hobbes is concerned with institutionalizing the state's monopoly of power: the state as model for political unity, "the bearer of the most astounding of all monopolies – the monopoly on political decision-

---

[21] C. Schmitt, *Der Leviathan in der Staatslehre des Thomas Hobbes* (Hamburg, 1938), p. 47.
[22] *Ibid.*, p. 113.   [23] *Ibid.*, p. 52.

making, that brilliant creation of Europe and of occidental rationalism."[24] The Hobbesian power state – *Machtstaat* – concerns what
Schmitt terms the strictly *political* aspect of the modern state, "the
positive decision about the form of political existence": an institutionalized monopoly apparatus for peaceful conflict-resolution within
a given society, binding exercise of political power and the efficient
implementation of political decisions. Such a state would have to have
a unique kind of authority, according to Hobbes. But in attributing to
this state an *absolute* authority, Hobbes proves his anti-liberalism.
The aim of the liberal *Rechtsstaat* is to bind the *Machtstaat* to general
norms – not to eliminate it. There still remains a problem from the
liberal point of view: as Hobbes remarked, a state strong enough to
protect everyone is potentially strong enough to repress everyone as
well.[25] According to Hobbes's *Leviathan*, sovereign state power is by
definition unbound by norms. For the sovereign power there exists but
one alternative: that of self-binding, and this does not make any sense
to Hobbes. No one can be bound to himself, "because he that can
bind, can release; therefore he that is bound to himself only, is not
bound."[26]

Carl Schmitt sees in Hobbes a classical example of *decisionist*
thought:

> All *Recht*, all norms and laws, all interpretations of the laws, all
> orders and arrangements – these are for him [Hobbes] essentially
> decisions of the sovereign: and "the sovereign" is not a legitimate
> monarch or competent authority, but precisely he who sovereignly
> decides. *Recht* is law, and law is the command which settles the
> dispute about what is *Recht*: *Auctoritas, non veritas, facit legem.*[27]

The sovereign decision is, writes Schmitt, the absolute beginning; and
this beginning is "nothing but sovereign decision-making" – i.e.,
"State dictatorship which creates law and order."[28]

---

[24] C. Schmitt, *Der Begriff des Politischen* (1932) (Berlin, 1979), p. 10.
[25] T. Hobbes, *De Cive*, in *The English Works of Thomas Hobbes*, vol. 2 (Darmstadt,
1966), pp. 175f.
[26] T. Hobbes, *Leviathan, ibid.*, vol. 3, p. 252.
[27] C. Schmitt, *Über die drei Arten des rechtswissenschaftlichen Denkens* (Hamburg,
1934), p. 27.
[28] *Ibid.*, pp. 28, 29.

In the scientific study of politics, Schmitt defends the principle of *methodical situationalism*: that is to say, all political concepts can be understood only on the basis of the concrete, polemic situation in which they belong. Otherwise, they become "misunderstandable, meaningless abstractions":

> Therefore, it is not admissable to abstract from the concrete situation – i.e., from concrete political antagonism. This applies to theoretical considerations of political phenomena as well. Every political concept is a polemic concept. Every political concept has a political enemy in mind, an enemy which determines much of its intellectual standing and power as well as its historical importance. Words like "sovereignty," "liberty," "*Rechtsstaat*" and "democracy" receive their precise import only by means of a concrete antithesis.[29]

In his *Der Begriff des Politischen*, Schmitt presents a critical summary of the idea of liberal constitutionalism:

> The systematic theory of liberalism is almost exclusively concerned with the internal struggle against state power; it consists of a series of methods by which to split, curb, balance or control this state power for the protection of individual freedom and private property. Liberalism seeks to make the state into a compromise and the arrangements and concerns of the state into a "safety valve." This cannot be termed either a form of government or a theory of government, even though it usually refers to itself as a theory of the "*Rechtsstaat*."[30]

The liberal theory of the *Rechtsstaat* must, he emphasizes, be understood on the basis of its polemic context, its "situation": the 1800s and their positivist faith in legality, "the belief in the rationality and ideality of systems of norms."[31] Initially polemical, positivism began as a struggle against any and every form of higher law, against any

---

[29] C. Schmitt, "Hugo Preuss – sein Staatsbegriff und seine Stellung in der deutschen Staatslehre," in *Recht und Staat in Geschichte und Gegenwart*, 72 (1930), 5.
[30] C. Schmitt, *Der Begriff des Politischen*, original version (1927), quoted from H. Hofmann, *Legitimität gegen Legalität* (Neuwied, 1964), p. 103.
[31] Schmitt, *Verfassungsrechtliche Aufsätze*, p. 270.

body of non-positive law. Gradually, positivism shifted the emphasis of its legitimization: from the intent of the legislator, via the intent of the law, and finally to the law itself, "the self-contained norm": "One subjects oneself only to the norm and to its specifiable content. On the face of it, this endows legal positivism with the greatest objectivity, stability, inviolability, certainty and calculability: in short, its very quality of positiveness."[32] Schmitt's claim that every political concept is also a polemical concept must also be applied to his own theory. For Schmitt, liberalism is the enemy, with its veiling of concrete political reality. Political reality is not governed by "abstract institutions and systems of norms," but ruled by tangible people and organizations.[33] Schmitt attacks what he regards as the neutralizing and de-politicizing effects of liberalism, its "negation of the political":

> The liberalism of the past century has singularly and systematically altered and denaturalized all political ideas ... Liberal thought completely avoids or ignores all questions relating to the state and politics. Instead, liberalism moves in a recurrent polarity between two heterogeneous spheres: ethics and economics; soul and commerce; culture and property.[34]

The liberal perspective is outdated given the new situation, i.e., the "metamorphosis" of the modern state from a liberal to a total state. In an article written in 1931, "The turn to the total state," Schmitt describes the present system of government as the product of a tension between the norms, values and institutions of the nineteenth century and a totally different, twentieth-century, situation. The underlying premise of liberal constitutionalism – i.e., the dualism of state and society – is no longer valid. It no longer has any meaning; it is "irrelevant." This distinction is under attack on both flanks: "The society-turned-state" becomes "the Economic State, the Culture State, the Caring State, the Welfare State, the Provider." At the same time, "the state-as-the-self-organization-of-society" intervenes in all aspects of social life. This erosion of the distinction between the previously discrete functions of state and society turns the liberal,

---

[32] Schmitt, *Über die drei Arten des rechtswissenschaftlichen Denkens*, p. 31.
[33] Schmitt, *Der Begriff des Politischen*, p. 72.
[34] *Ibid.*, pp. 68, 69.

neutral state into a "potentially total" state.[35] In an article from 1929, Schmitt claims that the leading industrial nations still cling to the traditional constitutional blueprint of 1789 and 1848. There are two exceptions: Bolshevik Russia and Fascist Italy. These are the only states to have attempted to "break away from the inherited constitutional clichés of the nineteenth century. Through their written constitutions they have expressed the great changes that have taken place in the economic and social structures of their nations in the very organization of the state."[36]

According to Schmitt the development toward a total state can be traced along two lines. First, there is the state that is total "in a purely quantitative sense, in the sense of sheer volume." This is the state that intervenes "indiscriminately" in all aspects of social life. In this sense, writes Schmitt at the beginning of the 1930s, the Weimar Republic is a total state. Its expansion is the result of weakness, not strength. It is total "because of weakness and lack of capacity to resist, because of its inability to stand up to the assaults of organized interests and factions."[37] Schmitt's terminology may seem confusing since he is suggesting that the result of these developments is the disintegration of the state's power: "This eventually leads to a plurality of moral ties and obligations, a 'plurality of loyalties' by which pluralist divisions are increasingly hardened, and the formation of state unity becomes steadily more endangered."[38] Schmitt sees Social Democratic theorists such as G. D. H. Cole and Harold Laski as the ideologists of pluralism. Their concern is not only with the pluralization of the power of the state, but also the vanquishing of the notion that this power is "in some way of a different and higher order" from other types of social organization: "The state becomes a social group of organization that at best stands at the same level as, never above, other organizations. In its ethical consequences this leads to the individual having to live in a multiplicity of disorganized concurrent social duties and loyalties."[39] Secondly there is the state that is total "in a qualitative sense."[40] This is the state that systematically exploits the possibilities of modern

[35] C. Schmitt, *Positionen und Begriffe im Kampf mit Weimar-Genf-Versailles 1923–1939* (Hamburg, 1940), pp. 151f.
[36] *Ibid.*, p. 111.   [37] *Ibid.*, p. 187.   [38] *Ibid.*, p. 156.
[39] C. Schmitt, "Staatsethik und pluralistischer Staat," in *Kantstudien*, (1930), p. 29.
[40] Schmitt, *Positionen und Begriffe*, p. 186.

technology to strengthen its own power. Both Fascism and Communism try in different ways to retain the "supremacy" of state power in this sense. Contrary to the assumptions of liberalism, there is, according to Schmitt, no distinct "political" sphere. The specifically political, from which all political actions and motives originate, lies in the dichotomy between friend and enemy. This, then, is the political equivalent of the dichotomy good/evil in morals, beautiful/ugly in aesthetics and profitable/non-profitable in economics. The friend/enemy dichotomy represents "the full range of intensity between union and separation, association and opposition." For Schmitt, politics is autonomous only in the sense that the validity of political categories is independent of moral, economic or other categories:

> The political enemy is not necessarily morally bad, nor is he necessarily aesthetically ugly. He need not appear to be a financial competitor; indeed, it may even be advantageous to do business with him. Essentially he is the "other," the alien. It is sufficient that he be existentially different and alien in a particularly intense way. Thus, in extreme circumstances, conflicts with him may occur. These will be conflicts which cannot be resolved either by reference to commonly held norms, or by the intervention of a disinterested – and therefore impartial – third party.[41]

The friend/enemy dichotomy has existential significance. Only the political actors themselves can, in a concrete situation, decide whether the "otherness of the alien" will threaten "to negate one's own mode of existence."[42] The friend/enemy distinction expresses "awareness of a serious situation": "The concepts 'friend,' 'enemy,' 'struggle' receive their true significance through the fact that they imply the real possibility of physical killing."[43] Schmitt emphasizes that the political enemy is not a private opponent: there is no personal antipathy. Rather, he is the public enemy – he is *hostis*, not *inimicus*; he is *polemios*, not *echthros*. Thus, having political enemies is quite compatible with the Christian commandment

---

[41] Schmitt, *Der Begriff des Politischen*, p. 27.
[42] *Ibid.*, p. 27.   [43] *Ibid.*, p. 33.

"Love thine enemies," for an "enemy" is here *inimicus* or *echthros*.[44]

Schmitt's political categories are existential ones insofar as politics is analyzed in existential terms and not in substantial ones. Such political existentialism is total in that it is universally applicable, the sole criterion being "that most intense of all distinctions – the grouping into friend and enemy":

> Existentially, this dichotomy is so strong and decisive that in the very instant that it arises it overshadows all previous non-political antagonisms such as those based on 'purely' religious, economic or cultural criteria and motivations. The situation becomes political, although from the purely religious or economic point of view its consequences and conclusions may often appear contradictory and irrational.[45]

Schmitt seeks to dig beneath the surface of liberalism's "fictions and normativity," beneath its "system of demilitarized and depoliticized concepts," to the brute fact of politics: the struggle between friend and enemy. Only in a real struggle do the final consequences of the friend–enemy relationship become clear: "the specifically political tensions in human life are gained in these most extreme circumstances." A world without this struggle between friend and enemy would be "a totally conciliatory world," that is to say, a world without politics.[46]

Schmitt looks to Hobbes for his theoretical position. But he sees Hobbes at best through the eyes of Rousseau. For Hobbes, the state of nature with its "war of all against all" was banished with the introduction of the political dimension, i.e., the state's monopoly on power. Schmitt, however, seeks to reintroduce the state of nature as the prevailing political condition. As a romantic Schmitt discerns behind the collapse of liberalism "a return to undamaged, uncorrupted nature," "silent and dark."[47] In this respect, then, it might be more accurate to describe Schmitt as a Rousseauian of the Hobbesian school.

Schmitt's political thinking combines existentialism's "intensity"

---

[44] *Ibid.*, p. 29.   [45] *Ibid.*, p. 39.   [46] *Ibid.*, p. 35.   [47] *Ibid.*, p. 93.

with militarism's "struggle." More than any other theorist of the twentieth century he champions the Machiavellian position: politics is a battle to conquer and retain political power, impatient of all normative bonds. Because of their hard-eyed political realism, Hobbes and Machiavelli are the ideal political theorists.

Schmitt aspires only to describe political reality as it exists behind the veil of normativism. However, in his attempt to remove this veil, Schmitt launches yet another normative theory: Machiavellian realism. Politics is ultimately and necessarily superseded by internal or external war, and thus by the possibility of "the physical killing of other human beings": "There is no objective so rational, no norm so correct, no social ideal so beautiful, no legitimacy or legality, that it can justify human beings killing one another for it."[48] In keeping with Machiavellian thinking, Schmitt believes that the *Machtstaat* overrides the *Rechtsstaat*. In a state of emergency, the *Rechtsstaat* must yield: "The state of emergency clearly reveals the nature of the state's authority. Here, the decision separates itself from the legal norm and (put paradoxically) authority shows that it creates *Recht* but does not have to be *Recht*."[49] Being a political existentialist, Schmitt is attracted to extreme and exceptional political situations. For example, the concept of sovereignty can be defined only in the light of such a situation: "whoever resolves the state of emergency is sovereign."[50] The state of emergency should not be regarded as a marginal or last-resort predicament, but rather as "a universal concept central to political knowledge": "Control over the emergency is in a very real sense the power to decide."[51] Seen from this point of view, the state of emergency cannot be regarded as a state of chaos or anarchy. It is, in a sense, order – order imposed by sheer power, not by justice: "The existence of the state proves here to be of greater importance than the validity of the legal norms. Decision-making is freed from all normative bonds, and becomes, in a real sense, absolute."[52] The power-wielder thus monopolizes the "ultimate" decision. Therein lies the "essence of state sovereignty," which Schmitt defines as a "decision-making monopoly" rather than

---

[48] *Ibid.*, p. 49f.
[49] C. Schmitt, *Politische Theologie* (1922) (Berlin, 1979), p. 20.
[50] *Ibid.*, p. 11.   [51] *Ibid.*, p. 11.   [52] *Ibid.*, p. 19.

a "monopoly of force or domination."[53] The state as a political unit has the power of *jus belli*, i.e., it can, in certain circumstances, define hostile elements "on the strength of its own decisions" and combat them.[54]

As an alternative to the dogmatism of constitutionalism, Schmitt espouses extreme scepticism. In *Politische Theologie*, he clarifies his form of scepticism, which he calls "decisionism": the validity of a political decision is established "irrespective of its content"; the decision is "from a normative point of view, born of nothing." Once a decision has been made, there can be no further discussion, "even though doubts may still endure."[55] A political decision is the outcome of a struggle between alternatives that cannot be supported by reasoning or discussion. Real politics, i.e., the struggle for power, starts where communication leaves off; in politics it is important *that* decisions are made, not *how* they are made. According to Schmitt's theory of *decisionism*, political decision-makers are bound neither from below by the demands of the citizenry nor from above by the norms of the law:

> The ultimate legal argument of all legal value and validity is to be found in the act of will – the decision – that as decisions in general first creates *Recht*, and whose force of law (*Rechtskraft*) is not derived from the force of law of decision rule, since even a decision not compatible with legal precepts is right. This force of law of antinormative decisions is part of all legal systems.[56]

Schmitt regarded his theories as part of what he called "counterrevolutionary political philosophy," which included de Maistre and Bonald, both critics of the French Revolution, and the Spanish Roman Catholic Dononso Cortes. Of Cortes, he has this to say: "Cortes is of a 'decisionistic' cast of mind: always expecting the worst, always awaiting Doomsday. This is why he despises the liberals, and regards atheist anarchist socialism as a respected, but deadly enemy, of diabolical stature."[57] Schmitt feels the same way. Sorel's anarcho-

[53] *Ibid.*, p. 20.
[54] Schmitt, *Der Begriff des Politischen*, p. 45.
[55] Schmitt, *Politische Theologie*, p. 42.
[56] Schmitt, *Über die drei Arten des rechtswissenschaftlichen Denkens*, p. 25.
[57] Schmitt, *Politische Theologie*, p. 80.

syndicalist work, *Reflections on Violence*, is the radical counterpart to Schmitt's theory. Sorel's "doctrine of direct action" is not only at odds with "the absolute rationalism" of marxism and its form of dictatorship, but also with the "relative rationalism" of liberalism with its "balancing, public discussion and parliamentarianism."[58] According to Schmitt the bourgeois ideal of "peaceful agreement" is, for Sorel, a "creation of cowardly intellectualism": "The bourgeois concept of balance is in direct contrast to another vision: the warlike ideal of a bloody, definitive, devastating, decisive battle."[59] The people, driven by their instincts, will one day smash "the rostrum of the Sophists," writes Schmitt, paraphrasing the words of Dononso Cortes, which in turn "word for word could have come from Sorel."[60]

For Schmitt all references to norms and rules is pure rationalization that conceals an underlying struggle for power. If politics has to refer to anything, then it must be to *Ordnung* or order, Schmitt wrote after 1932. The specific nature of this order varies according to circumstances. Schmitt launched a new theory, "Konkretes Ordnungsdenken," a doctrine of order, in response to the situation that now existed. This was an alternative not only to the normativism of liberalism, but also to his own theory of *decisionism*.[61] The watchword was now: "The *Führer* is the guardian of the *Recht*."[62] Liberalism's vulnerable combination of *Rechtsstaat* and *Machtstaat*, based on the dualism of state and society, now gave way to the "Führerstaat" with its "Staat, Bewegung, Volk."[63] Schmitt was for some years a legal ideologist to Hitler. The new theory, writes Schmitt, is based on the complete rejection of the general concept of constitutionalism, both in theory and in practice:

Among the great experiences and encounters that have driven me as legal theorist to the National Socialists is a conversation I had in 1932 with a celebrated, widely travelled, highly experienced lawyer from the U.S.A., a man over seventy years old. He gave me the

---

[58] Schmitt, *Positionen und Begriffe*, p. 11.
[59] *Ibid.*, p. 12.   [60] *Ibid.*, p. 12.
[61] Cf. Schmitt, *Über die drei Arten des rechtswissenschaftlichen Denkens*, pp. 57ff.
[62] Schmitt, *Positionen und Begriffe*, pp. 199ff.
[63] C. Schmitt, *Staat, Bewegung, Volk: Die Dreigliederung der politischen Einheit* (Hamburg, 1933).

benefit of his experience, and summed up his diagnosis of our current state of affairs in the following maxim: "we are today experiencing the bankruptcy of *idées générales*."[64]

III Machiavellianism and constitutionalism in conflict

Max Weber's major political concern is with the inexorable expansion of the bureaucratic apparatus and the possibility of political steering. Weber considered bureaucratic rule to be the purest form of rational–legal rule: the instrumental–rational, hierarchic system, organized around a cluster of special competencies, makes for extremely effective rule. The modern state bureaucracy, organized on the basis of the principles of the *Rechtsstaat*, functions – "at least in principle"[65] – in correspondence with general, rational calculable norms. It is thus predictable – like a "machine." What Weber feared was the possibility that lies "in the lap of the future," that this machine-like apparatus may receive all power. This bureaucratic machinery is already

at work, producing the cage of bondage of times to come, with which someday people, powerless like the fellahin of ancient Egypt, will be forced to comply, when a purely technical benefit – namely, a rational administration and provision – is the final and sole thing of value to determine the conduct of their affairs.[66]

In the face of this "basic fact of the inexorable progress of bureaucratization," the following questions concerning political forms of organization arise: firstly, how is it at all possible "in the face of this preponderance of the tendency to bureaucratization" to save the remnants of individual freedom of movement? And secondly, how can there be any guarantee "in the face of the increasing indispensability and thereby increasing power of state bureaucracy" that there will be forces capable of curbing and effectively controlling this superior force? How can democracy "even in this limited sense" be at all possible? And the third question, "the most important of all": granted

64 Quoted from Hofmann, *Legitimität gegen Legalität*, p. 167.
65 M. Weber, *Gesammelte politische Schriften* (1921) (Tübingen, 1980), p. 322.
66 *Ibid.*, p. 332.

that there are things the bureaucrats *cannot* do, and that the role of the political leader is different from that of the bureaucrat – what then is this role?[67]

The role of the state bureaucrat, says Weber, ends where that of the politician begins. He illustrates this difference with reference to the type of responsibility involved in the two roles: for the bureaucrat, de-personalized responsibility for his office, above and beyond conflicting sides, the question of "official duty"; for the politician, "individual and personal responsibility for his affairs," "the struggle for personal power" by means of taking a stand publicly.[68] The obligations of the bureaucrat concern an institution; those of the politician, his own affairs and positions.

When the bureaucratic universe determines the direction of politics, the very character of politics – struggle – vanishes in favour of a weak "Eudaemonism." The awareness of the normatively irrational nature of power is displayed by "that humanly lovable and praiseworthy, yet unspeakably petit-bourgeois softening of the mind which finds it possible to replace political ideas with 'ethical' ones, and then proceeds to identify these harmlessly with optimistic hopes of prosperity and good fortune."[69] Naturally enough, Weber's analysis of the power position of the bureaucracy was influenced by the German context, including the heritage of Bismarck. From a bureaucratic point of view, the situation in Wilhelmine Germany was close to perfect, according to Weber: the bureaucracy directed a dilettante monarch and an impotent parliament which had, ever since the days of Bismarck, repeatedly demonstrated its will to powerlessness. For Weber, however, the problem faced by Germany was but an example of a central dilemma of all modern mass societies.

Besides general and universal suffrage, there were especially two reforms which Weber proposed as possible antidotes to the bureaucratic spirit in politics: the parliamentarization of government activity, and the selection of the president by plebiscite. Weber's argumentation in connection with these two reform proposals documents his main political insight: namely, that the specific quality of politics can be saved from the encroaching bureaucratic trend only by

---

[67] *Ibid.*, pp. 333f.   [68] *Ibid.*, p. 335.   [69] *Ibid.*, p. 24.

concentrating political attention on the selection of political leaders.[70] Even persons possessing those qualities which, in Weber's opinion, mattered in politics – the power instinct and a sense of responsibility – lacked institutional arenas for developing their talents.

Thus, Weber's reasons for parliamentarization differ from the predominant liberal democratic view of parliament as the institutional mediation of the will of the people. What Weber sees in parliamentary democracy is first and foremost an efficient means of selecting and producing political leaders. With British parliamentarianism as his ideal, he presupposed that political leaders would so to speak be created through the parliamentary set-up – from the painstaking deliberations in committee work to the open fight for voter support. According to Weber, the British parliament has been "the place in which those politicians have been selected ... who have understood how to bring one-quarter of humanity under the rule of a tiny but governmentally well-versed minority. And indeed – the main point, in fact – this has to a considerable degree even been a voluntary submission."[71] Weber's second proposal for institutional reform concerned the selection of the president by means of direct elections. In parliamentarianism, he saw an antidote to the professional politicians of the bureaucracy and their monopoly on knowledge. It was his further contention that a president elected by plebiscite would counteract the increase in party bureaucratization and the related narrowing of the field of candidates for political leadership. In a direct competition for voter support, the "responsibility structure" of politics would emerge, clear and true. For that reason, Weber considered anything but direct election of the president to be "a mockery of the principles of democracy in the interests of parliamentary horse-trading."[72] In his view, the institutional system of direct election represents "the safeguard of true democracy – not powerless submission to a coterie, but submission to leaders chosen by the people themselves."[73] Under conditions of modern mass democracy, the "trust and belief of the masses" in their political leaders is established by mass demagogy. Every modern democracy tends toward what Weber calls "a Caesarean selection of the leader"; the most specifically Caesarean method

[70] *Ibid.*, pp. 351ff.   [71] *Ibid.*, p. 355.   [72] *Ibid.*, p. 498.   [73] *Ibid.*, p. 501.

is the referendum: "This is no ordinary 'voting' or 'election,' but the profession of a belief in the appointment of a leader for those from whom this acclamation is expected."[74] In discussions concerning the establishment of a new German republic after 1918, Weber proposed a political system combining both parliamentarianism and Caesarism. Caesarism in the form of the institution of Reichspresident would, in turn, represent a safeguard against "parliamentary absolutism," since the president would be a kind of parliamentarily controlled monarch.

Weber's proposal for a plebiscitary representative constitution may be seen as a variant of the classical idea of a *constitutio mixta*. In this respect, Weber's proposals are in line with a liberal concept of the dispersion of power by means of an institutionalized system of division of powers. But with his idea of a *Führerdemokratie* as an alternative to the *führerlose Demokratie*, Weber makes clear his scepticism about another liberal concept: the discontinuation – or at least minimalization – of dominion (*Herrschaft*). Weber's main concern is not to limit the power of the state but rather the expansion of *political* power. According to Weber, the alternative is either "*Führerdemokratie* with *Maschine*, or leaderless democracy, i.e., the rule of professional politicians with no profession, without those inner, charismatic qualities that are precisely what make a leader."[75]

In combating what he calls the bureaucratic iron cage of politics, Weber is willing to pay the price of Caesarism: extreme personification and irrationalization in the formation of political will. Characteristic of the Caesarean *Führerdemokratie*, Weber writes, is that there should in general be a highly emotional type of devotion to – and trust in – the leader. This accounts for a tendency to favor the type of individual who is most spectacular, who promises the most or who employs the most effective propaganda measures in the competition for leadership.[76] But despite such observations, Weber underestimated the danger that a Caesarean democracy might turn into a Caesarean dictatorship. In retrospect, one may say that Weber's view is pretotalitarian in a dual sense: firstly, it was formulated prior to the rise of modern totalitarian regimes; secondly, it is situated in a

---

[74] *Ibid.*, p. 394.   [75] *Ibid.*, p. 544.
[76] M. Weber, *Wirtschaft und Gesellschaft* (1922) (Tübingen, 1980), p. 157.

political no man's land between democracy and the discontinuation of democracy.

A general motif in Weber's political analyses is the concept of politics as power politics understood in the Machiavellian sense of the normatively unfettered struggle for power. As early as 1895, in his inaugural lecture, Weber announced: "Nicht Frieden und Menschenglück haben wir unseren Nachfahren mit auf den Weg zu geben, sondern den *ewigen Kampf* um die Erhaltung und Emporzüchtung unserer nationalen Art."[77] The subject of this lecture was "Der Nationalstaat und die Volkwirtshaftspolitik"; Weber emphasized that for the German state the *Staatsraison* is "the final measure of value" *also* in respect to economic policy too:

> wir wollen mit diesem Schlagwort die Forderung erheben, dass für die Fragen der deutschen Volkwirtschaftspolitik ... im einzelnen Fälle das letzte und entscheidende Votum den ökonomischen und politischen Machtinteressen unserer Nation und ihres Trägers, des deutschen Nationstaates, zustehen soll.[78]

And, more than twenty years after this, in his "Parlament und Regierung im neugeordneten Deutschland," Weber promulgates the same idea – struggle as the basic phenomenon of politics:

> Entscheidend wichtig ist: dass für die politische Führerschaft jedenfalls nur Persönlichkeiten geschult sind, welche im politischen *Kampf* ausgelesen sind, weil alle Politik dem Wesen nach Kampf ist.[79]

Like Carl Schmitt after him, Weber saw politics as the continuation of warfare by other means. In this tradition, the distinction between war and peace becomes diffuse, as when Weber discusses "peace" in inverted commas:

> Conflict (Kampf) cannot be excluded from social life. One can change its means, its objects, even its fundamental direction and its bearers, but it cannot be eliminated ... "Peace" is nothing more

---

[77] M. Weber, *Gesammelte politische Schriften*, p. 14.
[78] *Ibid.*, pp. 14f.   [79] *Ibid.*, p. 392.

than a change in the form of the conflict or in the antagonists or in the objects of the conflict, or finally in the chances of selection.[80]

Machiavellianism is decisionism transferred to the field of politics: strictly political decisions are the result of choices which cannot be justified by rational consensus. On the question of law and right Weber also takes a decisionist stand; but the legal decisionism of Weber differs from that of Schmitt in being, in certain respects, normatively modified.

According to Weber, it is not possible for there to be scientifically founded pleading for practical stands within the spheres of politics, jurisprudence or morals, "because the various spheres of the world stand in irreconcilable conflict with each other."[81]

Following the monotheistic intermezzo of rationalism, "polytheism" is returning, under scientific assumptions, in the form of a polytheism of *values*:

according to our ultimate standpoint, the one is the devil and the other the God, and the individual has to decide which is God for him and which is the devil. And so it goes throughout all the orders of life.

The grandiose rationalism of an ethical and methodical conduct of life which flows from every religious prophecy has dethroned this polytheism in favour of the "one thing that is needful." Faced with the realities of outer and inner life, Christianity has deemed it necessary to make those compromises and relative judgments, which we all know from its history. Today the routines of everyday life challenge religion. Many old gods ascend from their graves; they are disenchanted and hence take the form of impersonal forces. They strive to gain power over our lives and again they resume their eternal struggle with one another.[82]

Put in non-metaphorical terms, this polytheism means that "the ultimately possible attitudes toward life are irreconcilable, and hence their struggle can never be brought to a final conclusion."[83] This

---

[80] M. Weber, *The Methodology of the Social Sciences* (New York, 1949), pp. 26f.
[81] *Ibid.*, p. 147.   [82] *Ibid.*, pp. 148f.   [83] *Ibid.*, p. 152.

modern polytheism of Weber builds on the philosophy of Nietzsche and his reckoning with the moral theories of rationalism. In values, the decisive choice is left to the charismatic leader or the individual private human being.

The Machiavellian view of politics is so systematically and repeatedly stressed in the writings of Weber that any interpretation of Weber's works as being "steeped in the tradition of European liberalism,"[84] seems remarkably naive. Compared with this mild, liberal interpretation, the crass characterization of Weber provided by Lukács – who saw Weber as the ideologue of German imperialism – would appear far more adequate. According to Lukács, the democratization of Germany was for Weber "but a technical means for the purpose of a better functioning kind of imperialism."[85] But this interpretation makes the political theory of Weber undeservedly one-dimensional. In fact, the interesting thing about Weber and his theory of politics is precisely the unresolved tension – and thereby its "antinomian structure"[86] – between two competing elements: Machiavellian power politics and democracy; decisionism and constitutionalism; Caesarism and parliamentarianism. Weber as a political theorist is interesting precisely because he so uncompromisingly analyzes the problems of applying liberal–democratic ideas, originally formulated in bourgeois society, to conditions of modern mass society.

Weber rejects as utopian the concept of democracy as the free self-organization of the people. Likewise, he cannot accept another classical view of democracy, namely, as the institutionalized will of the people: "Concepts like 'the will of the people,' the true will of the people, no longer exist for me – they are *fictions*. It is just as if one were to speak of the will of the purchaser of a pair of boots as being authoritative for how the cobbler ought to pursue his craft. The buyer may know how the shoe pinches – but never how to make a better

---

[84] A. Giddens, *Politics and Sociology in the Thought of Max Weber* (London, 1972), p. 56.

[85] G. Lukács, *Die Zerstörung der Vernunft* (Neuwied, 1962), p. 536. See also H. Marcuse, "Industrialisierung und Kapitalismus im Werk Max Webers," in *Kultur und Gesellschaft*, vol. 2 (Frankfurt a.M., 1965), pp. 107ff.

[86] W. Mommsen, "Die antinomische Struktur des politischen Denkens Max Webers," in *Historische Zeitschrift* (1981), 35ff. See also Mommsen's pioneering study, *Max Weber und die deutsche Politik 1890–1920* (1959) (Tübingen, 1974).

shoe."[87] The question of democracy and its ordinances is for Weber a "state-technical" matter: democracy is the most expedient way of managing the selection of political leaders. This instrumental view of democracy has in fact led to the formation of two main schools within modern political theory: on the one hand Schumpeter and the realistic modernization of democracy;[88] on the other, Schmitt and the Caesarean discontinuation of democracy.

Weber's political theory remains vague on one central issue: the relationship between the two institutional arrangements for the selection of a leader, i.e., the parliamentary and the Caesarean. What Weber leaves as an unresolved institutionalized competitive relation is given a clear, unambiguous solution by Schmitt. From *Die geistesgeschichtliche Lage des heutigen Parlamentarismus* (1923) to *Der Hüter der Verfassung* (1931) Schmitt's work is highly critical of the concept of a liberal, debating, politically sovereign parliament. The activities of organized interest groups and the expansion of bureaucracy has, according to Schmitt, reduced parliament to a mere façade which conceals the political impotence of the institution. Neither does Schmitt regard parliamentary institutions as suitable instruments for performing what, for Weber, was a vital function: *Führerauslese* – the selection of a leader. The election of the President of the Republic by plebiscite was, for Schmitt, the only valid process by which a leader could be selected. Schmitt integrates Weber's concept of *Führerdemokratie* into his theory, assigning to the President of the Republic the role of the "Guardian of the Constitution."[89] Schmitt thus makes absolute Weber's idea of the directly elected *Führerdemokratie*, albeit in an altered context. Whereas Weber regarded the Caesarean or autocratic leader as a counterbalance to anonymous, leaderless bureaucracy, Schmitt saw in it an alternative to liberal democracy.

Weber's lack of clarity as a democratic theorist is further highlighted in his typology of the three legitimate forms of authority: the traditional, the charismatic and the legal–rational.[90] As mentioned above, legal–rational authority is the type of authority characteristic

---

[87] Max Weber in a letter to Robert Michels (1908), quoted from W. Mommsen, *Max Weber*, p. 421.

[88] On Schumpeter's political theory from this point of view, see R. Slagstad, *Rett og politikk* (Oslo, 1987), ch. 1.

[89] C. Schmitt, *Der Hüter der Verfassung*, (Tübingen, 1931).

[90] Weber, *Wirtschaft und Gesellschaft*, pp., 124ff.

of the *Rechtsstaat*. Authority is exercised in accordance with universal and formal norms, designed to ensure the greatest possible degree of predictability in their application. Legal–rational authority means government by officialdom, with its high degree of specialization and division of labor. According to Weber's analysis, bureaucratic authority – legal–rational authority in its purest form – is spreading in modern industrial societies, ousting traditional authority which had been accepted on the belief that its rules were decreed by divine authority.

Since the modern, democratic form of *Herrschaft* is by definition the opposite of bureaucracy, and the traditional forms of authority are also excluded, it would seem that Weber has no alternative but to include the democratic form of legitimacy as an aspect of charismatic authority. It is interesting to note that Weber's analysis of democratic authority does not appear in connection with either legal–rational or traditional authority. Instead, in *Wirtschaft und Gesellschaft* (1922), he deals with "democratic legitimacy" in an extension to the chapter on charismatic authority.[91] Charismatic authority is based on a belief in a leader's extraordinary personal qualities. As such it is the antithesis of bureaucratic authority, since it contains none of the characteristics essential to bureaucracy: predictability, impersonality and regularity. Weber's point here is that the principle of charismatic legitimacy, which must by definition be seen as authoritarian, "may be subject to interpretation or development in an anti-authoritarian direction."[92]

Given the inherent rationalization of modern societies (i.e. the elimination of the transcendent), the acceptance of charismatic leadership changes character. No longer is leadership accepted on the strength of its charismatic legitimacy; the acceptance itself becomes a basis for legitimacy, i.e., "democratic legitimacy": "The leader whose legitimacy rested on his personal charisma then becomes leader by the grace of those who follow him, since the latter are formally free to elect and elevate to power as they please, and even to depose . . . The chief now becomes the freely elected leader."[93] Democratic legitimacy becomes a by-product of charismatic leadership. The traditional relationship between the leader and his followers is maintained, even

[91] *Ibid.*, pp. 155ff.   [92] *Ibid.*, p. 155.   [93] *Ibid.*, p. 156.

though an anti-authoritarian shift has taken place in the charismatic type of legitimacy. In *Wirtschaft und Gesellschaft* Weber makes no clear distinction between elections (where a choice may be made between competing candidates) and acclamatory referenda. Thus in his typology of legitimacy he makes no allowance for democratic legitimacy in its classical, bourgeois sense: democracy as the institutionalization of the citizen's political role. This neglect of the civic dimension of politics is a central feature of Weber's political theory. He fails to take into account the ability of human beings to create a framework of promises and agreements, within which political battles are fought. In *Wirtschaft und Gesellschaft* Weber introduces this theory of "the phases of development" of law: its initial foundation in religious doctrines, the "natural law" tradition and modern positivist view:

> From this perspective, the formal qualities of the law emerge as follows: arising in primitive legal procedure from a combination of magically conditioned formalism and irrationality conditioned by revelation, they proceed to increasingly specialized juridical and logical rationality and systematization, sometimes passing through the detour of theocratically or patrimonially conditioned substantive and informal expediency. Finally, they assume, at least from an external viewpoint, an increasingly logical sublimation and deductive rigor and develop an increasingly rational technique in procedure.[94]

A positivist explanation of the factors contributing to the creation of legal systems must exclude a concept such as "natural law." Legal positivism has, writes Weber, "at least for the time being advanced irresistibly. The disappearance of the old natural law conceptions has destroyed all possibility of providing the law with a metaphysical dignity by virtue of its immanent qualities."[95] The collapse of natural law also means that questions of legitimacy must be analyzed in terms of their legality. Thus, political authority is legitimate if it is embodied in law. The consequences of this positivism are that any law can be

[94] Weber, *Economy and Society* (New York, 1986), p. 882.
[95] *Ibid.*, pp. 874f.

freely and sovereignly enacted or abolished, as long as the correct formal procedure is followed. According to Weber, legal legitimacy is based on "a belief in the 'legality' of patterns of normative rules and the right of those elevated to authority under such rules to issue orders."[96] The content of a law is arbitrary and may be established either "by agreement or by imposition."[97] The basis of all authority – and thereby also legal authority – is *belief*, "a belief by virtue of which persons exercising authority are lent prestige."[98]

Weber's political and legal decisionism is, however, tempered with normativism: even though legal and political norms may not be rationally justified, they still possess a very real power. Weber's fear of the expansion of bureaucracy is nothing less than a fear that these norms may become *too* binding. It will be remembered that for Weber the most favored alternative was *Führerdemokratie*, a charismatic leader elected by plebiscite.

[96] *Wirtschaft und Gesellschaft*, p. 124. [97] *Ibid.*, p. 125. [98] *Ibid.*, p. 153.

5. Democracy and the rule of law: some historical experiences of contradictions in the striving for good government

FRANCIS SEJERSTED

The rule of law and democracy correspond to the two different concepts of liberty, the negative, which makes liberty dependent on the curbing of authority, and the positive, which makes it dependent on the exercising of authority. These two concepts of liberty are, according to Isaiah Berlin, "two profoundly divergent and irreconcilable attitudes to the ends of life." The claims of each of them have, however, "an equal right to be classed among the deepest interests of mankind" (1958, pp. 51–2). With regard to political order, Berlin seems to take the somewhat pessimistic view that a synthesis is impossible, that there ought to be some sort of compromise. This same view is taken by, for instance, Robert G. McCloskey when he writes about the "dualism of the American mind": the propensity of the Americans "to divide their political hearts between the will of the people and the rule of law" (1960, p. 13). Is there really such a contradiction between democracy and the rule of law?

In the constitutionalist or rule of law tradition in the seventeenth and eighteenth century there was a marked tendency to see a contradiction. The opposites were despotism and rule of law and, as Kant for instance maintained, democracy was "im eigentlichen

This chapter was originally published in *Social Science Information* (SAGE, London and Beverly Hills), 18, 6 (1979), 945–60. The chapter is based mainly on two more comprehensive articles: "Rettstaten og den selvdestruerende makt: Noen refleksioner over det 19. arhundres embatsmansstat" ("The 'Rechtstaat' and self-destructive power: some reflections on the nineteenth-century civil servant state"), in Rune Slagstad (ed.), *Om staten* (Oslo, 1978), and "Demokrati og rettstat: Et perspektiv pa 1800-tallets politiske brytninger" ("Democracy and the 'Rechtsstaat': a perspective on the political conflicts of the nineteenth century"), *Historisk Tidsskrift* (Oslo, 1979). They have since been published in: Francis Sejersted, *Demokrati og Rettsstat* (Oslo, Univ. forlaget, 1984). More extensive references will be found in these articles. I have benefited from numerous discussions with colleagues, especially Ottar Dahl, Jon Elster, Per Maurseth and Jens Arup Seip.

Verstande des Worts notwendig ein Despotismus" (Kant 1976, p. 28). The authors in this tradition chose to favor rule of law so easily first, because when they talked about "democracy," which they did not do very often, they meant a plebiscitarian democracy. Secondly, the sovereignty of the people was taken care of, not by democracy, but by some sort of contract. The established order, the bound and limited government, was to be based on a voluntary abstention by the people from exercising *currently* their natural authority. This abstention or abdication act implied in itself an exercise of authority. Put simply, the will of the people was (or ought to be) the rule of law. Lastly, the constitutionalists, separated democracy and positive liberty in yet another way. In a more or less plebiscitarian democracy man was not free, he was a slave to his passions. Consequently, limited government was meant to take care of both negative and positive liberty; it was indeed an optimistic view.

The real core of the problem lies in the linkage between limited government and positive liberty. Today we can easily see the utopian element in the old constitutionalist position. To meet the needs for positive liberty in a modern society, it has been "necessary" to develop a democratic order. Thus the contradiction between democracy and rule of law has had a tendency to recur (as in the writings of Berlin and McCloskey). John Rawls's modern version of the contract theory can, I think, be seen partly as an attempt to reconcile the two claims for positive and negative liberty (Rawls 1973). At any rate, the problem of a possible contradiction between democracy and rule of law exists as a problem of normative political philosophy. In the following pages I shall, however, by and large be discussing the problem at the level of historical experience and with special reference to Norway. What were the alternatives in the different historical situations? Under which circumstances was the choice one between democracy and rule of law?

Democracy and rule of law can be seen as two different means to overcoming the inherent contradiction between state and society. State-building is necessary to society, but it also represents a threat. Rule of law was meant to curb state authority, while democracy was meant to mobilize society in the exercising of state authority. This contradiction between state and society must have been strongly felt in the centuries following the Renaissance. There was a need for peace, order and public security, and it went along with a general distrust of human nature. Man was governed by passions and could not withstand the temptations of power. On the other hand there was a growing belief in the possibility of constructing a state where the power was bound and the passions were kept under control.[1] This was the basis for all the intellectual energy which was put into the constitutionalist philosophy of that time. There were two main trends, the one recommending mixed government which opposed power with power, and the other recommending a separation of powers. The fundamental trait the two trends had in common was a purely negative approach to the exercise of power.[2] This rather intense process of ideologization seems to be important as a driving force behind the "spontaneous outbreak of constitution-making"[3] in the late eighteenth and early nineteenth century in the American states and in Europe. This "conservative element" is now commonly seen as an important element in the American Revolution.[4] Although the European case is not so clear, it seems as if the general tendency in this time of revolutions was the same, namely to block power rather than to *take* power. Hannah Arendt has argued that the constitutions were not the result of revolutions. "Their purpose was to stem the tide of revolution" (1963, p. 143). It is certainly true that constitution-making could have this counter-revolutionary appearance. In the American Revolution it seems, however, to have been weak, and this is also the case in Norway. Constitution-making was not a reaction to a revolutionary situation; if anything, it was a revolution in itself, directed against the power of the king and furthered by the openness of the situation (see below). The point is that constitution-making was directed against the power of the state, no matter who held power – a king or a democratically elected assembly.

The strength of the constitutionalist ideology lies partly in the fact that it could be both a revolutionary and a counter-revolutionary weapon. When one scrutinizes the Norwegian situation, the import-

[1] This interpretation of the ruling idea of the eighteenth century is emphasized in Lovejoy (1961), e.g. p. 38, and Hirschman (1977).

[2] These two trends of constitutionalism are the basis of analysis in a penetrating study by Vile (1967).

[3] The expression is taken from Arendt (1963, p. 139), where it has special reference to the American states.

[4] Greene (1968). The point is stressed in Greene's introduction. One of the most important works behind this reinterpretation is Bailyn's (1965).

ance of the constitutionalist ideology as based on a general need for security is at any rate evident from the high degree of consensus on the political and constitutional principle.

On the other hand, in order to explain why the rule of law had priority before democracy, it is important to look at the combination of special interest and general need. The strong and growing property-owning middle class had a special interest in predictability and constancy – in the security of property and of liberal rights – which represented the very essence of constitutionalism. This combination is particularly clear when it is maintained that passions could best be counterbalanced by allowing for the free pursuit of material again, "le doux commerce," as Montesquieu said (Hirschman 1977, p. 60). (In Adam Smith, the general and the special interests are combined in another way.) In all this there were elements of reality which in their turn strengthened the constitutionalist regimes. This was a pleasant reality for the most privileged, but nevertheless, a reality.

One of the main problems of the constitutionalists was to establish some sort of control over state power. This power was not only to be circumscribed, but also bound to general rules or standing laws: state action should be predictable, not arbitrary. In the words of Lionel Robbins, "what distinguishes the classical outlook from the authoritarian systems is not a denial of the necessity for state action on the one side and an affirmation on the other, but rather a different view of what kind of action is desirable" (1965, p. 192). To keep state power within the standing laws, it was necessary to establish a negative, controlling power. This was attempted by institutionalizing a separation of powers, by opposing power with power and by different ways of blocking state action through vetoes. But there was always the problem of the ultimate source of control. Public opinion was called upon to represent this ultimate source. The theory was developed by Kant, and was generally accepted (Habermas 1962). There should be an open disputing society with democratic elements based on the independent property-owners. "An opposition is so important, that if it didn't exist, we would have to create it in order to control the state," said Count Herman Wedel Jarlsberg, the leading Norwegian politician of the first half of the nineteenth century (Steen 1962, p. 38). The point to be stressed is that this public opinion, which was mobilized by making concessions to democracy, was primarily to be the basis of a negative, controlling power. Democratic elements were introduced to check, and not to legitimize, state power. They were to serve the *Rechtstaat* of the constitutionalist.

This aspect is most clearly seen in the "abdication aspect" of what was the main concern of the constitutionalists, namely, the making of constitutions. In principle, the constitutions were to be made once and for all. The more or less democratically elected Constitutional Assembly was to be dissolved after having made the Constitution. This was an abdication in favor of the principles laid down. The Assembly should not govern, the principles should. The constitutionalists had to create their own master – the law. The main distinction between the rule of Man and the rule of Law was the abolition of arbitrariness and consequently the ensuring of predictability and of "justice as regularity." The nongoverning character of the Legislative Assembly is likewise seen in its discontinuity. The Norwegian Storting, for example, was only to meet once every third year, while the government was a non-democratic body appointed by the king.

According to John Rawls, unevenly distributed political rights can be legitimized only by a maximin criterion. That means that under an uneven distribution those with least rights have more rights than under an even distribution of rights. Jon Elster has pointed out that a similar maximin criterion should be applied in the distribution of rights between generations (Rawls 1973; Elster 1978a). By giving to one generation the privilege of making a constitution and thus binding the following generations, greater freedom (less arbitrariness) will be ensured for all the generations than if each generation should have had the same privilege of making constitutions. This mode of thinking seems to have been general. It was always a pressing problem for the constitutionalists to weigh the advantage of a single reform against the general good of stability and predictability. In a more rule-skeptical age this problem is not felt to be so pressing.

The distinction between negative power to block action and positive power to take action is important in the constitutionalist tradition. The constitutionalists were very much concerned with the former, and they tied the notion of democracy to the latter. They did not initially use the term "democracy" for the constitutionalist regimes we find in, for instance, the U.S.A. and Norway, but after some time the term appeared. This seemed to have happened at the same time as the democratic institutions became a threat to the more strict rule of law (Christophersen 1966, p. 78; Stang 1833).[5] The distinction between negative and positive helps us, however, to explain why the constitutionalists so willingly introduced the democracy they feared, and which, later developed, showed they had at least some reason to fear.

In 1814 Norway shifted from absolute monarchy to a constitutionalist regime. The cession of Norway by the Danish king to the Swedish king after the Napoleonic Wars created an unclear and somewhat open situation in which a constitution was made on the basis of an astonishingly high degree of consensus. It just seemed as if this was the most natural thing to do, although there had been no opposition of any importance earlier (Steen 1951; Seip 1974; Mykland 1978).[6] The new Constitution was made very much on the American model. The main intention was clearly to bind the power of the king. The members of the Constitutional Assembly fought "upwards." In such a situation there was no contradiction between rule of law and the democratic institutions created according to the Constitution.

In the first decade after 1814, the democratically elected Storting stuck to the Constitution. They codified laws and checked the king by innumerable references to the Constitution. It was a controlling power acting on the part of the Constitution, but the roles changed.

From the late 1820s it was the king who made many references to the Constitution, while the Storting tended to take more initiatives and act more independently. A great leap forward was taken in 1869 when the Storting, from meeting only every third year, began to meet annually. As the position of the Storting was thus gradually changed from negative control into positive power, the problem of controlling positive state power changed from the problem of controlling the king into the problem of controlling the legislator. There are good reasons for arguing that the real democratic revolution lies in this gradually changing position of the democratic institution from a negative into a positive power position. This had clearly not been the intention of the early constitutionalists.

The parallel to the development in America is striking. It seems now to be commonly held that the American revolutionaries did not

[5] Stang uses the concept *demokratisk-monarchisk* to describe the Norwegian system.

[6] The main works on the Norwegian "revolution" are: Steen (1951), Seip (1974) and Mykland (1978).

fight for democracy, but "contributed to its coming,"[7] thus enabling a contradiction to develop between the rule of law and democracy. In Norway this contradiction became evident in the last decades of the nineteenth century.

While the *Rechtsstaat* was to the special advantage of the already privileged, we must somehow relate the development of the democracy to the emancipation of the underprivileged. Besides meeting the general need for participation or political freedom, the democratic development and the special interests of the underprivileged in a new redistributive state were strengthened by the ever-increasing general need for more state power in modern societies. Democratic institutions were called upon to loosen the ties which bound the old *Rechtsstaat*, and this often happened in periods of economic crisis.

In 1884, during the Great Depression, the negative power of the Norwegian government was reduced by the introduction of parliamentarianism. The government, which had originally been appointed by the king and which had gradually changed into a self-supplying corporation, was from now on to emanate from the majority in the Storting. The concrete issue in question was the right of the government to veto changes in the Constitution and to veto grants given by the Storting. The conservative leader, T. H. Aschehoug, saw the reforms as the abolition of the main guarantees for the rule of law. It was "the victory of the doctrine of the unlimited power and right of the state" (Aschehoug, 1885, pp. 1–2). According to Aschehoug, it was the same doctrine they fought against in 1814. The only difference was that the constitutionalists now had to fight "downwards." In the tradition inherited from the old constitutionalists, Aschehoug maintained that there was a contradiction between rule of law and democracy.

In the inter-war years the scene changed again: the alternatives no longer seemed to be *Rechtsstaat* or democracy. The doctrine of the unlimited power and right of the state no longer seemed to be typical for the liberal opposition of 1884, now in power. This was now the doctrine of the new Fascist and Communist regimes. When Lionel Robbins wrote the book referred to above in the late 1930s, he differed from the old constitutionalist tradition insofar as he could not see any contradiction between rule of law and democracy. Democracy

[7] The quotation is from W. H. Nelson. See Greene (1968), p. 58

now represented the guarantee for limited government. In this new situation democracy and stability seemed to be two sides of the same coin. New historical experience was poured into the old concepts.

The historical experience will of course be different in different countries. Almond and Verba, for instance, have found that there is a particularly strong combination of what they call "subject competence" and "political competence" in Britain. "Subject competence" means that people expect serious consideration of their cases from the officials, and this expectation is associated with independent government limited by the rule of law. "Political competence" means that people think they can do something about an unjust law (Almond and Verba 1963, pp. 173, 177). As we see, the two concepts correspond closely to the two concepts of liberty which we started out with. Both forms of liberty are presumably reasonably well taken care of in Britain, which means that there is no serious contradiction between democracy and the rule of law. The ideal situation as conceived by the constitutionalists is, then, to be found in Britain (?): the will of the people is the rule of the law. It is a paradox that this situation should be found in a country without a written constitution. The reason is perhaps to be found precisely in the Common Law tradition, where the norms can be interpreted with due regard to long-term changes in values. Conflicts can thus be played down.

In the U.S. there should, according to McCloskey, be more of a "dualism" – or what we call a contradiction – between democracy and the rule of law. This corresponds to what Almond and Verba have observed, that in the U.S. subject competence ranks low while political competence ranks high (more democracy than rule of law). In Germany they found that the opposite is the case: subject competence ranks high while political competence ranks low. As in the U.S. there should then be some sort of basic contradiction, but the "solution" is the opposite of that found in the U.S. This corresponds with an observation made by Richard Lowenthal, that there is in Germany a more or less general assumption that the fundamental rights of the citizens are constantly endangered by their elected representatives, while on the other hand the Constitutional Court is ready to "discover in the constitutional text a basis for detailed legislative precepts in a variety of fields" (Lowenthal 1978, 33). A fear of democracy strengthens the rule of law.

A great deal could probably be said about the particular historical experiences behind these differences between Britain, the U.S. and Germany. On the other hand the differences should not be overemphasized. The common experience is likely to be stronger – that democracy has after all been the best guarantee for limited government and the rule of law.

The changing relation between democracy and rule of law in different situations can partly be seen as an effect of some inner contradictions in the rule of law system as worked out in the nineteenth century. The use of democratic institutions to check and control state power and the gradual change of this negative power position into a positive one has already been mentioned, but there are some more points to be made along this line.

The notion of rule of law is usually looked upon as a conservative notion. However, if the idea is not so much that the state is limited and bound as that it should be by active encroachment limited and bound, it is really a radical idea. As we have seen, there is a tendency in the works of the American Revolution to regard the constitutionalist principle as a conservative element in itself. Viewed chronologically this is not necessarily so. To take upon oneself a historical mission to bind posterity is something different from being bound by the past. In the constitutionalism of the late eighteenth century, the idea acquired this radical form. One should and could in principle, once and for all, create a set of rules which would bind the state and guarantee a harmonious development of society. This is clearly seen, for instance, in the works of Jeremy Bentham. As a utilitarian, he held the view that it was in the power of man to create the norms of society. On this was based what has been seen as his interventionism, which was in contrast to the idea of natural law.

The idea that men were free to *create* their own norms should lead to the notion of positive law. The essence of this notion is the freedom to *change* law. A fully developed positive law means that there is no longer a claim that law should be general and standing. Positive law means that law has been an instrument of positive power, that the distinction between the setting of norms and the giving of commands is no longer clear. In a fully developed positive-law society the only standing norms are the metanorms, that is norms defining who has the power to change norms (Luhmann 1972; Hayek 1973–6).[8]

The distinction between "create" and "change" is important. Although the idea that men could create their laws stimulated the idea of positive law, this was clearly not the intention of utilitarian constitutionalists. They saw no good in a more or less perpetual changing of laws. The idea was that with an enlightened legislature, man could "go before events" (Bentham 1843, p. 205). This optimistic view on legislation permitted them to combine the idea of freedom to create laws with the idea of the rule of law. The combination of the old idea of the rule of law and the new idea of freedom to create laws was indeed a characteristic feature of the nineteenth century. Logically it meant an even greater element of abdication than if the basis had been the old notion of natural law, as it implied that there was a greater power from which to abdicate. That is perhaps one of the reasons why it did not work so well in the long run. The door was opened for the growth of positive law together with democracy.

On the other hand, it could be said that the rule of law system, as introduced in Norway at the beginning of the nineteenth century, was not a failure at all. It is not surprising that we can see certain contradictions within the system which in the course of time were to contribute to the changing of the system. The degree to which the system actually worked is perhaps more surprising. This was partly because of the institutionalized negative power and partly because of the general attitude toward the rule of law principle.

In Norway the typical bureaucrat held the most strategic positions. The bureaucratic inclination to act according to rules strengthened the system. Even the Storting was partly dominated by the bureaucrats in the first half of the nineteenth century, and by their tendency to set up rules and act accordingly. Faith in the possibility of binding the administration to general rules itself contributed to the binding of the system.

We cannot go into the historical details of this but the most

---

[8] Luhmann (1972), pp. 190ff., 211–12. See also Hayek (1973–6), especially ch. 4. Hayek maintains that the idea that "all law is, can be, and ought to be, the product of the free invention of the legislator ... is factually false ..." There is, according to Hayek, an "intentionalist fallacy" in the thought that man can create the norms of society (vol. 1, p. 73).

important and illustrative example besides the Constitution itself should be mentioned. It should cause no surprise that this example is the monetary system. In 1816 a private bank was established by law with the privilege of a monopoly of issuing bank notes. The bank was made private or lifted out of the political sphere in order to free the state from the temptation to "use" the bank. This reasoning was also used by David Ricardo. A banking company would be more "under the control of law" than the government. According to Ricardo, this distinction is important under "an arbitrary government." With an enlightened legislation, the state can run the bank, but only under the condition that it should be "totally independent of the control of ministers" (Ricardo 1963, p. 245). In the Norwegian case, however, the state or Storting was not confident that it could resist the temptation, so the bank was made private by an act of state abdication. In this manner the bank would be bound to the single aim of maintaining the par value of the notes. There should be no playing around with the currency.

This system was so well constructed in accordance with its intentions that it was kept intact through a devastating back-to-par policy in the 1920s (Sejersted 1973).[9] The system was not undermined until the devaluation in 1931, when Norway followed Britain. Many felt this to be the real breach with the old *Rechtstaat*. The attitudes of the men in strategic positions during the 1920s are illustrative. The governor of the bank argued by referring to the law: "The monetary system is established by law . . . The value of the notes is written on them . . . It is not enough to show that it is inconvenient to stick to what is once decided, it must be clear that it is not possible . . . the difficulties of keeping the law are severe, but the people live an eternal life."[10] On the other hand the Minister of Finance would not take action: "It is a fact that where the state has had the authority over the national bank, it has been a failure. The interests have been so pressing and the temptations so great that it has been impossible to resist them."[11] It was an important factor behind the back-to-par policy that nobody had the authority to do otherwise, and that was exactly what was intended by the system.

---

[9] Sejersted (1973) deals with the Norwegian back-to-par policy.
[10] Annual speech by the Governor of the Bank of Norway, February, 1927, p. 32.
[11] *Stortingsforhandlingene* (Proceedings of the Storting) (1926), vol. 7a, p. 129.

It was generally held, in particular by the social democratic opposition of that time, that the unhappy back-to-par policy of the 1920s
was partly the result of the excessive power of the governor of the
bank. This is a problematic statement. Although he could have
recommended another policy, the essentially negative character of his
power should be stressed. He did not represent an autocratic antidemocratic power. It was his duty, according to the rule of law idea, to
serve predictability by defending a decision previously taken by
democratic institutions. To do this, he was endowed with negative
power.

The nature of the negative power is more clearly seen in the
doctrine of judicial review. This is the right of the Supreme Court to
set aside a law by reference to the Constitution. This right was
exercised quite extensively in Norway after the fall of the veto rights of
the government in 1884 and till the 1930s (Seip 1968). It was a right not
to take action but to block action, which in this case meant a defense of
an earlier decision. We have returned to the important logical distinction between negative and positive power. The distinction is stressed
by Hannah Arendt: "It is seldom recognized and of some importance
that, to put it in Woodrow Wilson's words, 'power is a positive thing,
control a negative thing' and that 'to call these two things by the same
name is simply to impoverish language by making one word serve for a
variety of meanings' " (Arendt 1963, p. 300). Buchanan and Tullock
have made the same observation: "The relevant distinction between
the power of determining action and the power of blocking action has
not been sufficiently emphasized in the literature of political science"
(1965, pp. 258ff.). One must not conclude, however, that negative
power only has a general blocking effect. A. K. Sen has pointed out
that the exercise of negative power can, for instance, block an
antipollution move and thus positively impose external costs on others
(1970, p. 25). Negative power can also block negative power and thus
open the way for a "positive" development. (See example below.)
Negative power as embedded in the rule of law does not serve the
status quo. The institutionalized negative power to block state action
which we find in the constitutionalist regimes was thought necessary
not least because of the special character of the positive power
monopoly of the state. But it was a premise that this blocking of state
power would further the positive evolution of society as a whole. This

positive result would emerge from the many uncoordinated individual acts in the supposedly powerless private sphere. It is too easy to say that this line of reasoning was proved to be wrong by historical experience. In fact it was proved to be not altogether wrong.

The "positive" effect of the negative power was clearly seen in Norway in 1884, when the contradiction within the rule of law system was demonstrated. It was the Riksrett which voted for the abolition of the veto rights of the government. According to the Constitution, the Riksrett was composed of the judges in the Supreme Court and a certain number of members of the Storting. The judges from the Supreme Court were unanimously on the side of the rule of law principle and they thought the abolition of the veto rights of the government was contrary to the spirit of the Constitution. They also knew that they were a minority. Nevertheless they stuck to the formal rules, participated in the Riksrett and thus legitimized what they thought was an illegitimate act. In this way the democractic evolution was furthered by the institutions of the *Rechtsstaat.*

The clear-cut contradiction between democracy and rule of law which we started out with has been blurred, as a closer look at the nature of negative power has revealed contradictions within the rule of law system. We shall proceed to look at some aspects of the nature of positive power.

In the case of monetary policy, the taking of action was blocked by institutionalized norms. Apparently this was a conflict between negative and positive power. It should be kept in mind, however, that the institutionalization of negative power in the sense in which we have used the concept is in itself a positive power act of great bearing. Legislation such as the setting of norms and the abolition of authority to change these norms, not to mention the making of a constitution, represent the exercise of great positive power. Although to check and to control was what the constitutionalists first and foremost had in mind, they themselves had to go far beyond the limits of limited government in order to establish just those limits. From the outset even the Storting represented far more than a negative controlling power position. Not even the hierarchical order of norms according to which the Constitution should be derived from the natural law and the ordinary laws from the Constitution could veil the fact that the authority to set norms represented a positive power. It is on the whole important to note that the opposite of the rule of law was not the exercise of positive power, but the exercise of *current* power. It was current power which meant arbitrariness and which was the characteristic feature of despotism. The binding of the current despotic power of the state by legislation required a much greater positive power than that of the despot. To quote Bentham:

> With posterity the despot, as such, has no means whatever of communication. He has no names to call them by; he has no language in which to converse with them. But to the power of the legislator, time has no barrier to oppose: The *nati natorum et qui nascuntur ab illis* form but a small part of the multitude he has under his care: so that in this line alone the power of the latter is to that of the former as infinity to one. (1945, p. 176)

The power of the despot is self-destructive, as it can be opposed by later despots. But Bentham probably wants to go further than that and say that the power of the despot is opposed by his own power. If he was not free to change his mind, he would not be a despot. The power of the legislator is so much greater because it includes (in a system of standing laws) an abdication act which makes the legislator not a threat to, but an object of, his own power. The introduction of negative power by the constitutionalists was meant to protect the positive power performed by the legislators. Negative power was a precondition for – and not the opposite of – positive power. The limitation of the power of potential legislators in posterity was not the preoccupation of the early radical constitutionalists. They had, however, a clear understanding of the self-destructive aspect of current positive power. There is always in politics a problem of how to guarantee the following up of a decision. To follow a long-term strategy can require binding oneself in some way to one's own decisions, as did Ulysses in order to avoid the island of the Sirens. In the above-mentioned case, when the Storting voted for a private central bank, one of its main arguments was based on just that fear of being tempted – or fear of one's own irrationality – which made it rational to abdicate (Elster 1977, 469–526). The different abdication acts embedded in the making of a constitution, or the lifting of monetary policy out of the political sphere, or the different veto-institutions, were not only meant to give personal freedom under public security, but were also part of a long-term strategy for the development of society.

Democratic development has been closely linked to modifications in the rule of law or to more positive law and current power. It is easy to see the reason why this had to be so. Being bound to earlier decisions also meant that one was bound to the unintended and unfortunate consequences of the same decisions (or to the unfortunate, "positive" consequences of uncoordinated individual acts, not checked because the negative blocking power was blocked by a negative blocking power). Less predictability or modifications in public security have been regarded as a necessary price to pay for a better society. The only point to be stressed in this connection is that the claim to be independent of former decisions normally implies a limitation of the power to bind posterity (unless, as we have seen, one claims the right to execute a special historical mission). By not allowing some limitations set by former decisions one is undermining one's own power. Current power is self-destructive – "Instant power is objectless" (Elster 1978b, p. 128). Some sort of negative power is necessary not only to check, but paradoxically also to protect positive power.

The monetary-policy example displays the unfortunate consequences of a system based on absolute predictability within a limited sphere. The main idea behind a system of this kind was to establish a guarantee against uncertainty. It is questionable, however, whether absolute predictability within a limited sphere gives any general guarantee against uncertainty in a fast-changing modern society. Is it possible to give general, standing rules which can serve these intentions (predictability and personal freedom) in such a society? The positive answer runs: with an enlightened legislature one can "go before events." Today it is more common to give a negative answer, and to ask for more positive legislation. The monetary-policy example seems to support the latter view. We shall see, however, that this is not unproblematic.

How to stop inflation and how to limit the growth in public expenditure are two of the most pressing problems today. In the inter-war years these two problems were indeed solved – much too efficiently. The present difficulties are partly the result of a change in priorities. We are not willing to pay the price paid in the inter-war years to stop inflation. There are, however, other reasons for the present difficulties. Alan Peacock, for instance, has dealt with the problem of the growth in public expenditure, not as a problem of conflicting aims, but as a problem of the state's ability to make rational choices (Peacock 1979). According to Peacock, the revolution in expectations has developed faster than the state's ability to meet these expectations. As the state does not have the power to oppose the claims, the result is inconsistency and irrationality. It is tempting here to refer to Ricardo and to the Minister of Finance in the 1920s, who both maintained that inflation was the inevitable result if the state got the current responsibility for monetary policy. (Although these observations seem anachronistic today, they do have some value as predictions.)

Peacock has a tentative solution to his problem. The main point is that *a priori* a general rule should be established saying how great a part of the GNP should be used for public expenditure. This is the rule of law principle again, but from a slightly different angle than that from which we have viewed it so far. With the limitation of the authority of the state and the setting up of a general norm of conduct, state power is protected to some extent.

This is not to be confused with the sort of general rule advocated by, for instance, Buchanan and Tullock. They call for rules which link the benefit to the cost and thereby ensure rational expectations. As also pointed out by Buchanan and Tullock, such rules will not work when "redistributive objectives are of primary importance" (1965, p. 292). What Peacock must have in mind is a general rule which ensures the positive power to take rational decisions in a redistributive society where expectations are ahead of the current potential.

Peacock's solution acquired a general form in game theory. T. C. Schelling talks about the paradox that "the power to constrain an adversary may depend on the power to bind oneself; that in bargaining, weakness is often strength ... " (1960, p. 22). The "strong" policy of the bank governor was partly based on his lack of authority, which he himself referred to. Although it served an unfortunate policy, the governor had just what Peacock misses, namely, a standing rule to which he could refer. The problem in the case of Peacock is how to get the public to submit to the assertion that the state really is bound to the rule.

The practice of the International Monetary Fund in Washington illustrates the problem. It has often been said that the right of the Fund to intervene in the internal economic policy affairs in a country which has used its drawing rights beyond a certain limit is in reality a helping hand for the same government to carry out a policy which it wanted to carry out, but which it did not have the courage, or rather the political opportunity, to carry out by itself. The Fathers of the Constitution or the "gnomes in Washington" – such distant binding powers can be good to have in some cases.

J. M. Keynes, one of the greatest rule-skeptics in modern times, held that human intelligence should be free from fixed rules to find rational solutions to problems. On the other hand he assumed "that economic decision-making could be insulated from political pressures" (Skidelsky 1979, p. 37). When Peacock tentatively advocates a back-to-rules policy, it is obviously because he has found this assumption to be false. Fearing human weaknesses and irrationality he is led back toward the position of the old constitutionalists.

Some sort of binding or protection of positive power was necessary if the state was to act according to a long-term strategy. Now we have also seen that in certain cases this sort of negative power may even be a precondition for consistency and rationality.

Our analysis is in the constitutionalist tradition, insofar as it presupposes that the laws have a real binding effect. It is not uncommon to maintain that the fight for power in a society is a zero-sum game and that democracy should guarantee a more or less even distribution of this always present sum of power. The constitutionalists thought less of distributing and more of abolishing power – not by anarchy but by formalism. The rule of law was thought to further a powerless society. They thought of the abdication act we have referred to as a real abdication act for the benefit of all. Nobody should in principle have the competence to break or change rules, not even those who established them. It has rightly been pointed out that this idea partly served as a blind for a hidden exercise of power by those privileged in advance. In an extreme version the argument runs that when the powerful and privileged observed the rules it was because the rules served their purpose, and when the underprivileged observed the rules it was under the threat of reprisals. For a rule-skeptic, rules of the kind we are talking about are only a power instrument. It must be kept in mind, however, that there were difficult institutional barriers to overcome if one wanted the rules changed. Rules which were to the advantage of the powerful when established could be very difficult to change if they were later found to be to the disadvantage of the supposedly powerful. Examples are given above.

Of even greater importance is man's general inclination to act according to rules. "Man is a rule-following animal" (Peters 1958, p. 5). Very often rules are prior to action, which means that there is no choice of whether to act according to rules or not (Rawls 1955). This can obviously also be the case in the political sphere. In a stable society the privileged and supposedly powerful as well as the underprivileged will tend to act according to rules, not calculating whether this is in their own interest or not. In a changing society the rules will come under pressure and the tendency to exercise power will be greater, which means that man's tendency to follow rules is to a certain degree historically conditioned. It follows from this line of reasoning that the actual possibility of changing laws is also to a certain degree historically conditioned. F. A. Hayek is certainly right when he says that it is "factually false" to hold that *all* law "is, can be, and ought to be, the product of the free invention of the legislator."[12] On the other hand it is obvious that some law can be "produced" or changed by such free invention. The interesting point is, however, that this possibility of producing laws, or changing the norms of society, is in itself changing in the course of history.

There was some sort of self-reinforcing mechanism in the standing laws of the *Rechtsstaat*. And there was reality in the abdication acts. One got accustomed to looking at the laws as binding, and as the Governor of the Bank of Norway, one hesitated to change the laws. To understand the nineteenth century it is essential that one should understand the reality in the formalism – for better or for worse – of that century.

This has been an essay on power, but first and foremost on contradictions. Contradictions have something to do with the uninten-

---

[12] See n. 8 above.

ded consequences of human acts which constitute the very core of historical development. The modern state was set up to serve society, but it became a threat to the same society. Democracy was introduced to support the rule of law, but it also undermined the same rule. The standing laws of the *Rechtsstaat* were established to serve predictability, but they also tied society to the unforeseen and unfortunate consequences of the same laws. More current power was reintroduced to make democracy work better, but it also had some destructive effects on the same democracy. What I have sketchily tried to do is to move from a discussion of the contradiction between democracy and *Rechtsstaat* to a discussion of the contradictions within democracy on the one side and within the *Rechtsstaat* on the other. Thus I hope to have contributed to a better understanding of the relation between democracy and rule of law, as well as of the dynamics of the history of the period under survey.

References

Almond, G. A. and Verba, S. 1963. *The Civic Culture*. Princeton University Press

Arendt, H. 1963. *On Revolution*. London: Faber and Faber

Aschehoug, T. H. 1885. *Norges nuvaerende Statsforfatning* [Norway's Present Constitution], vol. 3. Kristiania: Malling.

Bailyn, B. (ed.). 1965. *Pamphlets of the American Revolution, 1750–1776*. Cambridge, Mass.: Belknap Press of Harvard University Press

Bentham, J. 1843. A general view of a complete code of laws, p. 205 in *The Works of Jeremy Bentham*, vol. 3, edited by J. Bowring. Edinburgh/London, W. Tait/Simpkin, Marshall

1945. *The Limits of Jurisprudence Defined*. New York: Columbia University Press

Berlin, I. 1958. *Two Concepts of Liberty*. Oxford: Clarendon Press

Buchanan, J. M. and Tullock, G. 1965. *The Calculus of Consent: Logical Foundations of Constitutional Democracy*. Ann Arbor, Michigan: University of Michigan Press

Christophersen, J. A. 1966. *The Meaning of Democracy as Used in European Ideologies*. Oslo: Universitetsforlaget

Elster, J. 1977. Ulysses and the Sirens: a theory of imperfect rationality. *Social Science Information*, 16 (5), 469–526

1978a. Demokrati og rasjonalitet. *Demokrati og samfunnsstyring belyst av humanistiske forskere* [Democracy and the leadership of society examined by social science researchers.] Oslo (Conference report NAVF).

1978b. *Logic and Society: Contradictions and Possible Worlds*. London: Wiley

Greene, J. P. (ed.). 1968. *The Reinterpretation of the American Revolution 1763–1789*. New York: Harper and Row

Habermas, J. 1962. *Strukturwandel der Öffentlichkeit*. Neuwied: H. Luchterhand

Hayek, F. A. 1973–6. *Law, Legislation and Liberty*. 2 vols. London: Routledge and Kegan Paul

Hirschman, A. O. 1977. *The Passions and the Interests*. Princeton University Press

Kant, I. 1976. *Zum ewigen Frieden*. Stuttgart: Reclam

Lovejoy, A. O. 1961. *Reflections on Human Nature*. Baltimore: Johns Hopkins Press

Lowenthal, R. 1978. Why German stability is so insecure. *Encounter* (December)

Luhmann, N. 1972. *Rechtssoziologie* [Sociology of Law] *I–II*. Reinbek: Rowohlt Taschenbuch Verlag (rororo Stud. 1/2)

McCloskey, R. G. 1960. *The American Supreme Court*. University of Chicago Press

Mykland, K. 1978. *Kampen om Norge* [The Fight for Norway]. *Norges Historie*, vol. 9. Oslo: Cappelen

Peacock, A. T. 1979. Public expenditure growth in post-industrial society, in *Post-Industrial Society*, edited by B. Gustafsson. London: Croom Helm

Peters, R. S. 1958. *The Concept of Motivation*. London/New York: Routledge/Humanities Press

Rawls, J. 1955. Two concepts of rules. *Philosophical Review*, **64**
1973. *A Theory of Justice*. Oxford University Press (1st edn 1971, Cambridge, Mass.: Harvard University Press)

Ricardo, D. 1963. *Principles of Political Economy and Taxation*. Homewood, Ill.: Irwin

Robbins, L. 1965. *The Theory of Economic Policy in English Classical Political Economy*. London: Macmillan (1st edn 1952)

Schelling, T. C. 1960. *The Strategy of Conflict*. Cambridge, Mass.: Harvard University Press

Seip, J. A. 1968. Den norske høyesterett som politisk organ [The Norwegian Supreme Court as a political institution] in *Tanke og handling i norsk historie* [Thought and Action in Norwegian History]. Oslo: Gyldendal

1974. *Utsikt over Norges historie* [Overview of Norwegian History], part 1, Oslo: Gyldendal

Sejersted, F. 1973. *Ideal, teori og virkelighet: Nicolai Rygg og penge-politikken i 1920-arena* [Ideal, Theory and Reality: Nicolai Rygg and the Monetary Policy of the 1920s]. Oslo: Cappelen

Sen, A. K. 1970. *Collective Choice and Social Welfare.* San Francisco: Holden-Day

Skidelsky, R. 1979. Keynes and the reconstruction of liberalism. *Encounter* (April)

Stang, F. 1833. *Om grundloven* [On the Constitution]. Kristiania: Cappelen

Steen, S. 1951. *1814.* Oslo: Cappelen

1962. *Konge og Storting* [King and Storting]. Oslo: Cappelen

Vile, M. J. C. 1967. *Constitutionalism and the Separation of Powers.* Oxford: Clarendon Press

6. Neo-federalism?

BRUCE A. ACKERMAN

I Reason and history

"It seems to have been reserved to the people of this country," or so the first of *The Federalist Papers* assures Americans, "to decide . . . whether societies of men are really capable or not of establishing good government from reflection and choice, or whether they are forever destined to depend for their political constitutions on accident and force."[1]

Two centuries onward, these proud words of Alexander Hamilton have been covered over with unintended ironies. Hamilton means, of course, to present the proposed Federal Constitution as the crowning achievement of the American Enlightenment. After countless ages of "accident and force," the first *Federalist* inaugurates a series of eighty-five essays by Hamilton, Madison and Jay that present a dramatic alternative. Adopting the evocative pseudonym Publius, the three statesmen present a remorselessly rationalistic defense of the proposed Federal Constitution. While the existence of *ad hoc* compromise is sometimes conceded,[2] it is not this aspect of the Convention's work that engages Publius' interest. Instead, he tries to defend almost every aspect of his Constitution through systematic political reasoning – seeking to convince himself, no less than his fellow Americans, that a new political world of "reflection and choice" is indeed at hand.

However flattering this image, it is precisely here that the passage of

This is a revised, and abbreviated, version of B. Ackerman, *The Storrs Lectures: Discovering the Constitution*, 93 *Yale L. J.* 1013 (1984).

[1] See *The Federalist*, ed. C. Rossiter (New York, 1961), no. 1, 33 (A. Hamilton). (All page citations will henceforth be from this readily available paperback edition.)
[2] See, for example, Publius' apologetic discussion of slavery in *ibid.*, no. 54, 336–41.

history has cast its ironic shadow. Publius' rationalistic experiment has become the oldest living constitution in the world. Each of the Philadelphia Convention's proudest creations has been transformed, and transformed again, during centuries of bitter political struggle. What, then, should we say of Publius' proud claim of triumph over history's "accident and force?" Is it still possible to find in *The Federalist* a political vision that might permit us to understand the American Constitution as a system worthy of "reflection and choice?"

The conventional answer, I think it safe to say, is No. Indeed, it is rare to find a subject upon which so many, and such powerful, voices agree. Thus, America's most influential political scientist, Robert Dahl, devotes the first chapter of his *Preface to Democratic Theory* to exposing *The Federalist* as "clearly inadequate" when viewed "as political science rather than as ideology."[3] Similarly, America's most influential constitutional theorist, Alexander Bickel, begins *The Least Dangerous Branch* by declaring *The Federalist*'s notion of constitutional government utterly "non-representational."[4] Beyond Dahl and Bickel lies the great shadow of Charles Beard and the Progressive historians.[5] On their familiar view, Publius is the spokesman for a propertied elite who were using the Constitution as a means of strangling the American Revolution before they lost control over it. On this interpretation, *The Federalist*'s effort to defend the new Constitution on its merits should be seen for what it is: sheer propaganda.[6] Little wonder, then, that Dahl and Bickel should begin

---

[3] R. Dahl, *Preface to Democratic Theory* (Chicago, 1956), p. 31.

[4] A. Bickel, *The Least Dangerous Branch* (New Haven, 1962), p. 16.

[5] C. Beard, *An Economic Interpretation of the Constitution of the United States* (New York, 1913). For an elaborate discussion of Beard's views of the American Revolution in particular, and those of the Progressive historians in general, see R. Hofstadter, *The Progressive Historians* (New York, 1968), 167–346. Since Hofstadter's book was written, American historians have become ever more skeptical of Beardian premises. For a thoughtful effort at rehabilitation, see J. Diggins, "Power and authority in American history: the case of Charles A. Beard and his critics," *Am. Hist. Rev.*, 86 (1981), 701.

[6] This is not to say that Beard was utterly dismissive of *The Federalist*. Instead, he proudly claimed the work as a precursor of his own effort to reduce politics to economics. See Beard, *An Economic Interpretation*, pp. 158–88. On this view, my emphasis on *The Federalist*'s distinctive contributions to democratic theory only obscures the work's genuine greatness. For other Progressive appraisals of *The Federalist*, see Beard, *An Economic Interpretation*, pp. 158–88; C. Merriam, *A History of American Political Theories* (New York, 1920), pp. 96–122; V. Parrington, *Main Currents in American Thought* (New York, 1927), pp. 284–8. For an earlier critique of the Progressive characterization of *The Federalist*, see B. Wright, *Consensus and Continuity, 1776–1791* (New York, 1958), pp. 40–60.

their great careers by declaring their intellectual independence from Publius. For it is only in this way that the thoughtful American may even begin to consider whether his constitutional heritage is worthy of "reflection and choice."

I mean to present a different view. I do not deny, of course, that *The Federalist* was indeed a part of a complex political and economic struggle. I simply insist that its ideas are also worthy of serious study in their own right. In taking *The Federalist* seriously, I hope to resist another familiar temptation. When scholars have risen above Beardian condescension, they have typically viewed *The Federalist* as a contribution to a kind of political engineering – offering brilliant new designs, it is true, but ones that depend upon more basic ideas manufactured earlier on the other side of the Atlantic. As a consequence, most of the best work tends to be a study of intellectual influence – tracing the contribution of Locke or Montesquieu or Hume on the final product.[7] While such work is essential, an exclusive concern with patterns of intellectual influence obscures a final possibility: was Publius something more than a political engineer? Did he, somehow or other, build a *distinctive* conception of constitutional government out of the rag-bag of Enlightenment ideas provided by history?

My answer is Yes. I hope to persuade you, moreover, that Federalist theory is not some curious antique, suitable for framing by the curators of our intellectual heritage. Instead, I mean to present the theory as a powerful set of ideas that still speak to the modern political predicament: hence the neo- in my title.[8]

Not that these neo-Federalist answers are the ones I myself would give if I were writing on a clean slate. Indeed, if I were only interested

[7] The best known of these enterprises is the effort to find links between *The Federalist* and David Hume. See G. Wills, *Explaining America* (New York, 1981) and D. Adair, *Fame and the Founding Fathers* (New York, 1974). As will appear, I believe that an overemphasis on the arch-conservative Hume seriously distorts the character of Federalist thought – though I certainly do not wish to deny the importance of the Scottish Enlightenment in the complex pattern of intellectual influence.

[8] This ambition may seem to run against the current of recent intellectual fashion – which prides itself in locating the meaning of texts in the particular historical contexts that gave them life. I believe, however, that first impressions here are misleading. On another occasion, I hope to show that the interpretation of Federalist thought advanced here usefully complements (and complicates) the most important contextual work attempted in recent decades. See, e.g., J. G. A. Pocock, *The Machiavellian Moment* (Princeton, 1975), pp. 506–52; G. Wood, *The Creation of the American Republic 1776–1787* (New York, 1969).

in describing the best of all possible worlds, I would not be wasting my time with Federalism, neo- or otherwise. I would instead be devoting all my energies elaborating the practical implications of my own political ideals as they appear in *Social Justice in the Liberal State*.[9] The fact of the matter is, however, that I am not writing on a clean slate. As an American living at the Constitution's Bicentennial, I find myself surrounded by an historical complex of constitutional symbols and institutional structures that originate in the Federalist period. Like it or not, it is these symbols and structures, not any of my own devising, that set the terms of my own efforts at political communi- cation with my fellow citizens. This fact cannot be lightly dismissed by a person, like myself, whose entire approach to political legitimacy centers on the possibility of successful dialogue. Indeed, it would be absurd for me to spend a lifetime in abstract praise of political dialogue while disdaining the continuing discursive practices of my fellow countrymen – merely because they did not conform to my own ideals of liberal conversation.

I propose instead a more complex journey to political self- understanding. Having glimpsed the structure of a better political conversation in *Social Justice in the Liberal State*, I shall spend the next few years examining the communicative practices in which, for better or for worse, I find myself immersed. *Is* there an organizing structure to the efforts of my fellow citizens to come to terms with one another?

What follows is only the beginning of an answer. When I elaborate it further, perhaps I will be in a better position to understand more deeply the complex relationship between dialogue-as-it-is and dialogue-as-it-might-be. For the present, though, my aim is not so much to criticize the organizing structure of American constitutional discourse as to understand it.

II The economy of virtue

A Revolution and constitution

Begin from the beginning: "We the People of the United States." We will get nowhere until we begin to appreciate the remarkable act of

---

[9] B. Ackerman, *Social Justice in the Liberal State* (New Haven, 1980).

authority required to write these opening words of the Constitution. Having emerged from a summer of top secret meetings, the Framers are not only announcing that "We the People" want to scrap America's first constitution, the Articles of Confederation. They also propose to ratify their new announcements on behalf of "the People" in a way that is plainly illegal. The Articles of Confederation explicitly required the agreement of all thirteen states before any constitutional change was to be considered valid; yet the Founders declare that their new Constitution speaks for "We the People" if only nine states give their assent. This revolutionary effort to redefine the rules of the game extends further – to the manner in which the nine states are to give their consent. As the Convention looked ahead to the struggle for constitutional ratification, it refused to permit existing state governments to pass judgment on its authority to speak for the People. Instead, only specially convened "constitutional conventions" would be allowed to determine the fate of the new Constitution. What in the world *justified* the Framers in asserting that this end-run around legal forms might give them a *better* claim to represent the People than the standing governments of the day?[10]

Now it is the first great merit of *The Federalist* that it does not allow us to view this assertion of authority as if it were the result of a counterrevolutionary coup d'état. Instead, Publius argues that the new Constitution is best seen as the culmination of the Revolutionary generation's entire experience in popular government.

It is this aspect of *The Federalist*, of course, that followers of Charles Beard look upon as blatant propaganda – a transparent effort to paper over the fact that we are witnessing the Ninth of Thermidor, not the Fourth of July. It is true, the progressive historian must wryly concede, that the Federalists proved far more successful in damming the popular tide with their counterrevolutionary Constitution than did their French and Russian counterparts. But this concession only leads the Beardian to doubt whether the assorted goings-on in eighteenth-century America added up to a genuine revolution at all. After all, we are by now familiar with the real thing: revolutions that devour their children in a sea of blood with the masses cheering on until, after

---

[10] For a fine elaboration of the Convention's anomalous status under preexisting constitutional law, see R. Kay, "The creation of constitutions in Canada and the United States", 7 *Can.–U.S. L.J.*, 111 (1984), 126–36.

popular passions exhaust themselves in an orgy of destruction, a Napoleon or Stalin emerges to rule the inert mass of his countrymen. If this is revolution, then surely the American Constitution *is* counter-revolutionary, and *The Federalist*'s invocation of the revolutionary tradition *is* sheer propaganda.

And yet, no less obviously, this conclusion depends on an unthinking acceptance of its master premise: why must Americans be embarrassed by the fact that their Revolution did not end in mass murder and political exhaustion? To put the point in terms so perceptively developed by Hannah Arendt:

It is odd indeed to see that twentieth-century American thought . . . is often inclined to interpret the American Revolution in the light of the French Revolution, or to criticize it because it so obviously did not conform to the lessons learned from the latter. The sad truth of the matter is that the French Revolution, which ended in disaster, has made world history, while the American Revolution, so triumphantly successful, has remained an event of little more than local importance.[11]

A "sad truth," but not an inevitable one. Rather than looking upon the American Revolution as an event of "local importance," I propose to read *The Federalist* against the background of a more general theory of revolutionary legitimacy. Rather than assuming that "real" revolutions must end in mass murder, I shall be asking whether anything in *The Federalist* helps us understand a very different possibility – that a period of revolutionary struggle might end in the creation of an enduring system of political communication.

1 The problematics of successful revolution To do *The Federalist* justice, then, turn your mind's eye to revolutionary scenes that, through remorseless repetition, have become a part of our common heritage. I do not want you to begin your act of reconstruction,

[11] H. Arendt, *On Revolution* (New York, 1963), pp. 55–6. My debt to Arendt in what follows far exceeds this single quotation. It would be silly, however, to attempt a footnote commentary on our innumerable points of agreement and disagreement. On a very general level, however, it should be clear that Arendt would reject the interpretation that follows, finding it far too appreciative of the values of civic privatism for her neo-Classical vision of the Founding.

though, at the climactic moment at which you and your fellow revolutionaries triumphantly explore the wreckage of the old regime. Instead, begin the action at a point when this final victory seems a far more doubtful matter.

Time One. You are surrounded by an ongoing regime – people occupying government offices, declaring themselves rightful rulers of the territory; others plotting and scheming to replace the present incumbents; the masses looking upon these goings-on with resigned indifference: politics as usual.

All this, so far as you are concerned, stinks. While the government *says* it represents the people, you think this claim is just plain wrong. Despite its undisputed mastery of established legal forms, you say that you – and your comrades – are the true representatives of the People. Now such a claim requires courage, no less spiritual than physical. Who, after all, do you think you are? The New Messiah?

It may be possible for religious zealots to stop conversation at this point. But for secular democrats, things are inevitably more complicated. Predictably, democratic revolutionaries will respond to the question of their own legitimacy in three different ways. First, they will say that the established government is systematically *subverting the public good*. This requires, of course, an ideology that specifies the public good that is being subverted. Secondly, they will portray themselves as possessing *special virtues* that entitle them to the position of the People's true representatives over other applicants for the position. Thirdly, the leadership's claims to legitimacy must be validated by the *concrete assent* given by faithful followers, who recognize them as the true representatives of the People despite the fact that their meetings lack the formal sanction of law. Without such validating conventions, you cannot be a revolutionary leader – only a leader in search of a revolution.

Time Two. The old regime has collapsed; the established forms of legal authority have disintegrated. You and your comrades have seized the commanding heights, and proceed with the business of government. Quite remarkably, you are now in control of the forms of legal authority. While this, in a way, was what the struggle was all about, victory brings its own embarrassments.

Revolution is a game any number can play. Just as you challenged established authority, so can the next fellow. He too can proclaim his

superior virtue and your subversion of the public good before irregular conventions who speak in the People's name. Vigilance, and the
effective use of force, is a part of the successful revolutionary's answer
to such rival pretensions. But there is another part too – an explanation of why it is wrong for others to usurp the usurper's crown.

There are two obvious answers to this obvious question of legitimacy. The first is "permanent revolution." Here, the revolutionary
elite deny that anything really important has happened as a result of
their accession to the legal forms of authority. After all, the elite did
not require legal forms earlier to declare themselves the People's true
representatives. It was enough to present themselves to irregular
assemblies as people of special virtue in pursuit of the public good.
And the "revolutionary legality" that was good enough for those great
times of glorious victory is certainly good enough today. So hip-hip-
hooray: onward in the People's service. Anybody who stands in the
way is a counterrevolutionary, who must be consigned to the past or
reeducated for life in a brave new world.

The other obvious answer is "revolutionary amnesia." Now that we
have seized power, let us forget how we got there. The law is the law.
If you do not like the law, then try to change it through the (newly)
established forms. Anybody who ignores the forms and violates the
law is a criminal. Criminals belong in jail.

2 The Federalist solution   Now the most important reason why *The
Federalist* is worth reading – not merely by Americans but by all
thinking people – is that it proposes a third way to solve the problem of
revolutionary legitimacy. While rejecting the possibility or desirability
of permanent revolution, *The Federalist* nonetheless places a high
value on public-regarding forms of political activity, in which people
sacrifice their private interests to pursue the common good in transient
and informal political association. While rejecting revolutionary
amnesia, *The Federalist* insists that the revolutionary form of politics
should become preeminent only under certain well-defined historical
situations. When these conditions do not apply, the claim of the
legally established authorities to speak in the name of the People must
be conceded by all thoughtful citizens.

For the moment, it is unnecessary to analyze the particular principles of Federalist constitutional science. The important points go

deeper. According to Publius, the beginning of revolutionary wisdom is to recognize that the future of American politics will not be one long, glorious reenactment of the American Revolution. Rather than preparing the way for permanent revolution, *The Federalist*'s task is to construct the constitutional foundations for a different kind of politics – where well-organized groups try to manipulate government in pursuit of their narrow interests. So far as *this* kind of politics is concerned, the new constitutional arrangements should trump ordinary political outcomes. Yet the very decision to masquerade under the name Publius indicates that Madison, Hamilton and Jay *do* believe in a kind of politics which, under certain conditions, justifies a change in preexisting constitutional principles.

It is, of course, the kind of politics exemplified by the Federalists themselves. A key paper is *Federalist* no. 40,[12] where Madison confronts the fact that the Philadelphia Convention acted illegally in exceeding the authority granted to it by Congress and the states under the Articles of Confederation.[13] After threading his way through several legal arguments, Publius drops his legalistic pose and asks how far "considerations of duty . . . could have supplied any defect in legal authority."[14] The answer is worth pondering:

> Let us view the ground on which the convention stood . . . They must have reflected that in all great changes of established governments, forms ought to give way to substance; that a rigid adherence [to forms] would render . . . nugatory the transcendent and precious right of the people to "abolish or alter their governments . . .," since it is impossible for the people spontaneously and universally to move in concert . . .; it is therefore essential that such changes be instituted by some *informal and unauthorized propositions*, made by some patriotic and respectable . . . citizens . . . [Indeed the Convention] must have recollected that it was by [this] irregular and assumed [method] that the States were first united against the danger with which they were threatened by their ancient government; . . . nor could it have been forgotten that no little ill-timed scruples, no zeal for adhering to ordinary forms, were anywhere

---

[12] See also *The Federalist*, no. 37, 226 (J. Madison) (describing "difficulties inherent in the very nature of the undertaking").
[13] See n. 10 above.   [14] *The Federalist*, no. 40, 251 (J. Madison).

seen, except in those who wished to indulge, under these masks, their secret enmity to the substance contended for. They must have borne in mind that as the plan to be framed and proposed was to be submitted to *the people themselves*, the disapprobation of this supreme authority would destroy it forever; its approbation blot out antecedent errors and irregularities.[15]

Hear the voice of the successful revolutionary. The highest form of political expression is to be found not in the formal assemblies arising under preexisting law, but through an "irregular and assumed privilege" of proposing "informal and unauthorized propositions." If such proposals were accepted by irregular, but popularly elected, assemblies, we are to understand that *the people themselves* – the words are italicized in the original[16] – had spoken; and if the People approved the revolutionary elite's considered proposals, this could "blot out . . . errors and irregularities."

Strong stuff. At present, though, I am less interested in evaluating the Federalist theory of constitutional law than in presenting it to public view. From this perspective, the critical point is that *The Federalist* elaborates a dualistic conception of political life. One form of political action – I shall call it constitutional politics – is characterized by Publian appeals to the common good,[17] ratified by a mobilized mass of American citizens[18] expressing their assent through

---

[15] *Ibid.*, no. 40, 252–5 (quoting Declaration of Independence, para. 2 [U.S. 1776]) (italics in original). While the central argument on this point is in no. 40, 251–5, important ancillary tests include nos. 39 and 43.

[16] Are the italics significant? I do not know. Certainly if *The Federalist* were a twentieth-century text, the distinctive patterns of typographic emphasis (which I have verified in the original editions) *could* fairly be said to have some significance. While I take note of the original italics in my discussion, I appeal to experts in eighteenth century typography to tell me whether it is appropriate to take them seriously here. In any event, nothing important turns on the question – the italics merely give typographic emphasis to meanings already evident in the text itself.

[17] See, e.g., *The Federalist*, no. 1, 33 (A. Hamilton); no. 46, 299–300 (J. Madison); no. 49, 316–17; no. 51, 323–5.

[18] Examples of *The Federalist*'s recurring affirmation of the Revolutionary past and its assertion of the ultimate need for mass mobilization may be found at no. 14, 103–5 (J. Madison) (need to continue Revolutionary tradition); no. 28, 181 (A. Hamilton) (separation of powers facilitates popular mobilization); no. 39, 240 (J. Madison) (need for form of government to maintain fundamental principles of Revolution); no. 46, 298 (division of powers permitting mass mobilization); no. 49, 314 (necessity of keeping open "a constitutional road to the . . . people . . . for certain great and extraordinary occasions"); no. 60, 367 (A. Hamilton) (revolutionary activity as a check).

extraordinary institutional forms.[19] Although constitutional politics is the highest kind of politics, it should be permitted to dominate the nation's life only during rare periods of heightened political consciousness. During the long periods between these constitutional moments, a second form of activity – I shall call it normal politics – prevails. Here, factions try to manipulate the constitutional forms of political life to pursue their own narrow interests.[20] Normal politics must be tolerated in the name of individual liberty;[21] it is, however, democrati-

[19] The extra-legal character of the Convention has already been discussed in n. 10 above. It will suffice here to note *The Federalist*'s recurring assumption that the People best express themselves through episodic and anomalous "conventions," and not through regular sessions of ordinary legislatures. See *The Federalist*, no. 37, 226–7 (J. Madison); no. 39, 243–4; no. 40, 250–5.

[20] These interests may, but need not be, narrowly materialistic. No less threatening were factions based upon narrow ideological ends – most notably the effort by sectarian groups to establish their own church despite the dissenting beliefs of their fellow citizens. Cf. *ibid.*, no. 10, 84 (J. Madison) ("a religious sect may degenerate into a political faction"). Indeed, Martin Diamond persuasively argues that, of all forms of partisan narrowness, *The Federalist* finds material narrowness the most readily controllable, and hence aims for a constitutional structure that seeks to channel factional politics into relatively harmless materialistic directions. See M. Diamond, "Ethics and politics: the American way," in *The Moral Foundations of the American Republic*, ed. R. Horwitz (Charlottesville, 1977), pp. 39, 52–6.

[21] This is, of course, the theme of the most famous paper in *The Federalist* no. 10. While the brilliance of Madison's analysis of factional politics is generally recognized, there is a tendency to approach *The Federalist* no. 10 as if it were a free-standing object, requiring relatively minor supplementation from other papers. For an example of this tendency, see D. Truman, *The Governmental Process*, 2nd edn. (New York, 1971), pp. 4–5. And yet the very definition of "faction" used by Madison in no. 10 suffices to establish the self-consciously partial character of the paper's analysis: "By a faction I understand a number of citizens, whether amounting to a majority or minority of the whole, who are united and actuated by some common impulse of passion, or of interest, adverse to the rights of other citizens, or to the permanent and aggregate interests of the community" (*The Federalist*, no. 10, 78 [J. Madison]). Rather than suggesting that all political groups are necessarily factional, this Publian formulation presupposes the reader's capacity to distinguish factions from movements that *do* aim to further "the rights of citizens" or the "permanent and aggregate interests of the community." While the genesis and character of these Publian groups are not elaborated in *The Federalist* no. 10, this shows only that no. 10's argument is self-consciously incomplete, and cannot be treated independently of other papers in *The Federalist* that undertake to deal with the nature of Publian politics. It is, of course, the object of this chapter to begin the requisite textual synthesis. To minimize the inevitable controversy that such a reading will generate, the chapter emphasizes papers that were also written by the author of *The Federalist* no. 10. While there are obvious differences between the Madisonian and Hamiltonian papers (see A. Mason, "The federalist – split personality," *Am. Hist. Rev.* 57 [1952], 625), I do not believe they involve the bedrock principles of dualistic constitutionalism developed here. Indeed, *The Federalist* no. 9, written by Hamilton, asserts its intimate connection with the subject of Madison's no. 10 – see *The Federalist* no. 9, 72–3 (A. Hamilton), and seeks to locate the fear of faction within the larger commitments of Publian politics. Moreover, my dualistic reading of the text parallels some of the larger dualisms others

cally *inferior* to the intermittent and irregular politics of public virtue associated with moments of constitutional creation.

B Federalist political science

Having established this dualism,[22] we next ask what *The Federalist* proposes to do with it. There are two conceptual possibilities. The first is fatalism. Here, the successful revolutionaries remain passive as they are engulfed by the tide of normal politics. There is nothing they can do during their moment of revolutionary triumph to prevent the future factional disintegration of the American polity. The cycle of constitutional politics/normal politics/constitutional politics will be played out endlessly to the end of human history. The second possibility is constitutional activism. Although there is no way to prevent the rise of normal politics,[23] perhaps the Revolutionary

have detected in Hamilton's political aspirations. See C. Kenyon, "Alexander Hamilton: Rousseau of the Right," *Pol. Sci. Q.*, 73 (1958), 161.

The best evidence of the fundamental unity of Publian thought lies in the fact that the democratic argument in support of judicial review, developed by Hamilton in *The Federalist* no. 78, only becomes fully intelligible when viewed in the light of the Publian texts, largely written by Madison, that are discussed in this chapter. See pp. 171–4 below.

[22] Indeed, Publius denies that he is developing a new conception, but insists that he is building upon a thoroughly familiar principle: "The important distinction so well understood in America between a Constitution established by the people and unalterable by the government and a law established by the government and alterable by the government, seems to have been little understood and less observed in any other country" (*The Federalist*, no. 53, 331 [J. Madison]). Recent historical work, moreover, tends to support Publius' confidence in his audience's mastery of this basic distinction. See Wood, *The Creation of the American Republic*, pp. 257–390.

[23] *The Federalist*'s pessimism on this matter is worth emphasizing. Publius' most elaborate treatment comes as part of an important paper explaining why not all constitutional disputes should be submitted to the general public for resolution: "Notwithstanding the success which has attended the revisions of our established forms of government and which does so much honor to the virtue and intelligence of the people of America, it must be confessed that the experiments are of too ticklish a nature to be unnecessarily multiplied. We are to recollect that all the existing constitutions were formed in the midst of a danger which repressed the passions most unfriendly to order and concord; of an enthusiastic confidence of the people in their patriotic leaders, which stifled the ordinary diversity of opinions on great national questions; of a universal ardor for new and opposite forms produced by a universal resentment and indignation against the ancient government; and whilst no spirit of party connected with the changes to be made, or the abuses to be reformed, could mingle its leaven in the operation. The future situations in which we must expect to be usually placed do not present any equivalent security against the danger which is apprehended" (*The Federalist*, no. 49, 315). Surely, one wants to say, Madison knows he is exaggerating both about the unity of the American People and the seriousness of the British threat? We must not

generation can take steps that will palliate the most pathological aspects of the normal condition. The aim here is to use the resources of constitutional law to channel the ebb and flow of normal politics in ways consistent with Revolutionary principle.

1 The problem It is plain that *The Federalist*'s Constitution takes this second path. It does not do so, however, in an optimistic spirit. Indeed, *The Federalist* is refreshingly free of claims that Americans are somehow immune to the diseases afflicting the rest of humankind.[24] Instead, there is a constant effort to reflect upon the lessons of modern and ancient political practice. And these lessons are anything but encouraging. European countries of American scale are veritable hothouses of despotism.[25] Ancient Greek democracies were transparently unequal to the military and economic challenges of aggressive empires.[26] Worse yet, they were notoriously unstable, constantly degenerating into turmoil and despotism

---

permit doubts about Madison's historical report to obscure the basic theoretical point: Americans can be expected to transcend factional politics only "in the midst of a danger which represse[s] the passions" (315). It is the old saw about the power of the hangman's rope to concentrate the mind wondrously, but raised to the level of collective political consciousness.

In case the point was missed, Madison devotes the next paper to variations on his theme. Since a *constant* appeal to the people on constitutional questions will permit the destruction of constitutional forms by self-regarding pressure-groups, Madison next considers the merits of a *regularized* legal procedure under which the public may undertake the task of constitutional review: every seven years, a group of Censors should be convened to discover and sanction all violations of the Constitution that have occurred since the People last assembled. Madison responds that the spirit of self-interested politics would simply degrade the constitutional forms of censorship, with the most powerful factions manipulating their amplified power to speak in the name of the People. Instead of using law to force a public-regarding politics into being, a collective effort to transcend faction should "be neither presumed nor desired, because an extinction of parties necessarily implies either a universal alarm for the public safety, or an absolute extinction of liberty" (*ibid.*, no. 50, 320 [J. Madison]). The first possibility explains the success of the Revolutionary generation; the second possibility can be avoided only if the Revolutionary generation takes advantage of Federalist constitutional science to bequeath its successors legal forms equal to the challenges of factional politics.

[24] A particularly eloquent assertion of this point may be found in *ibid.*, no. 6, 59 (A. Hamilton); see also no. 31, 196–7; no. 36, 218–19; no. 42, 268 (J. Madison).

[25] See, e.g., *ibid.*, no. 8, 66 (A. Hamilton); no. 41, 257–60 (J. Madison). The closest model is Great Britain. But, for obvious reasons, this is not a model that American Revolutionaries can follow with any great confidence. See, e.g., no. 69, 415–23 (A. Hamilton).

[26] See *ibid.*, no. 4, 49 (J. Jay); no. 18, 122–3, 124–5 (J. Madison and A. Hamilton).

as each group tried to seize exclusive power to oppress the others.[27]

In trying to channel the flow of normal politics, *The Federalist* cannot indulge in the old trick of adapting a blueprint that has succeeded elsewhere.[28] Upon considering the materials at hand, the greatest political scientist of the age, Montesquieu, concluded that republican government could not survive without constant calls upon its citizens' public virtue.[29] Yet it is precisely *The Federalist's* insight that *constant* appeals to public virtue could not be expected to sustain the normal politics of the American people.

2 The scientific solution   Against all of this, *The Federalist* can only place one weighty factor on the other side of the balance: the peculiarly modern institution of political representation. It was this invention of modern political science, not any increase in the quantity of human virtue, which permitted the rational hope that Americans might succeed where the Ancients had failed before them.[30] Representative institutions permit us to establish a regime encompassing millions of people with different religious and economic interests. Although each faction would gladly use political power to tyrannize over the others, their multiplicity permits the constitutional architect a new kind of political freedom. Rather than suppressing faction at the cost of individual liberty, the successful revolutionaries may hope to neutralize the worst consequences of faction by playing each interest off against the others.[31] Hence, the supreme importance of constitutional law. By manipulating the forms of constitutional representation, Publius hopes to drive normal politics into directions that do not endanger the principles of the American Revolution – principles elucidated by the irregular methods of constitutional politics.[32]

[27] It is this perception, of course, that generates the famous analysis of faction begun in *ibid.*, no. 9, 71–6 (A. Hamilton) and continued in no. 10, 77–84 (J. Madison).

[28] See *ibid.*, no. 14, 100–1 (J. Madison); no. 37, 228.

[29] C. Montesquieu, *The Spirit of the Laws*, ed. F. Neumann (New York, 1949), p. 21 ("The politic Greeks, who lived under a popular government, knew no other support than virtue . . ."), which *The Federalist* cleverly attempts to parry by citing Montesquieu against himself. See *The Federalist*, no. 9, 73–4 (A. Hamilton).

[30] See, e.g. *The Federalist*, no. 9, 72–3 (A. Hamilton); no. 10, 77–84 (J. Madison); no. 51, 320–5.

[31] The classic statements here, of course, in *The Federalist*, nos. 10 and 51.

[32] The dualist hope expressed in this sentence is developed most systematically in the six papers beginning with no. 46 and ending with no. 51. It is therefore essential to study these papers together in a single sitting, and resist the temptation to read them in one or another anthologized form.

How to do this is the master question of constitutional design. Only one thing is clear: disappointment awaits all those who fail to understand the distinctive character of representative institutions and who strive instead to create a national government that resembles, as much as possible, the face-to-face democracy of ancient Greece.[33] The temptation is strong to simulate the ancient *polis* by calling together a few hundred people to "represent" the rest of us and reenact the ancient rituals of direct democracy. This congress, not the people as a whole, will gather together in one place, discuss the pros and cons, count heads and declare the majority to be the winner in our name. The rhetoricians have a name for this solution to the problem of representation: synecdoche. In this figure of speech, the part (Congress) displaces the whole (We the People of the United States) for which it stands in the representational system. But if we mistake Congress for the People Assembled, and give it supreme power, it will act in a way that belies its rhetoric. In the words of *The Federalist*:

> The concentrating of [all power] in the same hands is precisely the definition of despotic government. It will be no alleviation that these powers will be exercised by a plurality of hands, and not by a single one. One hundred and seventy-three despots would surely be as oppressive as one ... As little will it avail us that they are chosen by ourselves. An *elective despotism* was not the government we fought for ...[34]

In short, political representation not only promises a solution to the ancient problem of democracy but provides the source of an entirely new problem – misplaced concreteness or reification. Once again, I quote: "The representatives of the people, in a popular assembly, seem sometimes to fancy that they are the people themselves and betray strong symptoms of impatience and disgust at the least sign of opposition from any other quarter ..."[35]

[33] For express, and repeated, rejections of the *polis* as a model for American constitutional theory, see *The Federalist*, no. 9, 72–3 (A. Hamilton); no. 10, 78–84 (J. Madison); no. 14, 100–1; no. 55, 341–2; no. 63, 384–5.

[34] *Ibid.*, no. 48, 310–11 (italics in original) (quoting Jefferson with approval).

[35] *Ibid.*, no. 71, 433 (A. Hamilton). Unlike the Publian texts quoted previously, this one is usually attributed to Hamilton. For another notable analysis of the problematic way in which legislatures represent the People, this time by Madison, see *ibid.*, no. 58, 357–61.

In contrast to the doctrine of legislative supremacy, *The Federalist* insists that *no* legal form can transubstantiate *any* political institution of normal politics into We the People of the United States. Madison is most explicit about this in *Federalist* no. 63. There, he rejects the popular belief that the ancient world was entirely ignorant of representative government. In doing so, he clarifies the distinctive conception of representation upon which *The Federalist* pins its hopes.

> In the most pure democracies of Greece, many of the executive functions were performed, not by the people themselves, but by officers elected by the people, and *representing* the people in their *executive* capacity ... [I]t is [thus] clear that the principle of representation was neither unknown to the ancients nor wholly overlooked in their political constitutions. The true distinction between these and the American government lies *in the total exclusion of the people in their collective capacity*, from any share in the *latter*, and not in the *total exclusion of the representatives of the people* from the administration of the *former*.[36]

Compare this text with the revolutionary pronunciamento, also written by Madison, that I have already discussed.[37] While Madison insisted there that the "irregular and assumed" procedures of constitutional politics provided access "*to the people themselves*," here he italicizes the claim that it is "*the total exclusion of the people in their collective capacity*" which is the hallmark of the American Constitution during periods of normal politics. In short, we must systematically reject the idea that when Congress (or the president or the Supreme Court) speaks during periods of normal politics, we can hear the *genuine* voice of the American people. Under normal political conditions, the political will of the American people cannot be "represented" by means of such naive synecdoche.

3 Master concept: the problematics of representation   Yet, at the same time, Publius insists that his constitutional creations – Congress, president, Court – *do* "represent" the People in some other way. If we are to understand this claim, however, we must use a more general

---

[36] *Ibid.*, no. 63, 386–7 (J. Madison) (italics in original).
[37] See pp. 161–2 above.

framework than that customarily employed in modern constitutional law. Too often, we address the problem of political representation as if it could be understood apart from a more general understanding of the problems involved in any and all efforts at representation – whether they be in politics, art or everyday language. Unless we attempt a more general analysis of representation, however, we shall never come to grips with *The Federalist*'s hopes for American government.

Imagine, then, that you were planning a long and hazardous journey and wanted to commission a painting which would "represent" you to your loved ones in your absence. You have two choices. On the one hand, you may find somebody with photographic aspirations, who might provide an image of you as you appear at the present moment. This mimetic kind of representation has familiar advantages and disadvantages. Precisely because it tries to present a realistic copy of your appearance, it is easy for others to read at a glance. Yet, for the very same reason, such a snapshot is unsatisfactory. Perhaps an artist who self-consciously appreciates that he *cannot* reduce your living reality to a piece of paper – that he is *only* providing a representation – will paint a portrait that, while less realistic, will nevertheless convey a deeper meaning to its audience. I will call this semiotic representation, because it is impossible to interpret the picture's meaning without self-consciously understanding that the picture is only a symbol, and not the thing which the symbol symbolizes.[38]

It is in this semiotic way that Publius sets about representing the People of the United States by means of a written text – the Constitution of the United States. To understand this document, we

---

[38] For purposes of gaining the broadest support for my argument, I have written this paragraph in a way that gives maximal credence to the mimetic aspiration. That is, by defining semiosis as requiring "the self-conscious understanding that the picture is only a symbol, and not the thing which the symbol symbolizes," I have allowed the proponent of mimesis to propose that *his* form of representation does not involve a similar form of symbolic self-consciousness. I do not believe, however, that this naively mimetic claim can withstand scrutiny. See A. Danto, *The Transfiguration of the Commonplace* (Cambridge, Mass., 1981), pp. 1–32, 54–89. In my view, the mimetic form of representation is best defined as the effort *to suppress* the interpreter's self-conscious recognition that the symbol is not really the same thing as the thing it symbolizes, while semiotic representation conveys meaning only by *provoking* the interpreter's self-conscious recognition of the representation's symbolic character.

must recognize that there can be *no* hope of capturing the living reality of popular sovereignty during periods of normal politics. Rather than trying for phony realism by supposing that Congress (or any other institution) *is* the People, the Federalist Constitution's first objective is to paint a picture of government which vigorously asserts that Congress is merely a "representation" of the People, not the People themselves.

The brilliant, but paradoxical, way that Publius makes this point is by proliferating the modes of representation governing normal politics. In Publian hands, the separation of powers operates as a complex machine which encourages each official to question the extent to which other constitutional officials are successfully representing the People's true political wishes. Thus, while each office-holder will predictably insist that *he* speaks with the authentic accents of the People themselves, representatives in other institutions will typically find it in their interest to deny that their rivals have indeed represented the People in a fully satisfactory way.[39] The result of the rhetorical interchange will be precisely the opposite of each partisan's hopes. Rather than allowing the House or Senate or the presidency to beguile us with the claim that it, and it alone, speaks in the name of the People themselves, the constitutional separation of powers deconstructs all such naive synecdoches. As it works itself out in practice, the system emphasizes that no legal form can enable any small group in Washington, D.C. to speak unequivocally for We the People during normal politics. The House and Senate and presidency merely represent the people in a manner of speaking; each is a metaphor that should never be confused with the way the People express their will during those rare periods of successful constitutional politics – when the mass of American citizens mobilizes itself in a collective effort to renew and redefine the public good.

Yet, while Publius begins his constitutional sketch by affirming its character as semiotic representation rather than living reality, he does not end there. So long as normal politicians are revealed as mere

---

[39] This idea is succinctly presented in a famous passage of *The Federalist*, no. 51, 321 (J. Madison); see *ibid.*, no. 60, 366–7 (A. Hamilton). Even more importantly, it motivates the last part of *The Federalist* – beginning with no. 52 – which seeks to show how the different branches of government will check each other's defects, and thereby yield a whole more "representative" than any of its constituent single parts.

"stand-ins" for the People, the Constitution also allows them to "stand-for" the People in a more straightforward way – by making its principal officials responsible, directly or indirectly, to popular election.[40] There is no inclination to deny the fundamental importance of recurring popular elections,[41] only an effort to establish that the pushings-and-shovings of normal politics are not the highest form of political expression.[42] Indeed, *The Federalist* tries to assure us that the new Constitution will encourage the selection of political representatives who, even during normal times, will rise above the parochialism of special interests.[43]

Nonetheless, the very effort to create institutions that will reward statesmanship during normal periods only emphasizes the difficulty of the task, the precariousness of the achievement. In the absence of a mobilized mass of virtuous citizens, there can be no guarantee that the constitutional machine will invariably produce tolerable results: "It is in vain to say that enlightened statesmen will be able to adjust these clashing interests and render them all subservient to the public good. Enlightened statesmen will not always be at the helm."[44]

This sober recognition drives *The Federalist* to a final institutional expedient. Given the danger that normal government will be captured by partisans of narrow special interests, Publius proposes to consolidate the Revolutionary achievements of the American people through the institution of judicial review. When normal representatives respond to special interests in ways that jeopardize the fundamental principles for which the Revolutionaries fought and died, the judge's duty is to expose them for what they are: merely "stand-ins" for the People themselves.

Not that Publius expects the Constitution to remain forever unchanged. To the contrary. *The Federalist* explicitly recognizes "that a constitutional road to the decision of the people ought to be marked out and kept open, for certain great and extraordinary occasions."[45] There will be future crises, new calls by future statesmen to put aside

---

[40] See *ibid.*, no. 39, 241–2 (J. Madison).   [41] See *ibid.*, no. 53, 331–6.

[42] See, e.g. *ibid.*, no. 46, 294–5; no. 48, 308–13; no. 65, 397 (A. Hamilton).

[43] See, e.g., *ibid.*, no. 10, 79–81 (J. Madison); no. 35, 214–17 (A. Hamilton); no. 62, 379–82 (J. Madison); no. 63, 384–9. For a recent elaboration of this theme, see G. Wills, *Explaining America* (New York, 1981), pp. 177–264.

[44] *The Federalist*, no. 10, 80 (J. Madison).   [45] *Ibid.*, no. 49, 314.

the quarrels of factional politics. If all goes well, the People will, in their irregular way, prove equal to the challenge.[46] Rather than trying to immobilize the People, the Supreme Court's task is to prevent the abuse of the People's name in normal politics. The Court's job is to force the People's normal representatives in Washington to engage in the special kind of mass mobilization required for a constitutional amendment if they hope to overrule the earlier achievements of the American Revolution.[47] In the famous words of *Federalist* no. 78, the *democratic* case for judicial review does not

> by any means suppose a superiority of the judicial to the legislative power. It only supposes that the power of the people is superior to both, and that where the will of the legislature, declared in its statutes, stands in opposition to that of the people, declared in the Constitution, the judges ought to be governed by the latter rather than the former.[48]

The problem with a Supreme Court, however, is obvious enough. What prevents it from misusing its constitutional authority to further one or another factional interest rather than to interpret the meaning of the past constitutional achievements of the American People?[49] Indeed, is it even possible to suppose any longer, as *The Federalist* plainly does, that something called judicial interpretation is an intellectually respectable activity?

My aim is not to answer these great questions here – if only because I do not think they *can* be answered satisfactorily until constitutional lawyers learn to recover the larger conception of constitutional government within which they are embedded. Rather than dismissing *Federalist* no. 78 as, in Alexander Bickel's words, "nonrepresentational,"[50] the challenge is to see how the concept of representation itself gives the text renewed meaning. This effort has permitted us to locate judicial review as part of a larger theme that distinguishes the

---

[46] *Ibid.*, no. 49, 314–17.   [47] *Ibid.*, no. 78, 469–70 (A. Hamilton).

[48] *Ibid.*, no. 78, 467–8.

[49] Publius himself plainly believes that the courts are "the least dangerous branch," (*ibid.*, no. 78, 465), and that the greater danger is judicial subservience to factions that have managed to gain a momentary ascendancy in the other branches (471).

[50] Bickel, *The Least Dangerous Branch*, p. 16.

American Constitution from other, less durable, frameworks for liberal democracy. In response to the perception that public-regarding virtue is in short supply, *The Federalist* proposes a democratic constitution *that tries to economize on virtue*.[51] The first great economy is purchased, of course, by the distinction between constitutional and normal politics. The second is gained by a scheme of constitutional separation of powers that normally gives elected officials powerful incentives to question the success with which rival "representatives" have embodied the political will of We the People of the United States. The third economy is obtained by designing an institution of judicial review that gives judges special incentives to uphold the integrity of earlier constitutional solutions against the pulling and hauling of normal politics.

In proposing a constitutional economy of virtue, however, Publius does not take a simple Hobbesian view of the human condition. To the contrary, the entire machine presupposes a dualistic psychology: "The supposition of universal venality in human nature is little less an error in political reasoning than the supposition of universal rectitude. The institution of delegated power implies that there is a portion of virtue and honor among mankind, which may be a reasonable foundation of confidence."[52]

The task is to create a structure of government that, in both normal and extraordinary times, will permit us to make the most of what virtue we have.[53] What more could constitutional law, or

---

[51] "The aim of every political constitution is, or ought to be, first to obtain for rulers men who possess most wisdom to discern, and most virtue to pursue, the common good of the society; and in the next place, to take the most effectual precautions for keeping them virtuous whilst they continue to hold their public trust" (*The Federalist*, no. 57, 350 [J. Madison]). The entire *Federalist* no. 57 is, of course, the most eloquent and profound statement of this theme.

[52] *Ibid.*, no. 76, 458 (A. Hamilton).

[53] This is the root of my objection to the most influential modern interpretation of *The Federalist*, to be found in Dahl, *Preface to Democratic Theory*, pp. 4–32. Dahl reads Publius as if he were seeking to solve the problem posed in B. Mandeville, *Fable of the Bees* (ed. F. Kaye, London, 1924), and design a system of government that could produce tolerable results without *any* appeal to the political virtue of its citizens. Unsurprisingly, Dahl finds Publius unequal to this challenge. His essay brilliantly examines each of the weak links in the Federalist argument when viewed as an effort to build a republic-without-virtue. Since Dahl's argument deserves serious consideration, I shall defer a detailed examination to another time. For now, though, it will suffice to say that I reject Dahl's guiding interpretive premise: *The Federalist* is not a failed solution to *The Fable of the Bees*, but a profound effort to solve a different problem.

constitutional lawyers, promise We the People of the United States?

III We the People?

A From successful revolutionary to private citizen

Thus far I have presented Publius as the epitome of the successful revolutionary – whose immersion in politics is rewarded not by a lifetime of failed hopes, but by a continuing exchange with the People that culminates in the collective affirmation of principles of national identity. For such a one as this, the good life *is* the political life; the paradigm of virtue is somebody, like George Washington, who gains his greatest fulfillment in sacrificing private interest for public good. And yet, despite this profoundly gratifying starting-point, Publius transcends his historical situation to glimpse another possibility: a world of private virtues inhabited by men and women who gain their deepest satisfactions in activities far removed from the public forum. Needless to say, Publius views this possibility with something less than complete enthusiasm. From his vantage-point, these private people spell public trouble – factional indifference to the public good. But it is a mark of Publius' greatness that he does not try to suppress forms of life he finds distasteful, but uses constitutional law to reach an accommodation with civic privatism in the name of human freedom. It is this act of self-transcendence that makes the Publian conception of dualist democracy relevant to people living in vastly different historical circumstances.

Notably ourselves. Putting aside all the obvious social and economic differences that separate us from Publius, the hard fact is that we do not live in the triumphant afterglow of the most successful revolution of all time. When we say virtue, we do not immediately think of George Washington or his living equivalent (and who might that be?). I do not wish to deny, of course, that we have had our political successes – and failures. My point, rather, is that the political domain, as such, does not at present dominate our moral consciousness. For the contemporary American, the life of political commitment is only one of many paths to value. Virtue and vice – meaning and meaninglessness – may be found in a bewildering variety of lives. So far as we are concerned, somebody who manages to preserve his integrity and make his mark in politics is, doubtless, a person who merits great praise – but any more so than the person who contributes to art, science or the less exalted business of decency, love and thoughtfulness?

In a sense, the ease with which we raise this question only makes the Publian economy of virtue more relevant to our political situation. If politics is not the preeminent path to virtue, it is all the more important for the Constitution to make the most of what little public virtue we can expect. Yet, on a more superficial level, the very fact that Publius takes public-regarding virtue *so* seriously is a stumbling-block for those moderns whose moral consciousness assigns it a more peripheral place. The principles of dualist democracy will be far more accessible if we show how they make sense within our own problematic of virtue.

This exercise in neo-Federalism, then, starts from a point very different from the one from which Publius began. Rather than the successful revolutionary trying to find a place for private life, I shall look at the Constitution from the vantage-point of the private citizen trying to locate the rightful demands of public life. In shifting interpretive field, I do not mean to suggest that Publius' vision is somehow obsolete. My aim is to show that, even if one changes starting-points dramatically, he can reason his way to the same dualistic conclusions that constitute the Publian heritage.

B The dilemmas of private citizenship

In taking the part of the private citizen, I hope to avoid easy caricature. The democratic dilemmas I shall elaborate do not arise in a cartoon world inhabited by privatistic zombies in search of the latest cheap thrill. Indeed, the best way to begin is by distinguishing the private citizen from someone I shall call the perfect privatist. The defining mark of the latter is his utter incapacity to take seriously the Publian effort to define a public policy that best fulfills the "rights of citizens and the permanent interest of the community."[54] Thus, when

---

[54] Cf. *The Federalist*, no. 10, 78 (J. Madison) (defining faction, discussed in n. 21 above).

confronting the question, "What is good for the country?," the perfect privatist acts as if this inquiry can be reduced to the question, "What is good for me?" While there are many Americans who take this strongly reductionist approach to political life, I will not try here to persuade them to abandon perfect privatism's manifold seductions. Instead, I propose to elaborate an alternative stance toward public life which remains accessible to most Americans. For most of us, our natural involvement with our personal destinies does not preclude self-identification as private citizens, capable of responding in a distinctive voice on questions involving the political community. Thus, in defending the views I announce as a private citizen, I cannot observe that a proposal will be to my personal advantage and leave the matter at that. When challenged, I must at least say that I have done more than consider my self-interest. Otherwise, I lose my standing as a private citizen and appear to my fellows as a selfish person bent solely on egoistic self-aggrandizement.

And yet, while most Americans answer to the name of private citizen, they have learned not to take their protestations of civic virtue *too* seriously. Indeed, even gaining a rudimentary empirical understanding of a national problem often requires a lot of work. While we may occasionally make this effort, a continuing commitment to informed citizenship may unduly deflect our energies from the innumerable struggles of everyday life. Beyond the problem of information, moreover, tower the moral dilemmas of American citizenship. A sober consideration of the national interest may well lead one to conclude that local interests must be sacrificed to the general good. Yet this message will be met with bewilderment, or worse, by friends and neighbors who fail to look beyond their parochial interests. It is little wonder, then, that few of us voluntarily shoulder the full burden of Publius.

However understandable his limited engagement in public life, the thoughtful private citizen must recognize that it generates three interrelated problems for a democratic polity. The first is apathy. The existence of many *private* citizens may demoralize those who otherwise would be attracted to invest greater energy in private *citizenship*: if so many others give only a passing concern to national politics, isn't it silly of me to maintain the struggle? The second problem is ignorance. Given their limited engagement, most people will not be in a position to make a considered judgment on most – sometimes all – of the issues that seem so important to the few who follow the pulling and hauling in Washington D.C. And finally there is the problem of selfishness. Without undertaking a serious examination of "the rights of citizens and the permanent interests of the community," isn't it all too likely that one's first political impressions will give too much weight to narrowly selfish interests?

C Coercive democracy

Apathy, ignorance, selfishness – without belittling these misfortunes, consider the disaster that would follow upon a serious effort at their eradication. Call the cure *coercive democracy*. If most people don't take national politics seriously, simply force them to pay attention. Every day or so, each adult citizen should be compelled to spend an hour or two discussing the issues of the day. Over time, this continuing confrontation with the issues will induce citizens to form considered political judgments. And if the discussions reveal that the masses are caught up in the protection of their petty local interests, doubtless we can train specially conscientious Public Citizens who will lead their fellows to a genuinely national and public-regarding view of the nation's problems.

It is easy, of course, to find this chilling vision of coercive democracy entirely unacceptable. Today's private citizen joins Publius in condemning coercive democracy as "a remedy ... worse than the disease."[55] Doubtless there are times when a liberal democracy may rightly call upon its private citizens to die in the defense of their country.[56] The demands imposed in times of crisis are not to be confused, however, with the normal place that citizenship occupies in the ordinary American's self-understanding. Generally speaking, it is up to each American to decide how much time and energy he will devote to private *citizenship*, how much to *private* citizenship. If this means that liberal politics will often suffer from apathy, ignorance and selfishness, we will all have to learn to grin and bear it.

[55] *Ibid.*, no. 10, 78.
[56] Doubtless, too, there are occasions upon which citizens, when faced with this demand, may conscientiously refuse to comply in the name of some ideal that is higher than democratic citizenship. My own views on this matter may be found in Ackerman, *Social Justice in the Liberal State*, pp. 293–301.

D Levelling democracy

While few ordinary Americans question these harsh political truths, American lawyers fail to struggle with them as they puzzle out the meaning of constitutional government in a liberal democracy. Instead, modern constitutional wisdom begins from a very different starting-point – one derived from the Progressive, as opposed to the Federalist, tradition. Instead of distinguishing between the constitutional conclusions reached by a mobilized citizenry and the ordinary outcomes of normal politics, the modern lawyer implicitly uses a model of the democratic process that precludes the self-conscious recognition of the ebb and flow of political involvement. This levelling approach to the Constitution sweeps aside the dualist's persistent anxiety about the problematic way in which normal democratic government "represents" the People during normal times. Instead, the leveller advances a single-track conception of law-making that drives the dualist's preoccupation with mass apathy, ignorance and selfishness to the periphery of constitutional thought. In this single-track view, there is only one place in which the political will of the American people is to be found: the Congress of the United States. If the Congress enacts a law, the People have spoken; if not, not. It's that simple, and no talk about the problematics of representation should be allowed to obscure this fundamental reality.

Not that levellers necessarily insist upon an utterly simplistic view of single-track law-making. They may, for example, remark upon the ease with which incumbent politicians can place their competitors at an unfair electoral disadvantage. Indeed, an elaborate concern with this problem can even reinforce the levelling ideal. It is almost as if the entire point of fair electoral ritual is to preclude any inquiry into the depth and breadth of the popular participation that lies behind a particular ballot count. If, in a formally free and fair contest, every voter chooses between the candidates on the basis of the winsomeness of their respective smiles, the leveller would treat this result no differently from another election in which every voter chose between the candidates on the basis of their position on black slavery. In each case all the leveller knows – and all he needs to know – is that by a vote of fifty-one to forty-nine, the People chose Candidate A over Candidate B; it is therefore Representative A who is *fully* empowered to rule in the name of the People until the next election.

This emphatic conclusion may be rendered rhetorically plausible by two diametrically opposed characterizations of the American electorate. On the one hand, the leveller may mythologize the citizenry, and treat each and every voter at each and every election as if he were Publius, preeminently concerned with the "rights of citizens and the permanent interests of the community." On the other hand, the levellers may adopt the stance of the hard-boiled realist and treat every voter as always out for himself.[57] The leveller may even flip back and forth between these very different images of the American voter. The critical point, however, is not the particular picture of the voter used by each leveller. Rather, it is the leveller's failure to discriminate between those rare occasions on which many people are investing heavily in their role as citizens and those frequent occasions of diminished political attention and concern. Thus the leveller's treatment of the voter as citizen parallels his treatment of Congress as law-maker. In neither case does the levelling constitutionalist provide a vocabulary that allows the private citizen or the politician/statesman to signal that he is taking his public-regarding responsibilities with special seriousness.[58]

Despite the reductionist character of the levelling approach, however, I do not wish to deny that it *does* offer a solution to the problem of civic privatism that is vastly superior to that of coercive democracy. Indeed, I shall be using the levelling conception of single-track democracy as a conceptual baseline in my efforts to assess the dualist alternative. Thus, I shall first emphasize the very important contributions that levelling makes to the theory of liberal democracy, and only then consider whether the dualist can do even better.

1 The leveller's contribution to liberal democracy Begin, then, with the symbolic and substantive contributions levelling makes to the

---

[57] While the classical work in levelling political philosophy takes a hard-boiled view of modern citizenship (see J. Schumpeter, *Capitalism, Socialism and Democracy* [London, 1942], pp. 250–83), the levelling tradition in American constitutional law sometimes adopts loftier, more Publian characterizations. This is the general tendency, for example, in J. Ely, *Democracy and Distrust* (Cambridge, Mass., 1980), discussed on pp. 189–90 below.

[58] For a recent essay that emphasizes this tendency for a more empirical point of view, see A. Hirschman, *Shifting Involvements* (Princeton, 1982).

liberal democrat's concern with the right of citizens to pursue a private life far removed from politics. On the side of symbol, the leveller assures each of us that our standing as full-fledged citizens is secure so long as we are willing to spend a few minutes at the polls once in a while. Even if we cast our ballots in ignorant or selfish ways, our votes are counted as if they were the product of the most conscientious examination of the nature of the common good. So far as the fundamental ritual of a mass democracy is concerned, the private citizen is allowed to reaffirm his citizenship without the need to ask himself any embarrassing questions about the quality of his commitments.

And then there is the matter of substance. The leveller *has* managed to avoid the transparent dangers involved in forcing people to be good citizens. Nobody is obliged to spend time tediously discussing the fate of the republic when he would rather be doing something else. Nobody is given the dangerous job of leading exercises in coercive consciousness-raising. While avoiding coercive democracy may seem too modest a goal for some, the liberal finds it an achievement of fundamental importance.

Now turn the coin to consider the liberal *democratic* arguments in favor of levelling. Beginning this time with substance, the levelling system makes it hard for a political clique to monopolize political control. While "ins" may beat "outs" in one, two or three elections in a row, a democratic electorate remains a notoriously fickle beast. In time, the ballot-box will yield a victory to the outs – if only because the opposing candidates have managed to convince the voters of the superior brilliance of their smiles or the greater profundity of their advertising copy. The most trivial levelling election, then, does serve important – indeed fundamental – functions. Even if elites are destabilized by almost-random electoral shocks, the system of levelling democracy does give reality to the notion of popular rule, and makes it harder for a closed circle to govern forever.

Levelling also promises the liberal *democrat* symbolic rewards. Rather than emphasizing the problematic character of the citizenry's engagement, the leveller can view each election day as yet another unambiguous triumph for the democratic ideal. Behold: millions upon millions of citizens have once again played their appointed part in the ritual of democracy. After all, nobody forced them to turn off their T.V. sets for the time it takes to go to the polls!

I do not wish to deny the important truth attached to the leveller's democratic symbolism. It *is* significant that so many of us have come together at the polls to show that we have not forgotten that we *can* speak as We the People of the United States.

2 Levelling and its inadequacies   Yet, for all its advantages, there is a darker side to the liberal democratic compromise that is levelling democracy. Begin, once again, with the liberal side of the story. True, the leveller does guarantee each private person his standing as a citizen even though he lives his life with only a passing glance at politics. Nonetheless, levelling democracy can be a very risky business. While most of us are focusing our concerns upon other matters, some of our fellow Americans work full time at the business of government. And they may well use their heavy political investments to maximize their advantage at our expense. By the time private citizens wake up to the threat to their fundamental interests, it may be too late for effective political action. The full-time politicos may have entrenched themselves on the commanding heights – all the while exercising the full legislative authority of the People, as is their right in a single-track democracy. At this point, it may be impossible for political mobilization to undo the consequences of earlier neglect. Moreover, even if countermobilization proves successful, the effort required will divert the *private* citizen from his most precious goals. By definition, these aims are not to be achieved in the public forum and will not be nourished by an all-consuming commitment to citizenship. In short, what the private citizen finds wanting in levelling democracy is adequate insurance against a political landslide engineered by well-organized special-interest groups speaking with the full authority of the People.

Although his diagnosis is very different, the liberal *democrat* can sympathize with his twin's dissatisfaction. However grateful he is for the leveller's real contributions to the symbol and substance of popular rule, there is more to democracy than the leveller will allow. Sometimes the private citizenry *is* trying to do more than simply express its displeasure with the ins by replacing them with the outs. Sometimes it is trying to work out a *considered judgment* on a matter of principle – a judgment reached only after years of popular mobilization and far-reaching debate. It is just this affirmative conception of democracy that transcends the limits of levelling theory. For, by definition, the leveller treats all acts of political participation as if they were accompanied by the same degree of civic seriousness. As a consequence, he cannot mark those rare occasions on which the American people do more than replace one set of ins with another and instead announce a fundamental change in the constitutive principles of the republic.

The problem, perhaps unsolvable, is this: can we design a regime which retains the very substantial achievements of levelling but which somehow ameliorates its liberal democratic disadvantages?

E The promise of dualist democracy

This is the promise of the dualist constitution. For the present, I want to defer all the vital detail required to make two-track law-making a credible constitutional reality. My aim here is to show how a dualist constitution – if it could be made to work in a legally credible fashion – would be superior to the levelling form of single-track democracy. And for this purpose, the simple concept of two-track law-making will suffice.

Begin, then, with the two-track system's promise to provide the *liberal* democrat with some political insurance for the millions of people who have better things to do than follow the goings-on in Washington, D.C. Most of the daily political action will predictably take place on the lower law-making track. And, by definition, nothing on this track can disturb the fundamental principles previously hammered out on the higher track. Thus, the private citizen is insured against a change in fundamental political principles – at least so long as no new political movement is making great progress in enacting its new principles into higher law.

At the same time, the dualist promises to satisfy the liberal *democrat* by institutionalizing the very distinction that is obliterated by the leveller's impoverished constitutional vocabulary. As in a levelling constitution, the democrat may continue to find meaning in the fact that Americans regularly go to the polls and sometimes replace one set of leaders with another. Yet he may find deeper meaning on those rarer occasions when the American people do even more – when, after sustained debate and struggle, they hammer out new principles to guide public life. For it is the very purpose of the higher law-making track to mark these occasions as possessing special and abiding significance in the life of the political community.

The existence of a higher law-making track, in short, has a liberal democratic value both on those rare occasions when a new mass movement succeeds in enacting new constitutional principles *and* during those frequent periods when no profound constitutional transformation is being seriously considered. When the higher track is empty, the liberal obtains insurance; when it is crowded, the democrat has a means of amplifying the voice of the People in a way that will arrest attention for a long time to come.

Despite its distinctive achievements, however, I do not pretend that dualism will magically dissolve all the difficulties that may be raised against it. Quite obviously, it will not satisfy the perfect privatist who demands an absolute right to ignore politics whenever he finds something better to do. Similarly, it will not satisfy the strong democrat who wants to have the People resolve all important questions all the time. More significantly, dualism does not even promise perfect satisfaction to the thoughtful private citizen. On the contrary, once a new political movement begins successfully to negotiate the obstacle course established on the higher law-making track, each of us will be faced with a hard choice. Either we may continue as relatively passive participants and run the risk of grave political defeat, or we may increase the level of our public involvement and sacrifice our more personal interests. Rather than deprecating the difficulty of this choice, the dualist merely seeks to create a system in which each of us can make our decision in a self-conscious and deliberate way.

F What does the Constitution constitute?

Until now, I have emphasized the extent to which a dualistic law-making system may reconcile competing aspects of the liberal democratic ideal. There is, however, a second way of approaching dualism's promise. Here, we move from the grand abstractions of political theory to the more particular difficulties that people encounter in the effort to communicate the ebb and flow of their citizenship involvements. To grasp the problem, put yourself in the typical position of the *private* citizen. So far as you are concerned, the victory of one or another political party in the next election will not typically transform the shape of your world. In contrast, your world *will* be shattered if your wife leaves you or your job loses its attraction, or you embarrass yourself before your friends in some shameful way. These are the things the private citizen normally takes with high seriousness; politics is a sideline, competing for his attention with countless other activities.

And yet you know that this sideline is different from others. Indeed, the ordinary irresponsibilities of normal politics sometimes begin to offend in a special way. Don't our so-called representatives recognize that there is something serious going on? Can't they see that business as usual won't suffice any longer?

Even as the private citizen says this, however, he must recognize a difficulty in rendering his heightened concern credible to his fellow Americans. For even now, he is not willing to sacrifice everything that makes his private life worthwhile in order to give his all for the republic. More abstractly, while the private citizen is categorically distinct from the perfect privatist, he is no less distinct from someone I shall call the perfectly public citizen, who insists upon the single-minded pursuit of the public good no-matter-what-the-private-sacrifice. This means that the private citizen confronts a special problem in engaging in political communication: how can he signify his concerns as a private *citizen* without undertaking the all-consuming commitment characteristic of a perfectly public citizen?

It is here that the American system of two-track democracy makes its signal contribution. The manner in which it does so, however, is rather complex. Call it the strategy of differential sacrifice. To see how it works, consider that a political movement takes to the higher law-making track only at a high cost. For in fixing its sights upon a higher law-making victory, it diverts energy from the lower law-making track, passing up the chance for cheaper victories that may further the more immediate interests of its followers. While this fact discourages most political groups from ever taking seriously to the higher track, it also gives those who do make the sacrifice a new way to signal their heightened civic concern – without, however, requiring them utterly to abandon their private lives. By allowing the movement ostentatiously to sacrifice lower law-making opportunities for the chance at higher law-making victory, a political movement can represent the concerns of a mass of private *citizens* with a credibility that cheap talk of virtue can never bring. The sacrifice implicit in higher law-making gives private citizens a credible way of saying to one another: "*This* time, we really mean it!"[59]

To forestall predictable misunderstanding, I am not suggesting that when a political movement actually succeeds in clearing all obstacles on the higher law-making track, a glimpse inside the innermost psychic recesses of the movement's partisans would reveal hearts entirely purged of self-interest and minds fully focused upon the "rights of citizens and the permanent interests of the community." Indeed, if it *were* possible for us to experience – and reveal to others – a pristine purity of motive, we could dispense not only with the strategy of differential sacrifice but also with the dualist constitution itself. Instead of the complex legal rituals of higher law-making, we might simply display the purity of our motives and get on with the public business at hand. It is precisely because we are psychologically complex creatures, however, that such "sincere" protestations of simon-purity seem naive ways of establishing our claims to private *citizenship*. The strategy of differential sacrifice, in contrast, provides a credible way in which psychologically complex private citizens can mark out those occasions when they mean to invest a certain aspect of their personality with heightened significance.

The symbolic uses of differential sacrifice may be illuminated by a glance at the way it works in more intimate spheres of life. Imagine, for example, that we lived in a place where the legal institution of marriage was unknown. In such a world, couples would still agonize over their decision to live together, and devise countless subtle mechanisms to signal to one another the special meanings they attach to their relationship. Yet this continuing effort at communication would be immeasurably enhanced by the legal form of marriage – through which parties self-consciously expose themselves to heavy

---

[59] Indeed, sometimes the added credibility gained by higher law-making may actually put the movement in a stronger position in the *lower* law-making system than it would have occupied had it concentrated exclusively upon lower-track law-making. This result is not inconsistent with the argument in the text; all that it suggests is that the credibility purchased by a group's willingness to bear the differential costs of higher law-making may sometimes prove an exceedingly valuable political investment – so valuable that its pay-off in lower law-making efficacy offsets the costs in time and money previously diverted to the higher law-making track.

costs if they later act inconsistently with their protestations of love and affection. The point of such a costly ceremony is not primarily to serve as a snapshot of the love and hate that attract and repel the parties to the continuing relationship; rather, it is to provide a symbolic system through which psychologically complex people can give a special meaning to a form of interaction and thereby *constitute* it as a special kind of community, distinct from the ordinary relations of everyday personal existence.

Constitutional dualism provides a similar symbolic system in the public realm. By providing a higher law-making system, the American Constitution succeeds in constituting something more than a government in Washington, D.C. It constitutes a system of political meanings that enable all Americans to indicate the rare occasions when they mean to present themselves to one another as private *citizens*, and mark them off from the countless ordinary occasions when they are content to understand themselves as merely *private* citizens – for whom political life is but one of many diversions in their continuing pursuit of happiness.[60]

Not that every effort at establishing our claim to private *citizenship* is fated to meet with Publian success. Instead, we must expect that most of our fellow citizens will look upon most political efforts at

[60] This formulation extends the original Publian insight into the semiotic character of representation (see pp. 167–71 above) to the one subject which somehow escaped Publius' attention – the representative pretensions of Publius himself. However much he insisted upon the merely representative character of normal politicians, Publius claimed a very different kind of status for the Federalist effort to represent We the People. So far as Publius is concerned, the Federalists were not mere representatives. They were the real thing: *the People themselves* (to recall Madison's italics).

And yet we cannot allow Publius to exempt himself from his own insight into the semiotic character of representation. Indeed, if we do so, we shall only succeed in providing grist for the neo-Beardian debunkers who aim to destroy the Publian tradition. For if the Framers are viewed as representing what was "really" going on in America in the 1780s, it is child's play to develop other snapshots that will place their depiction of We the People in a very different light. Not only will countless historians enumerate the countless patriotic folk who rejected the Federalist program, but in our privatistic age we would be downright disappointed if some psychoanalyst could not elaborate the darker impulses that "really" accounted for Madison's decision to take on the pseudonym Publius. It is only when we understand the Federalist exercise in higher law-making as a contribution to a semiotic, rather than a mimetic, system of representation that we may grasp its enduring significance. Rather than providing a snapshot of any reality beyond itself, higher law-making provides Americans with a vastly enriched vocabulary through which they can express the necessarily complex character of their relationship to the ebb and flow of political life in a liberal democracy.

national renewal with the apathy, ignorance and selfishness characteristic of normal life in a liberal democracy. And yet, from time to time,
some would-be Publians begin to strike a resonant chord; their strong
appeals to the public good are no longer treated as if they were the
ravings of fringe elements in American society. Instead of encounter-
ing ignorance or contempt, the new movement is taken seriously by
more and more Americans – even when they find its message deeply
repugnant. In turn, the movement's success in penetrating political
consciousness provokes a general effort to assess its ultimate significance: is it a passing fad or something of genuine public significance? Slowly the half-remembered rituals of higher law-making
begin to take on a deeper meaning, for it is through these rituals that
we may test the seriousness of our fellow Americans' effort at national
renewal and redefinition. Needless to say, most movements will fail to
generate the kind of widespread support for their Publian pretensions
that is required before they can constitutionally speak, once more, in
the special accents of We the People of the United States. But that, in a
sense, is just the point. If it *were* cheap and easy for higher law-making
to succeed, we would be debasing the remarkable collective achievement involved when millions of Americans do manage, despite the
countless diversions of liberal democratic society, to engage in an act
of self-government with a seriousness that compares to the most
outstanding constitutional achievements of the past.

G The intertemporal difficulty

It is within this context that I mean to locate the democratic function
of the Supreme Court. Begin with the levelling opinion that indicts the
Supreme Court as a "deviant institution of American democracy,"
doomed forever to bear the stigma of the "countermajoritarian
difficulty."[61] To put this familiar charge in dualistic perspective,
consider the obvious sense in which it is false. When the Court invokes
the Constitution, it appeals to legal enactments that *were* approved by
a whole series of majorities – namely, the majorities of those representative bodies that proposed and ratified the original Constitution
and its subsequent amendments. Rather than a countermajoritarian
difficulty, the familiar platitude identifies an intertemporal difficulty.

[61] See Bickel, *The Least Dangerous Branch*, pp. 16–17.

As befits a platitude, the truth on which the intertemporal difficulty stands is both simple and basic: courts are generally expected to follow the last word enacted into law. Judicial review, however, requires the Supreme Court to reverse this rule and insist upon its reading of the Constitution despite contrary instructions by later, popularly elected representatives. It is this reversal of the ordinary temporal priority that lies at the core of the charge of "deviance."

And surely the problem is a real one. Indeed, if taken with the usual *ceteris paribus* clause, the intertemporal difficulty is irrefutable. Call this the *principle of the last word*: other things being equal, it *would* be antidemocratic for the courts to reject a later decision of a representative government simply because it was inconsistent with an earlier one. The People must reserve the right to change their minds – otherwise we have ancestor worship, not democracy.

But are other things always equal? It is this, of course, that the dualist emphatically denies.[62] In his view, the American Constitution is one great effort to distinguish between those rare acts of representative government backed by the considered judgments of the mass of mobilized citizens and the countless actions based on something less than this. By contrast, the conventional wisdom takes a very different view of the intertemporal difficulty – one that is consistent with the levelling, or single-track, conception of democracy elaborated earlier. In contrast to the dualist's picture of constitutional peaks and statutory valleys, the leveller levels constitutional history to a single plane of legal significance. So long as legislators gain their seats through a process of fair and free democratic election, the leveller refuses to consider the quality of citizen involvement that supports a particular enactment. On this view, political decisions reached by one democratically elected assembly can never have greater legitimacy than those reached by another. It is, moreover, precisely this levelling premise that is required before the intertemporal difficulty may be translated into the countermajoritarian difficulty by a straightforward, four-step argument:

(1)   *Ceteris paribus*, courts should follow the last word enacted into

---

[62] Indeed, I understand the last three paragraphs to restate the point initially made by *The Federalist*, no. 78, 468–70 (A. Hamilton).

law by a popularly elected assembly. This is the principle of the last word.

(2) But, under the levelling principle, political solutions reached by a democratically elected assembly can never have greater legitimacy at one time rather than another.

(3) Therefore *ceteris* must be *paribus*, and a democratic court should always follow the last legally enacted word on the subject.

(4) Since judicial review violates this rule, it is presumptively antidemocratic.

Though it is rarely made entirely explicit, this bare-bones argument plainly motivates much of the most distinguished contemporary writing on the Constitution. To take an especially fine example, two features of John Ely's book *Democracy and Distrust* serve to mark it out as an archetypal product of the levelling approach.[63] The first is Ely's determined effort to trivialize the substantive principles that have, as a result of past generations' successful efforts in higher law-making, gained the status of constitutional principle. Indeed, so far as Ely is concerned, the history of our Constitution reveals that the very effort to guarantee substantive rights through higher law-making is a misconceived adventure.[64]

This first conclusion prepares the way for a second. For Ely does not propose to respond to his impoverished conception of higher law-making by abolishing judicial review. Instead, he seeks to give the Court a new mission by directing its attention to the machinery of lower-track law-making. In his view, private citizens can legitimately expect the courts to protect only those constitutional rights which keep our regularly elected representatives electorally accountable and suitably broad-minded in the exercise of their lower-track functions.[65]

No less remarkable than these conclusions is Ely's effort to present them as the most mature product of an "ultimate interpretivism" based upon the constitutional text itself.[66] After all, Ely asks, doesn't our Constitution devote far more of its language to matters of process than it does to matters of substance? Doesn't this textual concern with

---

[63] (Cambridge, Mass., 1980).   [64] Ely, *Democracy and Distrust*, p. 99.
[65] *Ibid.*, pp. 73–104, 135–80.   [66] *Ibid.*, p. 88.

process gain its fulfillment in Ely's image of a Supreme Court bent upon assuring the democratic legitimacy of an electorally responsive and broad-minded Congress?

It is here where the dualist must raise the cry of *non sequitur*. Granted, the Constitution speaks elaborately about democratic process. But the very complexity of the text belies Ely's interpretation of its overriding intent. Rather than reinforcing the democratic pretensions of our normal politicians in the manner of Ely, the Constitution makes their claim to speak for the People problematic – setting House against Senate and president against both, and staggering terms of office to make it extremely difficult for a single group of politicians to dominate all law-making organs on the basis of a single election. Rather than trying to make sense of all this textual and institutional complexity, Ely "reads" our Constitution as if the elaborate law-making relationships created by Articles I, II, IV and V somehow established a stripped-down version of British parliamentary government – in which plenary law-making authority was vested in a single House of Commons that renewed its electoral mandate periodically in a free and fair democratic contest.

Constitutional lawyers, however, can no longer allow Anglophile sentiments, inherited from the Progressive era, to blind them to the distinctive dualistic logic of their own democratic system.[67] While we may devoutly hope for the day when the Congress of the United States is dominated by men and women with the democratic values and broad vision of John Ely, we may never forget that the American Constitution, unlike that of the British, does not repose final law-making authority in any small group of representatives sitting regularly in the nation's capital. Nor, as *Federalist* no. 10 warns us, is it premised on the expectation that "enlightened statesmen will ... always be at the helm."[68] Only if our representatives move beyond normal politics and sustain a broad popular movement on behalf of their principles on the higher law-making track does our Constitution

---

[67] For some further reflections on the British model, see Ackerman and Charney, "Canada at the constitutional crossroads," 34 *U. Toronto L.J.* (1984), 117.

[68] *The Federalist*, no. 10, 80 (J. Madison).

allow them to make law with the full authority of We the People of the United States.[69]

H A dualist defense of judicial review

Rather than fixating upon the mechanics of single-track democracy, American lawyers must learn to take a less threatened view of the past higher law-making achievements of the American people. Quite simply, we are hardly the first generation of Americans to confront the ignorance, apathy and selfishness of normal politics, or the first to hope for a system of government that will represent the People despite the problematic character of their political involvement. Once we reflect upon the difficulties of this project, moreover, the fact that our predecessors are dead may come to seem less important than the fact that, on occasion, they did succeed in solving the very same problem we confront today in establishing a credible form of public-regarding discourse.

Of course, even the statesmen who created our Constitution or wrote its Civil War Amendments hardly convinced *all* their fellow Americans of the Publian character of their concern with the "rights of citizens and the permanent interests of the community." Universal consensus is not to be found this side of Final Judgment. The most a flesh-and-blood political movement can hope is that years of higher law-making activity finally generate a grudging, often bitter, recognition that it *has* earned the right to present itself as representative of a majority of private *citizens* on a few matters of basic principle, and that We the People have therefore spoken in a particularly authoritative way. It is upon these rare achievements of democratic politics that the dualist proposes to rest the democratic case for judicial review. Before our present politicians can convincingly establish that they are doing more than representing the judgments of perfect privatists or thoughtlessly *private* citizens, should we not test their claims against the paradigmatic higher law-making successes of the past?

When the Court tests some recent Congressional initiative against its interpretation of past constitutional solutions, it is not engaged in

[69] Not that Ely's concerns with the democratic fairness of normal politics have no place in our constitutional law. Indeed, I think that some of Ely's own principles will survive dualistic reinterpretation. My point is that only Ely's fixation upon a levelling conception of American democracy allows him to imagine that perfecting the democratic legitimacy of normal politics could possibly serve as the alpha and omega of constitutional law.

an antidemocratic form of ancestor-worship. By declaring a statute unconstitutional, the Court is discharging a critical dualistic function. It is signaling to the mass of private citizens of the United States that something special is happening in the halls of power; that their would-be representatives are attempting to legislate in ways that few political movements in American history have done with credibility; and that the moment has come, once again, to determine whether our generation will respond by making the political effort required to redefine, as private *citizens*, our collective identity. In short, the Court's backward-looking exercise in judicial review is an essential part of a vital present-oriented project by which the mass of today's private citizenry can modulate the democratic authority they accord to the elected representatives who speak in their name from the heights of power in Washington, D.C.

It is true, of course, that when faced with the Court's challenge, our elected representatives may find themselves unable or unwilling to overcome judicial resistance by successfully taking to the higher law-making track, to speak, once more, in the accents of We the People of the United States. Yet, once we begin to question levelling presuppositions, the mere fact that the People cannot be persuaded to overrule the Court hardly suffices to stigmatize the Court as undemocratic. Instead, the recurrent inability of normal politicians to succeed in higher law-making serves to express the hard Publian truth about the difficulty of mobilizing a majority of private *citizens* in a liberal democracy.

Nor will it do for levellers to respond to this dualist defense of judicial review by trading epithets and denouncing the Court as unduly conservative, if not downright undemocratic. For this easy condemnation ignores the extraordinary consequences that follow when, after years of long and hard struggle, a political movement *does* gain the right to speak in the name of We the People on the higher law-making track. Once a movement has succeeded in enacting a constitutional amendment, it will no longer be obliged to call so extravagantly upon the political energies of the American people. Its legal achievements will remain intact even when the mass of private citizens find, as they inevitably will, that they have better things to do with their time than continue the political struggle at fever pitch. Despite the inexorable return of normal politics, the movement's legal achievements will remain at the center of the consciousness of

America's constitutional lawyers, who should recognize a high responsibility to test the results of normal politics in the name of constitutional principle. From this point of view, the American Constitution is hardly a conservative friend of the status quo, but an implement of revolutionary questioning during the lengthy periods of apathy, ignorance and selfishness that mark the political life of a liberal democracy. By recalling to us the past occasions upon which We the People have managed to work out constitutional principles, the Court both frames the nature of our normal political struggles and allows us to test our own higher law-making ambitions with a discipline and democratic seriousness that the leveller can never understand, much less approximate.

IV Neo-federalism?

Constitutional lawyers do their fellow Americans an injustice, then, when they adopt a levelling attitude to the Supreme Court and ignore the dualist theory of democracy affirmed at the Founding. Rather than treating Publius as if he were an antique irrelevancy from a bygone age, we should recognize the Federalist constitution as offering a distinctive solution to a continuing problem of self-definition – one generated by two, quite distinct, traditions out of which the modern West emerges. The first, recalling the classical republican tradition, insists that the life of political involvement serves as the noblest ideal for humankind. The second, recalling a Christian suspicion of the claims of secular community, insists that the salvation of souls is a private affair, and that the secular state's coercive authority represents the supreme threat to the highest human values. When faced with this continuing struggle for ascendancy in Western thought and practice, the American Constitution does not seek an easy victory of one part of ourselves at the cost of suppressing the other. Instead, it proposes to use the conflict to provide the energy for a creative synthesis.

As Americans, we are neither perfectly public citizens nor perfectly private persons. The Constitution of the United States constitutes us as private citizens equipped with a language and process that may allow for liberal democratic self-government of a remarkably self-conscious kind – which is not to say, of course, that it *will* be used in any such spirit. Dualism's future prospects, however, are best left to another time.

7. Precommitment and the paradox of democracy

STEPHEN HOLMES

Il est absurde que la volonté se donne des chaines pour l'avenir.
Rousseau[1]

Laurence Tribe opens his influential treatise on constitutional law with a concise formulation of the countermajoritarian dilemma – the discord between majoritarian politics and constitutionally anchored restraints: "In its most basic form, the question . . . is why a nation that rests legality on the consent of the governed would choose to constitute its political life in terms of commitments to an original agreement . . . deliberately structured so as to be difficult to change."[2] The underlying problem has been posed in a variety of ways. How can the "consent of the governed" be reconciled with the preempting of subsequent consent by a Constitutional Convention? Why should a constitutional framework, ratified two centuries ago, have such enormous power over our lives today? Why should a minority of our fellow citizens be empowered to prevent amendments to the Constitution? Is judicial review, when based on a superstitious fealty to the intent of the Framers, compatible with popular sovereignty?[3]

I am indebted to Samuel Beer and Judith Shklar for comments on an earlier version of this chapter.

[1] "Du contrat social," *Oeuvres complètes*, edited by Bernard Gagnebin and Marcel Raymond, vol. 3 (Paris, Pléiade, 1964), pp. 368–9.
[2] Laurence Tribe, *American Constitutional Law* (Mineola, Foundation Press, 1978), p. 9.
[3] The Court, it should be noted, may run afoul of electoral majorities both when it worships and when it disdains the intent of the Framers. Thus, the countermajoritarian difficulty is broader than the conflict between strict interpretivism and judicial policy-making. Why should nine appointed judges – whether they follow or ignore the letter of the Constitution – have a right to nullify the decisions of democratically elected officials?

195

The tension between constitutionalism and democracy

These questions have a long history. In the Flag Salute Case of 1943, Justice Robert Jackson issued the following classical pronouncement:

> The very purpose of a Bill of Rights was to withdraw certain subjects from the vicissitudes of political controversy, to place them beyond the reach of majorities and officials and to establish them as legal principles to be applied by the courts. One's right to life, liberty, and property, to free speech, a free press, freedom of worship and assembly, and other fundamental rights may not be submitted to vote: they depend on the outcome of no elections.[4]

Constitutionalism, from this perspective, is essentially antidemocratic. The basic function of a constitution is to *remove* certain decisions from the democratic process, that is, to tie the community's hands.

But how can we justify a system which thwarts the will of the majority? On the one hand, we might – in the spirit of Justice Jackson – invoke fundamental rights: if such rights are somehow "inscribed in nature," they may simply override consent. Alternatively, we could focus on the self-defeating character of constitutionally unlimited democracy. This line of argument is pursued, for example, by F. A. Hayek.[5] A constitution, in his view, is nothing but a device for limiting the power of government.[6] Present-day citizens are myopic; they have little self-control, are sadly undisciplined and are always prone to sacrifice enduring principles to short-run pleasures and benefits. A constitution is the institutionalized cure for this chronic myopia: it disempowers temporary majorities in the name of binding norms. A constitution is Peter sober while the electorate is Peter drunk. Citizens need a constitution, just as Ulysses needed to be bound to his mast. If voters were allowed to get what they wanted, they would inevitably shipwreck themselves. By binding themselves to rigid rules, they can avoid tripping over their own feet.

A different, indeed contrary, perspective is provided by Martin Shapiro. Shapiro's position is subtle and difficult to summarize; but his

---

[4] *West Virginia State Board of Education* v. *Barnette*, 319 U.S. 624, at 638.

[5] Friedrich Hayek, *The Constitution of Liberty* (University of Chicago Press, 1960), pp. 176–92.

[6] This reductionist concept of constitutionalism will be challenged below.

essay on the meaning of the American Constitution concludes with a rhetorically memorable claim. When we examine a democratically enacted statute, he writes, we should not ask, like text-bound lawyers, Is it constitutional? Rather we should ask, like democratic citizens, Do we want it to be constitutional? We should not be enslaved by "certain dead gentlemen who could not possibly have visualized our current circumstances."[7] We should be guided solely by our collective decision about what sort of community we want to become.

Shapiro and Hayek typify the point and counterpoint of a continuing debate. Their disagreement neatly represents the quarrel – if I can put it this way – between democrats who find constitutions a nuisance and constitutionalists who perceive democracy as a threat. Some theorists worry that democracy will be paralyzed by constitutional straitjacketing. Others are apprehensive that the constitutional dyke will be breached by a democratic flood. Despite their differences, both sides agree that there exists a deep, almost irreconcilable tension between constitutionalism and democracy. Indeed, they come close to suggesting that "constitutional democracy" is a marriage of opposites, an oxymoron.

The existence of an irreconcilable "tension" between constitutionalism and democracy is one of the core myths of modern political thought. By calling it into question, I do not intend to deny well-known facts. Rather, by doubting a widely shared assumption, that is, by pursuing the (in some sense obvious) suggestion that constitutionalism and democracy are mutually supportive, I hope to shed light on some neglected dimensions of democratic and constitutional theory.

John Hart Ely, too, has argued that constitutional restraints, far from being systematically antidemocratic, can be democracy-reinforcing.[8] Democratic government, like all human creations, requires periodic repair. Its preconditions must be secured or resecured; and this cannot always be achieved by directly democratic means. The Court is thus constitutionally empowered to be the watchdog of democracy. Elected and accountable representatives must determine what "substantive values" are to guide public policy; but in matters of

[7] Martin Shapiro (ed.), Introduction, *The Constitution of the United States and Related Documents* (New York, Appleton-Century-Crofts, 1968), pp. xxi–xxii.

[8] John Hart Ely, *Democracy and Distrust: A Theory of Judicial Review* (Cambridge, Mass., Harvard University Press, 1980).

fundamental decision-making procedure, the Court bears major cus-
todial responsibility. It must strike down all legislation, no matter how
popular with electoral majorities, that undermines the conditions of a
well-functioning democracy: "unblocking the stoppages in the democratic process is what judicial review ought presumably to be about."[9]
This is a democratic (not merely paternalistic) arrangement. The
overall power of voters is enhanced when the electorate limits the
authority of its own elected officials over basic governmental processes.

Ely ably develops this thesis in the context of current legal controversies. But he provides his striking claim with little abstract
theoretical elaboration and almost no historical background. As a
result, he leaves depressingly untouched the myth of a fundamental
tension between constitutionalism and democracy. For a surprisingly
large number of serious thinkers, constitutional democracy remains a
paradox, if not a contradiction in terms. All working democracies, as
it turns out, operate within boundaries set by stabilizing constraints.
Ely's notion that constitutions can be democracy-reinforcing is therefore manifestly superior to the contrary idea that constitutions and
democracies are fundamentally antagonistic. Nevertheless, the myth
of an underlying "tension" lives on.

Discussion of this issue can be advanced by greater theoretical
abstraction and by a wider casting of the historical net. On the one
hand, the relation between constitutionalism and democracy can be
significantly clarified by an analysis of the way "constraints" in general
can produce or enhance "freedom." On the other hand, the dispute
about the relation between constitutionalism and democracy can be
traced back to the eighteenth century and even earlier. I will begin
with a foray into the history of ideas.

---

[9] *Ibid.*, p. 117. Ely's argument is persuasive in many respects; but, as others have
noted, he falls needlessly into a reductionist or single-purpose theory of judicial review.
The Constitution is not merely a procedural document, silent about all substantive
issues. And the Warren Court was concerned about a variety of values, such as fairness,
independently of its commitment to democracy. Some rights arise from the needs of
representative government; but others do not. The central weakness of his argument,
however, seems to lie elsewhere. Ely is right to object to justices who, wrapping
themselves in the veil of Reason, Natural Law, or the American Way, actually base
their decisions on subjective standards concealed safely beneath obfuscatory language.
But he is wrong to suggest that he has solved this perennial problem. His idea of
"democracy" is far from being a perfectly noncontroversial standard which could
liberate judges from the smudge of subjectivity.

The prohibition against binding the future

In the 1740s, David Hume noted a major contradiction at the heart of republican theory. Republicans universally relied upon the fiction of a social contract. But, wrote Hume, "this supposes the consent of the fathers to bind the children, even to the most remote generations, (which republican writers will never allow)."[10] Despite their concern to create an enduring framework for self-government, in other words, republicans generally insisted that a founding generation could never precommit its successors to a fixed constitutional scheme. In the Putney Debates, for example, one speaker says: "I presume that all the people, and all nations whatsoever, have a liberty and power to alter and change their constitutions if they find them to be weak and infirm."[11] And in the Declaration of Independence, Thomas Jefferson espoused the same principle: "it is the right of the people to alter or abolish" any "form of government" which has become "destructive" to life, liberty and the pursuit of happiness. No institution, however important, is unalterable; no law, however fundamental, is irrepealable.

This widely acknowledged taboo against constitutional precommitment was itself the generalization of a more fundamental prohibition: the principle that no father can bind his sons. Locke succinctly formulated the underlying rule: " 'Tis true, that whatever Engagements or Promises any one has made for himself, he is under the Obligation of them, but *cannot* by any *Compact* whatsoever, bind *his Children* or Posterity."[12] By the eighteenth century, even those attempting to construct an enduring political order drew the logical conclusion from Locke's premises. In Article 28 of the (unimplemented!) Jacobin constitution of 1793, for example, we discover the following incongruous but unambiguous statement: "Une génération ne peut assujettir à ses lois les générations futures."[13] At the end of the eighteenth century, in fact, the interdiction against precommitting

---

[10] David Hume, "Of the original contract," *Essays: Moral, Political, and Literary* (Oxford University Press), 1963, p. 457.
[11] "The Putney Debates" (October 28, 1647), *The Commonwealth of England*, edited by Charles Blitzer (New York, Putnam's Sons, 1963), pp. 72–3.
[12] John Locke, *Two Treatises of Government*, edited by Peter Laslett (New York, Mentor, 1965), book 2, ch. 8, sec. 116, p. 390.
[13] *Les Constitutions de la France depuis 1789*, edited by Jacques Godechot (Paris, Garnier-Flammarion, 1970), p. 82.

future generations boasted numerous theoretical advocates. To convey the flavor of their arguments, I shall focus at some length on the positions advanced by Jefferson and Tom Paine.

Paine and the consent of the living

In 1776, Paine had been the ardent advocate of a "Continental Charter" which he described as a "firm bargain" and "a bond of solemn obligation."[14] But in 1791, without dramatically changing his other views, he mounted a searing attack on the very idea of an inherited constitutional framework. According to Burke, the English parliament of 1688 had legally bound its posterity to the end of time. Paine countered that no such right or power existed: "[e]very age and generation must be as free to act for itself, *in all cases*, as the ages and generations which preceded it."[15] It is not only immoral but impossible to preempt the choices of successor generations. The fetters of the past are ropes of sand. Nevertheless, attempts to bind the future, while ultimately futile, can be quite irritating. They should therefore be denounced for what they are – open violations of natural justice.

In a way, Paine's blustering assault on constitutional precommitment follows logically from his conception of democracy. For him, democracy is the rule of the living.[16] More belligerently, democracy is a war against the past. The old European world of kings, aristocrats and hereditary entitlements is thoroughly rotten. The "fraud, effigy and show"[17] of the ancien régime must be relegated to the junk-heap of history – for history is a junk-heap. Tradition is not a storehouse of accumulated wisdom, the result of a thousand tiny adjustments embodying, as Burke suggested, more experience and knowledge than could ever be possessed by a single individual. Tradition, instead, is a pestilent sewer of abuses.

The sovereignty of the past is the reign of nobility, which actually means "no-ability." Competence cannot be inherited; so it is not

---

[14] Tom Paine, "Common sense," *The Life and Major Writings of Thomas Paine*, edited by Philip Foner (New York, Citadel, 1961), pp. 29 and 37.

[15] Tom Paine, "The rights of man," *ibid.*, p. 251.

[16] "It is the living, and not the dead, that are to be accommodated," and "as government is for the living, and not for the dead, it is the living only that has any right to it" (*ibid.*, pp. 251, 254).

[17] *Ibid.*, p. 366.

surprising that traditional societies heap power and rewards on imbeciles. Burke had dishonestly suggested that traditions, piously received, could relieve the present generation of making arduous choices. But even if such a shirking of responsibility were desirable (which it is not), it would be impossible, because the past is fraught with contradictions.[18] The settlement of 1688, for example, was an innovation forced on Englishmen by the irreconcilable conflict between religious and dynastic traditions. Burke knew this. While belittling the present and aggrandizing the past, he was actually serving the interests of a small elite – men very much alive.[19]

According to Locke, "an Argument from what has been, to what should of right be, has no great force."[20] Paine endorsed this view with a vengeance. Democracy, for him, was the routinization of impiety. There was no reason on earth why people should do things in the future the way they had done them in the past. Democracy was a tirelessly inventive system, oriented toward constant change and reform. The eighteenth-century battle against prescribed sentiments and nonvoluntary obligations gave no quarter to the earlier choices of an individual. Decisions made by one's past self came to appear imposed and thus illegitimate to one's present self. In Protestant countries, at least, marriage was no longer a sacrament. Thus, a perpetual contract began to appear unnecessary to the purposes of marriage, not to mention inconsistent with the human need to correct one's own mistakes.[21] The campaign for a loosening of the divorce

<hr>

[18] *Ibid.*, p. 273.

[19] In all fairness, Burke argued quite forcefully that constant reform was a necessity of government. His basic position, in fact, was wildly caricatured in Paine's account. Burke had written that it is difficult to be rational in politics: one must be thoroughly acquainted with numerous details in order to judge a situation correctly: "Abstractedly speaking, government, as well as liberty, is good; yet could I, in common sense, ten years ago, have felicitated France on her enjoyment of a government, (for she then had a government,) without inquiry what the nature of that government was, or how it was administered?" ("Reflections on the revolution in France," *The Works of Edmund Burke*, vol. III [Boston, Little, Brown, 1869], pp. 240–1). Paine "quotes" this passage, irresponsibly rewriting it to suggest that for Burke rationality is both impossible and undesirable in politics: "Mr Burke appears to have no idea of principles, when he is contemplating governments. 'Ten years ago' (says he) 'I could have felicitated France on her having a government, without inquiring what the nature of that government was, or how it was administered.' Is this the language of a rational man?" ("The rights of man," p. 258).

[20] John Locke, *Two Treatises of Government*, book 2, ch. 8, sec. 103, p. 380.

[21] See Milton's divorce tracts, *Complete Prose Works of John Milton*, vol. 2 (1643–8) (New Haven, Yale University Press, 1959); John Locke, *Two Treatises of Government*,

laws reflected a general unwillingness to allow the past to enslave the present.

Democracy was the collective counterpart to this personal institutionalization of precariousness:

> There never did, there never will, and there never can exist a parliament, or any description of men, in any country, possessed of the right or the power of binding and controlling posterity to the "*end of time*," or of commanding for ever how the world shall be governed, or who shall govern it; and therefore, all such clauses, acts or declarations, by which the makers of them attempt to do what they have neither the right nor the power to do, nor the power to execute, are in themselves null and void.

The present generation has an unlimited and illimitable right to new-model the institutions under which it lives. The only consent that legitimates any form of government is "the consent of the living."[22]

Paine's argument here presupposes an irresolvable tension between constitutionalism and democracy, between the inheritance of a fixed legal framework and the all-powerfulness of citizens currently alive. Just as Locke had denied fathers the right to shackle their children, so Paine (at least in these passages) denied the Founding Fathers the right to harness successor generations with a fixed constitutional scheme.

Jefferson and the self-sufficiency of generations

Thomas Jefferson explicitly denied the legislature the power to annul the personal liberties enshrined in the Bill of Rights. He endorsed "limited constitutions, to bind down those whom we are obliged to trust with power." And he even wrote, in lawyerly fashion, that "[o]ur peculiar security is in the possession of a written Constitution."[23] Like Paine, however, Jefferson was a fickle constitutiona-

---

book 2, ch. 7, secs. 80–3, pp. 363–5; Montesquieu, "Lettres persanes," *Oeuvres complètes*, vol. I, edited by Roger Caillois (Paris, Pléiade, 1949), letter 116, pp. 303–4.
[22] Paine, "Rights of man," pp. 251, 254.
[23] Thomas Jefferson, "Draft of the Kentucky Resolutions" (1798) and letter of September 7, 1803, *Writings*, edited by Merrill Peterson (New York, Library of America, 1984), pp. 454 and 1140.

list. He, too, launched an uncompromising attack on the very idea of constitutional precommitment. In September, 1789 (two years before Paine published *The Rights of Man*), Jefferson wrote to Madison addressing "[t]he question whether one generation of men has a right to bind another."[24] His answer was a resounding No.

Earlier, in his *Notes on the State of Virginia* (1781–2), Jefferson had made a modest effort "to get rid of the magic supposed to be in the word *constitution*." Virginia's ordinance of government was not "perpetual and unalterable" or, indeed, any more binding than ordinary legislation. He qualified these remarks, however, by arguing that a properly elected constitutional convention could place both basic rights and the form of government itself "beyond the reach of question."[25]

In a polemic published against Jefferson in 1788, Noah Webster poured scorn on these last-minute concessions to unalterable constitutions.[26] Jefferson apparently took Webster's biting sarcasm to heart. In this letter of 1789, at any rate, he adopted a more consistently majoritarian stance. Like Paine, he argued that "the earth belongs to the living and not to the dead."[27] Years later, he repeated the same argument in a somewhat more brutal fashion: "the dead have no rights. They are nothing." And "the particles of matter which composed their bodies, make part now of the bodies of other animals, vegetables, or minerals."[28] In his letter to Madison, Jefferson went so far as to deny all ordinary assumptions about historical continuity and (thus) national identity: "by the law of nature, one generation is to

---

[24] Letter of September 6, 1789, *ibid.*, p. 959; Jefferson's confusing belief that the majority both must and must not be limited is expressed concisely in his First Inaugural: "though the will of the majority is in all cases to prevail, that will to be rightful must be reasonable" (*ibid.*, 492–3).

[25] *Ibid.*, p. 251.

[26] "The contest for *perpetual bills of rights* against a future tyranny, resembles Don Quixote's fighting windmills; and I can never reflect on the declaration about an *unalterable constitution* to guard certain rights, without wishing to add another article, as necessary as those mentioned, viz. 'that no future convention or legislature shall cut their own throats, or those of their constituents' " (Noah Webster, "Government, Mr. Jefferson's arguments in favor of an unalterable constitution, considered," *American Magazine*, no. 1 [1788], reprinted as "On government" in *A Collection of Essays and Fugitive Writings on Moral, Historical, Political and Literary Subjects* [Boston, Thomas and Andrews, 1790], p. 67.

[27] Jefferson, *Writings*, p. 963.

[28] Letters of July 12, 1816 and June 5, 1824, *Writings*, pp. 1402 and 1493.

another as one independent nation to another."[29] A constituent assembly in Philadelphia, apparently, can no more legislate for future Americans than for contemporary Chinese.

The idea of "perpetuity" is morally repugnant, associated as it is with perpetual servitude and self-perpetuating monopolies. The very word *perpetual* should be swept aside with other debris inherited from the old regime: "no society can make a perpetual constitution, or even a perpetual law." People "are masters of their own persons, and consequently may govern them as they please." As a result, "[t]he constitution and the laws of their predecessors [are] extinguished then in their natural course with those who gave them being."[30] The physical death of the constitution-makers entails the spiritual death of the constitution.[31]

Lecturing in the 1760s, Adam Smith had told his students at Glasgow: "A power to dispose of estates for ever is manifestly absurd. The earth and the fullness of it belongs to every generation, and the preceding one can have no right to bind it up from posterity."[32] Writing from Paris in times of financial crisis, Jefferson echoed Smith's concern for this traditional way whereby one generation bound the next. Most of his analysis, in fact, revolved around the law of inheritance. He asked, for example, "[w]hether the nation may change the descent of lands holden in tail."[33] He also inquired if a father had the natural right to bury his children in a mountain of unpaid bills. More politically, he asked if one generation could justify contracting massive debts, while expecting succeeding generations to pay the toll. Jefferson's answer, similar to Smith's, was that successors are "by nature clear of the debts of their predecessors."[34]

On the basis of Buffon's actuarial tables, Jefferson calculated that

[29] Jefferson, *Writings*, p. 962; cf. letter of June 24, 1813, pp. 1280–1. For Noah Webster's earlier use of this argument, see Gordon Wood, *The Creation of the American Republic* (New York, Norton, 1972), p. 379.

[30] Jefferson, *Writings*, p. 963.

[31] In the same spirit, Jefferson expressed considerable disquiet about the antimajoritarian character of judicial review (e.g., letter of December 23, 1820, *Writings*, p. 1446).

[32] Adam Smith, *Lectures on Jurisprudence*, edited by R. L. Meek, D. D. Raphael and P. G. Stein (Oxford, Clarendon Press, 1978), p. 468 (see also pp. 69–70); cf. *The Wealth of Nations* (New York, Modern Library, 1937), p. 363.

[33] Jefferson, *Writings*, p. 963.

[34] Jefferson, *Writings*, p. 961. This seems to follow from the Lockian denial of inherited guilt (Locke, *Two Treatises of Government*, book 2, ch. 16, sec. 182, p. 436).

"half of those of 21 years and upwards living at any one instant will be dead in 18 years 8 months."[35] An individual can incur a debt only so long as he will repay it in person. Analogously, the political majority should contract no debts it cannot redeem within the course of nineteen years. Jefferson explicitly extended this argument to the question of binding constitutional frameworks. One of his clearest statements occurs in the letter of 1816:

> By the European tables of mortality, of the adults living at any one moment of time, a majority will be dead in about nineteen years. At the end of that period, then, a new majority is come into place; or, in other words, a new generation. Each generation is as independent of the one preceding, as that was of all which had gone before. It has then, like them, a right to choose for itself the form of government it believes most promotive of its own happiness.[36]

National plebiscites determining the form of government and enacting fundamental laws should be held every twenty or thirty years. The mere opportunity for constitutional amendment or repeal was completely inadequate. At set periods, all laws and institutional arrangements must lapse.[37] Only periodic and obligatory constitutional plebiscites can disenthrall the present from the past and assure every generation its proper say.

Precommitment and the growth of knowledge

Paine's impatience with the legacies of the past was fueled mainly by his bitter hatred of aristocracy. Jefferson, too, disliked hereditary monopolies. Just as important, however, was his veneration of science: "laws and institutions must go hand in hand with the progress of the human mind. As that becomes more developed, more enlightened, as new discoveries are made, new truths disclosed, and manners and opinions change with the change of circumstances,

---

[35] Jefferson, *Writings*, p. 961.   [36] Jefferson, *Writings*, p. 1402.
[37] Obviously enough, this rule, too, represents an attempt to bind posterity. When Jefferson wrote "let us provide in our constitution for its revision at stated periods" (*ibid.*) he was openly endorsing the imposition of unalterable arrangements on successor generations.

institutions must advance also, and keep pace with the times."[38] Modern science has made knowledge permanently unstable. The expectation that scientific progress will necessarily overturn current beliefs transforms precommitment into an epistemological absurdity.

This idea, like the others I have touched upon, has a long and intricate history. The brief remark cited from the Putney Debates already implied that the necessities of public learning must override constitutional pieties. If we discover that our constitution is weak and infirm, we should change it.[39] Similarly, Locke argued that the human capacity for learning and self-correction makes certain kinds of perpetual contract illegitimate. No promise to remain a lifelong member of a religious community, for instance, could possibly be binding. An individual has no right to enter into an irrevocable agreement of this kind: "[i]f afterwards he discovers anything either erroneous in the doctrine or incongruous in the worship, he must always have the same liberty to go out as he had to enter."[40]

Impatience with stupifying clogs to further learning was also voiced by Immanuel Kant:

> One age cannot enter into an alliance on oath to put the next age in a position where it would be impossible to extend and correct its knowledge, particularly on such important matters [questions of religion], or to make any progress whatsoever in enlightenment. This would be a crime against human nature, whose original destiny lies precisely in such progress. Later generations are thus perfectly entitled to dismiss such agreements as unauthorized and criminal.[41]

[38] Jefferson, letter of July 12, 1816, *Writings*, p. 1401.

[39] In the same spirit, Hobbes wrote that "No mans error becomes his own law; nor obliges him to persist in it" (Hobbes, *Leviathan* [Oxford University Press, 1965], part 2, ch. 26, p. 213).

[40] John Locke, *A Letter on Toleration*, translated by J. W. Gough (Oxford, Clarendon Press, 1968), p. 73. In early nineteenth-century America, institutional precommitment and majority rule collided over precisely this sort of religious issue. In several states, a legal battle raged over ecclesiastical trusts. Church founders had often granted land to a congregation on the condition that future parishioners would continue to embrace specific doctrinal beliefs. The legal question was: should a court enforce the will of defunct Trinitarians against the wishes of a majority of living Unitarians? This question is interestingly discussed in Mark DeWolfe Howe, *The Garden and the Wilderness* (University of Chicago Press, 1965), pp. 32–60.

[41] Immanuel Kant, "What is enlightenment?," in *Kant's Political Writings*, edited by Hans Reiss (Cambridge University Press, 1970), p. 57.

One pious generation is forbidden to bind the next to a doctrinal formula. Even more radically, an individual cannot precommit his own future selves: "it is absolutely impermissible to agree, even for a single lifetime, to a permanent religious constitution which no one might publicly question."[42]

To understand what abstract principle is at stake in these assertions, consider a parallel claim advanced in a different setting. Sixty-five years after Kant, John Stuart Mill wrote that "[t]he practical maxim of leaving contracts free, is not applicable without great limitations in case of engagements in perpetuity."[43] Mill was concerned here not with religion but with marriage. Present experience, he argued, does not provide the individual with sufficient knowledge to make an irrevocable lifetime engagement. A perpetual marriage vow does violence not only to the human capacity to change but also to the human ability to learn.

Precommitment is illegitimate when it stifles and mocks one's own learning capacity or that of subsequent generations. On this point, Locke, Kant and Mill concurred. Their common argument against precommitment, however, turns out to have surprising implications. With some effort, as we shall see, it can be upended into a powerful argument *for* precommitment.

Background to the Paine–Jefferson thesis

Discomfort with constitutional limits on democratic majorities dates back at least to the eighteenth century. Consciously elaborating on Lockian premises, both Paine and Jefferson argued that one generation had no right to bind the next. In other settings, however, both theorists advocated some form of constitutional precommitment; and they did so without doubting the ultimate sovereignty of the majority. The story as I have told it thus far is therefore obviously incomplete.

To put the eighteenth-century arguments of Paine and Jefferson into perspective, we need to ask what sixteenth- and seventeenth-century thinkers wrote about the status of inherited obligations. Most

---

[42] *Kant's Political Writings*, p. 58.
[43] John Stuart Mill, *Principles of Political Economy*, edited by J. M. Robson (University of Toronto Press, 1965), book V, ch. xi, sec. 11, p. 954.

early-modern theorists admired Solon, Lycurgus, Numa and the other great legislators of antiquity.[44] The most glorious achievements of the ancient world would have been impossible had one generation been unwilling or unable to bind the next. The question was not so much *could* a constitution-maker secure the conditions of good government by establishing more-or-less unalterable laws. The question was *how to justify* binding obligations to which subsequent generations had had no chance to consent.

Richard Hooker, to select a classic example, explained the binding power of ancestral decisions in a very simple way. Like an individual, he wrote, a kingdom retains its moral identity over time:

> And to be commanded we do consent, when the society whereof we are part hath at any time before consented, without revoking the same after by the like universal agreement. Wherefore as any man's past is good as long as himself continueth; so the act of a public society of men done five hundred years sithence standeth as theirs who presently are of the same societies, because corporations are immortal; we are alive in our predecessors, and they in their successors do live still.[45]

The present generation is bound by the decisions of its forefathers because the dead and the living constitute one people, linked by the same continuities which unite a single individual at the ages, say, of twenty and fifty. Hooker's defense of constitutional precommitment, in other words, was essentially analogical. Just like any other individual, a nation is bound by its original vows.

Promises create a prima facie obligation to fulfill them. According to Grotius, moreover, "[a]n association as well as an individual has the right to bind itself by its own act, or by the act of a majority of its

---

[44] The most remarkable example of an attempt at constitutional precommitment was the law Charondas established among the Thurians: "He commanded, namely, that the man who proposed to revise any law should put his neck in a noose at the time he made his proposal . . . but if the proposal of revision did not carry, the noose was to be drawn and the man die on the spot" (Diodorus Siculus, *The Library of History*, translated by C. H. Oldfather [Cambridge, Mass., Harvard University Press, 1946], book XII, ch. 17, p. 407).

[45] Richard Hooker, *Of the Laws of Ecclesiastical Polity* (1593) (London, Everyman, 1969), I, X, 8, pp. 194–5.

members."[46] Promises create a duty for the individual or collective promiser because they create a right for the promisee. Thus, the legal and moral problems which eventually surfaced in the polemics of Jefferson and Paine did not arise in cases of first-hand and two-part promises of the standard type: there was never anything controversial about an agreement by which one individual bound himself personally to another. Perplexities emerged in two special cases, however: (1) where one individual – or generation – tried to bind another, and (2) where there were not two parties, but only one, involved in the contract, i.e., where an individual tried to make a binding promise to himself. I have already discussed the first case; let me now consider the second.

Medieval "constitutions" such as Magna Carta were contracts between the king and various estates, especially the barons. The obliger and the obliged were distinct parties. Having made a promise to the nobility, the king was not free to release himself. The Whig settlement of 1688 was still styled as a compact between king and people. And even in the nineteenth century, American secessionists inclined to interpret the U.S. Constitution as a compact between sovereign states. In general, however, the modern constitutions which emerged in the United States and France toward the end of the eighteenth century were not conceived as negotiated truces between classes or factions. Indeed, as written, they bear a striking but neglected resemblance to proclamations by which an absolute monarch declares his sovereign will. Rather than being presented as an exchange of promises between separate parties, modern constitutions are typically styled as frameworks which "we the people" give ourselves.[47] In relations between an individual and himself, however, the power to bind entails the power to loose. (Psychologically, to take a trivial example, it is much easier to keep a date with your tennis partner than to keep a promise to jog made to yourself.) Legally, what you freely promise yourself, you can freely fail to deliver. What we the people give ourselves we the people can take away. From this

---

[46] Hugo Grotius, *De juri belli ac pacis*, translated by Francis Kelsey (Oxford, Clarendon Press, 1925), book 2, ch. 14, sec. 10, p. 386.

[47] The Weimar Constitution, for example, begins: "Das deutsche Volk . . . hat sich diese Verfassung gegeben" (*Die Verfassung des deutschen Reichs von 11. August 1919*, edited by Gerhard Anschütz [Berlin, Georg Stilte, 1933], p. xii).

perspective, a constitution which is both binding and democratic seems not merely paradoxical but incoherent.

No man can be obliged to himself

The principle at issue here can be traced back at least to Seneca. A binding promise requires two parties and cannot be performed by one party alone.[48] This position was elaborated by a host of later thinkers, including Bodin, Hobbes and Pufendorf, and eventually Rousseau. According to Bodin, for instance, "the sovereign prince" cannot "be bound unto the laws or ordinances he maketh himself; for a man may well receive a law from another man, but it is impossible in nature for him to give a law unto himself."[49] Hobbes nationalized this argument. Because no individual feels bound by a promise he has made to himself, no kingdom can be obliged by its own constitution:

> Neither can any man ... be obliged to himself; for the same party being both *the obliger* and *the obliged*, and the obliger having the power to release the obliged, it were merely in vain for a man to be obliged to himself; because he can release himself at his own pleasure, and he that can do this is already actually free. Whence it is plain, that the city is not tied to the civil laws; for the civil laws are the laws of the city, by which, if she were engaged, she should be engaged to herself.[50]

Bodin and Hobbes adduced the maxim, "a will cannot be bound to itself" to justify their thesis that the king is, more or less, *legibus*

[48] "The word 'owe' has no place unless two persons are involved; how, then, will it apply to one person, who, in the act of incurring a debt, frees himself from it?" (Seneca, "On benefits" v. 7, *Moral Essays*, vol. 3, translated by John Basore [Cambridge, Mass., Harvard University Press, 1935], p. 313). At v. 9 (*ibid.* p. 317), Seneca explicitly rejects the notion that a single individual, in any coherent sense, contains multiple selves.

[49] Jean Bodin, *Six Bookes of a Commonweale*, book I, ch. 8, pp. 91–9 (Harvard University Press, 1962) (punctuation, spelling and syntax modernized).

[50] Thomas Hobbes, *Man and Citizen*, edited by Bernard Gert (Gloucester, Mass., Peter Smith, 1978), ch. 6, sec. 14, p. 183; the same argument occurs in the *Leviathan*: "The Soveraign of a Common-wealth, be it an Assembly, or one Man, is not Subject to the Civill Lawes. For having power to make, and repeale Lawes, he may when he pleaseth, free himself from that subjection, by repealing those Lawes that trouble him, and making of new; and consequently he was free before. For he is free, that can be free when he will: Nor is it possible for any person to be bound to himself; because he that can bind, can release; and therefore he that is bound to himselfe onely, is not bound" (part 2, ch. 26, p. 204).

solutus.[51] Pufendorf explicitly extended this argument to include democracies. The people, in his view, held the same position of untrammeled constituent power occupied by Hobbes's absolute monarch. After stating in conventional fashion that "a man cannot become obligated to himself,"[52] Pufendorf went on to claim that "nothing" could prevent a democratic people from abrogating all their fundamental laws at any time.[53]

This argument was given its classic reformulation by Rousseau. A careful reader of Bodin, Hobbes and Pufendorf, Rousseau argued that "il est contradictoire que l'autorité souveraine se donne des entraves à elle-même," that "il est contre la nature du corps politique que le Souverain s'impose une loi qu'il ne puisse enfreindre," and that "il n'y a dans l'Etat aucune loi fondamentale qui ne se puisse révoquer, non pas même le pacte sociale."[54] The novelty of Rousseau's rejection of precommitment lies in his passionate concern for moral and psychological transformation. It is not so much that a sovereign nation has no right or power to bind itself, but rather that firsthand participation in the ritual of laying down fundamental laws lifts man up from animality and transforms him into a moral creature. The making and ratifying of regime-founding constitutions, one might say, changes an individual from "un animal stupide et borné" into "un être intelligent et un homme."[55] Periodic choice of the fundamental

---

[51] Ordinary subjects can be expected to keep their promises because the sovereign compels them to do so. But the sovereign's own promises, even his promises to others (to his subjects or to foreign princes) cannot be similarly binding because no superordinate enforcer is on hand.

[52] "A man cannot become obligated to himself, or enter into an agreement with himself, or promise himself something which concerns only himself. For whoever obtains a right by an obligation is at liberty to relinquish it, provided no injury is thereby done to a third party. In this instance the person obligating and the person obligated, that is, the one obtaining a right and the one giving it, are the same, and so, no matter how much a man may strive to obligate himself, it will be all in vain, since he can free himself at his own pleasure, without having carried out any obligation whatever, and the one that can do this is actually free" (Samuel Pufendorf, *De jure naturae et gentium*, translated by C. H. Oldfather and W. A. Oldfather [Oxford, Clarendon Press, 1934], book I, ch. 6, sec. 7, p. 94).

[53] Pufendorf, *De jure naturae et gentium*, book 7, ch. 6, sec. 8, p. 1064.

[54] Rousseau, "Sur le gouvernement de Pologne" and "Du contrat social" (I, 7 and III. 18), in *Oeuvres complètes*, vol. 3, pp. 981, 362, and 436 (see also the epigraph above). While claiming that absolutely nothing can bind the will of the assembled citizens, Rousseau also stipulated that the popular will can be expressed *only* through absolutely general laws. As has been noted, this is a limit, whether Rousseau chooses to call it that or not.

[55] Rousseau, "Du contrat social," p. 363.

law had a humanly redemptive function. This was much more important to Rousseau than the need for governmental flexibility so essential to *raison d'état* thinkers such as Bodin and Hobbes.

Nevertheless, Rousseau faithfully followed his great predecessors in mocking the very suggestion that the sovereign might have an obligation to keep a promise made to itself. In doing so, he explicitly assumed that nations can be adequately conceived as individuals. But this assumption is questionable. It is not obvious, for example, that the people can have anything like a coherent "will" prior to and apart from all constitutional procedures.

Why one generation *can* bind the next

The problems which obsessed Paine, Jefferson and other eighteenth-century radicals had not been neglected by previous European theorists. Earlier writers were especially concerned to establish whether a newly crowned king was obliged to pay the debts of his predecessor on the throne. Even a cautious monarch might sometimes be obliged to incur debts greater than he could repay during his own brief reign. Thus, there were pressing practical reasons for arguing that successors were, in fact, obliged to pay the debts of predecessors.[56]

In general, one individual's or generation's promise cannot oblige another. But this rule has a crucial exception: "the act of one generation can bind another only when some man [e.g., a creditor] has acquired a right from it."[57] More specifically, if you inherit another's property (e.g., his throne) you also inherit his debts. "By the strict law of nature no one is bound by another's act, except the one who inherits his property; for the principle that property should be transferred with its obligations dates from the establishment of proprietary rights."[58] Against the *legibus solutus* tradition, in other words, seventeenth-century natural law theorists argued that kings were obliged by the promises and contracts of their predecessors because they voluntarily accepted the kingdom to which these promises were attached.[59]

A thinly disguised version of this argument came to play a pivotal role in the *Two Treatises of Government*. Paine and Jefferson relied

---

[56] Pufendorf, *De jure naturae et gentium*, book 8, ch. 10, sec. 8, p. 1346.
[57] *Ibid.*, book 4, ch. 2, sec. 17, p. 518.
[58] Grotius, *De jure belli ac pacis*, book 3, ch. 2, sec. 1, p. 623.
[59] *Ibid.*, book 2, ch. 14, sec. 10, p. 385.

heavily on Locke's claim that a father could not bind his children. But, as Hume noted, this principle was not quite consistent with belief in an original compact. Locke circumnavigated the problem by invoking the concept of tacit consent. Only the original covenanters had consented expressly to the social contract. To explain why latecomers were nevertheless obliged to obey political authorities, Locke followed Grotius. Whenever he accepts a bequest, a nonsigner of the original contract implicitly consents to the political conditions which make enjoyment of that property possible.[60]

According to Sheldon Wolin, Locke employed "the institution of property inheritance to undercut the favorite notion of radicalism that each generation was free to reconstitute political society."[61] Alternatively, Locke's argument here could serve as powerful evidence of *his own* radicalism: if bequests alone justify the obedience of successor generations, inheritable property must become widely diffused as quickly as possible. Be this as it may, Lockian premises obviously do not compel Jefferson's and Paine's uncompromising view. Madison, too, was a Lockian, as we shall see.

Why a will *can* be bound to itself

In a sense, the prohibition against one generation binding the next is easier to overcome than the alleged impossibility of an individual (or nation) making a binding promise to himself (or itself). A striking contribution to resolving this problem was made in theology. God's capacity to bind Himself, so several late-medieval thinkers persistently argued, is an expression of His awesome freedom and power. Summarizing Ockham and others, Francis Oakley writes: "The only force, after all, capable of binding omnipotence without thereby denying it is the omnipotent will itself."[62] Hooker echoes this earlier tradition when he argues that God's commitments to himself are unchangeable: "Nor is the freedom of the will of God any whit abated, let, or

---

[60] Locke, *Two Treatises of Government*, book 2, ch. 6, sec. 73, p. 358 (see also sec. 191).

[61] Sheldon Wolin, *Politics and Vision* (Boston, Little, Brown, 1960), p. 311.

[62] Francis Oakley, *Omnipotence, Covenant, and Order* (Ithaca, Cornell University Press, 1984), p. 62. See also Berndt Hamm, *Promissio, pactum, ordinatio: Freiheit und Selbstbindung Gottes in der scholastischen Gnadenlehre* (Tübingen, J. C. B. Mohr, 1977).

hindered, by means of this; because the imposition of this law upon himself is his own free and voluntary act."[63] It is absurd, even blasphemous, to say that God cannot make a binding promise to Himself, for this would be to place a limit on God's freedom and power.[64]

The most important political version of this theological argument occurs in the *Six livres de la république*. As we have seen, Bodin explicitly asserts that no sovereign can be bound by promises he makes to himself. His basic position, however, is much more flexible than this rigid stipulation would suggest. At the heart of his great treatise is a list of restrictions which every sovereign should, indeed must, impose upon himself. The analogy with God's self-binding is striking: these restrictions are not *limits on* but rather *expressions of* royal freedom and power. Illicit when it involves a diminution of the king's authority, self-binding is permissible and even obligatory when it maintains and increases sovereign power. If the king can retain and extend his authority only by tying his own hands, then tie his hands he must.[65] In many circumstances, in fact, abdication of power is not an infringement of the prince's will but rather an indirect technique by which he can assert his will.

By accepting limitations on his own caprice, a prince can increase his capacity to achieve his ends. The idea that self-binding can be a strategy of freedom explains why Bodin – the advocate of absolute monarchy – nevertheless argues that the commonwealth "should by laws, and not by the prince's will and pleasure, be governed."[66] After all, there are only twenty-four hours in a sovereign's day. General laws are much less time-consuming, that is, yield greater return per unit of effort, than particular proclamations and decrees. Similarly, the king should precommit himself to coinage of a fixed value.[67] By so doing, he can increase his control of the economy, resist factional pressures to depreciate, and cultivate the confidence of creditors. Whether or not the sovereign is legally obliged to consult the Estates

[63] Richard Hooker, *Of the Laws of Ecclesiastical Polity*, book I, ch. 2, sec. 6, p. 154.

[64] The enormous influence of this tradition is confirmed by section 195 of the *Second Treatise*, where Locke argues that princes are subject to natural law because even the Almighty, who cannot be conceived as bargaining with His subjects, is bound by His own promises (Locke, *Two Treatises of Government*, book 2, ch. 16, sec. 195, p. 443).

[65] Bodin, *Six Bookes*, I.10, p. 162 and IV.4, p. 490; see also IV.3, pp. 469–70.

[66] *Ibid.*, IV.4, p. 490.   [67] *Ibid.*, VI.3, p. 687.

before levying a tax, he can significantly augment his revenues by granting such assemblies a role in the resource-extraction process.[68] Analogously, to ensure obedience to his own law, the sovereign must limit his own authority over the parlements and other officers of the realm.[69] In sum, Bodin overcomes his own injunction against self-binding by claiming that precommitment is a vehicle of royal freedom – the strategy by which a sovereign may most effectively assert his will.

Madison's defense of precommitment

When criticizing Jefferson's attack on constitutional precommitment, James Madison was able to resuscitate these earlier arguments. The two prohibitions (against one generation binding the next and against a will being bound to itself) had been challenged in the past, and with considerable success. While one man's promise could not bind another directly, it could do so indirectly by means of property bequeathed along with attendant obligations. A will, in the abstract, cannot be bound to itself; but self-binding is, in practice, an indispensable instrument of human agency.

In reply to Jefferson, Madison essentially denied that a constitution is a dead weight or obstruction. Bonds are not necessarily a form of bondage; constraints can promote freedom.[70] The American Constitution was an instrument of government, not an obstacle to government; it was not disabling, but enabling. The Framers had been moved to action when they saw the country suffering from a lack of governance and from inattention to common interests. By establishing a firm and energetic government, the Constitution they imposed would remedy these failings. It did not merely limit power; it also created and assigned powers and, of course, mandated governmental concern for the general welfare.

In England, at this very time, Burke was describing society as "a partnership . . . between those who are living, those who are dead, and those who are to be born."[71] But his argument was curiously medi-

---

[68] *Ibid.*, I.8, p. 109 (see also II.1, p. 192; III. 7, pp. 384–5; IV.6, p. 518).

[69] *Ibid.*, I.8, p. 103; I.10, pp. 159–60; III.1, p. 254; III.4, p. 323.

[70] As a Lockian, Madison agreed that "*Law* in its true Notion, is not so much the limitation as *the direction of a free and intelligent Agent* to his proper Interest" (*Two Treatises of Government*, book 2, ch. 6, sec. 57).

[71] Burke, "Reflections on the revolution in France," *Works*, vol. III, p. 359.

eval, appealing to the organic unity of the cosmos. Madison's similar-sounding idea of an intergenerational division of labor was much more secular and pragmatic. If we can take for granted certain procedures and institutions fixed in the past, we can achieve our present goals more effectively than we could if we were constantly being side-tracked by the recurrent need to establish a basic framework for political life. An inherited constitution can be democracy-enabling as well as democracy-stabilizing. It is not only and not essentially a hedge against arbitrary government. Because it is relatively hard to change, a constitution can disencumber, that is, emancipate the present generation. Thus, it cannot plausibly be characterized as an oppress-ive force, an autocratic attempt by the past to enthrall the future. Precommitment is justified because it does not enslave but rather enfranchises future generations.

In *The Federalist* no. 49, published three years before he formulated his rejoinder to Jefferson, Madison had already criticized the swing-door amendment procedure proposed in his friend's 1783 draft of a constitution for Virginia. Madison's objections to Jefferson's scheme were primarily psychological. He agreed that "the people are the only legitimate fountain of power" and that "a constitutional road to the decision of the people ought to be marked out and kept open, for certain great and extraordinary occasions."[72] But the frequent con-voking of constitutional conventions would periodically create a legal vacuum in which rational decisions, based on "the true merits of the question," were not likely to emerge. In this legally anomalous extraconstitutional condition, "[t]he *passions*, not the *reason*, of the public would sit in judgment."[73] Madison warned that the quite positive experiences of his own generation with constitutional conven-tions were not typical. In immediate post-revolutionary America, patriotic enthusiasm and universal resentment against Great Britain had created psychological conditions for trust and cooperation outside the framework of a written constitution. Such conditions were unlikely to endure.[74] In more ordinary circumstances, it would not necessarily be democratic to step casually outside the constitutional framework and pretend to ask "the people" to revise the ground rules.

---

[72] *The Federalist Papers*, edited by Clinton Rossiter (New York, New American Library, 1961), no. 49, p. 314.
[73] *Ibid.*, no. 49, p. 317.   [74] *Ibid.*, no. 49, p. 316.

Skeptical of republican theatrics and wary of informal coercion (i.e., the disproportionate power of self-selected elites, of the aggressive, outspoken and socially assertive) in systems of so-called direct democracy, Madison wanted to limit plebiscitary appeals. Because they threatened to nullify democracy-stabilizing constitutional precommitments, periodic plebiscites played into the hands of antirepublican forces. Madison opposed Jefferson's excessively relaxed amendment scheme for this reason alone.[75]

In his brilliant letter of February, 1790, Madison pursued the same line of attack. Jefferson's assertion that "a living generation can bind itself only,"[76] he wrote, is "not *in all respects*, compatible with the course of human affairs." The call for centennial plebiscites ignored certain basic features of republican politics. "However applicable in theory the doctrine may be to a Constitution, it seems liable in practice to some weighty objections."[77]

Madison's principal criticism stemmed from his worry, not shared by Jefferson, about the psychological conditions likely to prevail between the lapsing of one constitution and the ratifying of another.[78] Jefferson's plan for a constituent assembly every twenty years would make the government "too subject to the casualty and consequences of an interregnum." The attendant instability would surely decrease the significance of popular consent while markedly increasing the role

[75] What Madison described as his least important objection to Jefferson's amendment scheme is the one scholars cite most often. It is that "frequent appeals would, in great measure, deprive the government of that veneration which time bestows on everything, and without which perhaps the wisest and freest governments would not possess the requisite stability." The psychology of legalism has roots deeper than rational argument. For one thing, compliance with the law is contagious: "[t]he strength of opinion in each individual, and its practical influence on his conduct, depend much on the number which he supposes to have entertained the same opinion." Most people are not philosophers, and the habits of legality upon which social cooperation depends are an improbable and fragile achievement. Thus, "the most rational government will not find it superfluous to have the prejudices of the community on its side" (*The Federalist Papers*, no. 49, pp. 314–15).

[76] That is, a living generation of debtors can bind only itself to its creditors.

[77] James Madison, letter of February 4, 1790, in *The Papers of James Madison*, vol. 13, edited by Charles Hobson and Robert Rutland (Charlottesville, University Press of Virginia, 1981), p. 22.

[78] Here, as elsewhere, Madison revealed his indebtedness to Hume: "were one to choose a period of time, when the people's consent was the least regarded in public transactions, it would be precisely on the establishment of a new government. In a settled constitution, their inclinations are often consulted; but during the fury of revolutions, conquests, and public convulsions, military force or political craft usually decides the controversy" (David Hume, "Of the original contract," *Essays*, p. 461).

of chance and skillful demagoguery.[79] Frequent constituent assemblies would not be, as Jefferson imagined, transparent windows on to the wishes of the majority. Indeed, the hopeful or fearful anticipation of such periodic refoundings would exert a warping force on the political scene, creating otherwise nonexistent interests: "a periodical revision [would] engender pernicious factions that might not otherwise come into existence."[80] If the ground rules were placed beyond easy reach, by contrast, aggrieved parties would be encouraged to husband their resources. Citizens would benefit from having their hands tied in this regard: by avoiding a wasteful struggle over abstract rules, they could achieve more of their concrete aims than if a hotly contested amendment campaign were waged and won.

According to Jefferson, "[s]ome men look at constitutions with sanctimonious reverence, and deem them like the arc of the covenant, too sacred to be touched."[81] Madison was not one of these men. He did not wish to insulate the ground rules from all criticism and reform; he did not advocate an unalterable constitution. He merely wanted to make the amendment process complicated and time-consuming, requiring not a simple majority but rather a sequence of extraordinary majorities within various bodies over a period of time. In other words, he sought not an absolute but only a relative permanence. The unwieldiness of the amending power, he believed, would discourage frivolous attempts to revise the Constitution every time political deadlock occurred. The unavailability of constitutional amendment as an ordinary political strategy would encourage democratic processes of bargaining and mutual learning. Obligatory delays would also heighten the quality of successful amendments, because cumbersome procedures give all parties time for thought. Ultimately, Jefferson's scheme was unrealistic because it ignored the nerve-racking psychology of interregna and the way periodic opportunities to rescind the entire Constitution would both (mis)shape preferences and squander scarce resources.

[79] While acknowledging this aspect of Madison's argument, Bruce Ackerman also writes about "*The Federalist*'s recurring assumption that the People best express themselves through episodic and anomalous 'conventions,' and not through regular sessions of ordinary legislatures" (Bruce Ackerman, "The Storrs Lectures: discovering the Constitution," *Yale Law Journal* [1984], 93, p. 1022); but the passages he cites do not support this imaginative claim.

[80] Madison, *Papers*, vol. 13, p. 22.

[81] Jefferson, letter of July 12, 1816, *Writings*, p. 1401.

Madison also considered the question of the public debt and specifically Jefferson's claim that one generation never has a right to bind its successors to repay debts contracted earlier. Once again, Madison's objection was practical and had, as he cautiously suggested, "some foundation in the nature of things." Following the seventeenth-century natural law theorists, he wrote that financial obligations may descend from one generation to another because some essential national purposes can be achieved only on the basis of an intertemporal division of labor:

> Debts may be incurred with a direct view to the interest of the unborn as well as of the living: Such are debts for repelling a Conquest, the evils of which descend through many generations. Debts may even be incurred principally for the benefit of posterity: Such, perhaps, is the [Revolutionary War] debt incurred by the U. States. In these instances the debts might not be dischargeable within the term of 19 years.[82]

If benefits are distributed across many generations, burdens should be allotted in the same way. Such an arrangement corresponds to equity and provides rewards for all parties in an intergenerational alliance. True, future generations are seldom asked if they wish to accept a benefit (say, the defeat of Hitler) in exchange for assuming a debt. But if all civilized contracts required copresence then each generation would be reduced to a separate nation, that is, would be calamitously deprived of the advantages resulting from cooperation across time in which partners cannot, in principle, encounter one another. Practical considerations alone suggest that, in such cases, we should override the formal principle that no obligations can be incurred without express consent.

Madison next considered property law. The rights of property are not natural but "positive," that is, conventional and revocable. Even in the case of such lesser law, however, periodic assemblies for repeal or reaffirmation would have deleterious effects. On Jefferson's scheme, at twenty-year intervals "all the rights depending on positive laws ... become absolutely defunct" to be reenacted or not as the constituent assembly sees fit. Once again, such an arrangement would

[82] Madison, *Papers*, vol. 13, p. 23.

not merely register preference change over time. A constituent assembly is a thermometer which drastically alters the temperature of the room. In the case of property law, the anticipation of such assemblies would provoke "the most violent struggles ... between the parties interested in reviving and those interested in reforming the antecedent state of property." True, conflicting interests concerning property law exist with or without periodic constituent assemblies. But the inevitability of latent conflict does not imply that a cyclical outburst of violent struggles will necessarily work to the long-term advantage of, say, debtors. A "general uncertainty" would "discourage every useful effort of steady industry pursued under the sanction of existing laws" and, most important of all, would give an unearned and undemocratic advantage to those clever and unscrupulous enough to exploit social chaos for political gain.

Jefferson was dissatisfied with a formal opportunity to repeal laws and amend the constitutional order because he rejected the idea that tacit consent could legitimate rules and decisions. Consent can be inferred, according to the traditional doctrine, "from the omission of express revocation," say, from the non-invocation of the right of rebellion. In a modified form, Madison embraced this view. Resignation was not a sign of consent. But when citizens do not invoke their right of amendment and repeal, although they could do so easily and without being punished, they are implicitly agreeing to the framework in place. There is no need to schedule magical moments in which express consent must be proclaimed aloud, so long as the uninterrupted chance to protest and lobby for revocation is guaranteed.

The problems afflicting Jefferson's proposal were manifold and obvious. Only the doctrine of tacit consent could provide "relief from such embarrassments." Madison admitted that, in the past, the doctrine of tacit consent had had a "pestilent" effect. But he believed that its noxious side-effects could be more easily neutralized by a deftly designed constitution than could "the evils" necessarily ensuing upon Jefferson's scheme of periodic constituent assemblies.

Madison concluded by arguing that implied or tacit consent is essential to "the very foundation of Civil Society." Majoritarianism itself, so essential to Jefferson's scheme, depends on the assumption that individuals born into a society tacitly assent to "the rule by which the majority decides for the whole."[83] To require the express consent of every generation to the constitutional framework (or of every individual to majority rule) would introduce an element of nervous hysteria into the heart of democratic politics, weakening its capacity to resolve conflict and aggregate diverse interests without violence. To require express and constantly reiterated consent would decrease the influence of citizens over the direction of public policy and thus over their own lives.

Jefferson had associated his idea of government by the living with an unrealistic image of discrete present generations: "[l]et us suppose a whole generation of men to be born on the same day, to attain mature age on the same day, and to die on the same day, leaving a succeeding generation in the moment of attaining their mature age all together."[84] Unfortunately, this fantasy about citizens who are born and die in parade-like generational cohorts conveys an opposite message to the one Jefferson intended. Hume (affectionately described by Jefferson as a "traitor to his fellow men"[85]) was himself quite skeptical about the concept of tacit consent. But he drew a distinctly non-Jeffersonian conclusion from his observation that one human generation did not "go on the stage at once, and another succeed, as is the case with silkworms and butterflies."[86] Precisely because generations overlap, the living have no right to repeal, at set intervals, the legacy of the past. Closing the doors on our predecessors' commitments is impractical, because the members of every new generation must coexist with survivors of the old. Less fearful of innovation than Hume, Madison, too, was anxious that methods for registering public consent be compatible with the unsynchronized itineraries of human lives.

Founders and citizens

Unlike Rousseau's longing for a morally and psychologically transformative experience, the Paine–Jefferson formula has much to be

---

[83] *Ibid.*, vol. 13, p. 24.
[84] Jefferson, *Writings*, p. 960. Here again, the unexamined legacy of absolutism may be at work: while the sovereign people will obviously die in an unsynchronized and staggered manner, a sovereign monarch will die a single datable death.
[85] Jefferson, letter of June 5, 1824, *Writings*, p. 1481.
[86] Hume, "Of the original contract," *Essays*, p. 463.

said in its favor. The present generation lives in the world. Who else should be responsible for the workings of government if not its members? Ancestor worship must be kept under control.

As Madison suggested, however, the idea of government by the living is not as problem-free as it might at first seem. For one thing, repudiation of the past is a two-edged sword. Present decisions, made with the future in mind, will soon belong to the past. If we can assume that subsequent generations will treat our future-minded choices with sovereign contempt, why should we give more thought to the future than to the past?[87] We want to act responsibly toward succeeding generations, while we tend to reject the notion that previous generations are responsible for us. But is this really a consistent attitude to adopt? Adding the suggestion that those who are presently alive yearn to control the future, Jon Elster formulates this same *paradox of democracy* in the following way: "each generation wants to be free to bind its successors, while not being bound by its predecessors."[88]

Jefferson and Paine never squarely faced this problem. Imbued with the ideology of unlimited progress, they probably assumed that the future would take care of itself. Convinced that the genuine problems of politics were minimal and decreasing, neither perceived very clearly the advantages that might be reaped by an intergenerational division of labor. Viewing the past as a dead weight, they failed to appreciate that predecessors might disencumber successors. Neither was sufficiently impressed by the importance of organizing future democratic life. Neither recognized each generation's need to unclutter and systematize the agenda for solving present problems by taking for granted certain power-granting, procedure-defining and jurisdiction-specifying decisions of the past. In sum, neither managed to conceive the Constitution in a positive manner, as an indispensable instrument of government. Only theorists less intoxicated by the guarantee of progress became conscious of Elster's paradox and (more importantly) of the paradoxical dependence of the sovereignty of the present on the precommitments of the past. As a general rule, individuals tend to lose power and freedom whenever they attempt to solve all their problems alone. By accepting a pre-established consti-

---

[87] Burke made an analogous point: "People will not look forward to posterity, who never look backward to their ancestors" ("Reflections on the revolution in France," p. 274).

[88] Jon Elster, *Ulysses and the Sirens* (Cambridge University Press, 1979), p. 94.

tution, a people ties its own hands; but it also frees itself from considerable burdens.

Present decisions set in motion irreversible processes which, in turn, necessarily box in future generations. This is true whether we embody our decisions in "irrevocable" charters or not. We must adjust to this fact about historical continuity even if it violates Paine's and Jefferson's curious belief that each generation has an inviolable right to start from scratch, *ex nihilo*, with no inheritances from the past.[89] Jefferson himself helped foreclose the options of future generations by agreeing to deprive such states as Virginia of some of their sovereignty. This decision opened some doors by shutting others. Its impact, moreover, was far from negligible: it led, among other things, to a civil war fought explicitly over the legal perpetuity of the Union.

In his remarks on constitutional precommitment, Elster also suggests that there is a radical dissimilarity between the political action of the Framers and the political action of subsequent generations: "Only the constituent assembly is a political actor, in the strong sense of *la politique politisante*; all later generations are restricted to *la politique politisée*, or to the day-to-day enactment [i.e., acting-out or implementation] of the ground rules."[90] Elster does not claim, of course, that his analytical contrast is adequate to the realities of history. A constitution-maker can never be an unbound binder, any more than a sovereign can be an uncommanded commander. Myth-makers aspiring to legitimate a written constitution may invoke the analogy of God's creative act standing in a transcendent relation to acts within the created world.[91] But it would be unwise to repackage old myths as new theories. To influence a situation, an actual power-wielder must adapt himself to preexistent patterns of force and unevenly distributed possibilities for change. The influencer must be influenced: that is a central axiom of any realistic theory of power. The capacity to innovate and the need to adapt are never so sharply

---

[89] In retrospect, nothing could appear more laughable than the French Revolutionary attempt to restart the calendar at Year I.

[90] Elster, *Ulysses and the Sirens*, p. 94. Ackerman, too, argues for a radical dualism between constitutional politics and normal politics; even though many of his detailed comments suggest a smooth continuum and not an abrupt dichotomy (e.g., "The Storrs Lectures: discovering the Constitution," p. 1029).

[91] According to Hobbes himself, "the *Pacts* and *Covenants*, by which the parts of this Body Politique were at first made, set together, and united, resemble that *Fiat*, or *Let us make man*, pronounced by God in the Creation" (*Leviathan*, p. 8).

disjoined as Elster's distinction suggests.[92] The Framers of the American Constitution, for example, were slavishly indebted to the political theories of Harrington, Locke, Trenchard and Gordon, Hume, Montesquieu and Voltaire, to the experiences gained during the seventeenth-century English Commonwealth and to the preexistent and prelegitimized constitutions of the individual states. Moreover, they were faced with intractable realities (notably southern slavery) and only performed *la politique politisante* because they were simultaneously able to practice the art of compromise with unlovable realities, i.e., because they were engaged in *la politique politisée*.[93]

Individuals who set the side-constraints exercise greater influence than those who make particular decisions. Because a constituent assembly allocates authority and establishes decision procedures, it can, in some sense, be considered "privileged" with respect to succeeding generations.[94] But, on balance, it is not so clear who exerts more *power* in this relation. Elster expresses grave doubts about the concept of a continuous national "self" (such as Hooker assumed) exercising self-command through a constitutional framework.[95] But the idea that framers exert power over their descendants is no less controversial. The concept of power is difficult to apply in a situation where the power-wielder, being long defunct, can reap no possible benefit from modifying the behavior of his posterity.

Framers, at any rate, are not omnipotent angels intervening from outside the stream of history. Similarly, a subsequent generation, laboring within a framework established by law and custom, should not be likened to Pavlov's dog. While the Constitution has certainly shaped the course of American history, cultural drift and political crisis have returned the favor by reshaping the Constitution in unforeseen ways. Even though (and, in some cases, precisely because) they are precommitted by the past, descendants possess ample room for maneuver, innovation and reform. The chance for liberal construction – i.e., imaginative interpretation – of the Constitution, even

---

[92] Freedom cannot be plausibly conceived as the capacity to initiate action in a vacuum; human activity is unimaginable without some "passive" reaction to circumstances.

[93] Commenting on the less-than-omnipotent character of the Federal Convention, Max Farrand labeled the Constitution a "bundle of compromises" (*The Framing of the Constitution of the United States* [New Haven, Yale University Press, 1913], p. 201).

[94] Elster, *Ulysses and the Sirens*, p. 95.   [95] *Ibid.*, p. 94.

more than Article V, reconciles loyalty to the past with responsiveness to the present. To satisfy rival interests and muster majority support, participants at the Federal Convention incorporated conflicting and ambiguous provisions into the Constitution, thus delegating essential discretionary powers to their descendants.[96] They had no intention of sacrificing posterity to their own limited foresight.

The process of framing a constitution or *la politique politisante* continues long after a constituent assembly has been dissolved. Indeed, it never stops. Many of the basic features of the American Constitution (for example, the strength of the Union, the broad legislative responsibilities of the president and especially judicial review) were innovations introduced without the formal amendment procedure having been invoked. The Constitution is silent about political parties; but their subsequent development has decisively influenced the influence of the Constitution. Furthermore, fundamental terms such as "cruel and unusual" tend to alter their meaning from generation to generation. In comparative perspective, the "authorial" powers of later generations are probably greater than those of the Framers.[97] Successors, it could be argued, are not such hapless prisoners of the moment as were the Founders. They are no longer victimized by the urgent need to put an end to the chaos of a sovereignless nation – a need that may have made the Framers somewhat timid and conservative about change. Freed from the enormous task of launching and legitimating a new regime in a time of troubles, latecomers can devote themselves to achieving particular political goals.

Disabling and enabling rules

Paine and Jefferson were pleased that no generation had the ability to bind its successors irreversibly: the fact consecrated the right. After witnessing the "suicides" of several democratic regimes,[98] we cannot

---

[96] Carl J. Friedrich, *Constitutional Government and Democracy* (Waltham, Mass., Blaisdell, 1968), p. 140.

[97] The accumulated innovations introduced by later generations certainly rival the innovations of the Constitution over the Articles of Confederation (see *The Federalist Papers*, no. 40, p. 251).

[98] For instance, of the Second French Republic and, especially, of the Weimar Republic.

revive their complacency. The difficulty of binding the future is not always a cause for celebration. Our incapacity to precommit our successors in a semi-autocratic manner may lead to the destruction of democracy. True, the collapse of the Weimar Republic was ultimately due to the disloyalty of its elites, not to Article 48 or defective constitutional design. Still the catastrophe of 1933 suggests, once again, that constitutional precommitment and democratic politics may not be so antagonistic as Jefferson and Paine sometimes believed. There is a paradox but no contradiction here. Theorists who recognized the paradox, such as Madison, also embraced it.

A preceding generation cannot prevent a succeeding generation from saying: "No more freedom!" But this incapacity does not imply that predecessors have no right or reason to design institutions with an eye to making such decisions difficult. When attempting to bind the future, constitution-makers are not simply trying to exercise domination and control. Precommitment is justified because, rather than merely foreclosing options, it makes available possibilities which would otherwise lie beyond reach. The Paine–Jefferson formula, for example, is only convincing if we restrict our view to the short run, to relations between two generations. A wider perspective changes the equation. By means of a constitution, generation a can help generation c protect itself from being sold into slavery by generation b. To safeguard the possibilities of distant successors, constitution-makers restrict the possibilities of proximate successors. The Framers strove to create not merely a popular government but a popular government that (unlike the Greek republics) might endure. They had a right to bind us minimally to prevent us from binding our successors maximally. Recognizing the rights of its posterity, in turn, a current generation may voluntarily limit its own power over the future by submitting to the authority of the past. In other words, Madisonian precommitments are, in principle, both democratic and majoritarian. To grant power to all future majorities, of course, a constitution must limit the power of any given majority. Liberal constitutions, in fact, consist largely of metaconstraints: rules that compel each majority to expose its decisions to criticism and possible revision, rules that limit each generation's ability to rob its own successors of significant choices.

Paine and Jefferson shuddered at the idea of binding the future because they could not conceive of "binding" in a positive, emancipatory or freedom-enhancing way. Their blind-spot was due partly to a belief in progress. But it also resulted from their overly conservative conception of how constitutions function. The metaphors of checking, blocking, limiting and restraining all suggest that constitutions are principally negative devices used to prevent the abuse of power. But rules are also creative. They organize new practices and generate new possibilities which would not otherwise exist.

Constitutions may be usefully compared to the rules of a game or even to the rules of grammar. While *regulative* rules (e.g., "no smoking") govern preexistent activities, *constitutive* rules (e.g., "bishops move diagonally") make a practice possible for the first time. Rules of the latter sort cannot be conceived simply as hindrances or chains. Grammatical principles, for example, do not merely restrain a speaker, repressing his unruly impulses while permitting orderly ones to filter through. Far from simply handcuffing people, linguistic rules allow them to do many things they would not otherwise have been able to do or even have thought of doing. In other words, flexibility should not be contrasted with rigidity in the conventional manner for the simple reason that rigidities can create flexibilities. As I have been arguing, a democratic constitution does not merely hobble majorities and officials. It also assigns powers (gives structure to the government, guarantees popular participation and so forth), and regulates the way in which these powers are employed (in accord, for example, with principles such as due process and equal treatment). In general, constitutional rules are enabling, not disabling; and it is therefore unsatisfactory to identify constitutionalism exclusively with limitations on power.

Or perhaps we should rethink our concept of *limitations*. Limits do not necessarily weaken; they can also strengthen. For one thing, "that ill deserves the Name of Confinement, which hedges us in only from Bogs and Precipices."[99] Constitutions, moreover, can be binding in a possibility-engendering way. By having himself bound to the mast, Ulysses could enjoy an event (song without shipwreck) that he might not otherwise have experienced. His strategy of preventive self-incapacitation, however, is not precisely analogous to the designing and ratification of a constitution. In America, for example, if the Framers had not "bound" their successors, there would have been no

[99] Locke, *Two Treatises of Government*, book 2, ch. 6, sec. 57, p. 348.

country. That is why the Framers are also called the Founders. Ulysses bound himself; but he did not found himself. Constitutions do not merely limit power; they can create and organize power as well as give power a certain direction. Most important of all, limited government can subserve self-government by helping create the "self" (or national unity) which does the governing. That constitutionalism can contribute to nation-building is powerful evidence that it has a positive, not merely negative, function.

Enabling functions of the separation of powers

One of the main pillars of constitutionalism, the separation of powers, is routinely described in purely negative terms, as a machine for preventing encroachments.[100] Authority is divided to avoid excessive concentrations of power. One branch of government can "check" another, inhibiting despotism and disclosing corruption. But here, too, the negative connotations of constitutional binding obscure the positive purposes of institutional design.

As a corrective to the conventional view, it is useful to conceive the separation of powers as a form of the division of labor, permitting a more efficient distribution and organization of governmental functions. Specialization improves everyone's performance. According to Adam Smith, in fact, "[t]he separation of the judicial from the executive power seems originally to have risen from the increasing business of society, in consequence of its increasing improvement."[101] Initially, kings established quasi-autonomous judicial agencies in response to governmental overload. Originally, at least, an independent judiciary was not established to limit power but, on the contrary, to increase the capacity of the government to do its job.

Like other constitutional provisions, the separation of powers remains government-enabling: it disentangles overlapping jurisdictions, sorts out unclear chains of command and helps overcome a paralyzing confusion of functions. As a political version of the division of labor, it is creative because specialization enhances sensitivity to a diversity of social problems. The evolution of three distinct (though

---

[100] E.g., *Myers* v. *United States*, 272 U.S. 52, 293 (1926), Justice Brandeis, dissenting.
[101] Smith, *The Wealth of Nations*, p. 680.

cooperating) branches of government should probably be conceived by analogy with the development of the modern cabinet system. New institutions and offices were gradually developed to cope with a growing volume of diverse social problems. Each branch, moreover, recruits personnel in a distinct manner, thus increasing the variety of social interests and perspectives reflected in government decision-making.

The earliest justifications of the separation of powers emphasize its power-enhancing function. Bodin argued explicitly that an independent judiciary would increase the king's capacity to govern. Malefactors must be punished; but if the king exacts penalties personally, he will create resentments that will, in turn, weaken his authority. Thus, a clever sovereign will reserve to himself the distribution of rewards while delegating to independent magistrates the job of issuing condemnations and exacting fines: "In which doing, they who receive the benefits shall have good cause to love, respect, and reverence the prince their benefactor; and those who are condemned shall yet have no occasion at all to hate him, but shall still discharge their choler upon the magistrates and judges."[102] The separation of powers, according to this analysis, has important resentment-deflecting and responsibility-ducking functions. Montesquieu took over and refined this argument: a king who relinquished the power to punish crimes would actually increase his overall power because this arrangement would prevent involved parties from applying extortionate pressure on the crown.[103]

The separation of powers is not only power-enchancing; it is also democracy-sustaining. The maxim "divide and rule" was traditionally employed by the masters of mankind to keep their subjects in thrall. Democratic constitution-makers usurped this ancient principle and used it in a contrary way, as a strategy by which the governed might enforce their will upon their would-be governors. Rather than weakening government, the separation of powers helps secure the conditions of popular government.

Locke in particular emphasizes the representative function of the separation of powers. Why should not the legislative and executive

---

[102] Bodin, *Six Bookes*, book IV, ch. 6, p. 512.
[103] Montesquieu, "De l'esprit des lois," *Oeuvres complètes*, ed. Roger Caillois, vol. 2 (Paris, Pléiade, 1951), book 6, ch. 5, p. 315.

powers be combined in the same hands? If they were, the law-makers would know that the laws they enacted would never be applied to themselves (because they would be doing the applying). If the executive power rests in other hands, by contrast, legislators will make laws with the expectation that these laws will be applied to themselves as well.[104] In other words, the separation of powers ensures that the perspective of the ordinary citizen, subject to the law, is represented within the law-making process.

An additional, somewhat more speculative thought may be worth mentioning. The separation of powers is often described as a balance of powers. Perhaps under the influence of economics, political theorists have tended to conceive this equilibrium as inherently motionless and stable. But a "balance" may be better described as a situation easy to upset: a single straw will tip the scales. If the different branches of government balance one another, then the government as a whole may be much easier to influence from the outside. Hamilton makes this very argument about federalism.[105] The constitutionally imposed equilibrium may make the government as a whole into something like a barometer, much more sensitive to fluctuations in public opinion than any single-branch regime would be. In this sense, too, checks and balances may contribute directly to popular sovereignty.

Democracy-reinforcing restraints

Tribe asks: if we believe in the sovereignty of the people, why do we accept all these restrictions? The answer proposed by the American Framers was quite simple: these are not restrictions: they are the people.[106] The Constitution is an instrument of self-government, a technique whereby the citizenry rules itself. How else could a large community manage its own affairs? A collectivity cannot have coherent purposes apart from all decision-making procedures. The people cannot act as an amorphous blob.

[104] Locke, *Two Treatises of Government*, book 2, ch. 12, sec. 143, p. 410.
[105] "Power being almost always the rival of power, the general government will at all times stand ready to check the usurpations of the state governments, and these will have the same disposition towards the general government. The people, by throwing themselves into either scale, will infallibly make it preponderate" (*The Federalist Papers*, no. 28, p. 181).
[106] *Ibid.*, no. 78, pp. 467–8.

Carl Schmitt, an ardent opponent of liberal constitutionalism, explicitly spurned such considerations. Like many others, he subscribed to the myth of a fundamental opposition between constitutional limitations and democratic government: "the entire effort of constitutionalism was aimed at repressing the political."[107] Because the people are the ultimate constituent power, moreover, they must be conceived as an unstructured "Urgrund" or even as "das 'formlos Formende' " which cannot be precommitted by constitutional procedures.[108] But Schmitt's democratic mysticism, not to mention its practical consequences, suffices to discredit this entire approach. It is meaningless to speak about popular government apart from some sort of legal framework which enables the electorate to have a coherent will. For this reason, democratic citizens require cooperation from regime-founding forefathers. Formulated somewhat facetiously: without tying their own hands, the people will have no hands.

Decisions are made on the basis of predecisions. When they enter the voting-booth, voters decide who shall be president,[109] but not how many presidents there shall be. Fixed-calendar elections deny discretion to both public officials and popular majorities on a very important question. Democracy, in other words, is never simply the rule of the people but always the rule of the people within certain predetermined channels, according to certain prearranged procedures, following certain preset criteria of enfranchisement, and on the basis (to select a revealing example) of certain predrawn electoral districts. While placing supreme authority in an elected legislature,[110] Locke granted the power to reapportion the elected assembly to the unelected executive.[111] It would be unwise, he thought, to assign the task of remedying gross malapportionment to the very assembly created by this gross malapportionment. Such a negligent allocation of oversight-power would make legislators judges in their own cause.[112]

---

[107] Carl Schmitt, *Verfassungslehre* (Berlin, Duncker und Humblot, 1928), p. 41.

[108] Seizing the chance to dismay his legalistically minded colleagues, Schmitt wrote, quite unrealistically: "Ein geregeltes Verfahren, durch welches die Betätigung der Verfassungsgebenden Gewalt gebunden wäre, kann es nicht geben" (*ibid.*, pp. 81–2).

[109] Again on the basis of a preselection – which can be made more or less democratically – of the candidates.

[110] Strictly speaking, Locke's "legislative" was the king in parliament, and therefore only partially elective.

[111] Locke, *Two Treatises of Government*, book 2, ch. 13, secs. 157–8, pp. 418–20.

[112] Locke's argument, interestingly enough, was echoed by Chief Justice Warren in his majority opinion in *Reynolds* v. *Sims*, 377 U.S. 533 (1964), whereby the Court

Citizens can only enforce their will through elections held on the basis of a preexistent apportionment plan, a plan which may be unfair or obsolete. As a result, the responsibility for redistricting must be lodged outside the popularly elected legislature (e.g., in the Court). To preserve democracy, voters must partially abdicate the power of apportionment, that is, must remove it from the hands of elected and accountable representatives. This is a striking example of the paradox of democracy: citizens can increase their power by tying their own hands. Limited dedemocratization subserves continuing democratic rule.

Securing the conditions of public debate

The most obvious example of a constitutional limit which opens more doors than it shuts is the First Amendment. The primary function of constitutionalism, one could argue, is to protect liberty of discussion, not private property. Formulating a classic public-debate rationale for the First Amendment, Justice Brandeis wrote that the freedoms of speech, association and the press, including the right of legally dissenting from government policy, are "indispensable to the discovery and spread of political truth."[113] True, a troubled generation may succeed in abolishing freedom of speech for its immediate successors (it happened in Germany in 1933). But popular control will be decreased rather than increased by the loosening of this particular "restraint."

Among democratic theorists, none focused more persistently on the freedom-enhancing and citizen-involving nature of constitutional rules and institutions than John Stuart Mill. The burdens and opportunities of a written constitution were foreign to the English experience. But Mill devoted most of *Considerations on Representative Government* to a discussion of various semiconstitutional devices for organizing popular government. Such devices are stimulants as well as depressants. They mobilize decentralized information and imagination, encourage fact-mindedness, and create incentives for mutual criticism and learning. In advocating an institutional arrangement,

compelled Alabama to revise an obsolete districting scheme that had granted some citizens forty times greater influence on the choice of representatives than others.
[113] *Whitney* v. *California*, 274 U.S. 357, 375 (1927).

Mill typically stressed its creative functions: "it would not be exclusively a check, but also an impelling force."[114] He strove for a
constitutional balance between two sorts of mechanism: those that
ensured tolerance for poor performance (without being "idiot-proof,"
of course) and those that encouraged or induced high performance.
"Publicity" was a fundamental device in his scheme because it
functioned in both ways, as a mobilizer and as a hindrance.

The heart of Mill's constitutionalism was a system of incentives
encouraging thoughtful public participation.[115] His least successful
reform proposals, such as the public ballot and supplementary votes
granted to those holding university degrees, conspired not merely to
prevent the abuse of power but also to enlist intelligent citizen
participation: "the general prosperity attains a greater height, and is
more widely diffused in proportion to the amount and variety of
personal energies enlisted in promoting it."[116]

Democracy is government by public discussion, not simply the
enforcement of the will of the majority.[117] Public disagreement is an
essential instrument of popular government. Not any "will," but only
a will formed in vigorous and wide-open debate should be given
sovereign authority. The legally guaranteed right of opposition is
therefore a fundamental norm of democratic government; it provides
an essential precondition for the formation of a democratic public
opinion. Without being threatened or deprived of their livelihood,
citizens must be able to articulate and publicly defend heterodox
political views. Consent is meaningless without institutional guarantees of unpunished dissent. Popular sovereignty is meaningless
without rules organizing and protecting public debate.[118]

[114] John Stuart Mill, "Considerations on representative government," *Essays on
Politics and Society*, edited by M. M. Robson, vol. III (University of Toronto Press,
1977), p. 516.

[115] See, for example, *ibid.*, pp. 403–4.

[116] *Ibid.*, p. 404. Recent treatments of Mill often focus on his vaguely romantic and
narcissistic notion that participation beautifies the participant. More serious, however,
is his idea that public debate is the most effective way to mobilize decentralized knowledge and utilize the talents of citizens in solving common problems.

[117] A. D. Lindsay, *The Essentials of Democracy*, 2nd edn (London, Oxford University Press, 1951); also excellent on this point, Samuel H. Beer, "The strengths of liberal
democracy," *A Prospect for Liberal Democracy*, edited by William Lingston (Austin,
University of Texas Press, 1979), pp. 215–29.

[118] If a community decides by majority vote to disenfranchise a minority, we would
not wish to call their action democratic; but why not? If we define democracy simply by
reference to the will of the people, such civic expulsions seem democratic enough. But if

A constitution can prevent political elites from insulating their decisions from future criticism and revision. Powerful individuals naturally resent being contradicted and refuted in public. Rules forbidding the punishment of dissenters and gadflies[119] compensate for a lack of better motives. Similarly, by means of a constitutional provision ("Congress shall make no laws . . . abridging the freedom of speech"), a community can defend its own rational decision-making capacities against its inherent tendency to lapse into "group think."[120] Decisions made without canvassing diverse viewpoints are likely to be ill considered. Uninformed and uncritical deliberation has thus been described as a "mutilation of the thinking process of the community against which the First Amendment to the Constitution is directed."[121]

After a decision is made, the outvoted minority must in practice submit to the will of the majority. But the rules of the game allow losers to mount an aggressive campaign of public sarcasm and to focus public attention irritatingly on the unforeseen consequences of the decision reached. In the long run, such a momentarily annoying arrangement makes for better decisions. Rights, in other words, are not designed merely for the protection of the minority but also for the correction and instruction of the majority. No popular will worth taking seriously has a mystical preexistence; it is always the product of constitutional restraints. Because such limits tend to make government more intelligent, the majority may be willing to impose them upon itself.

Accepting this basic line of argument, both Mill and Madison rejected the claim that democracy is "based on the right to current intervention in all matters."[122] Democrats who advanced this view were unwitting heirs to the ideology of absolute monarchy. If the people is *legibus solutus*, if all the ground rules are perpetually on the

we define democracy as popular government through public discussion, then the disenfranchisement of a defeated minority would be a violation of a fundamental democratic norm. It would be a foreshortening of the discussion, a smothering of voices. In other words, the procedural rule that minorities must be permitted (so long as they obey the law) to continue protesting puts substantive limits on what the majority can decide.

[119] The narrowly legalistic definition of *treason* in Article III, section 3 provides another important protection for potential critics of the party in power.

[120] See Jon Elster, *Sour Grapes* (Cambridge University Press, 1983), pp. 39–40.

[121] Alexander Meikeljohn, *Political Freedom* (New York, Harper and Brothers, 1960), p. 27.

[122] The phrase is Elster's, in *Ulysses and the Sirens*, p. 93.

verge of being rescinded, there will be no possibility of recording or even forming an intelligent public will.

The idea of "possibility-generating restraints" helps explain the contribution of constitutionalism to democracy. It also helps clarify the relation between inherited obligations and express consent. The Framers assumed that future generations would want to live under a government in which most obligations arose from express consent. To make this possible, however, a constitution already had to be in place: a procedural document securing the preconditions for rational consent and dissent, public debate, conflict-resolution without violence and the thoughtful and cumulative revision of the constitutional framework itself. For such an imposed or inherited constitution, there could be no warrant other than hypothetical or presumed consent. In a democracy, ideally, everyone affected by a decision has a right to participate in making it. The unborn, however, are permanently disenfranchised. The Framers consciously acted on their behalf: to make subsequent consent meaningful, predecessors had no choice but to act without the leave of their successors. These traces of paternalism cannot be eliminated from the actions of the Founding Fathers. The constitutional "limits" they imposed, nevertheless, only remain binding so long as citizens continue to impose them upon themselves.

Autopaternalism

All members of a community can share an objective. But no individual will be willing to pursue it unless he can be assured that others will do their parts. According to Hobbes, peace is such a goal. Conservation of natural resources and relief of poverty are examples pertinent to developed societies today. Hume adduces the example of draining a meadow: " 'tis very difficult, and indeed impossible, that a thousand persons shou'd agree in any such action . . . while each seeks a pretext to free himself of the trouble and expense, and wou'd lay the whole burden on others."[123] To achieve their objectives, in other words, members of a political society must acquiesce in legal arrangements which bind their wills.

A democratically ratified constitution should be looked at in the

---

[123] David Hume, *A Treatise of Human Nature* (Oxford, Clarendon Press, 1978), p. 538.

same way. It seems, in many respects, a classic case of autopaterna-lism. People may voluntarily relinquish their ability to choose (in some matters) in order to accomplish their will (in other matters). Collective self-binding can be an instrument of collective self-rule. Rules restricting available options can enable individuals and commu-nities to achieve more of their aims than they could if they were left entirely unconstrained. Such is the democratic function of consti-tutional restraints.

In *The Strategy of Conflict*, Thomas Schelling examined how one party could exert power over another by means of self-incapacitation, for instance by chaining himself to a railroad track.[124] More recently, he has explored ways in which an individual can exercise power over himself by adopting comparable binding tactics: "We place the alarm clock across the room so we cannot turn it off without getting out of bed. We put things out of sight or out of reach for the moment of temptation. We surrender authority to a trustworthy friend who will police our calories or our cigarettes."[125] An individual can be crafty and strong-willed enough to bind his future selves even if he is too dim and weak-willed to act as he would prefer without precommitments. To achieve his desired ends despite his feeble resolve, an individual must restrict his available options. A voter, for example, can support compulsory seat-belt legislation in order to force himself to be free, i.e., to do what he really wants to do but would not otherwise be able to do because of laziness, absent-mindedness or social pressures to appear free and easy.[126] Similarly, laws which prevent employees from voluntarily consenting to work below the minimum wage may increase an individual's capacity to get what he wants by restricting what he can freely choose.

It is tempting to think of constitutionalism in these terms, as a cluster of techniques for collective self-management. By tacitly con-senting to judicial review, for example, electoral majorities volunta-rily abdicate power. They tie their own hands for what they pre-

---

[124] Thomas Schelling, *The Strategy of Conflict* (Cambridge, Mass., Harvard Univer-sity Press, 1960), p. 139.

[125] Thomas Schelling, "The intimate contest for self-command," *Choice and Con-sequence* (Cambridge, Mass., Harvard University Press, 1984), p. 58. See also "Ethics, law, and the exercise of self-command" (*ibid.*, pp. 83–112).

[126] Libertarians who protest that such legislation interferes with freedom of choice might be reminded that voting, too, is an instrument of choice.

sumably see as their own good. My entire analysis has been premised on the fruitfulness of this perspective. Nevertheless, we should pause before asserting, in a Schellingian way, that a constitution is basically a community's indirect strategy for self-command.

Nations are not individuals writ large; and constitutions may be misunderstood (not merely trivialized) by being compared with New Year's resolutions and explained in terms originally devised to describe the behavior of pigeons.[127] The Peter sober/Peter drunk analogy is not totally apt, because even a perfectly rational, clear-eyed and virtuous future generation could benefit from preestablished procedures for resolving conflicts. The Framers, moreover, did not have specific aims (to lose weight, stop smoking) which they wished to achieve despite the weakness of the will which would foreseeably afflict their posterity. They were neither forging chains to prevent future citizens from tumbling off a ledge nor tying on mittens to prevent them from scratching their hives. In general, Schelling's concept of self-command is much too negative to capture the enabling functions of constitutional precommitment. Among other things, the Framers wanted to guarantee that whatever decisions were eventually reached, alternatives were canvassed and counterarguments heard. As I said, the Constitution is in part an attempt to program fact-mindedness and self-criticism into American life. It represents not only an attempt by knowledgeable forefathers to prevent self-destructive behavior. The Constitution is also a set of incentives encouraging future citizens to think for themselves.

Autopaternalism is a very useful category for illuminating the democratic function of constitutional restraints. But there are, I think, at least three important disanalogies between constitutionalism and self-command as Schelling conceives it:

(1) Self-incapacitation is a bizarre metaphor to apply to nation-building. Constitutions contain various inducement mechanisms, devices for focusing attention, sharpening awareness of options, mobilizing knowledge, involving citizens and guaranteeing that future choices will be made under conditions where alternatives are discussed, facts are marshalled and self-correction is possible. When one of Schelling's individuals binds himself, he limits his preexistent ability to choose (even if, as a consequence, his subsequent range of choices

[127] As in Tribe, *American Constitutional Law*, p. 10.

is enlarged). When a constituent assembly establishes a decision procedure, rather than restricting a preexistent will, it actually creates a framework in which a nation can, for the first time, have a will.

(2) Constitutional devices, such as checks and balances, are not simply meant to compensate for a deplorable but predictable lack of moral fiber; they are actually conceived as superior to personal virtue and strength of character. The fat man who wishes to be thin would rather have a strong will. In lieu of inner fortitude, he binds himself. For liberal constitution-makers, by contrast, it would be positively undesirable to build political stability on the basis of collective virtue or an unflinching uniform will. This would overburden individual conscience, force a character standardization on citizens and deprive society of an extrapolitical variety of selves. Discussion would be pointless in such a preharmonized society. Thus, liberal framers do not want citizens transfixed on an overpowering common purpose. They reject virtue-based politics for a looser, less all-engaging, more procedural and discussion-stimulating sort of common framework.

(3) Without accepting Hayek's political views, we can admit the plausibility of his claim that "[l]ike most tools, [constitutional] rules are not part of a plan of action, but rather equipment for certain unknown contingencies."[128] While only partly accurate, this characterization of constitutional rules suggests a third disanalogy between constitutionalism and Schelling's strategies of self-incapacitation. The latter are monopurposive, while the former is polypurposive and intentionally designed to subserve future aims currently unknown.

The prohibition against self-enslavement

The very principle of voluntariness requires that certain options be foreclosed. Modern constitutions typically outlaw self-sale into slavery.[129] Slaves cannot enter into binding agreements. Thus, an act of voluntary self-enslavement would be a contract to relinquish, among other things, the right to make subsequent contracts. Accord-

---

[128] F. A. Hayek, *Law, Legislation and Liberty*, vol. 2 (London, Routledge and Kegan Paul, 1976), p. 23.
[129] Article 15 of the French Constitution of the Year III (1795), *Les Constitutions de la France depuis 1789*, p. 102; see also Locke, *Two Treatises of Government*, book 2, ch. 4, sec. 23, p. 325; and Montesquieu, "De l'esprit des lois," *Oeuvres complètes*, vol. 2, book XV, ch. 2, p. 491.

ing to Mill, this would be a practical contradiction: a willing to give up your will. By selling himself for a slave, a person

abdicates his liberty; he foregoes any future use of it beyond that single act. He therefore defeats, in his own case, the very purpose which is the justification of allowing him to dispose of himself . . . The principle of freedom cannot require that he should be free not to be free. It is not freedom to be allowed to alienate his freedom.[130]

Here we are faced with another fundamental norm of constitutionalism: you cannot voluntarily agree to give up your right voluntarily to agree.

One "solution" to the paradox of constitutional democracy may lie here. To preserve voluntariness, voluntariness itself must be restricted. The prohibition against selling oneself into slavery logically implies the acceptance of precommitment: openness in one respect presupposes closure in another. Precommitment is morally permissible whenever it reinforces the prohibition against self-enslavement. Among its other functions, constitutional binding is an attempt to foreclose the possibility that the nation (or any generation) will sell itself (or its posterity) into slavery. In this spirit, Article IV, section 4 of the U.S. Constitution purports to make a "Republican Form of Government" obligatory in the states and unalterable by future majorities. In general, a democracy choosing to destroy the framework in which nonviolent disagreement and conflict-resolution can occur would be acting suicidally. The Framers proposed, and subsequent generations have accepted, constitutional precommitment because it is a useful device for forestalling this sort of collective self-destruction.

Additionally relevant here is Bodin's assertion that "the prince cannot so bind his own hands, or make such a law unto himself [to] prohibit his grieved subjects from coming unto him with their humble supplications and requests."[131] Self-binding is illicit whenever it impedes the flow of information and squelches the learning capacity

---

[130] Mill, "On liberty," *Essays on Politics and Society*, vol. I, pp. 299–300; cf. Kant, "Perpetual peace," *Kant's Political Writings*, p. 75.
[131] Bodin, *Six Bookes*, book I, ch. 10, p. 169.

of the sovereign prince. By analogy, the sovereign people, too, cannot renounce its capacity to learn.

Originally directed against self-binding, this argument can easily be turned on its head. Once it is recognized that learning capacity can be enhanced by strategic self-binding, then self-binding becomes not only permissible but obligatory. Elected legislators must make no laws which interfere with voting rights, the free flow of information, freedom of assembly, and political access of minorities, i.e., activities "which can ordinarily be expected to bring about *repeal* of undesirable legislation."[132] The majority must limit its own powers to guarantee that it will remain a majority which can learn.

Paine and Jefferson believed that democracy was a system oriented toward change and innovation. Rationality itself requires future chances for reconsideration and self-correction. Like Madison, Mill accepted this principle but was convinced that beneficial change required a careful structuring of the conditions under which political reforms were evaluated and discussed. An institutional and legal framework must be devised for keeping open the widest gamut of alternatives for new and better decisions. Our humanity is best located in our capacity for choice, our ability not merely to decide but also to undo unsatisfactory past decisions and decide again.[133] A cleverly designed constitution can create a regime which is roughly adequate to the human capacity for self-correction. Only a rather inflexible precommitment to certain procedural rules (guaranteeing, for example, the continuing right of unpunished dissent) makes public learning possible. Constitutional democracy is the most "humane" political system because it thrives on the ability of individuals and communities to recognize their own mistakes. While prohibiting precommitments which obstructed further learning, Locke, Kant and others endorsed durable – though not unalterable – constitutional rules. They did so because they recognized that such rules can foster further learning. The dead should not govern the living; but they can make it easier for the living to govern themselves.

---

[132] So reads Justice Stone's famous footnote in *United States* v. *Carolene Products* (1938) 304 U.S. 144, 152 n. 4, my italics.

[133] "[An individual] is capable of rectifying his mistakes, by discussion and experience. Not by experience alone. There must be discussion, to show how experience is to be interpreted. Wrong opinions and practices gradually yield to fact and argument; but facts and arguments, to produce and effect on the mind, must be brought before it" ("On liberty," p. 231).

8. American constitutionalism and the paradox of private property

I

Property poses a paradox in the American constitutional system. Private property was for at least 150 years the quintessential instance of individual rights as limits to governmental power. Property set bounds between a protected sphere of individual freedom and the legitimate scope of governmental authority. But the rhetorical power and absoluteness of these bounds has been matched by their shifting permeability in practice. The legal concept of property – a symbol of stability and security – has undergone changes that amount to disintegration. Yet, paradoxically, property seems to retain its symbolic force as the foundation of American freedoms. It is still a central American value and an integral part of our system. But it has lost its traditional constitutional status: private property no longer serves as a boundary between individual rights and governmental power.

The paradox appears in theoretical treatments of property as well. It remains a subject of avid legal commentary, but commentators display a perception of property far different from its traditional meaning as boundary and a comfortable ignorance or disregard of the difference. And at the very time that property has lost its traditional status, it is the focus for the hopes of conservatives, liberals and radicals alike.

A striking number of different advocates of reform have proposed property as the vehicle for change. They want to reconstitute the constitutional meaning of property by tying it to the (related) values

Presented at the Annual Meeting of the Law and Society Association, Toronto, June, 1982. Revised for presentation at the North-East Legal History Colloquium at New York University Law School, December, 1982.

they want to promote, such as political participation, privacy and autonomy. The concept of property would be the means (by incorporation) of extending protection to these values, and the values would be the basis for defining and limiting the constitutional protection available to property. This focus on property reflects a faith in the possibility of using the tradition itself to effect radical change. The object seems to be to make property mean what the reformers want, and thus to turn the enormous rhetorical power of property to the ends of reform. C. B. Macpherson is bluntest about this enterprise: "What is the point of treating the right to a quality of life as a property right? Why not just put it forward as a human right? . . . If it is asserted as a human right separate from the property rights, the whole prestige of property will work against it rather than for it. We have made property so central to our society that anything and any rights that are not property are very apt to take second place."[1]

At the same time, conservatives use the tradition to resist egalitarian redefinitions of property rights and to oppose the changes that have already taken place. They urge a return to the good old days when the courts protected property rights and economic liberties, in keeping with "the intent of the Framers" and the basic values of the American constitutional system. In their view, property was, and should be, not only the symbol, but the source and guarantee of individual liberty. They argue that if we properly understood our constitutional system and the values underlying it, we would see that since 1937 the Court has betrayed that tradition, putting our liberties, our prosperity and the very essence of our constitutional system at risk. The resurrection of what they see as the traditional importance of property stands at the center of their program for reclaiming the tradition.

The conservatives are right in at least this respect: the key to understanding the changes in property and their implications for our system lies in the tradition. In this chapter, I try to use my understand-

---

[1] "Human rights as property rights," *Dissent*, winter, 1977, 77. Bernard Seigan provides an indirect confirmation of the ways in which protections for new rights, not conceived as property, are seen as standing in opposition to property rights: "when the courts attempt affirmative jurisprudence [the creation and protection of new rights requiring affirmative governmental action], they necessarily have to abandon their obligation to defend existing material rights." He does want property to work against, and certainly to take priority over, the new affirmative claims to welfare and equality. *Economic Liberties and the Constitution* (Chicago, 1980), p. 315.

ing of property's place in that tradition to make sense of the shifting and contested meaning of property today. This perspective provides a way of gauging the probable consequences of the changes (both actual and proposed) and of understanding the extent of their departure from tradition. The tradition allows us to see the ways in which property has been linked to the basic elements and structure of our system, and the way these links would be severed by new conceptions of property rights.

But my use of the tradition requires comment, for it is itself paradoxical. The very enterprise immerses us in the paradox of property – a paradox which I think lies at the heart of property's role in the American constitutional system.

My approach rests on the claim that there was a coherent structure to the Constitution at its origin, and that property had a central place in that structure. I argue that in crucial ways the foundations of our system were set between 1787 and 1830, and that these foundations provide an important perspective on changes in the concept of property. This argument reflects a belief in the integration and continuity of the Constitution and the system of beliefs which it reflects and sustains, such that a major change in a central part of the structure may be expected to have consequences for the other elements of the system. In many ways I think this belief is well founded.

But the history of property also seems to point in the opposite direction: our constitutional system has had an extraordinary capacity to absorb changes which, from a theoretical perspective, ought to be revolutionary – and which conservatives have decried as the portents of doom in 1787, the 1820s, the 1890s through the 1930s and again in the present. This immense flexibility points to one of the most interesting and puzzling aspects of property: the enduring and consistent rhetorical power of the sanctity of private property in American political thought – despite radical shifts in meaning and incursions on that sanctity in legal practice.[2]

What, then, is "the tradition" likely to be able to tell us about the consequences of current changes in the concept of property? And,

---

[2] See Morton J. Horwitz, *The Transformation of American Law* (Cambridge, 1977), and Harry Scheiber, "Property law, expropriation, and resource allocation by government, 1789–1910," *Journal of Economic History*, 33 (1973), 232.

more broadly, of what use is a conception of the tradition that proclaims its coherence and endurance yet acknowledges an apparently unlimited mutability in the purported core of the structure? The paradox itself suggests the answers: it is the *myth* of property, its rhetorical power, that has been crucial to our system, and current changes in the concept may threaten this mythic quality. The complex, paradoxical and mythical dimensions of property's importance in American constitutionalism emerge from an examination of change in the light of the tradition.

I begin this enterprise with one part of the tradition – the importance of property in the original formation of the conceptions, categories and institutions which constitute American constitutionalism – and contrast this original importance with the current constitutional status of property. I then move from changes largely accomplished to changes proposed, and offer caveats about property as a vehicle for egalitarian reform. Finally, I return to the other side of the tradition, its immense variability and enduring disjuncture between rhetoric and practice, to suggest the mythic quality of property, and to ask whether changes in the concept may finally undermine the myth itself – and with it constitutionalism as we have known it.

II

The Framers' preoccupation with the protection of property was the source of some of their most profound insights and of both the major strengths and most serious weaknesses of the Constitution.[3] The problem they saw was that an unequal distribution of property was the inevitable result of men's freedom to use their "different and unequal faculties of acquiring property."[4] Despite her vast resources and absence of a feudal past, America would not be immune from the age-old problem of the many and the few, the poor and the rich. The majority would be poor (ultimately propertyless, Madison thought), and property would thus be inherently vulnerable in a republican government. This vulnerability became the focus for the Framers'

---

[3] This discussion of property's importance in the political thought of the Framers and in the structure of the Constitution is a synopsis of the argument in my forthcoming book, *Property vs. Democracy: The Origins and Structure of the United States Constitution.*

[4] *The Federalist*, no. 10, ed. Jacob E. Cooke (Middletown, Conn., 1961), 58.

concern with the threat of majority tyranny. The recent history under the Articles of Confederation had shown that even duly constituted republican governments could violate the rights of their citizens, property rights in particular. Government by popular consent, far from being a complete solution to the problem of tyranny, brought with it its own inherent danger: majority oppression. The Framers' task was, then, to design a government based on republican principles but which could secure the rights of individuals and minorities. The security of property became the defining instance of the problem and the focal point for the solution.

The most thoughtful of the Framers saw the problem in terms of categories of rights. In Madison's terms, there were rights of property, which would be at risk if the propertyless held all the power, and rights of persons, which might be threatened if all power were in the hands of the propertied. But the threat was greater from the former than the latter because the propertied also had an interest in the rights of persons. The fundamental problem for Madison was providing adequate protection for each. The problem arose because of a third competing category and concern: political rights. The inevitably unequal distribution of property meant that if political rights were equally enjoyed by all, the rights of persons and the rights of property would not be equally protected. Part of the solution was to set up a hierarchy of rights: political rights were said to be mere means to the end of protecting civil rights.

These categories and hierarchy are important because they reflect a preoccupation with protecting private rights, particularly property, and a corresponding objective of containing and channeling the political power of the people. The Constitution was designed not to foster but to confine and undermine political participation. The highly mediated system was designed to turn the attention of the people to the pursuit of their private interests rather than to politics. Prosperity, not participation, would bind citizens to the government.[5] It was thus important for a great variety of reasons that the fundamental rules and structures of the system which would facilitate the pursuit of private

---

[5] See my argument in "Confining democratic politics: Anti-Federalists, Federalists, and the Constitution," *Harvard Law Review*, 96 (1982), 340. Alexander Hamilton was particularly explicit about the focus on private interests and the importance of prosperity rather than participation. See Forrest McDonald's *Alexander Hamilton: A Biography* (New York, 1979), ch. 5.

gain not be threatened by the fluctuations, irrationality or injustice of democratic legislatures. The basic rules of exchange and entitlement had to be secure.

This concern came together with a belief in "rules of justice"[6] which set limits to what even the majority could legitimately do. The experience under the Articles of Confederation brought home to the Federalists both the pragmatic concern with stability and prosperity (and, no doubt, the threat to the power of the elite) and the idea that in their political philosophy majority rule was not the sole criterion for legitimacy of governmental action. (Property in American political thought has always had this dual – sometimes conflicting – pragmatic and ideal quality.) Their ideal system required independent standards, conceptions of rights and rules of justice, which could confine the legitimate scope of governmental authority. This was the foundation for the American conception of limiting values, a conception which went far beyond, but was developed around, the problem of property.

But my presentation so far is one-sided. It is skewed, as was the original constitutional structure, toward the protection of property. But while the structure was skewed, it was not one-sided. It was the genius of the system to recognize a fundamental tension between the individual and the collective, between private rights and majority rule, and to institutionalize that tension. The Constitution is an effort, not entirely successful, to balance the rights of persons, the rights of property and political rights. The continuing tension between political rights and civil rights, between democracy and individual rights as limits on government,[7] is the most important and best characteristic of the American Constitution.

[6] The phrase "rules of justice" appears in *The Federalist*, no. 10, 57.

[7] This tension is sometimes characterized as that between democracy and constitutionalism (e.g., Walter F. Murphy, "An ordering of constitutional values," *Southern California Law Review*, 53 [1980], 703), sometimes as democracy and liberalism (Giovanni Sartori uses the terms "democracy" and "liberalism" in this sense in *Democratic Theory* [Detroit, 1962]). "Liberalism" seems problematic because it is such a vague and contested term. "Constitutionalism" has the virtue of capturing the particular form of the tension in the United States, where the rights conceived of as limits are seen as judicially defined and protected on the basis of the Constitution. But the term "constitutionalism" has drawbacks as well. At the broadest level, it seems desirable to find a more general expression of the values which "constitutionalism" captures in the United States. It should be an open question, not a presumption of the terminology, whether there are ways of defining and preserving limiting values quite different from the "constitutionalism" of the United States. The term "constitutional-

The forming of the Constitution and the institutionalization of the tension were completed with the development of judicial review.[8] This development gave institutional force to the importance of property as a symbol of limits to legitimate governmental power. The protection of vested rights from the encroachments of democratic legislatures was the central issue on which the courts asserted their power to protect individual rights from democratic attack. The inviolability of property was invoked to show that both the Constitution and natural rights required judicially enforced limits to the power of the majority. The Court became the guarantor and mediator of the basic tension of the system – a tension which held property rights at its center.

III

From this perspective the current state of judicial protection of property rights seems astonishing. Since roughly 1937, the Supreme Court has virtually abandoned all of the means it had established for preventing legislative interference with property rights. Statutes are hardly ever overturned as violations of the contract clause, and the commerce clause is almost never used to nullify legislative regulation. The standard of "rationality" used to determine the constitutionality of economic regulation is such that almost all legislation is found to have a rational basis. And the most obvious and direct protection, the prohibition against taking private property for public use without just compensation (found in the Fifth Amendment in the Federal Consti-

ism" also connotes not only the substance but the forms of decision-making which set limits to democratic action in the United States. This connotation is desirable in the sense that it reflects an important aspect of the American conception of limits to governmental power. But it is problematic as an opposition to democracy because it blurs the issue of whether the limits the Constitution embodies are substantive or purely procedural.

"Limiting values" seems a preferable term. It captures the core idea that there are values that set limits to the outcomes of the democratic process and, in juxtaposition to democracy, suggests that the values are neither derived from nor reducible to democratic values. And the term has the advantage of specifying neither the content of the values nor the means of giving effect to the limits. I shall use the term "constitutionalism" to refer to the balance and tension between democracy and limiting values in the American constitutional system.

I owe a greater clarity on these issues to conversations with Jeffrey Tulis of Princeton University.

[8] I spell out this argument at greater length in "Confining democratic politics," 340.

tution and in similar terms in most state constitutions) is in practice almost unrecognizable as a barrier to governmental power.

The dimensions of the shift in property's constitutional "status" may be most obvious in the law of "takings" and the academic comment it generates. There are two issues in cases arising under the Fifth Amendment prohibition (or comparable state constitutional prohibitions), "nor shall private property be taken for public use, without just compensation." The first issue is the strictly limiting part of the prohibition: the "public use" requirement. The courts have interpreted the "takings" clauses to mean that governments may take private property *only* for public use. If the intended use is not public, then a government has no authority to take private property even if it provides compensation. Thus when a government invokes its power of eminent domain (and offers compensation), the property-owner may challenge the expropriation as illegitimate because the property is being taken for private rather than public use. This is the clearest, most explicit, instance of property as a boundary to what the government can do. But in practice "public use" has long been defined so broadly that it is almost no barrier at all. The determination of what constitutes a public use is left largely to the legislature: "the role of the judiciary in determining whether [the] power [of eminent domain] is being exercised for a public purpose is an extremely narrow one."[9]

The Michigan Supreme Court's decision in the *Poletown* case provides a particularly dramatic example of how broadly public use can be defined.[10] (Most of the "takings" cases are state cases, and while there are variations among the states, the broad patterns I am discussing apply generally.) The Court upheld the expropriation of an entire neighborhood, which was to be razed and sold to General Motors so that it could build its new plant in Detroit. The entire plan was carried out according to General Motors' specifications at an estimated cost of 200 million dollars for the public and eight million for General Motors. The objective was to keep General Motors and its jobs in Detroit, and the rationale was that doing so would constitute a "public benefit." As the dissent vigorously argued, this broad interpretation of "public use" allowed the legislature to take property from one private party and give it to another – the very act repeatedly used

---

[9] *Bernman* v. *Parker*, 348 U.S. 26, at 32.
[10] *Poletown Neighborhood Council* v. *City of Detroit, Michigan*, 304 N.W. 2nd., 455.

to exemplify the limits of legislative power (although in fact a common practice in the nineteenth century).[11]

Public use has for so long ceased to be an effective barrier[12] that almost none of the extensive commentaries on the takings clause deal with it at all. The commentators are concerned with the issue of compensation, which arises when legislation – limiting land use, for example – that purports to be merely an exercise of the police power to regulate is challenged as amounting to a taking. Any interference with property rights which constitutes a taking must (by definition) be compensated; losses resulting from mere regulation are not compensable, presumably because they are treated as part of the inevitable cost of social order which all citizens must bear. The commentaries are devoted to sorting out these categories, to drawing the line between takings and regulation. This sorting out generally amounts to a discussion of when government has to (or should have to) pay for its interferences with private property.

Reading this commentary from the perspective of the formation of the Constitution, one is struck by the implicit transformation of property's place in our constitutional system. The literature is concerned not with limits to governmental power, but with the calculation and rationale for compensation. The basic question seems presumed to be "whether those who lose as a result of the redistribution of property bundles ought to be compensated."[13] This is a radically different question from whether or when a government has exceeded its legitimate authority.[14]

---

[11] See Scheiber, "Property law, expropriation, and resource allocation."

[12] There will soon be another Supreme Court ruling on the issue. The Court has agreed to hear a case challenging Hawaii's use of eminent domain to expropriate some of the enormous tracts of land held by the Bishop Estate in order to sell the land to the tenants now leasing it. The challenge here, as in *Poletown*, is that the taking is not for "public use." *Hawaii Housing Authority* v. *Midkiff* (80–141).

[13] Bruce Ackerman, *Private Property and the Constitution* (New Haven, Conn., 1977). In Laurence Tribe's terms, the two issues of compensation and public use have been conflated. "The public's willingness to pay, expressed through the legislative process, would serve as proof that the public had in fact been the beneficiary of what otherwise appeared to be a forbidden transfer of property from one owner to another" (*American Constitutional Law* [Mineola, New York, 1978], p. 458). Of course, if "public use" is defined by the legislative process, it no longer serves as a limiting requirement on the outcomes of that process. And it is this limit that property rights were traditionally proclaimed as.

[14] The question of "what is such a serious interference with property rights that it constitutes a taking" (and thus requires compensation) becomes inverted to, "what sort of thing do we think should be compensated and hence called a taking?" This inversion

The calculus of compensation approach may make sense given the presumption that whether an act is held to be a taking or a police power regulation, it is in either case within the scope of the government's power. One might then conclude that the only issue is when compensation ought to be awarded, and that this is an issue for distribution theories. But the distributional approaches are premised on the fact that the boundary issue, public use, has virtually dropped out of the discourse. My point is not that there is something wrong with the calculus approach, but that it constitutes a striking change in property's status in legal thought. In article after article on one of the main constitutional protections of property, the author is *not* concerned with limits to governmental power. The language of boundaries has been replaced by the language of distribution. And the authors seem largely unaware of the transformation or its significance. If the essence of the takings clause has (or should) become distributional calculation, then there has been an important shift away from property as the conceptual boundary to governmental power.

One can argue that property is in fact no longer suited to that role, that the original justification for its privileged position is now gone: property in its traditional meaning is no longer the source of autonomy for most people, and property cannot be conceived of as a boundary to state authority in a regulatory state. But while the Court's abandonment of most protections for property may reflect some such judgment, it seems as yet unwilling to replace a more traditional conception of property with the distributional calculation most commentators see as the rational approach.

Bruce Ackerman has made a lengthy argument about this in his book *Private Property and the Constitution.*[15] He sees a contrast

reflects the fact that the sole issue has become compensation, not limits on governmental power.

It is true that the requirement of compensation can serve as a practical limit if the costs are seen as prohibitive. Governments will not impose certain kinds of regulation if they are too costly. In Italy, for example, the requirement of compensation for losses in property values resulting from zoning threatened to bring city planning to a virtual halt. But the choice among competing claims on financial resources is very different from the focus on whether government has interfered severely or unduly with a private right. In both the distributional calculus approach and the focus on property as a limiting value, the practical question may in many instances be the same: when is compensation required? But the difference in focus and conceptual framework is extremely important for the role of property in American constitutionalism.

[15] (New Haven, Conn., 1977).

between the approach to property of the "scientific policy-maker" and that of the "ordinary observer." The rational calculations of the commentators, based on an understanding of property as a bundle of rights, and, generally, on utilitarian and economic models, are examples (though sometimes imperfect) of the "scientific policy-maker." The ordinary observer starts from the premise of the layman's understanding of property as "things." Ackerman thinks that what accounts for the seemingly unsystematic approach of the courts to the problem of takings is that they are essentially using the approach of the ordinary observer. This view is supported by Neal S. Manne's argument[16] that although the Supreme Court has said that it follows a balancing test of calculation of loss and benefit (as laid out by Holmes in *Pennsylvania Coal* v. *Mahon*, 1922, and premised on a bundle-of-rights theory)[17] it has really followed a straightforward approach of saying that a governmental action constitutes a taking when there is a physical invasion of property. This is clearly in keeping with the layman's understanding of property as "things."[18]

What, then, does takings law and its commentary mean for the position property holds in the American constitutional system? First, it may be that we should see the Court's approach as an effort to stop short of destroying the myth of property, of making it impossible for property to maintain its place in American political thought. If property is not a "thing," not a special entity, not a sacred right, but a bundle of legal entitlements subject, like any other, to rational manipulation and distribution in accordance with some "comprehensive view" (the basis for Ackerman's scientific policy-making), then it can serve neither a real nor a symbolic function as boundary between individual rights and governmental authority. Property must have a special nature to serve as a limit to the democratic claims of legislative power.

[16] Neal S. Manne, "Reexamining the Supreme Court's view on the taking clause," *Texas Law Review*, 58 (1979–80), 1447.

[17] 260 U.S. 393 (1922).

[18] I do not mean to adopt Ackerman's analysis in its entirety. There seem to be some unresolved problems with his categories. For example, we might expect a layman to consider an 80% diminution in the value of property to be a clear violation of property rights, even if the only systematic way of accounting for such a diminution is in terms of a bundle of rights. I expect that a refusal to hold that such a diminution is a taking runs counter to the ordinary layman's understanding, even though no physical invasion is involved.

The Court's position may reflect a tacit understanding of property's traditional constitutional status, and an unwillingness to destroy it. It may be, however, that despite the Court's efforts, the myth of property as thing, as sacred boundary,[19] may not be able to hold out much longer. Ackerman makes a persuasive case that the layman's concept of property as thing is breaking down. Too many people have to integrate into their daily experience legal technicalities of property which cannot be absorbed into the understanding of property as thing. Soon, he suggests, there will be no simple layman's concept for the Court to apply.[20]

Similarly, Thomas Grey makes a sophisticated and compelling argument that the concept of property has disintegrated.[21] Beginning with the concept of property as a bundle of rights (which he suggests was intended to have a disintegrating, de-moralizing effect), and leading to a set of conflicting theories of property, the once compelling idea of private property has broken down. Unlike most legal commentators he sees the political consequences of this disintegration: the disintegrated concept loses its specific moral force, and as it does so, its special place in legal and political thought.

This brings me back to the puzzle I posed at the outset. This idea of private property as a basic individual right and a fundamental value in the American political system has withstood 150 years of alternating

[19] There is a connection between the literal concreteness of property as many people experience it and the sense that property was vital to the republic, to individual freedom, to limited government. Although analytically there is a conflict between the notion of property as a literal thing and property as a boundary to governmental power, I think it is the concreteness of property that gives it its force as a concept which is seen as something more than a (rearrangeable) collection of legal entitlements. Property was seen as a specific, identifiable, knowable entity which held a special place in law, republican theory and "society." Property was "something" which was important, which required and was entitled to protection, which could be threatened and whose destruction or violation would cause far-reaching damage.

It is as though property rights have remained infused with a natural-rights quality long after natural-rights theories were no longer generally accepted. Legal as well as political rhetoric implied that property rights gave effect to some preexisting natural phenomenon – whose concreteness gave an intuitive certainty and substance to the legal construct. Lawyers' and judges' daily work with the mutability, variety and multiplicity of property rights seemed (for at least 150 years) not to have shaken their sense that property rights were different from other legal entitlements and deserved a special and protected status.

[20] It seems to me, however, that the conditions for this breakdown of the layman's understanding have been around for a long time.

[21] "The disintegration of property," in *Property: Nomos XXII*, ed. V. Roland Pennock and John Chapman (New York, 1980).

judicial redefinition, neglect and abuse (if one wants so to characterize the Court's use of property and contract to strike down social welfare and regulatory legislation in the first part of this century). Should the courts' and commentators' approach to takings make us think that the concept and people's experience have finally been so transformed that property can no longer serve its traditional role?

It seems to me at least possible that the cumulative changes have finally gone to what really matters to the importance of property for political thought – not its precise (and shifting) legal definition, or even the extent of judicial protection accorded to it, but its mythic quality, its rhetorical power. If property is finally perceived to be merely a legal entitlement, indistinguishable in nature from any other, if it loses its moral force both among the populace in general and the judiciary, then it seems to me that the consequences are likely to be far-reaching. Either some other concept or value will have to replace it as a symbol of limited government, as the core of constitutionalism, or we may be facing a change in constitutionalism itself.

While the conservatives are fighting such a development, in both scholarly argument and popular rhetoric calling upon the traditional values of property as a limit to government, there is another set of theorists who seem deliberately interested in taking advantage of the disintegration of property to reshape it to new ends. These efforts raise, from a different angle, the question of the consequences of redefinition.

IV

A wide range of writers have argued that fundamental egalitarian and democratic reform requires a restructuring of the system of property. The authors of proposals for new conceptions of property rights range from those who clearly intend the redefinition to be the basis for a radical transformation of the society, to those who are making an explicitly constitutional argument about the meaning of property. I am interested here in the arguments for using property as a vehicle for providing greater protection for certain values within the basic structure of the American constitutional system. This holds all the appeal of radical reform without revolution, of taking the best of the system and making it better by removing its inequities and strengthening its most attractive values. The appeal is particularly powerful because the arguments suggest the possibility of taking a concept which has traditionally been the basis for inequality and limits on democracy and turning it around to be the basis for equality and democracy. If it could work, this sort of reform by redefinition, transformation through constitutional interpretation, would have a great deal to recommend it. But I wonder about it for a number of reasons.

All of these arguments for redefinition (including those outside the American Constitutional framework, like C. B. Macpherson's) are characterized not only by a recognition of a need to reconceive property rights, but a choice to make the concept of property the vehicle for implementing the values they want to protect.[22] A limited instance of such a choice (although one with potentially far-reaching consequences) is the suggestion by a Federal District Court Judge that "the law can recognize the property right of the community to the extent that U.S. Steel cannot leave . . . the Youngstown area in a state of waste, that it cannot completely abandon its obligation to the community, because certain vested rights have arisen out of this long relationship and institution."[23] In 1964 Charles Reich made the now famous argument that various forms of government largess should be treated as "the new property" and thus provided with appropriate legal protections.[24] Frank Michelman has argued that property should be regarded as "an essential component of individual competence in social and political life," particularly stressing, in a recent article,

---

[22] My purpose here is to consider the kinds of arguments being made (rather than to offer detailed analysis of each) and to indicate the problems I see with their common approach.

[23] The statement is from the District Court Judge in pretrial hearing, cited in the decision by the U.S. Court of Appeals, *Steelworkers, Local 1330* v. *U.S. Steel Corporation*, 105 LRRM 2312, at p. 2324. The District Court ultimately concluded that "Unfortunately, the mechanism to reach this ideal settlement, to recognize this new property right, is not now in existence in the code of laws of our nation" (103 LRRM 2925, at 2931–2). If such a property right were to be recognized, its effect would be to take the issue of plant closings out of the "market place" and into the political realm. This is a particularly interesting aspect of the property debate which I have not had time to go into here. Some arguments, like this one, would use property to remove issues from determination by the market and "private" bargaining. Other arguments, like those of Demsetz, see property as the vehicle for bringing decisions *into* the market. The concept of property seems, in turn, to be central to this very distinction between state and market, public and private. As the concept of property disintegrates, it may be that this distinction will be harder to maintain.

[24] "The new property," *Yale Law Journal*, 73 (1964), 733.

property as the basis for effective participation.[25] Steven Munzer suggests that traditional private property is especially well suited to securing the values of control, privacy and individuality, and is working on ways of reconceiving property so that these goods can be equitably distributed.[26] There is, finally, a set of arguments calling not for redefinition of property rights, but a reinvigoration of their judicial protection. One version of this argument belongs among these other approaches because it suggests that greater judicial protection of property, properly understood, would provide greater protection for equality.[27]

What are we to make of this intriguing constellation of arguments? The first thing that is striking about the choice of property as the concept through which we can usher in a new era of greater equality (aside from the fact that it turns the traditional concept on its head) is that this attention to property takes place in the context of the disintegration of the concept. In some ways this makes sense. If the meaning of property is disputed, if it is in effect fluid, what better time to try to restructure it in the direction of one's preferred values? Property has the advantage of being a concept that apparently retains its rhetorical power, while its content is indeterminate and available for reshaping. On the other hand, there is something peculiarly anachronistic about making property the vehicle for change at the very time that it seems to be losing its place in the constitutional structure.

As I argued above, property no longer serves as the primary limit to the scope of governmental authority. Although the Court has not formally abandoned property as a barrier to governmental action (and one can still easily imagine some governmental takings or regulations which would be held to be illegitimate invasions of property rights), neither property nor its sister concept of contract have in fact been effective means of challenging legislation for many years now.[28] And,

[25] "Property as a constitutional right," *Washington and Lee Law Review*, 38 (1981), 1097.

[26] "Control, privacy, and individuality in justifications for property," presented at the Jurisprudence Section, Convention of the Association of American Law Schools, Philadelphia, January, 1982.

[27] Richard Funston, "The double standard of constitutional protection in the era of the welfare state," *Political Science Quarterly*, 90 (1975), 261. Not all arguments against the "double standard" of stricter protection for personal liberties than economic liberties have this egalitarian thrust.

[28] There is some possibility that the Court might move away from this position. Rhenquist, for example, has shown an inclination to use both property and contract to

as I noted, there are good reasons for arguing that property, as it was traditionally understood, can no longer serve the functions which originally made it the centerpiece of American constitutionalism. But the recognition that the concept of property is disintegrating and that it is losing its place in the constitutional structure (if not in the popular imagination) could lead in more than one direction.

One could, for example, focus on the ways in which property has become divorced from the values of, say, autonomy, which originally lent it its importance. One could focus on how property has been tied to inequality in our tradition, and on the consequences of that inequality for our political system and for the distribution of goods associated with property. From this perspective one might watch the further disintegration and decline of the concept with some satisfaction, hoping to give the values once associated with property a primacy now unencumbered by the inequalitarian tradition. This would lead one to consider alternatives to property and replacements for it, which could both foster preferred values and sustain constitutionalism. (A difficult combination, to which I will return shortly.)

But this is not the direction taken by those whose arguments I have referred to. They seem to have chosen to build on the long-standing tradition of property and its continued importance in popular rhetoric and understanding of politics. In each case, the author has correctly identified values that have traditionally been associated with property in legal and political thought, and has then argued that these values should become the defining features of property. Thus if the central value underlying property is autonomy or the capacity for effective participation, then the determination of what constitutes constitutionally protected property could be made on the basis of whether it promotes those values.

As a strategy for change, this is compelling in many ways. A successful redefinition of property could call upon both continued popular support for "property" and a well-established legal tradition of protection. There are, however, serious strategic problems with this approach. One danger is that it may underestimate the power of the

limit the scope of state power. *Penn Central Transportation* v. *New York City*, 438 U.S. 104 (1978); *United States Trust Co.* v. *New Jersey*, 431 U.S. 1 (1977); *Allied Structural Steel Co.* v. *Spannaus*, 438 U.S. 234 (1978).

concept to be manipulated. The concept of property has a long tradition, one which may not be easily severed, and which runs counter to the equalitarian and democratic thrust of most of the arguments I have been examining.

I think we can see one indication of this danger in the history of the "new property." Charles Reich argued that private property has traditionally provided a sphere of privacy and independence necessary for individuality and liberty. Now that people are increasingly dependent upon government largess for their material well-being, this largess should be treated as "property" so that it can provide, rather than undermine, the security and independence for which property was traditionally the source. He argued that this security should be ensured by providing procedural protections against withdrawal of government largess. The Supreme Court accepted this argument in *Goldberg* v. *Kelly*,[29] adopting Reich's phrase "the new property," and holding that a welfare recipient was entitled to a hearing before his benefits were cut off.

This case was the beginning of revolution in procedural due process. But this revolution has been curtailed, and one vehicle for its curtailment has been the very concept of property with which it began. Having accepted the argument that the rights in question were entitled to protection because they were *property* rights, the Court then argued that only those rights which really involved property-like entitlements required the procedural protections in question. And state benefits, the Court said, constituted property-like entitlements only when the state chose to grant them in terms that looked like property.[30]

There is a certain logic to this apparently circular, and highly restrictive, "positivistic" approach: what makes something which doesn't at all resemble traditional property "property-like"? Why, the state's deliberately granting it with property-like entitlements. But there was nothing necessary about this line of reasoning. (Indeed, its positivism runs counter to the tradition.) The Court could surely have proceeded with the reconception of property it started in *Goldberg*. The use of the term "property," however, gave the Court a convenient handle for retrenchment. The conventional, limited concep-

[29] 397 U.S. 254 (1970).   [30] *Regents* v. *Roth*, 408 U.S. 564 (1972).

tion of property provided a rhetorically consistent basis for pulling back from advances made in the name of property.

The very strength of the tradition of property makes it in some ways a precarious base for innovation. When one chooses to use property, redefined, to provide new kinds of constitutional protection for rights of autonomy, participation or material well-being, one runs the risk that temporary advances will fall back before a long, and much narrower, tradition.

Strategic problems with property as a basis for egalitarian reform are also evident in Richard Funston's argument. He urges that returning to greater judicial protection for property rights would generate a greater attention to the need for a material, economic base for the enjoyment of rights.[31] Both equalitarian reformers and hard-line conservatives agree that liberty requires an economic base. But they draw very different conclusions from this premise, and part of the difference lies in their understanding of the relation between property, liberty and inequality.

Funston argues that judicial neglect of property rights arises from a "double standard"[32] of judicial review based on a division between personal rights and property rights. He maintains that this division is at odds with a legal and philosophical tradition which insisted upon the "equality of the values of property and liberty."[33] More importantly, the double standard fails to recognize the integral connection between property and liberty which is, in his view, both part of our tradition and an important political reality. (He is right in the general sense about the tradition, except that, as I have argued above, the Framers did see a tension between property rights, personal rights and political liberty, and ranked them in that order.)

Funston sees two promising indications that the Court may be moving away from this double standard toward greater protection for property. He cites Justice Stewart's argument in *Lynch* v. *Household Finance* that "[T]he dichotomy between personal liberties and property rights is a false one ... a fundamental interdependence exists between the personal rights to liberty and the personal right to

[31] "Double standard."

[32] The classic critique of the double standard is Robert McCloskey, "Economic due process and the Supreme Court: an exhumation and burial," *Supreme Court Review* (1962).

[33] "Double standard," 262.

property. Neither could have meaning without the other."[34] Funston also finds "a heightened sensitivity to property claims" in the Court's willingness to uphold "property interests against First Amendment and equal protection claims."[35] He sees all this as promising not only because it may redress an unjustifiable imbalance in contemporary jurisprudence, but because appropriate protections for property will provide a basis for fuller, and more egalitarian, protection for liberty.

Funston is not simply talking about protection for the "new property." He also suggests that a renewed recognition of the relation between property and liberty, of the necessary economic basis of liberty, would generate a greater judicial scrutiny of laws that seem to discriminate on the basis of wealth. He argues that a court that was willing to make real inquiries into "the rationality of legislation affecting property-related interests" (as opposed to accepting whatever the state claims the purpose and effect of the law would be) might have come to different conclusions in cases where discrimination against the poor was alleged: in the *Rodriguez* case, where the Court rejected a challenge to the local property tax system of financing public education on the (equal protection) grounds that it disadvantaged children from poor districts,[36] and in the *Valtierra* case, where the Court upheld a special requirement for submitting low-income housing proposals to prior referenda.[37] He seems to think that a court used to scrutinizing legislation interfering with property and sensitive to the interrelation between property and liberty would be sympathetic to the dangers of discrimination against the (powerless) poor and perhaps even to arguments that some kind of material equality is necessary for the exercise of the rights the Constitution guarantees.

Without going into it here,[38] I simply note that the argument that civil or political rights require, and therefore entitle one to, economic equality implies a radical leap from our traditional liberal conceptions

---

[34] 405 U.S. 538 (1972), cited in "Double standard," 276. The case involved garnishment of the plaintiffs' credit union account. The issue was whether there was a federal jurisdiction over cases involving property rights brought under Section 1982. This ruling provides a new avenue for judicial protection of property rights.

[35] "Double standard," 277.

[36] *San Antonio Independent School District* v. *Rodriguez*, 411 U.S. 1 (1973).

[37] *James* v. *Valtierra*, 402 U.S. 137 (1971).

[38] I elaborate this argument in "Law, legitimacy, and the transformation of the liberal state," presented at the Canadian Political Science Association, Halifax, 1981.

to rights.[39] This is the leap which conservatives fear lurks behind arguments like plaintiffs' in *Rodriguez*, and the emphatic conservative rejection of that leap indicates why we should not be sanguine that a renewed judicial interest in property would lead to an egalitarian approach to the need for an economic basis for liberty.

Inequality has been at the center of the traditional American understanding of the relationship between property and liberty. Liberty, according to the tradition, generates unequal property through the free exercise of unequal faculties. The protection of liberty thus requires a protection of inequality with all its political consequences (consequences whose threatening aspects the Constitution was designed to mitigate). C. B. Macpherson also regards this inequality as inevitable, given our prevailing definition of property. "Property as an exclusive right of a natural or artificial person to use and dispose of material things . . . leads necessarily, in any kind of market society . . . to an inequality of wealth and power that denies a lot of people the possibility of a reasonably human life. The narrow institution of property is bound to result in such inequality, in any society short of a genetically engineered one that would have ironed out all differences in skill and energy."[40] His solution is a radically nonmaterial definition of property which is not premised on exclusivity.

I note these arguments to indicate that the conservatives rest on solid ground when they argue that their understanding of proper protection for property and liberty militates against what they see as a dangerous drive toward equality. It is clear that Bernard Seigan, for example, does not think increased security from legislative interferences with property would or should lead to a different outcome in *Rodriguez*. He *wants* property to stand in the way of, to take priority over, affirmative egalitarian measures.

Had *Rodriguez* and *Maher* [another case on discrimination on the basis of wealth, which held that the Constitution does not require

[39] There have, of course, been proponents of this position, from the Anti-Federalists' call for a republic with only moderate disparities of wealth, through the demand for "forty acres and a mule" for the former slaves, to the contemporary arguments by liberal academics that greater economic equality is necessary to make good on liberal claims. But none of these has prevailed, and virtually all claims for economic *entitlements* derived from civil or political rights have been strenuously and successfully resisted.

[40] "Human rights as property rights," 73.

public funding for abortions] been decided differently, any societal structure with serious wealth inequalities would have been threatened. At some point the Court would have had to decide that a person does not have a fundamental right to food, clothing, medicine, housing, legal assistance, or other "just wants." If it did not in time so hold, the Court would have imposed a guaranteed annual income that would have been supplied from the pockets of people not represented in the making of these decisions.[41]

From the conservative perspective, the purpose of a return to judicial protection of property and economic liberties is to prevent such ill-conceived egalitarianism. In the eyes of conservatives, claims to substantive equality imply not only redistribution but major shifts from negative to affirmative concepts of rights, from allocation by the market to allocation by political process, and from a limited state to an all-encompassing bureaucracy. Egalitarianism threatens property and liberty. Conversely, property protected by the judiciary can serve as a barrier to such undermining of our tradition.

The conservatives have cogent (though limited) arguments and the weight of history on their side. They do not always take adequate account of the ways property has changed over the years; their conception of property as the source of autonomy and boundary to the legitimate scope of state authority is often anachronistic. Nevertheless it seems more likely that a renewed interest in property rights would follow along a deeply laid groove of inequality rather than serve as a path toward an egalitarian conception of the material base for liberty.

The meaning of property and its proper place in our constitutional structure is contested domain. The fact that conservatives as well as radicals and reformers are urging greater attention to property suggests that one ought to be wary about using property as a vehicle for egalitarian conceptions of rights. It is certainly the case that property has traditionally been associated with the values of independence, privacy, autonomy and participation. But in our tradition that association has always been shaped by premises of inequality. Even today, when the rhetoric of egalitarianism is commonplace, the inequality of property still seems to be widely accepted. The old categories still prevail, in modified form. The distinction between

41 *Economic Liberties and the Constitution*, p. 310.

economic and political rights remains strong. And while political equality is now accepted, it has never interfered with the basic acceptance of (sometimes commitment to) economic inequality.[42] The effort to build on the concept of property in order to foster an equal distribution of its associated values may turn out to work against one of the most powerful elements in the tradition: the link between inequality, property and liberty.

V

So far I have been using the tradition to make arguments about strategy, suggesting that efforts to use property as a vehicle for egalitarian reform may be dangerously ineffective.[43] But, paradoxically (as is appropriate with property), I have equally serious concerns about the consequences should such radical redefinitions take hold. These redefinitions are potential threats to the mythic quality of property that has sustained the central tension between democracy and limiting values in American constitutionalism. This mythic quality is best revealed by the paradoxical nature of property in our tradition, and so it is to that dimension of the tradition that I now turn.

The American conception and practice of constitutionalism developed together with private property – in our categories of rights, in our conception of limited government and in the institutionalization of rights as limits in judicial review. The picture is not, however, a simple one. After the Court had successfully established the power of judicial review and the sanctity of property and contract, there followed a period of some fifty or sixty years in which the courts fostered and allowed the redefinition of the basic rules of exchange and entitlement which they had so carefully claimed as their domain in the first decades of the nineteenth century. Property was, in effect, neither stable, nor

[42] See Jennifer Hochschild, *What's Fair: American Beliefs About Distributive Justice* (Cambridge, Mass., 1981).

[43] There is a countervailing strategic benefit which I have not discussed. Attention drawn to the need to redefine property may have an important educative function. Redefining property may have the advantage of getting people to rethink their understanding of this basic right, rather than frightening them, as a frontal attack on private property would. It is hard to know how to weigh the dangers of inadvertently giving additional support to traditional, inegalitarian, restrictive conceptions of property against the advantage of changing people's presumption about the nature of their basic rights.

sacred, nor a barrier to governmental authority. The redefinitions of property amounted to violations of vested rights,[44] and the courts placed practically no limits on the use of eminent domain, even by private corporations.[45] Yet throughout this development, the rhetoric of property did not change. There was no major redefinition of property as contingent on the public good, or as a matter for legislative rather than judicial determination.[46] And the rhetoric of property as the foundation of the republic and the guardian of individual rights was picked up again in the period about 1880 to 1930 and used in striking down a wide range of social welfare legislation and economic regulation. By 1937 both the practice and rhetoric had shifted. The Court abandoned its "economic due process" of the previous period, and, as we have seen, property is today in a state of disintegration and indeterminacy. If property still serves as some kind of outer limit to what legislatures would try to do, or courts would tolerate, it is not a boundary against which government routinely pushes (or when it does, the boundary is routinely pushed back). Property is not the basis on which the Court tries to draw the line between individual rights and governmental power.

Nevertheless, this judicial practice does not seem as yet to have shaken the popular force of the idea of property as a limit to the legitimate power of government. However much the "layman's understanding" of property as things is being blurred by increasing contact with legal abstractions, the idea that "government can't take what's mine" seems to be holding fast.[47] This belief may in fact be the last vestige of a popular understanding of constitutionalism. In an era

---

[44] See Horwitz, *Transformation of American Law.*

[45] See Scheiber, "Property law, expropriation, and resource allocation."

[46] Some of the nineteenth-century cases, eminent domain in particular, contain comments about the need to balance private rights and public good, and occasionally even a broad claim that property is always held subject to the needs of the community. But these comments do not amount to, or lead to, an overall reevaluation or redefinition of property. The basic conception of and rhetorical stance toward property seem to remain the same, despite intermittent statements of contingency. The judiciary of the "economic due process" era was able to call upon the sacred tradition of property in part because the conception of property as a limiting value remained dominant despite practice and occasional pronouncements to the contrary.

[47] This is, of course, based largely on impressionistic evidence. For example, the advertisements urging citizens to think of social security as something which is *theirs*, which they have paid for, suggest that some people clearly think it is a forceful argument. The resistance to the idea of inheritance tax is another such indication. See generally Hochschild, *What's Fair.*

when the language of democracy dominates political rhetoric, there does not seem to be widespread appreciation of the nuances of constitutionalism. "The government can't take what's mine" may, however, still serve, as it originally did, as a basic limit on the idea that "the majority rules." The Court's virtual abandonment of property as a barrier has not brought with it a public crisis of constitutionalism.[48] Perhaps that is in part because the *idea* of property as a limit endures in popular belief. And the enduring power of this idea may be the single most compelling reason for building upon property to establish new values as the foundations of constitutionalism.

I raise the issue of the popular conception of property in part because the whole idea of property as the basis for liberty and limit to government rests on a myth; it is not the intrinsic nature of legal rights to property or the actual practice of their protection which accounts for this idea, but the special hold which the concept of property seems to have on people's imagination.

In some ways property is the ideal symbol or focus for the limits to governmental authority because of its concrete character. Physical invasion of private property is a particularly obvious kind of public violation of private rights; one's property can form a literal material boundary to the legitimate scope of state power. But this represents only part of property's paradoxical nature. Property is held out as a symbol of rights which are independent limits to the scope of governmental authority. At the same time, property is, of all the basic rights, perhaps most obviously the creation of the state. If a purpose of government is to protect property, that is in part because property (unlike freedom of conscience, for example) could not exist without the mechanism of government.

Property takes its very meaning from the definition given to it by the state. Even classic American invocations of natural rights and limits to legislative power have been coupled with acknowledgements that property is a matter of positive law.[49] Property is thus the boundary to governmental power, but it is a boundary government itself draws. Through property and its definition by the judiciary, the state creates,

---

[48] It is hard to assess how much the disintegration of property has contributed to the academic crisis of faith in the coherence of all legal doctrines. It seems more likely that the disintegration of property is merely one part rather than the cause of this crisis.

[49] See, for example, *Calder* v. *Bull*, 3 Dall. 385 (1798).

and shifts, and recreates its own limits. This is the American form of the essential problem of self-limiting government.

Self (state)-defined limits only work to sustain constitutionalism if the reality of self-definition is obscured by the mythic quality of those limits. Rights can only be effective as a boundary if the belief in their independent constitutional status is maintained. At least within legal circles, property's claim to this status has been seriously shaken. I will return shortly to the question whether something else has taken its place.

The other mythic element of property is perhaps even more important. The claim that the institution of private property is the only sound basis for individual liberty rests on the belief that the legal entitlement to property is somehow qualitatively different from any other form of legal entitlement. Consider, for example, the argument that freedom of the press can be truly secure only under a regime of private property. This translates into a claim that the protections the state provides for property (protections which enable one to be secure in the ownership of a press and thus independent of government pressure) are more reliable than the protections a state could provide directly against censorship or interference from other public or private sources. This is the essence of all forms of the claim that "the only dependable foundation of personal liberty is the economic security of private property."[50] The claim is repeated so often, and in such surprising contexts (Reich, for instance, refers to "the need for a property base in civil liberties"[51] despite the fact that he has a clear understanding of the ways property is the creation of the state) that one can only assume that it has enormous intuitive appeal.

There is, however, nothing obvious about why legal entitlements to property should be intrinsically more secure than legal entitlements to other rights. There is almost certainly no intrinsic difference in the nature of the legal entitlements themselves to justify the claim that protections of property rights are more reliable and provide greater security. The reason for property's special status seems to be the sense that property secured by the power of the state provides a greater *experience* of security, independence and autonomy than, say, guar-

---

[50] Walter Lippman, quoted in Seigan, *Economic Liberties and the Constitution*, p. 330.
[51] "The new property," 777.

antees of noninterference with editorial decisions or income provided by the state. Although the legal protections could be comparable, people feel, or think they would feel, more confident in the security of a relationship defined as ownership than in the security of direct legal entitlements or guarantees. Certainly the role of the state is more obvious in such entitlements or guarantees than in ownership. And direct state action will be invoked less frequently in securing property than dispensing income. But these differences also seem to be matters of psychological experience rather than differences intrinsic to the vulnerability of the entitlements or to the power they confer.[52]

If I am right that this experience lies at the heart of why people believe property rights bear a special relation to liberty,[53] then the impressive and enduring power of this experience is not to be underestimated. It leads me to ask whether any conception of rights which is not rooted in or symbolically associated with something concrete like material goods can ever have the hold on people's imagination which property has had for centuries.[54] With this question in mind, I return to the implications of changes in the conception of property for American constitutionalism.

If property has been central to the basic tension between democracy and limiting values on which American constitutionalism rests, what happens to the tension and to the system when the pivotal concept of property changes? Implicit in this question is the much larger problem of how flexible the American constitutional system is: whether, for example, the tension can be realigned without undermining its basic structure. The issue of property points in the direction of answers.

---

[52] If, for example, it is a question of how many steps government would have to go to to deprive one of one's property as opposed to one's income, or what kinds of institutions (legislatures, courts, or administrative bodies) would make the decision, then there seems no reason why the institutional procedures in both cases could not be virtually identical.

[53] As the conflict between conservatives and liberal egalitarians shows, the belief in the special relation between property and liberty is something quite different from the claim that there are many rights which cannot be enjoyed unless one's material needs are taken care of and one is not subject to the power of another.

[54] While this attitude toward property is hardly unique to the United States, it is possible that its vigorous endurance here is one of the ideological triumphs of the American constitutional system. Judicial review has provided for an extraordinarily effective mutual reinforcement between ideology and the structure of power. It is of course conceivable that the reconception of property by the courts, commentators and publicists of various kinds could gradually reshape people's experience of the relation between property and liberty.

Part of the answer lies in the legal issues to which the Court has turned its attention since its virtual abandonment of property. This is itself a large subject which I can only touch on here. In short, however, I think that the Court has increasingly been interested in matters of procedure and that the substantive rights, such as privacy, which it has protected have neither the material base nor the intuitive clarity of property rights. It seems possible that while this shift is in many ways entirely appropriate, it may entail a threat to constitutionalism as we have known it.

The abandonment of property as barrier and the increased attention to matters of procedure and process may have shifted the balance of our constitutional structure. There may now be less emphasis on limiting values and more on democracy, not because the Court no longer overturns legislation, but because of the kind of legislation it overturns and the grounds on which it does so. This trend may suggest that property has lost its original place because the idea of sharp boundaries between the sphere of individual rights and legitimate governmental authority is not tenable in a regulatory welfare state.[55] It remains to be seen whether a new balance can be struck, whether the new rights being protected can sustain the tension necessary for constitutionalism, or whether we shall have to rethink our notion of limited government altogether.

All of these questions become clearer when examined in light of proposals for change. Michelman's proposal provides an illuminating focus since his arguments are made in an explicitly constitutional context. He sees a "puzzle" of property similar to the one I have outlined above:

> it is both an implicit premise of the constitutional system that individual holdings are always subject to the risk of occasional redistribution of values through the popularly ordained operations of government, both active and regulatory, and an explicit premise of the system that people can have property, be owners, not only as among themselves but also vis-à-vis the state.[56]

[55] This is an argument I spell out in "Individual autonomy in the bureaucratic state: toward a reconception," presented at the 1983 meeting of the American Political Science Association.

[56] "Property as a constitutional right."

He seems to see this puzzle as reflective of the necessary tension of constitutionalism or what he refers to as "the deeper contradiction in our best attitudes towards popular rule and individual worth, infinitely valuing them both." He suggests that he respects this tension and seeks only a partial resolution, one "that allows us to experience the contradiction as generative tension rather than a dead end."[57]

The premise for his resolution is that "rights under a political constitution, including property rights, are first of all to be regarded as political rights." This premise provides a basis for assigning a meaning to the property rights which the Constitution promises to protect, but does not define: "what one primarily has a right to is the maintenance of the conditions of one's fair and effective participation in the constituted order ... Loss – and even great loss – of the economic value of one's holdings may not as such violate these conditions ... What does, perhaps, violate them is exposure to sudden changes in the major elements and crucial determinants of one's established position in the world, as one has come ... to understand that position."[58] Michelman suggests that the determination of what constitutes a constitutionally impermissible encroachment on individual "property" rights may be made on this basis.

Assuming the practicality of such a standard, what are its implications? Michelman's proposal purports not to eliminate the tension of constitutionalism, since it offers a standard against which to measure the action of a democratic legislature. He does not simply say that property means whatever the state says it does. But the premise on which the proposal rests seems to eliminate the distinction between political rights and civil rights which was once fundamental to our system. While the justification for all the checks and restraints on democracy was once that political rights are only means to the end of protecting the rights of persons and property (and these restraints are particularly necessary to protect property), we are now told that all our constitutional rights, including property, should be seen primarily as political rights. Even though the right to effective participation is to serve as an independent, judicially enforceable, standard for legislative action, the collapsing of categories of rights seems to threaten the tension of constitutionalism as it has existed in our tradition. At the

[57] *Ibid.*   [58] *Ibid.*

very least, Michelman turns the original hierarchy upside down: political rights are primary and the rights of property are to be defined in terms of what will safeguard and promote these political rights.

A departure from the original tradition may be appropriate. A political theory which is more democratic than that of the Framers may require a shift in emphasis on political rights. It may be necessary to abandon genuinely substantive limits on the legislature (as opposed to those aimed at protecting the political process) in an era when there is faith neither in natural rights nor in the existence of a unitary common good, certain to be best for all. (Interestingly, the conservatives who advocate a return to traditional protections of property rights seem to have faith that there is a clear common good. They seem confident that their preferred system of economic liberties and free enterprise is genuinely in the best interest of all.) It is important for us to consider, however, that the redefinition of property rights Michelman proposes would reshape the structure of our system by giving a very different meaning to constitutionalism than it has had, and than the system was designed to implement. This brings me, finally, to the question of whether the proposed redefinitions of property could sustain constitutionalism in the light of my argument about the psychological basis for the rhetorical power of property.

The idea of constitutionalism need not be based on natural rights, but it does require a commitment to the limiting values which is deep and strong enough to resist the force of majority rule. The values which are to serve as enforceable limits on the will of the majority must command such commitment or either they or the system of constitutionalism built on them will, in the long run, fall before the compelling and legitimate power of democracy. This is surely even more true today than when the Constitution was formed.

In 1787 property was a perfect candidate for such a value. It had an impressive philosophical tradition behind it: both Locke and the republican thinkers such as Harrington stressed the importance and value of property. The protection of property had been an important issue in the rhetoric of the Revolution, "No taxation without representation" being the most famous instance. It was a right with which most Americans had some immediate, personal connection, and it had a concrete quality which made it an ideal symbol for the barrier between individual rights and legitimate governmental power.

This is the tradition upon which those who want to redefine property hope to draw. My closing question is whether the proposed redefinitions will be able to sustain the link with tradition or have sufficient force of their own to serve as effective limiting values.

One of the potential problems is that the new definitions remove property from the concrete, material quality the concept has traditionally had. It is certainly not the case that the traditional conceptions of property – either constitutional or Common Law – have been simple or exclusively material.[59] But they have had a clear material base which is the core of both the legal and popular conceptions. The problem is that the effectiveness of the new conceptions may depend on the extent to which they are rooted in the material quality which has given property its special, enduring power. It may be that only such rootedness could give them the force, the hold on people's imaginations, to serve as a basis for constitutionalism. Not just the population at large, but judges require a concept, a value with at least some of the mythic, rhetorical power which property has had. And this may prove problematic for the new conceptions.

The very extent to which the new definitions are egalitarian seems to be the extent to which they depart from the material base of property. Egalitarian reconceptions thus not only fly in the face of a major part of the tradition, they may undermine the most compelling part of the concept of property. And Macpherson, as I noted earlier, suggests that this conflict is inevitable. As long as property is essentially material (and exclusive) it will generate inequality. Those who want to redefine property to make it the basis of equitably distributed goods of autonomy, privacy or effective participation may have to give

[59] Indeed it is part of the Common Law's claim to fame that its concept of property was divisible and abstract enough from a very early stage to allow for such useful concepts as trusts and remainder interests. The proposal in the Youngstown case that a community has a property claim on an industry that has "drawn the life blood" of the community is an instance of an effort to build on the less material elements of the traditional concept. (This is also, to use Macpherson's terms, not an exclusive right, but a right not to be excluded.) Thus the plaintiffs refer to their property claim as an easement (the most common instance of which is a right of way over another's property). This proposal was intended to meet a particular need, not to redefine all of property. It thus need not be able to carry the weight of constitutionalism. While the Youngstown proposal is clearly at odds with other concepts of property (U.S. Steel's rights to use and dispose of its property), this seems to me to be the kind of stretching of the concept which would contribute only slightly to its disintegration. Precisely because it is less ambitious, it does not pose the problems for constitutionalism which the more complete redefinitions do.

up the link to property's most compelling aspect. And to the extent that they do so, they may create a concept so abstract that it will not have adequate force as a limiting value.

The question which the perspective of the tradition then poses is whether property radically redefined can continue to serve its original function as a pillar of constitutionalism – as the focal point or symbol for the limits to legitimate state power. The efforts at egalitarian redefinition raise questions about whether any abstraction, such as autonomy, could serve as an effective limiting value and whether there is something about egalitarianism itself (perhaps its necessary abstractness) which threatens constitutionalism as we have known it. My point is not that there is any theoretical or intrinsic reason why a concept like autonomy (or property redefined to mean autonomy) could not be the limiting value – as opposed to participation, which by its democratic, process-oriented nature threatens to collapse the tension between democracy and limiting values upon which American constitutionalism has rested. My suggestion is rather that property seems to have held its place in American constitutionalism for as long as it has because of its rhetorical, mythical power. If it is to be replaced or redefined, the alternative may have to have the same intuitive appeal, evoke a comparably powerful response, command the same kind of allegiance which property has traditionally been able to. If property redefined loses this force, it may lose as well its effectiveness as the symbolic limit to governmental power.

VI

The reader may by now see the paradoxical elements of my argument: property has so disintegrated that it can no longer serve its constitutional functions; property is so important to constitutionalism that we ought not risk redefining it in a way which would weaken constitutionalism; property has been such a pernicious force in our constitutional tradition that it would be a grave error to use the concept to effect egalitarian reform.

This paradoxical quality is, I think, generated first by the paradox of property – that there has always been a striking gap between rhetoric and legal reality – and second, by my judgment that property is, in fact, at the root of both what is best and what is worst about the American constitutional system.

But paradox does not, I hope, mean incoherence. The disintegration of the concept of property and its at least partial displacement as the primary limiting value do not render any further discussion purely academic for two reasons. First, my concern throughout this paper: it seems important to understand that, given property's place in the basic structure of the Constitution and in the conception of constitutionalism, a radical change in this status may signal far-reaching consequences in the best as well as the worst of the system. The history of property in the tradition suggests that the impact or likelihood of such changes probably rests not just with some increasing gap between rhetoric and reality (for we know that the system has sustained dramatic gaps), but with the undermining of the very rhetorical power of property.

Secondly, the disintegration of property does not render it irrelevant because there are compelling arguments to reinstate property – suitably redefined – as a fundamental, limiting value.

It is the call for reinstatement which brings out the real double edge to my views on property and the Constitution. I am completely persuaded that any fundamental egalitarian and democratic transformation of the system requires a radical reconception of property. I am doubtful whether the constitutional right of property, or indeed the American Constitution, can be a vehicle for such reform. The system was designed neither to facilitate participatory democracy nor to cope with the problem of the overlap between economic and political power. While I believe that both of these basic weaknesses stem from the original preoccupation with the protection of property, I am not at all sure that one can eliminate them by superimposing a radical redefinition of property on to the existing system. And in the meantime, a reinvigoration of property may give new force to its traditional limitations.

On the other side, I think that the original concern with protecting property generated an appreciation of what I take to be a fundamental and enduring political problem: the tension between the individual and the collective. The American solution to this problem is deeply flawed: it is skewed, as I noted earlier, by its origins in property. But I am nevertheless reluctant to embrace an alternative which seems not to acknowledge this tension, or which would eliminate the institutional tension between democracy and limiting values. The proposed redefinitions seem to threaten to do this by destroying property's rhetorical power and thus weakening its efficacy as a limit, or by collapsing the distinction between civil and political rights, thus undermining the very idea of rights as substantive limits to the outcomes of democratic processes.

If, as I sometimes think, not merely a redefinition of property but a major restructuring of our institutions is necessary for a truly democratic and egalitarian society, then the lesson of property and American constitutionalism is this: the ideal system requires some conception of individual rights which provides a countervailing, limiting value to democracy. The necessary tension can probably be sustained only if the value is not conceived in terms of political rights and if it has the rhetorical power of myth. If property redefined is to be the route to radical reform, it must be redefined with this in mind.

9. From liberal constitutionalism to corporate pluralism: the conflict over the enabling acts in Norway after the Second World War and the subsequent constitutional development[1]

FRANCIS SEJERSTED

In 1945 all the political parties represented in the Storting (the Norwegian parliament) put up a joint program for the reconstruction period. The only party not to sign the program was the Communist Party. The setting up of a joint program has led to the conclusion that there was an exceptionally high degree of political consensus in Norway in the late forties. There are, however, some factors which complicate the picture. On the one hand it is correct that there was a general reaction against the old party feuds and a general feeling of unity in the nation. On the other hand there was what may be seen as conflict to win leadership over the unified nation. Thus we find a curious blend of conflict and unity. While the joint program expressed unity, the conflict over laws regulating prices and production revealed deep ideological divisions. Political strife concerning these laws started in the Norwegian War Cabinet in London in 1944 and continued up to 1953. We shall return to the "solution" found in that year.

The laws mentioned above were enabling acts by which the Storting gave broad discretionary powers to the government and to the public administration for intervention in economic life. There was general agreement that the administration should have discretionary powers. The conflict concentrated on the extent of these powers. In the early phase of the debate, however, it appeared that constitutional questions were not significant issues for some participants. This applies to

A first draft of this chapter was presented at a conference at Ustaoset in January, 1983. I benefited greatly from the debate at the seminar. In particular I want to thank Torkel Opsahl and Rune Slagstad for their comments.

[1] This chapter was originally written in 1983 in connection with the work on a history of the Conservative Party. The discussion of the Labor Party is based mainly on second-hand sources.

the case of the young power elite in the Labor Party which attained an absolute majority in the Storting in 1945. This group represented a generation full of enthusiasm, courage, plans for the future and also, to a certain degree, desire for dominance. The binding power of the rule of law and complicated procedures and the ability of the courts of justice to test the decisions of the administration were felt to be unnecessary hindrances. Discretionary power conceded by the far-reaching enabling acts, on the other hand, provided opportunities and freedom for action.

The tendency toward more enabling acts was a natural part of the growing state power. A modern society needed more government. A strong state could also serve as an instrument in the emancipation of underprivileged groups. However, whereas the latter looked upon the growing state power as a good in itself, others looked upon it as a problem and a threat to liberty. Both sides could agree, however, that the development pointed out a new way of governing society. The old liberal state of the nineteenth century was built on distrust of state power; state activity had to a large degree been concentrated on law-making. According to the principle of legality, every decision made by the government or the administration should be based on laws given by the Storting. And these laws should be of a kind which minimized the necessity (or possibility) of the government's or the administration's using discretionary power. This implied that many decisions would be predictable and that they could be controlled by the courts of justice. There would always be some need for discretionary power, but the tendency toward more enabling acts which ultimately led to the constitutional conflict in the years following the Second World War involved an expansion of the discretionary power beyond the limits of the old rule-of-law state. The change implied a new role for the administration, which should no longer limit itself to the nondiscriminatory establishment of a general framework within which private interests could take initiatives.

The old rule-of-law state had already been fundamentally modified through the development of political and social rights in addition to the original civil rights (to use T. H. Marshall's threefold typology of rights). While the state had been regarded as a potential threat to civil rights, it was the guarantor of social rights. So the developments of the first decades of the twentieth century involved a more state-positive attitude in general. The idea that the state should be the main initiator in economic life was, however, new in Western societies. Nevertheless, it was relatively easily adopted in the Keynesian macro version. But state dirigism on the micro level was a different question: it was bound to be felt as more of a threat to the normative structure of the liberal society than either the growth of social rights or Keynesian economics.

The conflict over the enabling acts had its roots in the debate over concession laws immediately before and after the First World War. This conflict was followed by a conflict over the laws on price and production regulation in the twenties. The Trust Commission reported from 1921 that "there has been a concentration and an organization in industry by which the free competition has been modified."[2] This development could be met in two ways, according to the report. The state could either reestablish free competition by prohibiting agreements on the regulation of competition, or it could control, or perhaps even take part in, the management of the trusts and monopolies in question. The commission recommended a combined solution.

A young commission member, Wilhelm Thagaard, emphasized more strongly than the rest of the commission that the trusts and monopolies represented a necessary cooperation and organization in industry. To ensure that industry worked for the common good, there had, however, to be efficient control and perhaps even "a change to public management."[3] Thagaard was inspired by the minority vote in the British Trust Commission report written by Ernest Bevin, J. A. Hobson, W. H. Watkins and Sidney Webb.[4] He was appointed head of the Trust Control Commission and later of the Directorate of Prices. In these positions he practiced the Trust Laws according to his own views on the bad effects of competition and the good effects of cooperation in industry and trade.

Thagaard came to London in 1944, where he became the architect of the governmental decree on price and production regulation named after him: the "lex Thagaard." This was by all standards a very radical decree by which the administration was given power to regulate

---

[2] Report 1921. *Parl. pap.* 1924. O. prp. 46. Appendix, p. 8.
[3] *Ibid.*, p. 48. [4] *Parl. pap.* 1924. O. prp. 46. Appendix.

FRANCIS SEJERSTED

prices, to forbid reduction or stoppage in production, to order the manufacture of certain goods, to forbid the establishment of enterprises or the shutting down of factories and to impose taxes to be used for price regulation. The decree immediately met with heavy opposition. The only reason it did not blow up the Norwegian War Cabinet was that it was passed in the Cabinet on Liberation Day in May, 1945.[5] Thagaard aimed at nothing less than a new function for public administration. A new type of civil servant was needed. The old system in which the majority of civil servants did not have any decision-making powers had undermined their ability to take initiative according to Thagaard. What were required in the new system were competent, alert and innovative civil servants who would be able to see the wider implications of what they were doing. For economists this demand was not difficult, it was thought. Since there were very few economists in the public administration, Thagaard suggested a reschooling program.[6]

We find enabling acts in many other countries in the interwar years. In some nations we get a clearer demonstration of the more doubtful implications than in Norway during this period. Johs. Andenæs, a professor of law, had this to say in the concluding phase of the Norwegian debate:

Enabling acts can be used as means of putting the democratic constitutional system out of function. This was what happened in Germany when the Reichstag by an act of March 24, 1933 decided not only that legislation could take place as prescribed in the constitution, but also that the government could act as a legislator. The enabling act was a form chosen to give the transition from democracy to dictatorship an appearance of legality.[7]

The growing need for state power collided with the requirements of democracy and public security. Obviously there was room for compromise based on different concepts of a good society.

5 *Parl. pap.* 1947. Vol. 5. Doc. 6. F. Sejersted, *Opposision og posisjon* (Oslo, 1984), p. 18.
6 W. Thagaard, "Den offentlige administrasjon under et system med statsregulert næringsliv," *Nordisk Administrativt Tidsskrift* (1946), 166–7.
7 Johs. Andenæs, "Domstolenes stilling til Stortingets delegasjon av myndighet" (paper presented in 1953), in *Avhandlinger og Foredrag* (Oslo, 1962), p. 289.

The debate in 1947

The committee which prepared the lex Thagaard emphasized that the decree should only be valid for a very short and difficult transitional period. This was also stressed by the Ministry of Finance, which, in addition, stated that the "drastic decree" should only be used "with the utmost care."[8] Such comments were not sufficient to prevent bitter accusations from the opposition that the Labor Party wanted to introduce "Nazi dictatorship in economic life."[9] The precondition was, however, that the decree should be presented for the new Storting as soon as possible. The Labor government asked Thagaard himself to make the preparations for the presentation. For different reasons this was delayed until June 1947.[10]

In the meantime other enabling acts were passed in the Storting. The provisional decrees from the Norwegian War Cabinet in London on export, import and currency were replaced by temporary acts which gave the government and the administration free hands in a detailed regulation of foreign trade. These acts were by and large carried unanimously, but not without a deep feeling of uneasiness on the part of the opposition. One of the leading Conservatives, John Lyng, proposed that the acts should be made valid for only one and a half years, because, as he said, "general enabling acts such as those in question could only be defended under absolutely exceptional circumstances." The only way to prevent them from being permanent was to set a time-limit, according to Lyng. A fundamentally different view was expressed by the Communist representative Kittil Berg, who wanted an ordinary permanent law. The result was a provisional law which lasted for many years.[11] The uneasiness of the opposition was thus accentuated before the great debate on the laws on price and production regulation in 1947. It felt that it had already been pushed quite far.

The proposals put forward by the Labor government in 1947 followed, by and large, the radical pattern of the lex Thagaard. The proposals provoked a very heated general debate. According to the

---

[8] *Parl. pap.* 1947. D 5. Doc. 6, p. 67–8.
[9] General Committee. Cons. Party 26–5–45.
[10] Thagaard's report. *Parl. pap.* 1945/46. Appendix to O.prp. 152.
[11] *Parl. pap.* 1946. Tid. O., pp. 715, 716. John Lyng, *Veksten i statens makt* (Oslo, 1958), pp. 110–16.

Conservative Party leader, C. J. Hambro, they "unmasked the totalitarian views of the Labor Party." Concessions to Hambro's view were indeed given by one of the Labor Party leaders, Sverre Støstad: "When it comes to the fundamental question of how we shall organize our production, our economic life in the future in order to create the maximum happiness for as many people as possible, then it must be permitted to use means of regulation which are also used by totalitarian regimes, if necessary."[12] The strongest attacks were directed against laws on production regulation which simply gave the government a free hand to regulate production by direct measures. The attacks were so severe that the more lenient Conservative representatives, Lyng and Sjur Lindebrække, dissociated themselves from them in the Storting.

The members of the opposition were not absolutely unanimous, but came close to an agreement in principle. The Liberal Party representative, Lars Ramndal, asked whether it was the intention "to regulate people into a new order of society."[13] Lyng, who was the main speaker from the Conservative Party, had three counterarguments. First, he maintained that the proposals represented a threat to political democracy by moving "important issues away from the open and free forum where they should be argued with the opposition and over to decisions behind closed doors and drawn curtains in the offices of the administration." Secondly, he meant that the proposals would lead to such fundamental changes in the relations between parliament and government that it could not be in accordance with the Constitution: "Furthermore, the proposal gives legal authority to encroachments on the rights of the individual of a kind which raises doubts about its constitutionality." Thirdly, there were the objections "on the basis of purely economic–political considerations": "When the administration is endowed with the full power of attorney to take fundamental and unpredictable measures within the field of labor relations and basis of existence of most of the professions, an atmosphere of unsafety and uncertainty will be created which in its turn will suppress the creative initiative."[14] The counter-

[12] *Morgenbladet* 24–2–47. According to Nils Ragnar Kamsvåg, *Høyre og den økonomiske politikken 1945–53* (Cand. philol. thesis, 1980). This section of the present chapter is partly based on Kamsvåg. *Parl. pap.* 1947. O., p. 498.

[13] *Parl. pap.* 1947. Tid. O., p. 452.

[14] *Ibid.*, pp. 459–61 and Innst. O. X 1947, p. 16.

arguments of Lyng were both constitutional and economic, but with the main emphasis on the former.

Vested interests were of course involved in the conflict, and the Conservative Party was in danger of being isolated as a party for the business class. The organizations of business and industry had been deeply involved in the public debate, and the party leaders feared that the party could be too closely associated with these organizations.[15] This was the main reason why the Conservative Party wanted a coordinated opposition by all the nonsocialist parties; that did not, however, materialize.[16] This fear of being isolated as a party for business interests shows the limitations of the constitutional arguments. It could be held that the issue was not whether the decisions concerning price and production regulation should be taken by the Storting or by the administration as maintained by Lyng, but whether they should be taken by the state or by the businessmen. The Labor Party attacked the opposition along these lines, holding that the planned economy with state regulations was the most democratic solution.

There were influential people in the Conservative Party who warned against the constitutional arguments and emphasized the economic arguments of free enterprise.[17] To use economic arguments was, however, to meet the Labor Party on home ground. The main strategy of the Labor Party was to use practical and down-to-earth arguments for a planned economy. According to the Minister of Finance, Erik Brofoss, the issue had nothing to do with political principles; it was just a matter of finding practical solutions to common problems: "The political debate is like a burst of cannon fire over no-man's-land."[18] The strategy was effective not least because the special needs of the reconstruction period coincided with the general policies of the Labor Party. The special need for regulations in the reconstruction period was the greatest problem for the Conservative Party. Exceptional circumstances forced the party to give more concessions to planned economy and to the discretionary power of the administration than it would have done under more normal

---

[15] See *inter alia* a letter from six business organizations, *Parl. pap.* 1947. D. 5. Dok. nr. 5, pp. 7, 12.

[16] Cons. parliamentary group 19–3–47.

[17] Bernt Ingvaldsen and Sven Nielsen. Kamsvåg, p. 85.

[18] *Parl. pap.* 1947. Tid. O., p. 482.

circumstances. It should be noted, however, that there were influential Labor Party members who agreed with the opposition insofar as they saw the conflict as representing a basic ideological conflict.[19]

The acts were passed according to the proposals from the Labor government. There was a deadline of one year. To prepare a permanent law, a committee was appointed with trade union lawyer Gustav Sjaastad as chairman and Thagaard as vice-chairman. It took almost five years before the committee managed to present a proposition for a permanent law on price and production regulation. In the meantime there had been some quite serious conflict over proposals for other enabling acts.

First there was the proposition for an employment act put forward in 1947.[20] The proposition contained clauses stating that those who wanted to hire a person first had to get the permission from the Employment Directorate, and a clause saying that all persons fit for work had to obtain permission from the same directorate if they wanted to go abroad. The latter was withdrawn before the proposition was presented before the Storting. The opposition maintained that the proposition represented the first step toward total control of the labor force. Besides stressing the difficulties of the reconstruction situation it is necessary to emphasize that even the opposition did not expect the Labor government to use these acts for all they were worth. The idea was rather that an institutionalized opening up for such wide discretionary power would *sooner or later* lead to the abuse of that power. The legal guarantee lies in the removal of such institutionalized temptations to use power.

There was also a proposition for a law on the maintenance of price regulation put forward in 1948. According to this proposition there should be a special price police force, and it was furthermore said that the duty to give evidence in price regulation cases was not subject to the limitations and exceptions in the ordinary criminal law.[21] Besides provoking demands for an inquiry and denouncement by the opposition, the case also shed light on the more fundamental conflict.[22] The idea behind the law was of course that in the difficult reconstruction period there should be no opportunity of getting away with a criminal

[19] *Ibid.*, p. 466 (Meisdalshagen).   [20] *Ibid.*, pp. 378ff.
[21] *Parl. pap.* 1948. O. prp. 83. § 7, p. 7.   [22] *Parl. pap.* 1948. Innst. O. I, p. 2.

economic offense against the community. The opposition leader, John Lyng, found it necessary to remind the Labor government that the idea behind the many complicated rules of procedure and the limitations of the duty to give evidence in the ordinary criminal law was the protection of the weak.[23] The nonsocialist argument in both these cases was based on the old constitutional principle according to which the law should be a guarantee against the abuse of state power. In reply to this the Labor Minister, Sven Oftedal, said that the opposition, in spite of all its talk of liberty and liberties, did not lay enough stress on freedom from poverty.[24] Economic efficiency meant freedom from poverty. The last proposition was withdrawn by the parliamentary leader of the Labor Party, Oscar Torp. This was one of the first signs of a "retreat" or of the "second thoughts" of the Labor Party, to which we will return.

In 1948 the problem was raised again at the political level through the proposal of a prolongation of a house requisition law from 1946. There was still a severe housing shortage and all agreed that a prolongation was necessary, but there was disagreement about the formulation of the law. The Conservatives argued that the public requisition of accommodation in private houses was a very delicate matter and that it had to be executed with the utmost care. A committee of lawyers suggested rules based on "the principle of contradiction."[25] This meant that the house-owner should have the right to see all the relevant documents and to give a statement before any decision was reached. In their minutes the requisitions committee should give an account of the premises of the final decision, and the minutes should be sent to those who had been involved. In principle this meant that procedural rules from the courts of justice were introduced to the decison-making process of the administration as a substitute for the lack of control by the courts. This was a way of "solving" the constitutional problems which should be gradually developed.

When the Labor Party conceded to house requisition more easily than the opposition, it was not only because it laid more weight on the solving of social problems, or on social rights as opposed to liberal civil

<hr />

[23] *Ibid.*, Tid. O., p. 98.   [24] *Parl. pap.* 1947. Tid. O., p. 401.
[25] Ragnhild Øvrelid, *Rettssikkerhet eller demokrati* (Oslo, 1984), p. 59. *Parl. pap.* 1948. Tid. O., p. 757.

rights. Some Labor Party representatives had a tendency to look upon house requisition as a good thing in itself. It could be a first step toward a more collective way of life. The Labor representative Jacob Friis recalled his stay in Moscow before the war when he lived in a flat where "many women shared one kitchen. This led to a social attitude which is rare in certain parts of our population. To be forced into a social attitude, into a situation where one has to associate with people, is not only a phenomenon of scarcity, but is also a phenomenon of progress for the people."[26] There was in the Labor Party a vague skepticism toward the individualism of the liberal tradition which weakened their objections to the law.

The conflict over the emergency acts[27]

In 1950 the Labor government proposed the emergency acts. In these proposals there were statutory provisions on internment without legal procedure, on press and other censorship, on summary procedures by special courts and on the reintroduction of capital punishment. These laws were to be applied in case of war, which did not raise any problem. They could also be applied "under threat of war," which some found more difficult to accept, and finally they should be applied when "the independence or the safety of the nation was in danger as a consequence of war or threat of war between other countries or for some other reason," which was what met with the greatest opposition – in particular the vague phrase "for some other reason."[28] It was a clause saying that the sanction of parliament should be obtained "if possible," which means that the act was not an enabling act in a strict sense. The arguments from both sides were, however, in principle of the same kind as in the cases discussed above.

To understand why these propositions were put forward it is necessary to remember the general fear of war at the time. The propositions had been prepared in 1948, just after the coup in Czechoslovakia. After having been worked out, however, they were

[26] *Parl. pap.* 1948. Tid. O., p. 777.
[27] Almar Elvebakk, *Krigsfrykt, demokrati og lovgivning* (Cand. philol. thesis, 1970). Steinar Sjølyst, *Krigslov og dødsstraff* (Cand. philol. thesis, 1971). John Lyng, *Brytningsår* (Oslo, 1972), pp. 204–12.
[28] *Parl. pap.* 1950. O.prp. 78, p. 10. See O.prp. 79.

put aside. After the outbreak of the Korean war they were again put forward. The immediate response was positive. There was obviously a general feeling that far-reaching provisions of this kind were a necessary part of the national defense. It was held that the total war had blurred the distinction between war and peace and so it could be necessary to apply the provisions in time of peace. Total war demanded total defense.

In the press strong criticism was expressed only in the Communist paper, *Friheten*, and in the far right-wing paper, *Farmand*. Fear of war was mixed with fear of Communism, and *Friheten* looked upon the proposals as directed against the Communists, and not without reason. *Farmand* feared "the totalitarian authority" given to the Labor government.[29] After some time a more general criticism gained momentum. A particularly strong criticism was expressed by some well-known intellectual leaders. The most dedicated defender of the liberal creed was the famous socialist author, Sigurd Hoel. The government had, he wrote, "turned its back on the Norwegian Constitution and on all free democratic rights, and marched along the broad road to dictatorship."[30] Most of the lawyers who took part in the discussion generally supported the propositions. This was the case with Professor Andenæs, mentioned above, who was ordinarily an ardent defender of liberal ideas, and the well-known professor Frede Castberg. They based their view on the supposition that the provisions were only a codification of constitutional emergency law.[31] Or as the Public Prosecutor, Andreas Aulie, said, "It is impossible to disarm a belligerent enemy by rule-of-law ideals."[32] Among the more influential lawyers, only one, Kristen Andersen, disagreed in principle. He maintained that the propositions "undermined the very basis of Norwegian and Nordic constitutionalism."[33]

Among the Conservative Party members the conflict between constitutional principles and the efficiency of national defenses was felt. Traditionally the party favored a strong defense policy, and most of the Conservative press had supported the propositions. On the other hand they had their scruples. The issue is first mentioned in the minutes of the parliamentary group in connection with the

[29] Sjølyst, p. 41.   [30] *Ibid.*, p. 72. *V.G.* 13–9–50.
[31] Appendix to O.prp. 78 and 79.   [32] Elvebakk, p. 74.   [33] *Ibid.*, p. 28.

reintroduction of capital punishment. There is only a summary remark saying that they "agreed to vote against the proposition as it was too strong a reminder of the conditions in the people's democracies."[34]

The growing criticism put the government in a difficult position. The difficulties were solved by the intervention of Lyng. As a member of the parliamentary committee on judicial affairs, he took the initiative of cooperating within the committee and with the Ministry of Justice in order to work out a modified version of the propositions which all the large political parties could agree upon. A modified version finally carried the majority vote.

There was some discussion about whether the final laws implied any concessions to the criticism. The laws said nothing about capital punishment, special courts, internment or censuring. But they gave the government authority to take appropriate measures "when the nation was at war or under threat of war, or when independence or security was in danger." In the premises it was said explicitly that the laws legitimated the same measures which had been specified in the original propositions. The difference was said to be that by not explicitly specifying the measures, the extraordinary character of the measures was emphasized.[35] It was obviously difficult to find the right compromise between constitutional principles and the effectiveness of national defenses. This illustrates the liberal dilemma: To meet the threat from outside against constitutional democracy it was necessary to take measures which in themselves threatened the principles of constitutional democracy. At least that was what many felt at the time.

It is difficult to say where the dividing-line should be drawn. There was of course a sharp distinction based on fundamental differences in political views between those who held that there was a danger from the East and those who did not. But one can hardly say that it was the latter who represented constitutional democracy. As pointed out by Rune Slagstad, we find an opportunistic attitude among those to the left of the Labor Party. The constitutional arguments they used to fight the emergency acts were the same arguments they repudiated in the debate over the laws on price and production regulation. There is a similar kind of opportunism among those on the far right wing, who

[34] Board of parl. group 18–9–50.   [35] Sjølyst, p. 94.

used the arguments the other way round.[36] As for the Conservative Party, it went a long way towards accepting the harsh measures in the acts, but at least it did so in acknowledgement of the liberal dilemma and sought a compromise. This was politics of a conservative type. Those who were not accustomed to consider politics as a choice between evils had more difficulty in acknowledging the dilemma. In the defense of the original propositions from the government there was a clear tendency to disregard the constitutional problems. It was maintained that it was only a question of confidence. People ought to be confident that the government used its enlarged authority and great discretionary power in a reasonable way. There was no opportunism in the arguments of the Labor Party. It was consistent in its disregard of the constitutional arguments, at least in the issues in question and at least so far.

The last fight over the laws on price and production regulation

It took a long time to work out the propositions for a permanent law on price and production regulation. The committee presented its report in 1952, five years after it had been appointed. In the meantime it had been necessary to renew the temporary laws four times. But there was general agreement that the real fighting should be postponed until the propositions for a permanent law had been presented. The report with these propositions triggered off one of the most heated general debates in modern Norwegian history.[37] There were propositions for two laws, one on price regulation and one on production regulation. While Thagaard had been the strong man behind the price regulation law, the production regulation law was in the main formulated by the chairman of the committee, Sjaastad.[38] There had been a general debate on the basis of the temporary laws concerning the necessity for constitutional guarantees. We shall return to that debate below. The majority of the committee, including Thagaard and Sjaastad, gave concessions to the constitutional

---

[36] Rune Slagstad in a paper presented on January 17, 1983 at Ustaoset.

[37] Tore Agin Nilsen, *Den politiske strid omkring Prisloven. Hvorfor ingen Rasjonaliseringslov?* (Cand. philol. thesis, 1971).

[38] Information given by Trond Bergh.

counterarguments, at least by discussing them at some length.[39] Their main conclusion was, however, that legal security had to be sought in better procedures within the administration rather than in specific rules. This was the argument we found in the debate on the house requisition law, and it was quite a common view in 1952.

It must be added that Sjaastad had included some constitutional guarantees in the proposition for a production regulation law.[40] This was in principle the more radical of the two propositions. But the guarantees were rather feeble and not nearly enough to dampen the revolutionary character of the law. As for the price regulation law formulated by Thagaard, it contained an absolute open and general enabling clause saying that the king or those given the power of attorney by the king could take such action as they found necessary in order to "counteract unreasonable or harmful conditions in business, unnecessary or costly trade activity, irregular competition, doubtful business methods or other business dispositions or conditions which can be said to be unreasonable or harmful to common interests."[41] There is also reason to note the strange wording in the report to the effect that the issue was the security of the citizens in relation to "faults" made by the administration.[42] This wording unmasked the tendency by the majority to overlook what was the real constitutional problem at hand, at least from the point of view of the opposition. It was not a question of guarantees against "faults," but of guarantees against the abuse of power, which is a different thing altogether. By and large the majority vote of the committee continued the policy laid down in the temporary acts. It opened up the possible execution of wide discretionary power by the government and the administration. Whether one agrees with the majority vote or not, it must be clear that the propositions implied a serious attack on the liberal, normative structure of society. The issue concerned much more than the appropriate means of reaching more or less agreed goals. Here was a basic conflict of an ideological nature, as was the fight over the same issue in 1947. The solution in 1947 was in reality a postponement, and many felt that it was the final and decisive fight which took place in 1952.

---

[39] The Report from the committee is printed as an Appendix in three volumes to O. prp. 60. *Parl. pap.* 1952. Vol. I, pp. 71ff., 244ff., and vol. II, pp. 84–135.

[40] The proposition for an act on production regulation: *ibid.*, vol. I, pp. 277ff.

[41] *Ibid.*, vol. I, p. 191.   [42] *Ibid.*, vol. I, p. 246.

And the conflict was over the general trend in the development of the system of society.

As mentioned above, the propositions led to a very heated general debate. It was started by the minority in the committee:

> To read the motives gives a depressing impression that the majority wants a certain goal, a certain system, not to say a certain order of society. On the basis of political conviction and with the aid of a very vivid imagination the majority has tried to construe a need for the unprecedented far-reaching system for public regulation and control which it proposes.[43]

The arguments were the same as in 1947. On the one hand there were the arguments based on the idea of a planned economy, and on the other the accusations of totalitarianism which flourished again. The two more substantial counterarguments were the "rule of law" argument against discretionary power and the economic argument emphasizing the damaging effects of the unpredictability of public measures. Again the Conservative Party ran into difficulties because of the tendency to identify the party with the business class.

The most important difference in relation to the debate in 1947 was that the more formal question concerning the constitutionality of the enabling acts had been solved. According to the principle of judicial review, the Norwegian Supreme Court has the competence to test the constitutionality of any law in connection with a specific case. The case in question was an extra duty imposed on the whaling companies in connection with a general price regulation and with the authority of the temporary lex Thagaard. In 1952 the Supreme Court decided that the constitutionality was quite in order although, as it is said, "the delegation of the power of attorney to impose extra duty on the citizens in this case goes much further than in any previous case in peace time."[44] It has been maintained that this decision by the Supreme Court represented a definite victory of "the new view" that parliament had the right to delegate its legislative power.[45] The

---

[43] *Ibid.*, vol. III, p. 99. [44] *Norsk Retstidende* 1952, p. 1098.
[45] Torkel Opsahl, *Delegasjon av Stortingets myndighet* (Oslo, 1965), p. 37. See also a similar decision by the Supreme Court, *Norsk Retstidende* 1956, p. 952.

decision of the Supreme Court meant that the opposition lost one of its best arguments at the start of the last great fight over the enabling acts. With the Labor Party in absolute majority in the Storting and with the blessing of the Supreme Court, it looked as if there should be no barriers to the enactment of the Sjaastad committee propositions. But this was not what happened. It soon became evident that the opposition was strong even within the Labor Party. The association of cooperatives, which was close to the party, maintained for instance that the majority vote of the committee was "a voluminous affair much more dictated by the necessity to give the public administration instruments for all conceivable situations than to protect those who will be the subjects of the law against these wide powers of attorney."[46] And when the new Labor government of Oscar Torp took over in 1952, it first presented a proposition for a law on price regulation which was very moderate compared to the proposition of the Sjaastad committee. The wide enabling clauses were replaced by much more specific paragraphs.[47] Later the Prime Minister even declared that the government had no intention of presenting any proposition with regard to regulation of production.[48]

The "retreat" of the Labor Party in the debate on price and production regulation has been a much-disputed topic among Norwegian historians. Some historians have sided with the dominant opinion of the Labor Party in maintaining that it was not a "retreat": it was only a question of appropriate measures to reach common aims, in particular post-war reconstruction. In 1952 the reconstruction period was over, and so the "retreat" was only an adjustment to a new situation.[49] It ought to be clear from what has already been said that we tend to interpret the standpoint of the Labor Party in the debate on price and production regulation in 1952–3 as a "retreat" in the sense that the constitutional counterarguments were taken seriously in the party in a way they had not been before. The Labor Party developed its second thoughts on constitutionalism, and I shall examine the way this came about.

---

[46] *Parl. pap.* 1952. O. prp. 60. Appendix, vol. II, p. 29.
[47] *Parl. pap.* 1952. O. prp. 60, p. 152, §24 and §25.
[48] *Parl. pap.* 1953. Tid. S., p. 240.   [49] Nilsen, p. 91.

The Labor Party's second thoughts

If we go back to the bitter political conflict of 1947, we will see that while the Sjaastad committee started to work out its radical propositions, the constitutional aspects of the conflict were taken up for critical examination by lawyers. This attention proved to be of importance later. Professor Andenæs took the initiative in a speech given at a meeting of the Association of Barristers. His topic was the control of the administration by the courts of justice. According to Andenæs this control represented an important constitutional principle. The opening up of a discretionary power by the enabling acts tended to change this control into a mere formality:

> It could not be denied that at the same time as a progressively larger part of our economic life has been subject to public control by administrative bodies established for that purpose, the control by the courts of law and thereby the principle of a law-bound public administration has tended to be undermined. This is not only the case in the dictatorship countries, but also in our society. The ideal drawn from the principle of the rule of law, that the public administration should be strictly bound by the law and subject to the control of the courts of law, has gradually lost ground to the claim for more efficient administration.[50]

A compromise had to be found with due consideration both for the principles of the rule of law and for the efficiency of the administration.

According to Andenæs there were two ways in which to save the principles of the rule of law. One was the traditional way of avoiding general enabling acts and keeping to substantive law; this made control by the courts of justice possible. Andenæs's points in effect asked for a further examination of arguments concerning rule of law by the young and ambitious Labor party elite. He argued that there should be no more enabling acts than was strictly necessary. Since some were necessary, Andenæs suggested safeguarding the rule-of-

---

[50] Johs. Andenæs, "Domstolene og administrasjonen" (paper presented in 1947), *Avhandlinger og Foredrag* (Oslo, 1962), pp. 278, 280. See also Øvrelid, p. 50.

law principles by enacting rules for better and more adequate procedures within public administration. This issue was taken up by a
committee jointly appointed by the Association of Barristers, the
Association of Judges and the Association of Lawyers in Public
Administration. The committee was asked to work out proposals for
such procedural rules.

The issue was later taken up on a broad Nordic basis. It was *inter
alia* the main topic at a Nordic conference in 1951. The introductory
paper was written by Professor Andenæs. It was in the main an
extension of his speech from 1947 with particular concentration on the
decision-making procedures in public administration.[51] The most
characteristic feature of the debate was the unanimous support for the
notion that "the very life nerve of control by law of the public
administration was in danger," to cite the Swedish professor Nils
Herlitz.[52] This was also the basic concern of the judge of the
Norwegian Supreme Court, Terje Wold. The difference between
Wold and Andenæs was that while Andenæs emphasized the conflict
between efficiency and security by law and sought a compromise with
special care for the latter, Wold was still more uncompromisingly on
the side of security by law. According to Wold, no decision should be
taken by the public administration if the legal rights of the individual
citizen were thereby affected. He also referred to "the fruitful
discussion about the claims for security by law" which had taken place
in connection with the emergency acts and which had had "a great
impact on the final version of the acts."[53]

The interesting point is that Wold was a prominent member of the
Labor Party. He had been Minister of Justice in the Norwegian War
Cabinet in London and he was later appointed Chief Justice of the
Supreme Court. Wold's opinion was not exceptional. As the debate
developed among the lawyers and forced clarification of points at
issue, a high degree of consensus was reached. In other words, the
lawyers in the Labor Party shared the general anxiety among
lawyers with regard to constitutional development and liberal
rights.

[51] Johs. Andenæs, "Garantier for rettssikkerheten ved administrative avgjørelser."
Appendix IV to *Förhandlingarna å det Nittonde Nordiska Juristmøte i Stockholm 23–25
august 1951* (Stockholm, 1952).
[52] *Ibid.*, p. 244. [53] *Ibid.*, pp. 250–1.

All the influential Labor Party lawyers who turned out to be skeptical toward the enabling act in the last phase had earlier been active in the fight for similar acts. As the Minister of Justice in the War Cabinet, Wold had been the man to launch the lex Thagaard. According to C. J. Hambro, the Conservative leader, he had referred to Soviet impulses. When the laws were passed in the Storting in 1947 he had rejected all the constitutional arguments as nonvalid.[54] This was also the case with Erik Brofoss, who, as a Minister of Trade, was the main figure behind the 1947 laws. As the Minister of Justice, O. C. Gundersen launched the propositions on the emergency acts in 1950. These were the men who were the first to reexamine their initial positions. As lawyers they developed "second thoughts" when confronted with the general opposition within the lawyers' profession. The social democratic attitude toward the constitutional questions was not clear, and even the Labor Party lawyers could go quite far in using the law as an instrument of political power. However, when the basic constitutional questions on legal security were posed, they had to make their position clear. It appeared then that they as lawyers in a liberal society identified with the liberal constitutional views on law as a guarantee against the abuse of power. With the lawyers as mediators the Labor Party clarified its views on these same questions in the early fifties.

The Conservative leader, John Lyng, who was himself a distinguished judge, was among the first to develop the constitutional arguments. He maintains in his memoirs that these arguments were decisive in the end, and he is probably right. As pointed out by Ragnhild Øvrelid, it was when the opposition from the business class against the laws on price and production regulation coincided with the constitutional arguments that the breakthrough of the opposition was achieved.[55] The precondition was, however, that the constitutional arguments had been taken out of the hands of the political parties and expanded within the nonpolitical lawyers' profession.

Although the part played by the lawyers seems reasonably clear, the whole process within the Labor Party which led to the retreat has not yet been analyzed. As already mentioned, the "retreat" was carried out by a new Labor government. This is not to say that the old Prime

---

[54] *Parl. pap.* 1947. Tid. O., p. 514.　　[55] Øvrelid, p. 121.

Minister, Einar Gerhardsen, who was the dominating figure in the party at that time, was in opposition to the new party line. The explanation must rather be that Gerhardsen saw the necessity for a new policy and that by withdrawing from his position as Prime Minister, he made the change easier. The two lawyers Gundersen and Brofoss remained in the government while the radical Minister of Finance, Olav Meisdalshagen, left along with Gerhardsen. It was the new Minister of Finance, Trygve Bratteli, who presented the modified proposition for a law on price regulation.

The influence of the lawyers and the new government should be seen against the background of some more fundamental attitudes within the social democratic movement. This means that the changing attitude of the Labor Party calls for further comment about the balance between liberal constitutionalism and socialism within the party.

The historians who have argued against the "retreat"-theory have emphasized the fact that the government never used much of the discretionary power it was entrusted with by the temporary laws from just after the war. That applies in particular to the power to regulate production by direct measures. There had turned out to be no need for such strong measures, and so the "retreat" was not only a consequence of the fact that the reconstruction period was over, but was also an adjustment made in the light of experience. This argument can be turned on its head, however. Why pass such far-reaching enabling acts if they were not necessary? If the constitutional arguments had been taken seriously, it would certainly have been a better strategy not to entrust the government and the administration with more power than was needed at the moment. The very fact that the enabling acts went so much further than necessary nurtured the notion that they represented much more than just convenient measures for administration.

Looking back at the different enabling acts from after the war it seems clear that the Labor Party, and in particular the Labor government, had given weak objections to the extension of their own discretionary power. The majority vote in the Sjaastad committee was the logical outcome of Labor Party policy after the war. Constitutional control had to give way to administrative efficiency. We have referred to courageous youthfulness and lust for power in order to lead society on to a better future. This self-assured youthfulness could, with indignation, reject traditional constitutional claims for guarantees against abuse of power. The government had no intention to abuse its power ... There was a tendency to reduce the constitutional problem to a question of confidence. It was "ridiculous" to imply that the wide powers of attorney could be misused.[56] The whole matter about "confidence" shows that the liberal distrust of human nature, the very thought that power corrupts, which lies at the bottom of liberal constitutionalism, was not shared by the social democrats, at least not in 1947.

The Labor Party wished to expand political power, or the power representing the community. Limitation of the private sector was not only designed to promote efficiency, but was also a good in itself from a collectivistic point of view. In the social democratic tradition law was regarded as an instrument of political power rather than as a guarantee against the abuse of power, which is the liberal constitutional view. That is the reason why the Labor Party could go so much further than the nonsocialist parties which were more closely attached to the liberal ideology.

It is, however, necessary to distinguish between two fields for the expansion of political power. In the first place, there is the question of expanding political power in economic life, as with laws on price and production regulation. These laws implied state control over the means of production. As we have seen, the Conservative Party had difficulty in defending its constitutional standpoint on these matters, as the constitutional guarantees coincided clearly with the interests of a particular economic group. The party could easily be isolated as purely an interest organization of "the capitalists," although the party argued, of course, that what was best for the capitalists was also best for society at large. The standpoint of the Labor Party was based on a distrust of the market mechanism, which went further than the question of an efficient and just allocation of material resources. As maintained by Ulf Torgersen, there was in the Labor Party a populistic tendency to reject the market mechanism on moral grounds.[57] The reason was not only that it functioned badly, but also that it was based

---

[56] *Parl. pap.* 1948. Tid. O., p. 93. See also 1947. Tid. O., pp. 412, 479, 490, 504. In general the argument played a prominent part in the debate in 1947.

[57] Ulf Torgersen, "Arbeiderpartiet – fra populisme til systemmanipulering" (paper presented at Ustaoset, 1982).

on a principle of doubtful moral value – the profit motive. The notion of private vices becoming public virtues was not strong in the labor movement.

The anti-liberal element in Labor Party policy is perhaps clearest in the issues which did not have anything to do with the conflict between political and economic power. The laws on house requisition had to do with distribution of material goods, but it had nothing to do with control over the means of production. Freedom of speech and movement was of course a still more delicate issue. It was touched on, although somewhat unwittingly, in the propositions on the emergency acts.

In Norway as in many countries, a sharp distinction has developed between the constitutional guarantees in the economic field and the guarantees in fields which represent civil rights in a more restricted sense. The mixed economy means that the formerly private economic sphere has been opened to widespread public interference. But even in this field there has been a perceived need for some limitations and constitutional guarantees. The last major confrontation in 1952–3 was over the establishment of these limitations and guarantees. It was in this connection that the Labor Party developed its "second thoughts."

In addition the Labor Party has, of course, felt obligations toward the liberal, constitutional tradition. These obligations have always been there, but they have not always been felt to be so binding by everyone in the party. After the Second World War there were so many pressing tasks for the government that such things as security by law were more or less pushed aside by those elements in the party tradition which stood for the expansion of the political power. At the start of the fifties the situation changed. Those who had been young in 1945 had grown older. The economic development had been positive. Moreover the Labor Party hesitated when confronted with the fierce opposition of business interests. The party chose not to provoke, but rather to cooperate with these interests. Some will say that the Labor Party chose to be the administrator of bourgeois society. There was, at any rate, a far better understanding in the party for the constitutional arguments. The changing external conditions seem, however, to be insufficient to explain this change in attitude.

What is most striking is the growing argumentative power of the opposition against the enabling acts. There is a possibility that the leading part of the Labor Party reacted opportunistically, realizing that the party could lose votes if it really pressed on for a more radical constitutional change. Constitutional liberalism was deeply rooted in Norway. It is very difficult to distinguish opportunistic reactions of this kind from situations where people really have been convinced by arguments. Some will tend to believe that the latter never happens. If the indications are that it really did, it must be the changing attitudes toward the constitutional arguments in the Labor Party which were responsible. We can follow the process by which the arguments were taken over from the opposition by the lawyers, who expanded and elaborated them and finally persuaded the inner circle of the party. The argument worked because they met with liberal sentiments in the party cadres.

The outcome of the conflict over the enabling acts was, as Andenæs has written, "a turn of the tide." And he continues:

> Before the permanent law on price regulation was passed this year the laws on regulation gave in practice the public administration full authority to take all the general and individual decisions it found necessary or appropriate. The new law on price regulation represents a change, a reaction against what could be said to be a tendency to overstep boundaries.[58]

There is, at any rate, good reason to maintain that the constitutional development took a new course from 1953, but it was not just a retreat to the old order. I shall argue that the final solution was after all more in line with the traditional Labor Party attitudes than seemed to be the case in 1953.

A new constitutional development

The question of enabling acts did not provoke such sentiments or such conflict after 1953 as it did before. This did not mean that there were no more enabling acts. On the contrary, there were quite a lot of them after 1953, and it was generally held that they were necessary measures. The reason why these regulations did not stir up more intense conflict was that the government went along the second road

[58] Andenæs, "Domstolenes," p. 286.

pointed out by Andenæs in 1947. That is, the result of the conflict in 1952–3 was not only that the law on production regulation was withdrawn and that only propositions on absolutely "necessary" enabling acts were to be put forward in the future, but also that the work to develop better and "safer" procedures for decision-making in the public administration was started. A large commission was appointed for that purpose and Terje Wold became the chairman. In the course of time this constitutional reform movement led to the establishment of an *ombudsman* (in 1962), to an Administrative Procedure Act (in 1967) and to a Freedom of Information Act (in 1970). Taken together these acts represented quite extensive constitutional reforms on which there was a large degree of political consensus. Although these reforms had their origin in what may be called a liberal concern for legal security, they broke away from liberal constitutionalism in some important respects.

The problem is that the legal security derived from these procedural rules is something different from the traditional liberal legal security. In the liberal tradition the preoccupation is with the protection of individual human rights and the rights of the minority in relation to the majority. In other words, the preoccupation is with the limitation of political power – how far can political power go? The ombudsman and better procedures and publicity in the administration will no doubt contribute to a better security by law in the traditional sense. But the characteristic feature of Andenæs's "second road" is nevertheless that the expansion of discretionary political power is taken for granted. The legal security lies not in the limitation of that power, but rather in the right to take part in and influence the decisions which are related to oneself. The new procedural rules were in a way more concerned with democratization than with preserving the legal security in the traditional sense. The effect was rather contrary to the latter in so far as the democratization of the administration gave legitimacy to further expansion of public power.

When so many lawyers were so easily led on to the "second road" it was probably because of the strong influence of *legal realism*.[59] The legal realism school holds that decisions – in courts or administration – are based more on personal values, social background, interests and

[59] On "legal realism" see R. Dworkin, *Taking Rights Seriously* (Cambridge, Mass., 1977), p. 3.

so on than on explicit substantive rules. References to rules tend to be rationalizations. This rule-scepticism of the legal realism school is parallel to the rule-scepticism in the socialist tradition. According to this the liberal notion that positive power can be blocked by negative power is based on fiction. The notion has only served a strategy by which the privileged have been able to defend themselves against democratization. The tendency in liberal tradition to see a potential conflict between democracy and the rule of law is opposed by this school of thought. The law cannot be a guarantee of the weak against the strong, as was Lyng's contention in the debate on the administration of price regulation. Positive power can only be opposed by positive power, which means that the only way by which the weak can get guarantees and security is by making themselves strong. Legal security must consequently be based on the right to take part in the decision-making process. Legal security and democratization are two sides of the same coin.

The enabling acts raised two problems. One was the introduction of arbitrariness and unpredictability about what the public power could do. The other was the problem of democracy raised by the delegation of power from the democratically elected Storting to the administration. The latter problem was obviously of greater importance to the Labor Party than the former. The democratic problem explains why the party had its "second thoughts." It is important to note, however, that in the Labor Party the legal security problem coincided with the democratic problem. Both could be solved by democratic participation. And participation, or the right to influence the decisions for those involved in the particular cases, was what the principle of contradiction in administrative procedures was about.

This principle is in conflict with the liberal notion of the impartial judge saying that those who have particular interests in a case should be regarded as disqualified to decide in the case.[60] Andenæs touched on the problem in 1951, saying that it could be difficult to apply the principle of contradiction to the administration.[61] In court proceedings there will always be two parties confronting each other. In decisions by the administration there are seldom confrontations of that kind. The danger is that there can turn out to be no explicit

---

[60] Johan P. Olsen, *Politisk Organisering* (Oslo, 1980), pp. 58f.
[61] Andenæs, "Garantier," p. 20.

contradiction and consequently no balanced compromise between conflicting interests. In particular it may be difficult in concrete cases to articulate the common interest of a rational overall system.

It is also important to note that the delegation of the authority of the Storting was not only a delegation of the legislative power. It implied also outlines of a new concept of legislation. The rule-scepticism of legal realism meant a scepticism toward a rule-of-law concept in general. The tendency was that the decision in a concrete case should not be taken on the basis of substantive law rules but rather on its own merits. Legislation should not concentrate any longer on substantive law giving an *a priori* indication of *what* will be the outcome of a specific decision, but rather on the distribution of competence, or on *who* should take the decision.[62] We are all along talking about tendencies, of course. But the trend away from substantive laws and toward competence norms and procedural rules is quite clear.

The idea is then that all parties and interests involved should be heard. As pointed out by Øvrelid in her detailed study of the practice of the Administrative Procedure Act, this has meant the introduction of a special form of corporativism, or rather of what Stein Rokkan called "corporate pluralism."[63] So corporate pluralism is the main outcome of the constitutional reform movement which sprang from the conflict over the enabling acts. The public administration was opened up, and it was opened up initially for the well-organized interest groups.

Corporate pluralism means that a growing part of the decisions are taken at the intersection line between the administration and the organized interest groups. It has been commonly held that the trend toward corporate pluralism has come by itself, that there has not been

[62] Opsahl, *Delegasjon*. Opsahl is emphasizing the fact that legislation is about to withdraw from the setting of norms in the traditional substantive sense and into the setting of "competence norms" *inter alia* by passing enabling acts (pp. 25–6). According to Nils Kr. Sundby the withdrawal into the setting of competence norms implies a changing attitude toward the setting of substantive norms which will be the object of adjustments "from day to day" (Nils Kr. Sundby, *Om Normer* (Oslo, 1974), pp. 153f.). The threat toward legal security lies in the fact that laws are losing their character as norms either by being reduced to mere decisions in concrete cases as is the true implication of the development described by Sundby, or by being lifted up into the thin air of the meta-norms which by definition are not real norms. For a comment on Sundby on the relation between real norms and meta-norms, see F. Sejersted, "Rettsstaten og den selvdestruerende makt," in Rune Slagstad, ed., *Om staten* (Oslo, 1978), p. 61.

[63] Stein Rokkan, "Numerical democracy and corporate pluralism," in Robert Dahl, ed., *Political Oppositions in Western Democracies* (New Haven, 1968).

any planned policy of corporativization. The driving force has been the needs from case to case.[64] A complicated modern society with growing public regulations has, in order to function, had to be based on a cooperation between the regulators and the regulated. This is undoubtedly a correct observation, but it doesn't tell the whole truth. As we have seen, corporativist arrangements were also the outcome of a conscious search for solutions to constitutional problems. The need of the administration to cooperate with the organized interest groups coincided with the political wish to control the administration through the same interest groups.

The idea of corporativism was certainly not bound only to the debate over the enabling acts. In 1945 the Labor Party launched a comprehensive program for an overall corporativist economic structure. The idea was to build up a democratic economic structure along with the political democracy. This plan was never realized except for some minor reforms, one reason being that the Labor Party took over the political power positions and thereby lost much of its interest in an alternative channel of power. It is also of special interest in our context to note that in the preparatory documents to the lex Thagaard there is reference to a planned corporativist structure: the delegation of authority by enabling acts will be balanced by the participation of business organizations and trade unions in the decision-making process.[65] The same idea was expressed by Thagaard in 1946: democratic guarantees should be sought in the cooperation with interested groups.[66] The idea of corporativism had followed the propositions on laws on price and production regulation right from the beginning.

Even if the corporativist structure of the Labor Party was never realized, the idea of corporativism was close at hand. It is noteworthy that the Conservative Party also picked up the idea very early. The young vice-chairman of the party, Sjur Lindebrække, was an especially keen advocate of the introduction of a more informal corporativism or of a corporate pluralism.[67] According to Lindebrække, it was absolutely necessary with a certain degree of coordination in the economic life, and corporate pluralism was a better alternative than centralized state intervention. The notion of plural-

---

[64] Jorolf Moren, ed., *Den kollegiale forvaltning* (1974), p. 21.
[65] *Parl. pap.* 1947. D 5. Dok. 6, p. 68.   [66] Thagaard, p. 169.
[67] Sjur Lindebrække in *Morgenbladet*, 25–4–60.

ism was also very much in line with liberal thought. All this helps to explain why the Conservative Party so easily accepted the new trend. The actual development came in fact very close to the sort of informal corporativism advocated by Lindebrække. Evidently there was a basis for a constitutional development in the direction of more corporativism. The conflict over the enabling acts actualized the need for more corporativism. For the Conservative Party corporate pluralism turned out to be a convenient way to solve the constitutional problems created by the enabling acts, and so it was for the Labor Party. The conflict over the enabling acts accelerated the development toward corporate pluralism *inter alia* by creating a general ideological basis for it.

It is doubtful whether corporate pluralism really solved the problems at hand. It has already been pointed out that control by the courts of justice and so the security by law in the traditional sense is weak. It is also open to question whether the democratic effect has been supposed. Ragnhild Øvrelid has argued that this has not been the case. She is in line with a commonly held view that corporate pluralism has created a partnership of the elites. In the last years there is also a vague tendency to ask for constitutional reforms of a more traditional liberal colour. In short, the constitutional development of the future is an open question.

So far, however, we see the outlines of a new constitutional system based on legal realism and social democratic traditions. In some respects it is different from the old liberal constitutionalism. It is in a way more democratic, but with fewer restraints on the public power. This means that the retreat of the Labor Party in the early fifties was followed up by a new constitutional development, so in the long run it was a case of one step backwards and two steps forwards.

10. Arguments for constitutional choice: reflections on the transition to socialism

JON ELSTER

Many people believe that socialism – some form of political and economic democracy – would be a good thing, if only it could work. But they do not believe the socialist ideals are compatible with economic efficiency. Others believe that socialism might well work, if only we could get there. But they do not believe there is a feasible path from capitalism to socialism. This chapter is addressed mainly to the second group of objectors, but to some extent also to the first. It is only marginally addressed to those who think socialism would be a bad thing if we got there and it worked.

In my view socialism must not only be democratic: it must be reached in a democratic way. The opposite view was stated by Alfred Sauvy in 1949: "Just as capital goods take precedence over today's welfare in order to ensure tomorrow's, so truth must be shelved during the unhappy period in order to let the full truth burst forth tomorrow ... In this light, Communism represents an enormous effort to achieve truth in the long term and freedom on tick (*liberté à crédit*)."[1] False analogies and wishful thinking apart, what are the flaws of this argument? On what premises could it be refuted?

The conception I am arguing against can be decomposed into two statements: (1) One may rationally count on being able to achieve full democracy by the temporary abolition of democracy; (2) This path is not only rationally grounded, but also morally defensible. The main thrust of my argument is directed against (1). Even if (1) were granted, however, I would still object to (2) on the grounds that the current generation has *rights* that set limits to the sacrifices one can impose on it for the benefit of later generations. On the positive side I shall argue that only democratic processes are feasible and legitimate paths to

[1] Cited after Aron (1983), p. 309.

socialism. Briefly stated, my view is that the process must be legitimate in order to be feasible. If the general tendency of socialist
reforms is perceived to be fundamentally just, people will have the
motivation to endure the extensive trial-and-error procedures that will
be needed to implement them.

To refute (1) one might adduce two arguments, one general and the
other more special. The general argument is that it is impossible to
predict with certainty or even quantified probability the consequences
of a major constitutional change. The special argument is that
democracy is an especially unlikely outcome of a process that begins
by abolishing democracy. Although, if the general argument is
accepted, we cannot tell what the outcome would be, we can at least
exclude that it would be democratic. The special argument rests on the
idea that the means must partake of the nature of the end, since
otherwise they would subvert it. Although attractive, this argument is
not very robust. It must be balanced against the opposite view, that
means too similar to the end will never get us to it, since they
presuppose that it has already been reached.[2] Hence I shall only rely
on the general argument.

For the transition to socialism to be democratic, it must take place
within the framework of existing constitutions. It can be defined as the
choice of a socialist constitution within the framework of a nonsocialist one. Or, to phrase the question slightly differently, it is a question
of changing the constitution in a constitutional way and in the
direction of socialism. I am not concerned here with legal philosophy,
but with the moral basis for political action. I focus on constitutions
because they are the embodiments of legitimacy in most democratic
societies. It will be objected that constitutions are only the accidental
remains of the past, which ought not to constrain the shaping of the
future. While in one sense indisputably true, this assertion in another
sense misses the point. A constitution gains legitimacy from what has
been called "the normative power of the factual": compared to the
alternatives, which are contending with the status quo and with each
other, it has the privilege of *existing*. There is, however, this important
core of truth in the objection: one ought not, or so I shall argue, to feel
constrained by a constitution that makes change impossible.

---

[2] For an elaboration of this argument, see Elster (1985a), pp. 119–20.

I Three approaches to constitutional analysis

In *Democracy in America* Tocqueville set himself the task of looking at the social and economic consequences of the democratic institutions he had found in place in America.[3] His analysis was not oriented toward political action, at least not within the country he was observing. As observer rather than participant, he studied the consequences of democratic institutions *ex post* and at a distance.

This perspective may be contrasted with two approaches to constitutional choice *ex ante*. One relates to the choice of a constitution where none exists, another to the change of a constitution already in place. If a revolution or war has destroyed the old political fabric, the need for a constitution is imposed – at least if there is agreement that the system shall be a constitutional one and disagreement at most over which constitution to choose. If, however, a legitimate constitution is in place, it usually imposes formal and substantive constraints on what changes can be made. These, typically create a bias *de jure* for the existing constitution over the alternatives. In addition there is a bias *de facto* which follows from the uncertainty surrounding the choice and from the plurality of alternatives. Rational individuals may not want to embark on a process of change if they are unable to anticipate the outcome; and even if they are able to, they may not reach agreement on which direction to choose. (In addition there are various socio-psychological mechanisms tending to favor the status quo. I discuss these matters in Section III below.)

In this chapter I am concerned mainly with the latter bias. I want to add a comment, however, on the formal constitutional constraints on constitutional change. According to one extreme school of theorists, only unanimously adopted changes ought to be allowed.[4] A single person would in principle have the power to block a change desired by everyone else, with the consequence that accident is given near-total primacy in the theory of legitimacy. The unanimity principle would enjoin us to accept the status quo even if it had, say, strongly inegalitarian features that (1) were neither intended nor foreseen when the constitution was originally adopted, (2) would have blocked

---

[3] See chapter 3 above.   [4] See for example Buchanan (1975).

its adoption by unanimous rejection had they been foreseen and (3) are considered today by almost everybody to be decisive reasons for abolishing it. A society that found itself saddled with a constitution requiring unanimity for all changes, including change of that requirement itself,[5] might feel tempted to override the text of the constitution, yet hesitate to do so because of fear that a precedent might be set for disregarding the constitution on other, less justified grounds. *A fortiori* this would hold in the less extreme case where the constitution has a clause requiring a qualified majority for any constitutional change, including change of the clause itself. Is there a way out of this dilemma?

Consider what a defender of unanimity would answer if asked how the ground rule of unanimity should be adopted. He could hardly answer that it would be chosen by simple majority; for consistency he would have to say that the rule itself must be adopted unanimously. This suggests the following generalization. At any given moment of time we may assume that there is a well-defined percentage $f(x)$ of the assembly that wants the majority required for a change in the constitution to be at least $x\%$ of the votes. $f(x)$ must be a decreasing function of x; also we may assume that $f(50) > 50$ and $f(100) < 100$. Then there must be some percentage x^* such that $f(x^*)$ approximately equals x^*. This self-supporting percentage is the one that ought to be incorporated in the constitution.

This reasoning could lead legitimacy to by-passing the constitution. A country that by an accident of history finds itself endowed with excessively conservative restrictions on constitutional change, compared to what the citizens currently think they ought to be, could violate the constitution without loss of legitimacy. This would amount to a small revolution, but it would not be a breach of democracy.[6] It would on the contrary, be directed against the undemocratic notion that the few should have veto power over change even when only a few wish them to have that power.

---

[5] For a demonstration that there need not be any paradox in such self-referring laws, see Hart (1964). He does not, however, suggest that a self-referring law ought also to be self-supporting.

[6] Marx's argument for the "dictatorship of the proletariat" may, with some important qualifications, also be understood as advocating a breach of constitutionalism but not of democracy; see Elster (1985b), pp. 435–6, 447–8.

II Consequentialist arguments for constitutions

Assuming, then, that constitutional change is not blocked by the veto power of a small minority, how could one argue for it? In this section I consider consequentialist arguments for constitutional change, while in the next section I take up the argument from justice. Although I mainly have in mind changes in the property rights in the means of production, much of the argument applies to other changes as well.

There are several types of consequentialist arguments for constitutions. First, one may argue that a proposed constitution will lead to better decisions being made, compared to some existing or proposed alternative. To assess this view, we must first make it clear what we mean by "better." It could mean that decisions will be better on the average, or that the worst decisions that could be made will be better. I return to this distinction below. Next we must make it clear what it means to say that a single decision is better or worse than another. Since a political decision is the choice of certain means to realize a certain end, the quality of the decision might be linked either to the quality of the means, given the end, or to the quality of the end itself. The quality of the end may be judged in the light of the preferences of the participants in the political process, if we consider the constitution as a mechanism for aggregating preferences, or in the light of further criteria as well. One might, for instance, evaluate a constitution for its ability to protect the interests of later generations, even when these are not internalized in the preferences of the current one.

Secondly, one might attempt to justify the proposed constitution in the light of other consequences than that of leading to better decisions. One might argue, for instance, that certain decision-making processes have better consequences for the participants – not because the outcome is better, but because the very process of participating improves them in some way. There is a wide range of theories that advocate politics as the good life for man, and assess specific institutional arrangements by the scope they allow for the self-realization of the individual.[7] A related yet somewhat different idea was advocated by Tocqueville. He remarks that "democracy does not provide a people with the most skillful of governments," but justifies it by the argument that "it spreads throughout the body social a restless

[7] See Elster (1985a) and Elster (1986) for a critical survey of some of these theories.

activity, superabundant force and energy never found elsewhere."[8] Politics affects the participants in a way to be valued not for itself, but for its further, nonpolitical consequences.

Self-realization and economic progress may be valued as by-products of a constitution, and provide additional arguments for choosing it. They cannot, however, constitute the only argument for the choice of a constitution. They are *essentially* by-products, in the sense that one can only count on them to arise as side-effects of actions undertaken for some other purpose.[9] It is only on the condition that the participants take the decision-making process seriously that the beneficial side-effects will be forthcoming. This implies that Tocqueville's argument, which makes good sense as an assessment *ex post* of democratic institutions, cannot easily be transformed into an argument *ex ante*, because he explicitly denies that they are to be valued because of the quality of democratically made decisions. It would be a pragmatic contradiction if one were to enjoin a people to espouse democracy in the following terms: "Although in the process of governing democratically you will make a mess of it, compared to aristocratic or monarchic regimes, the process will also shake you out of the rut of ordinary routine and generate economic progress that will benefit everybody." For one thing, the exhortation would come up against an obvious free-rider problem; for another, it would undermine the motivation and the seriousness of the participants and thus ultimately defeat itself.

This difference between arguments *ex ante* and assessments *ex post* is, however, of secondary importance. The main difference is that the first approach comes up against the massive difficulty of predicting the consequences of major institutional changes. To appreciate this difficulty, we may draw upon Tocquevillian methodology. I shall present a series of reasons, four altogether, why the limits on our predictive abilities may be such as to block any purely consequentialist argument for reform. I have presented the reasons in chapter 3 also, but I apply them here to a different set of problems.

The skeptical tenor of the argument will be evident. Methodologically it is closer to the pessimism of Hayek than to the moderate optimism of Popper, and very far removed from any belief in planned

---

[8] Tocqueville (1969), p. 244. The passage is more fully quoted in chapter 3 above.
[9] See Elster (1983a), ch. 11 for the notion of states that are essentially by-products.

social change. On the one hand I argue that the state of the social sciences is light-years away from allowing us to predict the *global net long-term equilibrium effects* of major institutional changes. On the other hand I argue that piecemeal social engineering, through incremental planning or trial and error, is of little help as a remedy to this theoretical deficit, since this method only allows us to estimate local, partial, short-term or transitional effects. The skepticism is, however, balanced by a positive argument from justice, set out in the next section.

(a) Local versus global consequences

The goal of a constitutional change is, almost by definition, a general, society-wide reform. In the present case we are also talking about major constitutional changes, relating to the basic structure of property rights. It is very difficult indeed to assess before the fact what the consequences will be of a reform which is both large and general. The direct and indirect ramifications will be endless and feed upon each other in a way that very soon becomes too complex to grasp. It may be possible to assess the consequences of the general implementation of a small reform, or of the partial implementation of a large one, but there is in general no reason to believe that the consequences will be the same or similar for a general large-scale reform. It is probably true that if all men became good it would be good for everybody, but "It may just be that a Sodom with ten righteous men is *not* better than a wicked Sodom where the war of all against all prevails."[10] Similarly it may be better if all men are selfish than if all become moderately altruist, yet better still if they become strongly altruist.[11]

To illustrate the first point – the difference between implementing large changes in the small and in the large – we may consider two proposals for changing the ownership and incentive structure of the firm. On the one hand, there is the market socialist proposal that firms be owned and managed by workers. It is at least arguable that the very mixed success of small-scale market socialism, i.e. individual workers' cooperatives in a predominantly capitalist economy, tells us nothing about the prospects for large-scale market socialism in which all or

---

[10] Margalit (1983), p. 80.   [11] Kolm (1984), ch. 11.

most firms are run by workers.[12] On the other hand there is Martin Weitzman's "profit-sharing" proposal, according to which employers and workers would bargain over the percentage of the net product rather than over the wage rate. Weitzman's proposal is motivated by various macro-economic properties of profit-sharing that could never act as an incentive for the individual firm,[13] hence the paucity of isolated experiments in profit-sharing does not tell against the viability of a profit-sharing *economy*.

Weitzman's proposal may also be used to illustrate the second point, namely, the difference between implementing small changes on a large scale and large changes on a large scale. Between a pure wage economy and a pure share economy there are many intermediate forms, each of which would have a base wage and a profit-sharing percentage. Assume that one attempted to implement the profit-sharing proposal by making it mandatory for all firms to have a small bonus – i.e., a share of the profit – on top of a fixed wage, and that the system worked better than the pure wage economy. One would not be justified in concluding that it would work even better with a larger bonus and a lower base wage. Conversely, if the small-bonus system performed worse than the pure wage system, one could not conclude the possibility that a system with a larger part of the workers' income paid as a share of the profit might outperform the latter.

(b) Partial effects versus net effects

The *ceteris paribus* methodology of the social sciences tends to diminish its usefulness as a tool for planning and reform. Although within a given model, holding various things constant, one may predict that a proposed reform will have certain effects, it could well happen that the things held constant will in reality be affected by the reform. In particular, this is likely to happen in the case of major institutional and constitutional changes. For one thing, even with given motivations the new institutions may modify behavior in unexpected ways; for another, they may affect the motivations themselves.

[12] This view is argued in Miller (1981). For a (subtly qualified) defense of "stable polymorphism," see Krouse and McPherson (1985).
[13] Weitzman (1984), ch. 9.

The first problem is that of strategic adaptation to reform by those affected by it. Moral hazard is the most important problem of this kind, with applications to social as well as private insurance. A reform that creates a security net under the competitive market will also lead to more people needing the net, by reducing the incentive to survive without it.[14]

A deeper and more difficult problem is that of the endogeneity of preferences, illustrated by the following example.[15] A reform movement to increase the scope for self-realization in industry, in the work process itself or through industrial democracy, might fail because there is no widespread desire for self-realization, as opposed to a life oriented toward consumption broadly understood. Yet one might speculate that the lack of desire for self-realization is mainly due to the lack of opportunities for self-realization in capitalist societies. By the mechanism of adaptive preferences,[16] one often dismisses as undesirable what is unattainable anyhow. If more opportunities for self-realization become available, they may liberate the latent desire for this mode of life.[17] Hence one could argue that an institutional reform in this direction would create its own need, so that the full set of consequences would go much beyond that of satisfying the desires of those who already want it.

While plausible, this argument is not compelling. Adaptive preference formation is not the only mechanism that shapes our wants and desires. Even if more opportunities for self-realization are created, the desire might lag behind. Or – to take the converse possibility – the desire for self-realization might outrun the opportunities, with a net loss in welfare. All of these effects are possible, none of them certain. After the fact it may be possible to tell which of them is operating and in what combination, but the social sciences are in no state to predict *ex ante* what the outcome will be.[18]

---

[14] It is not obvious, however, that linedancers who perform with a net can be expected to fall off the line more frequently than those who work without a net. Danger may concentrate the mind, mortal danger may unnerve it. Moreover, different people may be attracted to linedancing under the two regimes.

[15] For a fuller argument see Elster (1986).

[16] For the concept of adaptive preferences, see Elster (1983a), ch. 3.

[17] One ought to retain the option of consuming, however, since otherwise one would not know whether the new desire for self-realization is itself an adaptive one.

[18] For related arguments see Granovetter (1979) and Boudon (1984).

(c) Short-term versus long-term consequences

The effects of an institutional framework can be assessed within different time perspectives. In particular one must distinguish between the static and the dynamic efficiency of different economic systems. Static efficiency is defined as the optimal use of existing resources, dynamic efficiency as the optimal creation of new resources. The latter includes an optimal investment policy and, even more fundamentally, an optimal rate of technical innovation. A system that performs well in the first respect may fare badly in the other, and vice versa. Again we shall have to look at the net effect. A very dynamic system may be so wasteful that the gains from innovation leak away; conversely, a very careful husbandry of resources may paralyze the growth of the system.

We may compare, from this perspective, the three forms of market production: wage capitalism, profit-sharing capitalism and market socialism. By far the most important aspect of static efficiency in this context is the ability to maintain full employment.[19] More precisely, the system has to be judged (a) by its ability to absorb new workers and (b) by its ability to retain old workers in the face of a recession. Real-world capitalism, i.e., wage capitalism, performs badly on both counts, whereas on theoretical grounds one could expect profit-sharing capitalism to do well on both, since the system is set up in such a way that employers always have an incentive to hire more workers. Market socialism would, again on theoretical grounds, be expected to do well on the second count, since workers would not have an incentive to fire themselves, but badly on the first, since they would not want to share the revenue with more workers. On the other hand we know that wage capitalism has performed well as regards dynamic efficiency. It has been argued on theoretical grounds that self-managed firms will have less incentive to invest and innovate, unless the individual worker plans to remain in the firm for a very long time. The prospects for a profit-sharing economy are more unclear in this respect.

It is perhaps possible to have some confidence in purely theoretical or *ex ante* arguments about static efficiency, although I have some doubts. We may note that Schumpeter argued in 1942 that "whatever

---

[19] I am indebted to Karl O. Moene for helpful discussions of this problem.

the economic goals desired by whoever is in the position to give effect to his desires, socialist management could attain them with less disturbance and loss without necessarily incurring the disadvantages that would attend attempts at planning progress within the framework of capitalist institutions."[20] It is hard to believe that he would have written these words today. (Remember that the form of socialism he had in mind was centrally planned state socialism.) In any case, arguments about dynamic efficiency must remain highly speculative. The determinants of innovative activity, in particular, are as elusive and unpredictable as the "animal spirits" in which Keynes found the explanation of investment behavior. The problem of predicting innovative activity involves that of predicting how firms in (what is now) the future will predict (what will then be) the future, when they face uncertainty both with respect to what the activity will yield and with respect to what other firms are doing. There are very strong arguments against the possibility of anticipating the outcome of what will essentially be a nonrational decision.[21]

(d) Transitional effects versus steady-state effects

When assessing a reform on consequentialist grounds, one must take care not to perform the assessment before the dust raised by the change has settled, and it is possible to see what the new equilibrium looks like. It would be pointless, for instance, to evaluate the success of a revolution by considering the state of the economy immediately after it has taken place. It is not simply that capital which has been destroyed must be replaced, and that opponents of the change must come to accept it. Expectations and motivations must adjust to the new opportunities and constraints, and plans made on that new basis must have time to come to fruition. We must be able to assess dynamic as well as static efficiency.

At this stage in the argument there is no need to insist on the massive difficulties of predicting ahead of time what the equilibrium outcome will be. Let me, instead mention four special problems that arise. First, any serious reform proposal must take account of the time needed to reach equilibrium, not just of the properties it is expected to

---

[20] Schumpeter (1961), p. 195.
[21] For a defense of this assertion, see Elster (1983b), especially chs. 4 and 5.

have when we get there. The goal to reform ought not to be the best possible society, but the best possible development of society *from now on*. Hence if *per impossibile* we had a reliable theory affirming the existence, accessibility and optimality of a general social equilibrium, we still ought not to embrace it unless we knew what would happen during the traverse. The legacy of Marx includes not only the intellectual *hubris* of believing with total certainty that the advent of Communism was inevitable, but also the moral error of thinking it justified any sacrifice imposed on the intermediate generations.

Secondly, one must consider the possibility that the reform might set in motion a process that has no equilibrium, or at most a cyclical one ("limit cycles"). If the tendency to counteradaptive preference formation ("the grass is always greener on the other side") is widespread, this is what we would expect to observe.[22] The ugly aspects of capitalism might lead workers in capitalism to prefer socialism, and vice versa.[23] The goal of social planning, to match desires with opportunities, may prove to be a will-o'-the-wisp. The lack of an equilibrium could also be due to problems inherent in the mechanism for aggregating preferences. Even assuming that individual preferences remain the same, cyclical majorities might undermine the existence of equilibrium.[24]

Thirdly, it may be the case that the process has an equilibrium that would be reached within a reasonably short time *in a constant environment*, but that the latter changes so rapidly and unpredictably that the process of approaching the equilibrium is constantly thrown off course and has to start all over again. Social planning is somewhat like trying to hit an unpredictably moving target. When the solution is finally produced, the problem may no longer exist.

Lastly, there is a specifically political difficulty involved in predicting the outcome of a political reform movement. Because the success of a reform and the belief that it will last are mutually dependent on each other,[25] the ultimate result could be very sensitive

---

[22] For the notion of counteradaptive preferences, see Elster (1983a), pp. 11–12.

[23] Dunn (1984).   [24] Riker (1982), especially pp. 206ff.

[25] For a striking, if extreme illustration of this problem I can do no better than cite the following comment on monetarist reform by F. Bates (1981): "Can a democratic government credibly commit itself to adhere to a policy no matter what its consequences – to guarantee that the monetary base will not be allowed to grow faster than $x\%$, even if the optimists should turn out to be wrong, and the policy leads to massive unemploy-

to small and unpredictable differences in popular confidence during the early stages. To the extent that instrumental success depends on confidence and legitimacy, which must in turn be generated by instrumental success, reformist politics becomes an art rather than a science. To the extent that the legitimacy derives from other sources, this particular problem becomes less acute.

One upshot of this discussion is that constitutional choice is clouded in uncertainty, in the sense that we cannot attach any probabilities to the various possible outcomes of the reform. Although there is no unique rule of rational decision-making for such contexts, most people would choose the maximum principle of acting as if the worst were the case. They would choose the constitution the worst possible consequence of which would be better than the worst consequence of any alternative, thus justifying Hume's "maxim, that in contriving any system of government, and fixing the several checks and controls of the constitution, every man ought to be supposed to be a knave, and to have no other end, in all his actions, than private interest."[26] Hence "a constitution is only so far good, as it provides a remedy against maladministration."[27] The last statement, surely, is too strong, but for our purposes a weaker version suffices: a constitution can only so far be *rationally expected* to be good, as it provides a remedy against maladministration.

This is a distressing conclusion, but there is worse to come. The obvious retort to the Humean sceptic is that we can, after all, *learn* about the effects of constitutions, by trial and error or piecemeal social engineering. Edmund Burke was no great believer in the power of reason to legislate *a priori*, but he was not without faith in stepwise reform: "By a slow but well-sustained progress the effect of each step is watched; the good or ill success of the first gives light to us in the second, and so, from light to light, we are conducted with safety through the whole series. We see that the parts of the system do not clash. The evils latent in the promising contrivances are provided for as they arise. One advantage is as little as possible sacrificed to another. We compensate, we reconcile, we balance."[28]

---

ment and idle capacity quickly, and slows down inflation only very gradually? Catch 22: maybe the theory is right, but the only way to test it is to convince people that the government would persist even if it is wrong."

[26] Hume (1963), p. 40. [27] *Ibid.*, p. 25. [28] Burke (1790), part 2, ch. 1.2.

We have seen, however, that this proposal will not do. On the one hand it is clear that by requiring local and initial viability of institutional reform, the set of possible changes is severely restricted. By piecemeal social change we can at most achieve local maxima,[29] since many institutions which are viable in the large and in the long term may not be so in the small or in the short term. True, we may stumble upon the global maximum by trial and error, but we cannot rationally count on finding it. On the other hand it is no less obvious that one cannot conduct experiments which involve the whole society and whose results will not emerge for decades, even centuries. Uncertainty and transition costs will block the adoption of any such proposal. People will have no motivation to participate in massive and protracted experiments of uncertain efficacy, unless the reform is perceived to be inherently fair and just. I now turn to this consideration.

III The argument from justice

In modern democratic societies the perceived justice of social institutions and policies is a condition for their long-term viability. This proposition, while intuitively plausible, is not easy to document empirically. The importance of "the justice motive in social behavior" equals its elusiveness.[30] Like all norms, those of justice and fairness are extremely context-dependent in the way they are interpreted and applied.[31] They are, in particular, highly sensitive to framing and reframing.[32] The important norm of equality, for instance, can be implemented in very different ways, depending on the reference group – equality with whom? – and the dimension along which people are required to be equal – equality of what? Almost any policy can be

[29] The view that any global maximum can be achieved by incremental change is as mistaken in biology as in politics. In view of Popper's well-known espousal of this view in his political theory (Popper 1957, pp. 64ff.), it is interesting to note that he also applies it to biological evolution, arguing that "the mechanism of natural selection ... can simulate rational human action directed towards a purpose or aim" (Popper 1972, p. 267). For a refutation of this view, see Elster (1984), ch. 1.3.

[30] The sociology of justice and injustice does not seem to be in a very advanced state, as judged from the contributions to Lerner and Lerner (1981) or such articles as Jasso (1980) or Tallman and Ihinger-Tallman (1979). The historical approach in Moore (1978) yields more substantial insights, but is of limited value for theoretical purposes.

[31] See Yaari and Bar-Hillel (1984).

[32] See Tversky and Kahneman (1981); also Elster (1985c).

both criticized and justified on grounds of equality, by suitable choice of reference group and dimension. These ambiguities easily lead to self-deception, manipulation and, after a while, to cynicism. It is easy to argue that ideals of fairness, equality and justice are mere window-dressings for self-interest.

I believe, nevertheless, that some norms of justice are more robust and stable than others. Specifically, I shall argue that there are *negative* norms of justice which are constraints or *necessary* conditions for consequentialist reforms in democratic societies, and *positive* norms which are *sufficient*, nonconsequentialist conditions for reform. Both sets of norms are defined in terms of the central democratic value of *equality*: equality of treatment in the negative case, equality of influence in the positive case.

(a) Negative justice

This could also be called "justice as fairness," although not quite in the Rawlsian sense. Assume that we are dealing with a reform which is proposed and justified on consequentialist grounds. For each citizen the reform will imply a temporal stream of burdens and benefits; for simplicity I assume that the net discounted value is positive for everybody, hence excluding purely redistributive measures. I further assume that the reform is only one among a set of proposed measures that would provide a Pareto-improvement over the status quo. Typically each proposal would confer special advantages on some groups of citizens, in addition to the general benefits provided to everybody. A paradigm example could be property laws: it is in the interest of everybody that there be *some* stable set of property rights, and in the interest of each group to have one particular set chosen.

In such situations we may observe the paradoxical outcome that *the very plurality of cooperative arrangements prevents any one of them being chosen*. For each proposal there is some group which will think it unfair, compared to some other proposal under which it would be better off. We have, in other words, a bargaining problem, in which the outcome may very well be the breakdown of negotiations and the perpetuation of the inefficient status quo, which has, at least, the advantage of existing. The formal branch of bargaining theory, stemming from the work of John Nash, is not very helpful in dealing with this issue. It does not try to explain *whether* an efficient outcome will be reached, only to determine on axiomatic foundations *which* efficient outcome ought to be chosen.[33] This class of theories also rests on assumptions that are not observed in real-life bargaining situations. For one thing, the assumption that the outcome of bargaining does not depend on interpersonal comparisons of utility is clearly unrealistic.[34] For another, the assumption that the set of outcomes can be rendered continuous by admitting lotteries between physically discrete outcomes does not in general apply to real-life situations.[35]

A less general but more useful theory of bargaining is that pioneered by Thomas C. Schelling.[36] It turns on the immensely fruitful idea that in inherently conflictual situations the only way to reach agreement may be to hit upon a naturally salient outcome, a "focal point" as Schelling called it, or a "Schelling point" as it has since come to be called. What is naturally salient depends on perceptual psychology, social conventions and shared history, not on formal features that can be stated in terms of rational-choice models. Typical focal points in bargaining are "allow no exceptions," "divide equally," "do as we did last year" or "do nothing." A more complex example is a price and income freeze as a tool for economic stabilization.

Focal points in democratic politics do not always – *pace* Tocqueville[37] – embody substantive equality, but they have to represent formal equality, in the sense of impartiality or fairness. The feature of price and income freezes by which they gain legitimacy is not that everybody suffers equally, but that the distribution of suffering is perceived to be blind, mechanical and impersonal. The (relative) gainers gain by accident, not because someone intended them to gain. Although there is great reluctance to the overt use of lotteries, there is also great acceptance for any policy that can be justified by such notions as "the great lottery of life" or "you win some, you lose some." By contrast, fine-tuned policy measures are easily suspected of intentional bias, an outstanding example being "trickle-down" pres-

---

[33] For a recent survey see Kalai (1983).

[34] Roth, Malouf and Murnighan (1981); see also Yaari and Bar-Hillel (1984).

[35] See Fishburn (1978), pp. 136ff. for a discussion of the conditions under which lotteries are likely to be used in social decisions; see also Broome (1984a,b).

[36] Schelling (1963).

[37] See Tocqueville (1969), pp. 651–2, cited in chapter 3 above.

criptions for economic growth. Even simple measures may of course be suspected of bias if it is transparent that they will systematically benefit some groups more than others. Proposals for flat tax rates are an example. The ideal focal policy, in additional to being simple in its conception and efficient in its result, must be opaque in its operation; like grace it must fall upon the deserving and the undeserving alike. In actual cases efficiency must often be compromised to achieve fairness and legitimacy. Simple policies are rarely optimal in the unrestricted policy set, although they may come out on top when constraints on political feasibility are added.[38]

To find local policies which represent a reasonably good approximation to efficiency is the major task of political leadership in democratic societies with highly organized interest groups. Many of these groups have effective veto power if they feel that a proposal is substantially worse for their members than some alternative policy that could also be chosen. This blocking power of organized minorities can only be overcome through proposals which (1) are better for everyone than the perpetuation of the status quo and (2) do not benefit people differentially in ways that are intrinsically correlated with membership in any particular interest group.

(b) Positive justice

The argument from negative justice applies mainly to small- or medium-sized reforms, which can be justified on consequentialist grounds provided that the side constraint of fairness is respected. For major institutional changes an argument from positive justice is needed, since the argument from (II) above then blocks any purely consequentialist reasoning. It is my contention that the nonconsequentialist values of justice, liberty and democracy have been the major proximate causes of social change over the last few centuries. To be sure, the efficacy of these values must in turn be explained by material conditions, but this is different from saying that they are themselves material in content.

If a reform is perceived as fundamentally just, people will be

---

[38] Note that this trade-off between equity and efficiency differs from the more frequently discussed one, which arises because of the negative incentive effects of redistributive measures.

motivated to endure the costs of transition and the extensive trial-and-error procedures that may be required before a viable implementation is found. The historical experience provides some evidence for this view. Universal suffrage was widely believed to be a dangerous system, but once the injustice of restricted suffrage came to be felt, the system had to go – before anyone knew what the consequences would be. The contemporary crisis of authority at many levels of society – in the family, the enterprise or the organization – also arose because of the perceived injustice of the old patriarchy and hierarchy. There is no doubt that the new forms of organization and decision-making have created a lot of chaos, waste and inefficiency. Yet people are prepared to put up with these difficulties, because they go together with a clean gain in justice. They perceive, more or less clearly, that the problems are temporary rather than permanent, and that the steady-state effect of diffuse authority structure may look very different from the transitional effect of diffusing authority.

The two reforms compared above – profit-sharing and workers' self-management – fare very differently in this respect. The profit-sharing proposal does not pretend to embody values that differ from those of wage capitalism. The private ownership of the means of production is left in place, as is the system of bargaining between workers and owners. Moreover, there is no pretension that the long-term equilibrium outcome of the bargaining will be more just or fair than under wage capitalism. The argument is strictly limited to the proposition that the change from bargaining over a wage to bargaining over the share of the net product will have desirable short-term consequences with respect to full employment. My question, then, is the following: if the profit-sharing proposal was implemented and turned out to have various perverse, unanticipated side-effects, as it very likely would have, would there be a widespread consensus to persist in the experiment until one had got rid of the bugs? My claim is that there would not be any motivation to endure the difficulties. The gains would be perceived as too abstract, uncertain and remote, compared to the immediate costs and obstacles. Indeed, the very anticipation that this will be the case is likely to block even the initial implementation.

By contrast, the case for workers' self-management rests on the intuitively appealing idea that any joint or cooperative enterprise ought to be governed in common, by the equal influence of all concerned and to the equal benefit of all concerned. Because the proposal rests on the nonconsequentialist value of autonomy, it is more resistant to practical difficulties of implementation. If one particular realization of self-management turns out to be too clumsy or inefficient, this will provide a motivation not to abandon the whole enterprise, but to search for another, more viable form. Thus if it proved difficult to find a form of direct democracy that is neither too demanding on the participants nor too detrimental for productivity, one could experiment instead with representative economic democracy. In particular, workers might prefer self-realization in the work process itself over self-realization through participation in decision-making.[39] It could turn out that they valued the possession of the right to self-management more than its actual exercise, much as one can value the freedom of mobility without ever desiring to use it.[40] The democratic right to choose what rights and what kind of democracy to have could lead in many directions, except that total abdication of the right to self-government would have to be proscribed.

There is one reason, however, why the movement toward economic democracy is slower and more unsure than the earlier struggle for political democracy: the injustice of private ownership of the means of production is less self-evident than that of restricted suffrage. Capitalism as a steady state tends to generate its own justification in which the result of past injustice appears to legitimate present injustice. Or, in one phrase, capitalist exploitation appears as just because of workers' alienation. The appropriation by the capitalists of the product of labor is exploitation. The workers' belief that the capitalists have the right to appropriation because of their legitimate possession of the means of production is alienation, in one sense of that term.[41] Exploitation and alienation reinforce each other in a steady-state process that has been well described as follows: "Attention is focused not on past labor but on the present value of the embodiment of past labor, and its current productiveness can be taken to provide a justification for the appropriation of the surplus of current output over the wage bill to those

---

[39] Elster (1986), section V.   [40] See also Elster (1983a), ch.3.2.
[41] For a survey of the various senses of "alienation" in Marx, see Elster (1985b), ch. 2, especially pp. 74ff., 100ff.

who have appropriated the embodiment of past labor, thereby providing the current basis of future appropriation."[42]

All social systems tend to generate patterns of belief that sustain them, either because the cognitive dissonance would otherwise be too painful or because the angle of vision is so restricted that alternatives are not perceived as feasible.[43] The mechanism just cited for the case of capitalism comes in addition to these general tendencies. It all adds up to a massive bias in favor of the status quo, but for a very different reason from the one cited earlier. There I argued that the status quo often serves as a focal point that survives not *faute de mieux*, but rather because of an *embarras de richesses*. None of the existing alternatives attract sufficient support, although each of them taken singly is perceived as superior to the existing system. Here the argument is that the status quo may generate the belief that it is actually better than any alternative.

To break down this bias in favor of the present is not an easy task, but an indispensable one if the system is to be changed in a legitimate way. In one of the preparatory manuscripts for *Capital* Marx states the idea as follows: "The recognition [by labor] of the product as its own, and the judgment that its separation from the conditions of its realization is an injustice – forcibly imposed – is an enormous awareness, itself the product of the mode of production resting on capital, and as much the knell to its doom as, with the slave's awareness that he *cannot be the property of another*, the existence of slavery becomes a merely artificial, vegetative existence, and ceases to be able to prevail as the basis of production."[44]

The passage is atypical, since Marx does not normally emphasize so strongly these cognitive conditions for the abolition of capitalism. In another respect it is highly typical, namely, in the belief that capitalism will itself produce the conditions that lead to its abolition. The present analysis points toward the same conclusion, but from very different premises. Marx argued that the increasing gap between the possibilities for want satisfaction created by capitalism and the actual extent which it allows for would become intolerable and lead to the violent abolition of the system. In the light of the century which has

[42] Nuti (1970), p. 57.   [43] See notably Veyne (1976) for a magisterial analysis.
[44] Marx (1861–3), p. 2287.

passed, the following scenario is more plausible. By promoting *actual* want satisfaction, capitalism also lays the foundation for political democracy and, ultimately, for an extension of democracy to the economic realm.

References

Aron, R. 1983. *Mémoires*. Paris: Julliard

Bates, F. 1981. The sins of wages. *The Economist*, March 21, p. 24.

Boudon, R. 1984. *La Place du désordre*. Paris: Presses Universitaires de France

Broome, J. 1984a. Uncertainty and fairness. *Economic Journal*, **95**, 624–32

1984b. Selecting people randomly. *Ethics*, **95**, 38–55

Buchanan, J. 1975. *The Limits of Liberty*. University of Chicago Press

Burke, E. 1790. *Reflections on the Revolution in France*. Many editions.

Dunn, J. 1984. *The Politics of Socialism*. Cambridge University Press

Elster, J. 1983a. *Sour Grapes*. Cambridge University Press

1983b. *Explaining Technical Change*. Cambridge University Press

1984. *Ulysses and the Sirens*, rev. edn. Cambridge University Press

1985a. The market and the forum. In J. Elster and A. Hylland (eds.), *Foundations of Social Choice Theory*, pp. 103–32. Cambridge University Press

1985b. *Making Sense of Marx*. Cambridge University Press

1985c. Rationality, morality and collective action. Forthcoming in *Ethics*.

1986. Self-realization in work and politics. To be published in *Social Philosophy and Policy*

Fishburn, P. 1978. Acceptable social choice lotteries. In H. W. Gottinger and W. Leinfellner (eds)., *Decision Theory and Social Ethics*, pp. 133–52. Dordrecht: Reidel.

Granovetter, M. 1979. "Advancement" in theories of social evolution and development. *American Journal of Sociology*, **85**, 489–515

Hart, H. L. A. 1964. Self-referring laws. In *Festskrift til Karl Olive-*

crona, pp. 307–16. Stockholm: Norstedts. Reprinted as ch. 7 in H. L. A. Hart, *Essays in Jurisprudence and Philosophy*, Oxford University Press, 1983

Hume, D. 1963. *Essays: Moral, Political and Literary*. Oxford Univeristy Press

Jasso, G. 1980. A new theory of distributive justice. *American Sociological Review*, **45**, 3–32

Kalai, E. 1983. Solutions to the bargaining problem. Discussion Paper No. 556, Department of Managerial Economics and Decision Sciences, Northwestern University (to appear in *Social Goals and Social Organization: Essays in Memory of Elisha A. Pazner*)

Kolm, S.-C. 1984. *La bonne economie*. Paris: Presses Universitaires de France

Krouse, R. and McPherson, M. 1985. A "mixed" property regime: equality and liberty in a market economy (typescript, Williams College)

Lerner, M. J. and Lerner, S. C. (eds.) 1981. *The Justice Motive in Social Behavior*. New York: Plenum Press

Margalit, A. 1983. Ideals and second-best. In S. F. Fox (ed.), *Philosophy for Education*, pp. 77–89. Jerusalem: The van Leer Jerusalem Foundation

Marx, K. 1861–3. *Zur Kritik der Politischen Ökonomie (1861–63)*. In *Marx-Engels Gesamt-Ausgabe*, vol. II.3.6. Berlin: Dietz, 1982

Miller, D. 1981. Market neutrality and the failure of co-operatives. *British Journal of Political Science*, **11**, 309–29

Moore, B. 1978. *Injustice: The Social Bases of Obedience and Revolt*. White Plains, N.Y.: Sharpe

Nuti, D. M. 1970. Capitalism, socialism and steady growth. *Economic Journal*, **80**, 32–57

Popper, K. 1957. *The Poverty of Historicism*. London: Routledge and Kegan Paul

1972. *Objective Knowledge*. Oxford University Press

Riker, W. H. 1982. *Liberalism against Populism: A Confrontation between the Theory of Democracy and the Theory of Social Choice*. San Francisco: Freeman

Roth, A., Malouf, M. W. K. and Murnighan, J. K. 1981. Sociological versus strategic factors in bargaining. *Journal of Economic Behavior and Organization*, **2**, 153–78

Schelling, T. C. 1963. *The Strategy of Conflict*. Cambridge, Mass.: Harvard University Press

Schumpeter, J. 1961. *Capitalism, Socialism and Democracy*. London: Allen and Unwin

Tallman, I. and Ihinger-Tallman, M. 1979. Values, distributive justice and social change. *American Sociological Review*, **44**, 216–34

Tocqueville, A. de. 1969. *Democracy in America*. New York: Anchor Books

Tversky, A. and Kahneman, D. 1981. The framing of decisions and the psychology of choice. *Science*, **211**, 453–8

Veyne, P. 1976. *Le Pain et le cirque*. Paris: Seuil

Weitzman, M. 1984. *The Share Economy*. Cambridge, Mass.: Harvard University Press

Yaari, M. and Bar-Hillel, M. 1984. On dividing justly. *Social Choice and Welfare*, **1**, 1–24

11. Constitutions and democracies: an epilogue

CASS R. SUNSTEIN

Among those involved in the events leading to the American Constitution, Thomas Jefferson was most concerned about the conflict between democracy and constitutionalism. For Jefferson, periodic constitutional amendment was a necessary part of a well-functioning democracy. "Each generation is as independent of the one preceding, as that was of all which had gone before. It has then, like them, a right to choose for itself the form of government it believes most promotive of its own happiness . . . [T]he dead have no rights." For James Madison, by contrast, constitutions must be insulated from the ordinary operation of politics. Jefferson's proposal, he wrote, would produce "the most violent struggles . . . between the parties interested in reviving, and those interested in reforming the antecedent state of property." In Madison's view, a reduction of factional strife justified the insulation of constitutions from the ordinary functioning of politics. The debate between Jefferson and Madison has often been recapitulated in discussions of the relationship between constitutionalism and democracy.

Constitutions operate as constraints on the governing ability of majorities; they are naturally taken as antidemocratic. But constitutional provisions serve many different functions. They may be liberal or illiberal; different constitutions, and different parts of the same constitution, protect different interests. We may distinguish, for example, between structural provisions and rights provisions. Structural provisions are usually intended to minimize the pathologies associated with one or another conception of democracy. Thus, for example, a system of separation of powers is typically intended either

I would like to thank Bruce A. Ackerman, Douglas G. Baird, Frank H. Easterbrook, Stephen Holmes, Michael W. McConnell, Richard A. Posner, and David A. Strauss for valuable comments on a previous draft.

to limit the power of factions – powerful private groups – or to reduce the likelihood that representatives will pursue their own interests rather than those of the public generally. The twin fears of factional tyranny and self-interested representation have often been important motivating forces behind structural provisions. Even if such provisions are insulated from the workings of majoritarian politics, they may be understood as democratic insofar as they attempt to ensure that government will act in the interest of the public at large.

Rights provisions are designed to fence off certain areas from majoritarian control, but they also serve different functions. The protection of some rights is rooted in a desire to protect democracy, however understood. The right to freedom of speech and the right to vote are examples. The fact that majorities cannot intrude on such rights should not obscure their democratic nature. But rights might also be antidemocratic, in the sense that they interfere with democratic processes for reasons that are independent of a desire to preserve the functioning of democracy. Consider the right to freedom from unreasonable searches and seizures, the right of privacy, perhaps the right to property[1] – or the insulation of the slave trade from Congress. The status of such interests as rights reflects, to a greater or lesser degree, a distrust of democracy.

There are thus dramatically different forms of constitutionalism – just as there are widely disparate conceptions of democracy. It would be a mistake to identify constitutionalism with (say) its eighteenth-century version, or to assume that democracy must be understood (say) in terms of modern interest-group pluralism. The purpose of the discussion that follows is to explore the relationship between different conceptions of democracy and different approaches to constitutionalism, with particular reference to the chapters in this volume. Section I discusses pluralist conceptions of democracy and the limitations imposed on pluralism by some forms of constitutionalism. Section II

---

[1] The right to property is part of a class of rights that serve dual functions. Sometimes that right derives from principles of "natural right," generating a check that is deliberately antidemocratic. Sometimes private property is justified on democratic grounds: it prevents constant factional struggle over the distribution of wealth, and it also creates a safeguard against an unduly powerful and hence tyrannical public sphere. The right to freedom from unreasonable searches and seizures might be similarly understood in democratic terms.

examines various reasons for removing issues from the public sphere. Section III explores the relationship of private property and limited government to constitutionalism. Section IV deals with the problem of preference formation. The ultimate goal of the discussion is to suggest the possibility of constitutional structures that promote nonpluralist forms of democracy and at the same time escape some of the pathologies that can be associated with eighteenth- and nineteenth-century constitutionalism.

I Against pluralist democracy

The Framers of the American Constitution operated against a background set by the republican tradition. Classical republicanism understood politics to be a system of widespread public participation in the governmental process.[2] Properly understood, politics was not a process in which people attempted to satisfy their consumption choices. Selection of values was instead the object of the process. Civic virtue, understood as dedication to the public good rather than the pursuit of private interest, was to be the animating principle for political participation. A small republic would thus be preferred to a large one: both virtue and participation would be less likely to be achieved in a large territory. The ultimate ideal was one of an active citizenry, engaged in politics to decide the terms of social life.[3]

This understanding might be contrasted with modern pluralism, which sees politics as a struggle among self-interested groups for scarce social resources (Stigler 1971; Dahl 1956; Bentley 1908; Truman 1951). Under this understanding – often positive, sometimes normative – political participation is fueled by self-interest. Laws should be understood as a kind of commodity; the goal of the system is to reach an equilibrium that accurately reflects numbers and intensities of citizen preferences. Political behavior is in its essence no different from market behavior. In this view, the absence of political activity or unrest might be understood as an affirmative good,

---

[2] This brief summary is stylized and ignores some of the unattractive features of traditional republicanism – in particular, the limitations on the class of people permitted to participate in politics. See Pitkin (1981).

[3] In the early period of the United States, of course, there was not a large scope for governmental action – in part a reaction to experiences in Europe with the infusion of religion into government.

suggesting contentment with the existing order. Under these premises, there is little or no room for constitutionalism, except to set up the basic rules to govern the struggle of interests. The purpose of politics is to aggregate preferences, and checks on the process of aggregation are not easy to understand.[4]

One of the principal tasks for the Framers of the American Constitution was to synthesize traditional republicanism with emerging principles having pluralist features. In chapter 6, Bruce Ackerman argues that the Federalists managed to combine the two in a "two-track" theory of democracy. Under that theory, "higher law-making," in the form of *constitutional politics*, produces the particular norms placed in the Constitution itself. Constitutional politics is characterized by both mass mobilization and civic virtue. Thus the protection of free speech, for example, is the result of widespread public participation and an exercise of virtue on the part of the public generally.

The other, lower track of law-making consists of *normal politics*, which amounts to pluralist bargaining. For Ackerman, the day-to-day workings of politics are necessarily pluralist in character. Normal politics is characterized by an absence of widespread participation and by self-interest. In the light of human selfishness, apathy and ignorance, the ideals of civic virtue and citizen participation are impossible to achieve.[5] To be sure, the processes of bargaining are constrained by various structural devices, most notably by the backdrop of constitutional law. Pluralism is checked by constitutionalized norms, both structural and rights-based; lower-track law-making must always yield to higher-track law-making where there is a conflict. But the Framers recognized that normal politics would necessarily dominate the territory. In the light of human nature, normal politics could be overcome only by "coercive democracy," a cure worse than the disease.

Ackerman's chapter is intended to do three things at once: to capture the Federalist vision of politics; to set out a more subtle and attractive conception of democracy than either the republican or the pluralist alternative, standing by itself; and to justify the role of the

---

[4] This understanding represents a prominent strain in American constitutionalism. It underlies, for example, the thought of Oliver Wendell Holmes (see Rogat 1964). For a modern illustration, see Posner (1986).

[5] To the extent that preferences are endogenous, this conclusion might be questioned. See (V) below.

American Supreme Court in the face of the "countermajoritarian difficulty" produced by the existence of judicial power to invalidate legislation. On all three fronts, I think, the attempt is unsuccessful; and an exploration of the difficulties will provide a helpful introduction to the problem of constitutionalism and democracy.

Federalist politics.

The Federalist vision of politics was indeed designed to incorporate elements of republicanism and pluralism, but there was no sharp distinction between two kinds of politics in their ultimate product, and the mix was different from that described by Ackerman. One of the Federalists' principal goals was to cabin the reach of normal politics, which they understood in terms of faction, whether based on interest or ideology.[6] The system of national representation was designed to ensure that politics would have a deliberative character. This understanding can be found throughout the writing of Hamilton and, even more pervasively, Madison. Thus Hamilton suggested that the "aim of every political constitution is, or ought to be, first to obtain for rulers men who possess most wisdom to discern, and most virtue to pursue the common good of the society; and in the next place, to take the most effectual precautions for keeping them virtuous whilst they continue to hold their public trust." Hamilton tied these understandings to the theme of deliberation in many places in the Federalist papers.

Madison's views on the matter are set out most carefully in *The Federalist* no. 10. There he suggested that small-scale republics should be distrusted, since they would be peculiarly vulnerable to the influence of private factions. A large republic, for Madison, would have two features that would diminish the likelihood of factional tyranny. First, the various groups would be able to offset one another; any particular one would be unlikely to be able to capture government in order to distribute wealth or opportunities in its favor. Secondly – and for present purposes this is the central point – national representatives in a large republic would be more likely to be able to escape parochial pressures. For Madison, representatives were to "refine and enlarge the public views by passing them through the medium of a

6 See n.7 below.

chosen body of citizens, whose wisdom may best discern the true interest of their country and whose patriotism and love of justice will be least likely to sacrifice it to temporary or partial considerations." The Federalists hardly intended to promote a system of politics as pluralist bargaining.

In the same vein Madison attacked members of Congress as "advocates for their respective constituents," and preferred large election districts and length of service, which would "render the Body more stable in its policy, and more capable of stemming popular currents taking a wrong direction, til reason and justice could regain their ascendency." In all of these respects, one finds a powerful Burkean strand in the Framers' theory of representation. The principal purpose of that strand was to ensure that representatives would perform deliberatively, and not react mechanically to the interests of their constituents. Responsiveness was, in this view, not an ambiguous good; it often operated to promote the power of private factions. The Federalist hope was that representatives would have the virtue associated with republican citizens. Theirs was therefore a hybrid conception of representation: public officials would be accountable to the public, and they would neither conduct their deliberations in a vacuum nor be subject to the sway of well-organized private groups.

Of course the Federalists were aware that the scheme might go astray and that the various safeguards were imperfect. In *The Federalist* no. 10, Madison recognizes that "enlightened statesmen will not always be at the helm." *The Federalist* no. 51 may be understood as an elaboration on this theme, attempting to control representatives who lack virtue by opposing "ambition to ambition." The distribution of national powers was designed to furnish a supplemental check.

These various understandings fit well with a number of features of the American Constitution. The system of national representation is the most obvious example. But it is important too that of the various political actors, only the House of Representatives was to be elected directly. The president was to be selected by the electoral college, a deliberative body. The Senate would be appointed by state representatives. In addition, the system of separation of powers further attenuated the authority of well-organized private groups; it thus operated as an additional check against factional tyranny[7] and self-interested representation. Finally, the existence of judicial review, guaranteeing enforcement of the Constitution in the face of popular will, served as a final safeguard. All of these features were designed to ensure that national politics would be genuinely deliberative (Bessette 1980); indeed, the creation of a deliberative democracy (*ibid.*), combining a measure of insulation with significant popular control, was a central purpose of the Framers.[8]

Ackerman's description of the Federalist vision of politics understates the central effort to confine normal politics and to ensure a measure of deliberation quite apart from the rare moments of constitutional politics. Ordinary politics, for the Framers, was to be infused to the extent possible with features of republicanism. Ackerman reads into the Federalist vision a twentieth-century conception of politics, heavily influenced by modern economics, that was quite foreign to the Framers' hopes and expectations for the constitutional system.

The problems of normal politics

Normal politics is not an attractive conception of governance; and it is not the best that a constitutional democracy might do.[9] To understand the point, it is necessary to explore pluralist approaches to politics.

The pluralist understanding sees the political process as a kind of market. Laws are simply commodities; they should reflect numbers and intensities of preferences. The pluralist approach thus takes the existing distribution of wealth, the existing set of entitlements and existing preferences as exogenous variables; all of these form the basis for pluralist struggle. The goal of a political system is to ensure that the various inputs are reflected accurately in law. This under-

---

[7] Factional tyranny may come both from private groups seeking to promote their economic interests and from ideological groups whose nonmaterial interests are at stake. In the United States, the problem of faction has generally stemmed from the former set of groups, but many nations have suffered most as a result of the latter.

[8] Sometimes these features of the original framework are invoked to support the claim that the Framers were antidemocratic. See, e.g., Hofstadter (1948).

[9] For varying views on the descriptive accuracy of the pluralist approach in contemporary American politics, see Kalt and Zupan (1984), Peltzman (1984), Mayhew (1974) and Maass (1983).

standing carries with it a particular conception of representation, in which officials respond mechanically to constituent desires.[10]

The appeal of the pluralist understanding stems from its utilitarian underpinnings, its effort to respect current preferences and the desire to avoid the risks of tyranny associated with active preference-shaping by government. But if some preferences can be shown to be objectionable, the case for pluralism becomes much weaker. Indeed, a significant purpose of politics may be to decide on preferences and to reveal objectionable preferences as such through processes of political discussion and debate (Goodin 1986). Consider laws prohibiting discrimination on the basis of race or gender. Such laws owe their origin, at least in part, to a perception that the preferences that give rise to discrimination are objectionable or distorted. The distortion may come from two sources. The first is the phenomenon of adaptive preferences on the part of victims – preferences that are based on the absence of available opportunities (Elster 1983). In the context of gender, the phenomenon is especially pervasive. The second source of distortion is interest-induced beliefs on the part of the beneficiaries.[11]

Sometimes, in short, politics has a deliberative or transformative dimension. Its function is to select preferences or to provide opportunities for preference-formation rather than simply to implement existing desires. The point is a quite general one, extending beyond discrimination law to environmental measures, regulation of broadcasting, welfare expenditures and many others. Such laws represent, to a greater or lesser degree, an effort to select preferences through politics.[12] Under the pluralist understanding it is not clear why laws should not be bought and sold like commodities in a market place; such a process of sale would accurately aggregate preferences. But for those who believe in a deliberative function for politics, the market place metaphor will be unsuccessful.

Much of the appeal of pluralism stems from its connection with utilitarianism. The goal is accurately to aggregate private preferences, and to the extent that some preferences are rejected, the appeal of

[10] Those desires may themselves be based on different things – for example, ideology or interest. In the pluralist model, interest is the usual motivating force of political conduct.

[11] This is a complex phenomenon. For a skeptical treatment, see Elster (1985).

[12] To a degree, of course, some such laws are interest-group bargains, or represent efforts by some groups to impose their preferences on others.

pluralism is undermined. But even if one believes that a utilitarian approach to politics is desirable, it is by no means clear that the pluralist system should be accepted. First, accurate preference-aggregation through politics is unlikely to be accomplished in the light of the conundrums in developing a social welfare function (Riker 1982; Arrow 1963). Public choice theory has shown that cycling problems, strategic and manipulative behavior, sheer chance and other factors make majoritarianism highly unlikely to provide an accurate aggregation of preferences (cf. Offe 1985). Pluralist approaches, despite their foundations in public choice theory, tend to overlook these difficulties.[13]

Even if these problems might be surmounted, one would have to be optimistic indeed to believe that there is an identity between the result that would be reached by the considered utilitarian and that which would be reached by a legislature responding to constituent pressures as they are generally imposed. In any representative democracy, there is simply too much slippage between legislative outcomes and constituent desires. Much of the slippage comes from two sources. The first is financial expenditures on politics. Such expenditures have influence on governmental outcomes, but it is hard to maintain that there is a close connection between the level of expenditures on a proposed law and the amount of utility[14] to be gained by it. Willingness to pay and utility are at best imperfectly correlated at the individual level (Dworkin 1980); at the level of legislation, the correlation is extremely weak.

The second and perhaps more fundamental source involves transaction-cost barriers to the exercise of political influence (Hardin 1982). These barriers play a critical role in determining the nature and amount of influence imposed on representatives. In particular, unorganized groups are unable to exert much in the way of political influence. These factors make it hard to believe that legislative outcomes accurately reflect numbers and intensities of preferences.

It follows that a system of normal politics would hardly deserve complete sympathy, even if it did capture the understanding of the Framers of the American Constitution. One of the purposes of constitutionalism is to insure against normal politics or at a minimum

---

[13] Some of Arrow's assumptions may, however, not hold in the political process.
[14] I put to one side the difficulties with the concept here.

to limit its reach and effects. In particular, a well-functioning nonpluralist democracy might attempt, in Federalist fashion, to insulate
national representatives in order to promote the performance of their
deliberative tasks.[15] An alternative strategy, drawing from traditional
republicanism, would be to provide spheres for political action by
citizens generally, a course that would require a large measure of
decentralization and that is occasionally reflected in American Federalism (see Barber 1984). Both of these strategies carry risks of their
own, but they are a partial response to the defects in normal politics.
Neither of them need posit a belief in a unitary common good; but
they do require a large measure of debate and discussion before
compromise is undertaken.

Judicial review

Many of the problems raised by judicial review derive from the
discretionary character of interpretation, not from the intertemporal
problem raised by the fact that the Framers and ratifiers are no longer
living. Constitutional texts are often open-ended, and the act of
interpretation will be highly discretionary. It is, for example, by no
means clear whether "freedom of speech" is abridged by laws
regulating disclosures by government employees, restrictions on por-
nography or laws prohibiting disclosure of confessions during a
criminal trial. Nor is it obvious whether "the equal protection of the
laws" is denied by a law treating spouses of men differently from
spouses of women for purposes of social security, a measure prohibiting women from performing in combat or a law requiring people to
retire at age sixty-five. In these cases, the problem for constitutional
democracy is why the discretionary power necessarily implied by this
interpretive task should be conferred on unelected judges.

Ackerman's distinction between constitutional and normal politics
is not helpful here. To be sure, it does help to handle problems raised
by judicial review when the Court can claim to be acting in the service
of a (particular) value judgment made by the Framers and ratifiers of
the Constitution. Hamilton also provided a justification for this

---

[15] It is a mistake to read Madison as if his only fear were the civil strife that would
come from factional struggle; national representatives were to insure as well against
government as interest-group deal.

practice in *The Federalist* No. 78, invoking the independence brought about by life tenure as a guarantor of fidelity to the constitutional text. Even if Hamilton's argument is vulnerable because of the intertemporal problem (see Brest 1980), the more pressing task is to develop a theory that would justify (and discipline) judicial review in cases in which the Constitution makes no particular value judgment. The process of constitutional "interpretation" is not explained by Ackerman's theory.

One can point to notable efforts in recent years. One such effort understands judicial review as a kind of "antitrust" measure designed to ensure the appropriate functioning of pluralist politics (Ely 1981). In this view, courts do and should intervene into majoritarian politics when the political process is defective – either because minorities are systematically excluded from participation or because some right having to do with political participation has been abridged (*ibid.*). The rights to vote and to freedom of expression are the classic examples. Competing efforts argue that courts, as politically insulated institutions, should be better suited to define and elaborate "fundamental rights," which are to be derived from political theory, tradition, social consensus or some other source (Bickel 1962; Perry 1982). But all of these efforts have proved vulnerable (Brest 1981).

Perhaps surprisingly, the Federalist understanding of politics and of representation turns out to be useful here as well. An important justification for national representation, it will be recalled, was to ensure a deliberative role for government – a system in which existing preferences and attachments would not be taken as exogenous variables but would instead be made subject to general criticism and debate. Since the founding of the American Constitution, that role has been limited, with direct election of senators, the declining role of the electoral college, changes in communications and technology and other factors that have sometimes made it difficult for representatives to worry about anything other than reelection. Some studies of representative behavior suggest that constituent pressures play a dominant and nearly exclusive role (see, e.g., Mayhew 1974; Peltzman 1984; but also Maass 1983; Kalt and Zupan 1984).

In many Western democracies, it is constitutional courts that have assumed the deliberative function through the process of constitutional adjudication. It is in the process of judicial review, and through the culture to which judicial review contributes, that existing social practices must be justified. Judicial insulation from politics has thus made a deliberative or transformative[16] role – in Ackerman's terms, constitutional politics – far more likely. The function of the American courts in the antidiscrimination movements associated with blacks and women are prominent examples, and there have been parallel developments elsewhere.

There are of course risks in such a course. The courts' lack of accountability poses significant dangers. Moreover, judicial action, even if deliberative, suffers from the significant defect that it necessarily excludes the citizenry from political processes. But it may be that a firm judicial hand has at least on occasion served an important and distinctly Madisonian role, minimizing the power of self-interested groups and ensuring a measure of scrutiny of the existing set of preferences and the existing allocation of power.

II Private and public

For those who believe that there is a conflict between constitutionalism and democracy, the tension stems from the fact that constitutions remove certain topics from public scrutiny and review. The basic institutional arrangements may be changed only with extraordinary difficulty; the rights protected by a constitution are not subject to political revision. For some, the resulting stability is bought at an enormous price, which is the insulation of fundamental choices from collective struggle or deliberation (see Unger 1987). This point amounts to another version of the attack on the distinction between public and private: the decision about what will be public and what private is necessarily a public choice, and the problem with some or all constitutions, it may be said, is that they ignore the implications of that fact.

In his two provocative chapters, Stephen Holmes argues that constitutionalism and democracy can be highly compatible. In particular, Holmes suggests that when constitutions remove subjects

---

[16] Deliberation need not, of course, be allied with transformation. In the Federalist vision, they were to some degree opposites: deliberation was designed to help insulate the status quo. The notion that deliberation will often lead in the direction of transformation thus depends on controversial premises. See below.

from the public sphere, the removal might be justified, not as a means of protecting "rights," but instead in order to ensure the proper functioning of the democratic process. Echoing Madison, Holmes contends that public discussion and debate of certain subjects will make democracy unable to function. The exclusion of religion from politics might be thus understood. Religious disputation might factionalize the system, make enemies of friends and (eventually) prevent the operation of a democratic public sphere entirely. If one removes religion from politics, one will make it less likely that factions will coalesce around a particular issue, and increase the likelihood that people will be able either to deliberate on the public good or to achieve mutually acceptable accommodations. The removal also diverts resources from unresolvable problems to soluble ones. So too, the decision to generate a basic institutional structure, and to immunize it from revision, might promote rather than undermine democracy. For Holmes, this strategy – voluntary foreclosure of choices – is liberating, not confining; the decision to create and immunize an institutional arrangement will leave future generations freer to address other issues.

The phenomenon is reflected at both the individual and the social level. Just as neighbors may not discuss some issues that will threaten a friendship, a political system may impose "gag rules" on itself. Holmes argues neither that there is a natural or prepolitical private sphere nor that the creation of such a sphere need be based on a belief in any theory of rights. His category of rights is derived from a desire to maintain a well-functioning democracy.[17]

The basic argument is persuasive, and it suggests that conventional approaches to the problem, posing an inevitable conflict between constitutionalism and democracy, are naive. But there are two difficulties here, which suggest that the basic problem cannot be dissolved.

The first problem is that, as Holmes recognizes, privatization through constitutional decision is a two-edged sword. It may promote democracy in the way Holmes suggests; but it may also immunize an issue from public inspection and debate and at the same time – and this is the central problem – resolve it favorably to one or another side. Consider three examples: abortion, redistribution of property and

---

[17] It is thus continuous with the arguments offered in Ely (1981), though the focus is somewhat different.

slavery. Privatization of such issues may have its benefits, and indeed the removal of all three from politics has been justified on grounds like those invoked by Holmes. But privatization through constitutional law also immunizes the question from public scrutiny and resolves it by a kind of fiat. For Madison, the removal of property from democratic control was justified precisely on the grounds suggested by Holmes;[18] consider his opposition to frequent constitutional amendment. But the example suggests that at times privatization through constitutional law is profoundly antidemocratic. One need go no further than the experience of the Supreme Court in the early part of this century, in which legal doctrines were used to check the redistribution of property.[19]

Other examples come to mind: the role of women in society, gun control, the rights of racial minorities and homosexuals. Often those who urge social transformation are told not to raise their complaints in the democratic sphere precisely on Holmes's ground: their advocacy is disruptive, upsets the peace and makes the ordinary operation of politics far more difficult. When the large questions are debated publicly, the risks of factionalization and conflict are greatest, and hence Holmes's arguments are most likely to be applicable. The response to the arguments is that politics sometimes operates at its best when the fundamental questions are opened up to collective conflict and deliberation (Arendt 1965; Unger 1986). Movements in favor of women and racial minorities are important examples here. A system that immunized from collective control the issues that produce the most conflict would hardly be democratic; under such a system, democratic processes would operate only when the stakes were low, and the largest issues would be resolved behind the scenes or by particular groups.

There is a further difficulty. Holmes argues that privatization through politics will decrease factional struggle, but (as he recognizes) the opposite may occur. If resolution through political processes is unavailable, people may press all the harder, become less likely to avail themselves of political remedies generally, lose faith in the system and resort to extralegal means. This was the experience of the

---

[18] Thus it was not primarily justified as protecting a natural or prepolitical right to private property.

[19] See below.

United States after the decision of the Supreme Court in the *Dred Scott* case, which privatized slavery; it may also be the case with abortion. The distinction between issues that produce conflict and issues that do not, while relevant, is thus inadequate to decide which issues to remove from the public sphere.

Holmes's chapter on "precommitment" (chapter 7) has similar virtues and a similar weakness. To be sure, constraints may be liberating; if some issues are resolved, a person or policy may go about its business more freely. The ability to proceed against the backdrop of set institutional arrangements allows government to resolve political questions without revisiting the basic questions. In this respect, Holmes is persuasive in challenging the notion that constitutional democracy is an oxymoron. But precommitment has a dark side as well. To close off from politics decisions about basic institutional arrangements is also confining. Consider the view that the modern system of checks and balances operates to insulate private property and privilege from democratic control. That system may have other effects as well; but there can be no doubt that redistribution is rendered more difficult by virtue of the existence of the institutional checks, and that inaction as well as action may be a product of factional power. In these circumstances precommitment across generations remains a serious problem for democratic theory.

The point brings up a further difficulty – the problem of identification. Which issues should be privatized in the interest of ensuring the proper functioning of the public sphere? The answer cannot be made to depend on the importance of the issue. The fact that an issue is important is hardly a reason to prevent it from reaching the public domain; indeed, importance may argue the other way. Surely it is relevant whether the effects feared by Holmes – factionalization and draining of public resources to insoluble problems – are likely to occur. It is important, too, whether the issue sought to be privatized by constitutional law can be considered a "right." The traditional justification for removal of issues from politics is that some matters do not belong in the hands of (potentially oppressive) majorities, regardless of whether factionalization would occur. The contemporary understanding of freedom of religion is based at least as much on this concern as on the fears of factionalization.

All this suggests that privatization will sometimes promote the proper functioning of the public sphere, but that it sometimes will not, and that fears about factionalization are often voiced most vociferously by those committed to the status quo. If there is no independent argument that the matter to be removed from politics should be considered a "right," the category of cases justifiably privatized because of the fear of factionalization should be relatively small.

III Property, limited government and deliberative politics

One of the purposes of eighteenth- and nineteenth-century constitutions was to insulate private property from self-interested government officials and from factional tyranny. Indeed, the concept of faction was closely associated – if not identified – with the phenomenon of private groups seeking to redistribute resources or opportunities from the wealthy to the poor.[20] The constitutional embodiment of this perception can be found in both the structural and the individual rights provisions of constitutions from the period. Thus the structural provisions of the American Constitution protect property by making government action difficult. Agreement among the several branches is necessary in order for redistribution to be carried out. Many of the individual rights provisions of the American Constitution are designed to safeguard property. The contract clause, protecting private contract, and the eminent domain clause, requiring compensation for "takings" of property, are the most prominent examples, and the due process clause has also been used as a barrier against the redistribution of wealth and income.

In American law, the tension between constitutionalism and democracy reached its high point in the early twentieth century, when an aggressive Supreme Court, relying on the due process clause, invalidated a wide range of regulatory and redistributive legislation, including minimum wage and maximum hour laws (see Kennedy 1976; Tribe 1978). The period is often described as "the Lochner era," after the decision in *Lochner* v. *New York*, the most famous case of the era. In this period, the Court reasoned that minimum wage and maximum hour laws were an effort to take property from employers and to

[20] See the little-remembered close of *The Federalist* no. 10: "A rage for paper money, for an abolition of debts, for an equal division of property, or for any other *improper or wicked project*, will be less apt to pervade the whole body of the Union than a particular member of it" (my italics).

transfer it to employees. This form of "naked" interest-group transfer was, in the Court's view, prohibited by the Constitution.

There were two critical steps to the Court's reasoning. The first consisted of a limitation of the category of permissible government ends. Efforts to redistribute resources and paternalistic measures were both constitutionally out of bounds. Measures that prohibited force or fraud, or attempted to help the public generally,[21] were permissible. Only the latter measures could be fit within the state's authority, known as the "police power." This limitation on the category of permissible ends of course had important implications, excluding a wide range of measures enacted by majorities.

The second step in the Court's approach consisted of careful scrutiny of the relationship between any permissible end invoked to support a statute and the means chosen by the state to promote that end. Thus, for example, maximum hour legislation was invalid as an effort to promote the health of bakers, since the state was unable to demonstrate to the Court's satisfaction that maximum hour legislation would in fact improve health. Under this framework, minimum wage legislation was an easy case for the Court: the health rationale seemed quite weak and the legislation purely redistributive. The limitation in the category of permissible ends, in conjunction with vigorous means–ends scrutiny, served to "flush out" impermissible bases for government action. In cases decided in this era, the Court continued the original eighteenth-century fusion of concerns about redistribution and private property with the fear of faction (for a modern example, see Epstein 1985). But for the Lochner Court – unlike for Madison – private property was to be protected mainly for antidemocratic reasons. The goal of the Lochner majority was to preserve the existing distribution of wealth and entitlements, not to prevent the disintegration of the public sphere into civil strife.

The downfall of the Lochner era understanding has led to a decline in the centrality of private property to American constitutionalism. This decline has occurred on two fronts. First, courts have concluded that redistributive or paternalistic measures are permissibly "public." This phenomenon derives in part from a recognition that the existing distribution of resources is not natural but is in part a creation of government (Sunstein 1987). In these circumstances, efforts to reallo-

[21] This category was not, however, well defined.

cate entitlements and wealth do not interfere with a system that should be taken as prepolitical or inviolate. Second, courts have demanded much less in the way of a close connection between the public end and the means chosen by the state to promote that end. A minimal connection will suffice. A law forbidding opticians to perform certain services, for example, will be upheld if a rational legislature might believe that some opticians will not be able to perform those services adequately. Both minimum wage and maximum hour laws are defensible as redistributive measures. The expansion in the class of permissible ends and the need for only a weak means–ends connection have ensured that social and economic legislation will almost always be upheld against constitutional attack. The decline of the Lochner-era understanding fits comfortably with Madisonian premises. It is no longer necessary to preserve the existing distribution of property in order to prevent the kinds of class warfare that Madison feared.

In her contribution to this volume, Jennifer Nedelsky claims that the Supreme Court has "abandoned" private property as a constraint on government. In her view, private property has been central to the constitutional order since its inception; once it is abandoned, she suggests, constitutionalism will itself be jeopardized. Without property, the distinction between civil and political rights may collapse, and the "necessary tension" between constitutionalism and democracy will be threatened. For Nedelsky, private property has served an important ordering function, checking democracy and vindicating the claims of constitutionalism. Unlike Holmes, Nedelsky sees considerable tension between constitutionalism and democracy, and to that extent she is not altogether displeased by the abandonment of property as an ordering principle. But she is ambivalent about whether property-based constraints on democracy are desirable.

In my view, Nedelsky overstates the decline of private property in American constitutional law. The Court continues to require compensation for "takings" of property – at least when there is a physical invasion by government, and sometimes even when there has been no such invasion. The abandonment, such as it is, means only that regulatory measures – zoning legislation, rent control, labor laws, land use regulation – will rarely be held to require compensation. The reasoning depends in part on conventional understandings of the term "taking," in part on the perception that redistribution does not cause class warfare and in part on the theory that has resulted after the downfall of the *Lochner* period. Regulatory measures, even if redistributive, are based on purposes that are plausibly public; and the means–ends connection is sufficient to satisfy a court. Because private property continues to receive protection, it is a mistake to interpret modern doctrine as an across-the-board abandonment of earlier understandings.

We may doubt, moreover, whether private property, understood in eighteenth- or nineteenth-century terms, is central to what Nedelsky calls the "myth" of constitutionalism (Baker 1986). A general respect for private property is usually important for a democracy, but such general respect need not be undermined by regulatory and redistributive measures. In the current period, far more important to constitutionalism than an absolute right to property are, first, the traditional political rights, including the right to speak freely, to vote, to associate; secondly, rights of freedom from discrimination on certain grounds, primarily race, religion and gender; and perhaps above all, the various institutional safeguards protecting against government action at the behest of well-organized private groups. As we have seen, the traditional fears that underlie constitutionalism involve factional power and self-interested representation, producing either corruption or tyranny. The absolute protection of property, at least in its original incarnation, is no longer closely associated with either of those goals. Indeed, private property may itself be seen as a product of factional power: the refusal to reallocate entitlements and wealth may stem from the power of well-organized private groups. It is for this reason that various paternalistic and redistributive measures can comfortably coexist with modern constitutionalism.

Finally, it is doubtful that the "abandonment" of private property – at least in its current form – poses a serious risk for constitutionalism. There is no reason to believe that the existing system – insofar as it offers less than complete protection to private property – will generate serious crises of legitimation. It should not be forgotten that judicial protection of private property once produced such crises. Changing conceptions about the relationship of the individual to the state have made the absolute sanctity of private property a doubtful proposition. There is no sign that constitutionalism in general – as distinct from a particular species of constitutionalism – is thereby jeopardized.

Nedelsky is correct in suggesting that private property has served an important ordering function and that it may be difficult to come up with a feasible alternative. Her fear may be that without firm protection for private property, we are left with pluralism; and as we have seen, pluralism and constitutionalism do not go well together. But American constitutional doctrine does reflect a unifying theme that may eventually turn out to be an important surrogate for private property (Vining 1978). It will be recalled that even in the post-Lochner era, courts require a plausible argument that legislation has resulted from something other than the political power exercised by particular groups. Under many constitutional provisions – most prominently, the due process and equal protection clauses – the imposition of a burden or the differential distribution of a benefit must be defensible in public terms (Sunstein 1984). The Court requires some showing that legislation can be defended as responsive to some public value; it must be more or other than a naked interest-group deal. Thus, for example, when legislation treats optometrists more favorably than opticians, it must be possible to point to something other than political power to justify the differential treatment.

This idea reflects a powerful antipluralist thrust in modern consti-tutional law; it also reflects a Madisonian conception of represen-tation. To be sure, the norm is not vigorously enforced. The Court is willing to hypothesize legitimate bases for classifications and upholds them even when an interest-group explanation is highly plausible. But there is a norm, constitutional in status, that rejects the idea that legislation can be solely a product of private power.

Sometimes, in fact, the Court goes further, requiring that the value at issue survive critical scrutiny designed to ensure that it is not itself a product of existing relations of power. Thus in the contexts of gender and race, it is insufficient to be able to point to a widely held value as a basis for differential treatment. Racist and sexist preferences may not stand as a basis for a classification, even if they are generally held. The idea appears to be that such preferences are themselves a product of power, or represent "ideology," and therefore cannot serve to justify legislation.

Underlying these decisions is a distrust of pluralist politics and a belief that private preferences should be "laundered" (Goodin 1986;

Sunstein 1986) through political scrutiny and debate. The understanding here is that naked wealth transfers are undesirable and that the requirement of discussion in terms of the public good will have a deterrent effect on their occurrence (cf. Elster 1983). It is thus necessary to show that some value and not merely power – or values based on power – accounted for the legislative enactment. Whether the prohibition of naked preferences or of beliefs based on power will ultimately generate a coherent substitute for the property-based foundations of previous doctrine remains to be seen (Sunstein 1985). But whether or not such a substitute might be generated, the declining solicitude for private property does not pose a significant threat to constitutionalism.

It is true, however, that traditional notions of limited government and of the rule of law might be in tension with democracy – a point emphasized by Francis Sejersted in chapter 5, and reflected in Slagstad's discussion of Carl Schmitt in chapter 4. Traditional liberal understandings of constitutionalism grew in part out of a perceived need[22] for predictability, stability and security of persons and property. Sejersted describes these as "the very essence of constitutionalism" – an overstatement revealed as such by Holmes in chapters 1 and 7, but a description with some truth nonetheless. And modern defenses of constitutionalism, made in similar terms, assume considerable force in the light of recent and current experiences with governments that do not limit the operation of the public sphere. None of these governments is democratic. A government unchecked by constitutional safeguards or a healthy and independent private sphere may be tyrannical. Sometimes constitutional checks work to prevent private groups from usurping governmental processes; sometimes they cabin the authority of government officials, who have their own interests to promote.[23]

To be sure, such limitations carry risks of their own insofar as they remove subjects from the public sphere. And in some circumstances, a well-functioning democratic system, instead of or in addition to limited government, may operate as a check on these dangers. Sejersted makes the point in suggesting that democracy may serve

[22] For present purposes one need not say whether this need applied to all or only to particular social classes. Cf. chapter 2.
[23] The economic literature on "agency costs" should prove helpful here.

rather than undermine the rule of law. But both his first chapter and Slagstad's discussion of Schmitt suggest that constitutional barriers – like the general right to property and to freedom of contract – that limit democracy may end up strengthening democracy even when they cannot be defended straightforwardly in democratic terms.

V Preference formation, constitutions, and democracy

One of the most promising developments in recent economic and political thought is the exploration of the processes of preference-formation. Traditional economic theory takes preferences as exogenous; the same is true of traditional pluralism and of some forms of constitutionalism (Bork 1971; Posner 1986; Ackerman, this volume). But sometimes legal structures – including constitutions – will generate preferences, a point with a number of implications. For example, if the legal structure produces the preference, it is impossible to defend, without circularity, the structure by reference to the preference. Theories of constitutionalism and democracy that depend on preference satisfaction will thus be less plausible. Any system will tend to generate private preferences that it can satisfy (see Roemer 1985).

The phenomenon of endogenous preferences thus has considerable importance for democratic and constitutional theory (Roemer 1986). In particular, it should increase understanding of the frequent claim that political outcomes should be different from consumption choices. Consumption choices may depend, for example, on the lack of available opportunities (Elster 1983). In these circumstances a purpose of politics is not simply to implement preferences, but instead to select them, in a forum in which various distortions may be discussed and brought to light – not by a political elite but by the public binding itself, outlawing certain preferences or ensuring the availability of a range of choices. The distinction between markets and politics, discussed above, thus depends in part on a belief that preferences should not be taken as exogenous variables. This view is closely associated with a conception of individual freedom that understands the term to refer to selection rather than implementation of ends. The associated understanding of political freedom understands the term to refer to a deliberative process in which the citizenry in general selects social ends.[24]

That understanding of political freedom leads naturally to the distinction between ordinary preferences and "preferences about preferences" and the related phenomenon of voluntary foreclosure of consumption choices through law, whether constitutional or statutory. People may implement their second-order preferences – "preferences about preferences" – with structural and rights provisions.[25] Sometimes constitutions themselves represent an effort by past or current majorities to foreclose future choices in the service of some other end. Holmes discusses the desire to ensure the smooth functioning and to prevent the self-destruction of later governments; one might point as well to individual rights provisions designed to ensure that future majorities, swept up in some momentary cause, do not embark on a misguided course of action. The institution of judicial review might be justified and understood in precisely these terms. This conclusion holds regardless of whether the process of interpretation is discretionary or sharply constrained. If it is constrained, courts are enforcing second-order as against first-order preferences. If it is discretionary, the institution of judicial review might nonetheless be understood in Madisonian terms, as an opportunity to refine as well as reflect private preferences.

Using recent writing on preference formation, Jon Elster argues that constitutional change can be justified only on grounds of justice, not for its consequences. Consequential arguments, Elster says, are likely to be either speculative or self-defeating. They are speculative because it is hard to know the actual consequences of major institutional changes; one cannot predict their "global net long-term equilibrium effects." Elster suggests, for example, that a remedy for the phenomenon of adaptive preferences may be unsuccessful. One cannot know whether a particular preference is adaptive or not; and it is unclear what the remedy should be even if one does know. Consequentialist arguments may be self-defeating because (for example) to urge a constitutional change on the ground that it will

---

[24] There are of course risks of tyranny associated with this approach, captured in Rousseau's notion of "forcing people to be free."

[25] Note, however, that some second-order preferences may be distorted, nonautonomous, or otherwise objectionable. Consider a preference not to prefer to marry someone of another race, captured in a law prohibiting racial intermarriage.

increase the citizenry's energy for economic development or promote self-realization may undermine those effects. Those effects, as Elster has suggested before (Elster 1983), are essentially by-products. Consider the injunction to "be spontaneous."

Arguments based on justice do not, in Elster's view, suffer from any such defects. Economic democracy is an example. The principle of justice may persuade people to seek democracy in the workplace, even if the consequences are obscure. Elster concludes that constitutional change is likely to be both explained and justified on nonconsequential grounds.

Much of what Elster says is persuasive, but there are several gaps in the argument. First, the distinction between consequential arguments and arguments from justice is hardly clear cut. Sometimes consequential arguments are arguments from justice, and vice versa. Consider – to take recent random examples from American constitutional history – the debates over school prayer, abortion, gender discrimination and school busing to achieve desegregation. All of these debates reflect, on both sides, a mixture of consequential arguments and justice arguments; sometimes those arguments are one and the same. Even if the two might be distinguished, it is hardly clear that consequentialist arguments cannot justify constitutional change. Consider, for example, the original ratification of the American Constitution, which was urged predominantly on consequential grounds. The basic argument was that an expansion in the powers of the national government would reduce factional struggle, promote commerce and increase both prosperity and security (see Stone, Seidman, Sunstein and Tushnet 1986). Events preceding ratification suggested that a notional government was necessary for precisely these purposes. On the conventional account, the consequential arguments turned out to be not only persuasive to those who listened, but also correct.

In recent years, two of the most prominent (and nearly successful) efforts at constitutional change in the United States have been the balanced budget amendment and the equal rights amendment. The balanced budget amendment is defended and criticized on largely consequentialist grounds (see, e.g., Elliott 1985). The argument is that national representatives are unable to escape interest-group pressures and that a balanced budget amendment might, in the fashion of Ulysses and the Sirens, serve as a sensible means of precommitment on the part of the public and its representatives. The argument is probably incorrect, but the example should show that consequentialist arguments for constitutional change can be made and evaluated.

Consider, too, the consequentialist aspects of the arguments for the equal rights amendment, which would prohibit state discrimination on the basis of gender. Of particular interest here is the fact that many women, especially those of the earlier generation, are hostile to the equal rights amendment. But it should not be controversial to suggest that their hostility derives in part from adaptive preferences – preferences resulting from the absence of available opportunities. The goal is to reduce cognitive dissonance by rejecting new conceptions of the role of women in society. In these circumstances, it may be appropriate to be suspicious of those preferences,[26] based as they are on relations of power, and to argue in favor of constitutional change on consequentialist as well as justice grounds. All this suggests that consequentialist arguments for constitutional change may well have force; it all depends on the context and the particular change.

Elster suggests as well that capitalism paves the way toward socialism because it promotes the actual satisfaction of wants. But his own discussion of adaptive preferences undermines the point. Any political system is to some degree self-perpetuating, because wants are conditioned by the perception of available opportunities.[27] The point suggests that the absence of widespread dissatisfaction with a political system need not be a dispositive argument against change – consider the apparently widespread and long-standing acceptance of totalitarian regimes in some nations. This phenomenon provides another reason to reject pluralist approaches to democracy insofar as they take the absence of political activity as a reason not to question the existing regime.

The phenomenon of adaptive preferences joins with collective

[26] Consider in this regard Montesquieu's discussion in the *Persian Letters* (Montesquieu 1973) of the processes by which women in a harem become content with their fate; and consider also the phenomenon of the "happy slave," captured in historical accounts of the ambivalent reaction of some slaves to emancipation after the Civil War.

[27] The mechanisms that produce constitutional change remain somewhat mysterious. It should not be forgotten that the duration of most constitutional systems tends to be quite short.

action problems to make significant change extremely difficult to achieve. An understanding of cognitive processes thus helps to explain why and when constitutions and institutional structures generally lay the foundation for their own perpetuation. But this is an area in which much work remains to be done. It should not be surprising if increasing knowledge about the processes of preference-formation turns out to provide the next set of advances for democratic and constitutional theory.

VI   Conclusion

Democracy is not a unitary concept; the same is true for constitutionalism. If democracy is understood in pluralist terms, constitutionalism and more particularly judicial review are difficult to defend. But there are reasons to be suspicious of pluralist politics, which take the existing distribution of wealth and the existing set of preferences as exogenous and which is hard to defend even on its own premises. One of the functions of constitutionalism is to guard against pluralist politics or at least to limit its most pernicious features.

Constitutionalism of various sorts is highly compatible with nonpluralist conceptions of democracy. Some such conceptions attempt to promote deliberation about preferences, not merely to implement them. Other forms of constitutionalism, sensitive to the risks of factional power and of self-interested representation, pursue several different strategies: the creation of spheres of private autonomy of various sorts in order to limit government power, to protect private and public rights and to ensure the smooth functioning of the public sphere; the use of structural limitations, like the system of checks and balances, to restrict the government's ability to act; and the development of institutional devices to reinforce democratic processes as a check on both factions and representatives. All of these strategies have risks as well as benefits. But for all of them, a central goal of constitutional democracy is to secure a realm for public discussion and collective selection of preferences while guarding against the dangers of factional tyranny and self-interested representation.

All this suggests that it is difficult to discuss the relationship between constitutionalism and democracy in the abstract. Some constitutions might promote democracy; others might subvert it. There is no inevitable tension between democracy and constitutionalism. The tasks for the future are to devise appropriate conceptions of democracy, and to design constitutional provisions that will support rather than undermine them.

References

Arendt, H. 1965. *On Revolution*. New York: Viking

Arrow, K. 1963. *Social Choice and Individual Values*, 2nd edn. New York: Wiley (1st edn 1951)

Baker, C. E. 1986. Property and its relation to constitutionally protected liberty. *University of Pennsylvania Law Review*, **134**, 741–816

Barber, B. 1984. *Strong Democracy*. Baltimore: Johns Hopkins University Press

Bentley, A. 1908. *The Process of Government*. Chicago: University of Chicago Press

Bessette, W. 1980. Deliberative democracy: the majority principle in republican government, in *How Democratic is the Constitution?* edited by R. Goldwin and W. Schambra. Washington, D.C.: American Enterprise Institute, pp. 102–16

Bickel, A. 1962. *The Least Dangerous Branch*. New Haven: Yale University Press

Bork, R. 1971. Neutral principles and some First Amendment problems. *Indiana Law Journal*, **47**, 1–31

Brest, P. 1980. The misconceived quest for the original understanding. *Boston University Law Review*, **60**, 204–38

    1981. The fundamental rights controversy: the essential contradictions of normative constitutional scholarship. *Yale Law Journal*, **90**, 1063–1109

Dahl, R. 1956. *A Preface to Democratic Theory*. Chicago: University of Chicago Press

Dworkin, R. 1980. Is wealth a value? *Journal of Legal Studies*, **9**, 191–226

Elliott, E. E. 1985. Constitutional conventions and the deficit. *Duke Law Journal* (1985), 1077–1110

Elster, J. 1983. *Sour Grapes: Studies in the Subversion of Rationality.* New York: Cambridge University Press

1984. *Ulysses and the Sirens: Studies in Rationality and Irrationality.* New York: Cambridge University Press

1985. *Making Sense of Marx.* New York: Cambridge University Press

Ely, J. H. 1981. *Democracy and Distrust: A Theory of Judicial Review.* Cambridge, Mass.: Harvard University Press

Epstein, R. 1985. *Takings: Private Property and the Law of Eminent Domain.* Cambridge, Mass.: Harvard University Press

Goodin, R. 1986. Laundering preferences, in *Foundations of Social Choice Theory*, edited by J. Elster and A. Hylland. New York: Cambridge University Press, pp. 75–101

Hardin, R. 1982. *Collective Action.* Baltimore: Johns Hopkins University Press

Hofstadter, R. 1948. *The American Political Tradition.* New York: Random House

Kalt, J., and Zupan, M. 1984. Capture and ideology in the economic theory of politics. *American Economic Review*, **74**, 279–300

Kennedy, D. 1976. Form and substance in private law adjudication. *Harvard Law Review*, **89**, 1685–1778

Maass, A. 1983. *Congress and the Common Good.* New York: Basic Books

Mayhew, D. 1974. *Congress: The Electoral Connection.* New Haven: Yale University Press

Montesquieu 1973. *Persian Letters.* New York: Viking Penguin

Offe, C. 1985. Legitimation through majority rule?, in *Disorganized Capitalism: Contemporary Transformation of Work and Politics*, edited by J. Keane. Cambridge, Mass.: MIT Press, pp. 259–99

Peltzman, S. 1984. Constituent interest and congressional voting. *Journal of Law and Economics*, **27**, 181–205

Perry, M. 1982. *The Constitution, the Courts, and Human Rights.* New Haven: Yale University Press

Pitkin, H. 1981. Justice: on relating public to private. *Political Theory*, **9**, 327–52

Posner, R. 1986. *Economic Analysis of Law*, 3rd edn. Boston: Little, Brown

Riker, W. 1982. *Liberalism against Populism: A Confrontation Between the Theory of Democracy and the Theory of Social Choice*. San Francisco: W. H. Freeman

Roemer, J. 1985. Optimal endogenous preferences (unpublished manuscript)

1986. 'Rational choice' Marxism, in *Analytical Marxism*, edited by J. Roemer. Cambridge University Press, pp. 191–201

Rogat, Y. 1964. The judge as spectator. *University of Chicago Law Review*, **31**, 213–56

Stigler, G. 1971. The theory of economic regulation. *Bell Journal of Economics and Management Science*, **2**, 3–21

Stone, G., Seidman, L., Sunstein, C. and Tushnet, M. 1986. *Constitutional Law*. Boston: Little, Brown

Sunstein, C. 1984. Naked preferences and the Constitution. *Columbia Law Review*, **84**, 1689–1732

1985. Interest groups in American public law. *Stanford Law Review*, **38**, 29–58

1986. Legal interference with private preferences. *University of Chicago Law Review*, **53**, 1129–74

1987. Lochner's legacy. *Columbia Law Review*, **87**, 873–919

Tribe, L. 1978. *American Constitutional Law*. Mineola, New York: Foundation Press

Truman, D. 1951. *The Governmental Process*. New York: Knopf

Unger, R. 1987. *Politics: A Work in Constructive Social Theory*. Cambridge University Press

Vining, J. 1978. *Legal Identity: The Coming of Age of Public Law*. New Haven: Yale University Press

Index

357